Conflict of Laws:
Mexico and the United States

A Bilateral Study

Studies in Inter-American Law

Vol. 1

Conflict of Laws:
Mexico and the United States

A Bilateral Study

by

S. A. BAYITCH
Professor of Law
University of Miami School of Law

and

JOSÉ LUIS SIQUEIROS
Professor of Law
Universidad Nacional Autónoma de México

UNIVERSITY OF MIAMI PRESS
Coral Gables, Florida
1968

Copyright © 1968 by

University of Miami Press, Coral Gables, Florida

Library of Congress Catalog Card No. 68-31040

Printed in the United States of America

Foreword

Habent sua fata libelli. This one had its full share. Written in Summer 1964, the manuscript became involved in a series of happenings too unbelievable to relate. Finally, the book found its proper place in this new series published by the University of Miami Press, along with other studies dealing with inter-American legal research.

The present study is descriptive rather than comparative, with emphasis on Mexican law while the discussion of the corresponding law in force in the United States is limited to situations related to Mexico and to some basic principles in order to facilitate understanding.

My sincere thanks go to Lic. Siqueiros not only for his dedicated and valuable cooperation but also for his friendship over the years.

Coral Gables
April 1, 1968

S. A. BAYITCH

Contents

PART TWO

NATIONALITY

PART FOUR

CRIMINAL LAW

PART FIVE

JURISDICTIONAL CONFLICTS

PART SIX

Introduction

Mexico with its more than forty six million people inhabiting an area one fourth the size of the United States is the only Latin American country having a common boundary with the United States, a line of some fifteen hundred miles dividing two territories rather than separating two nations.

The first on the American continent to be conquered by Spain and one of the earliest to achieve independence, Mexico has had throughout its history important ties with the United States: political, economic, social and cultural. Common hemispheric interests, congenial political ideas and extensive cooperation in matters economic, particularly by vast American investments in Mexico, have established a climate of cooperation and respect. But this is not all: the United States numbers among its nationals many of Mexican descent while, on the other hand, Americans show an apparent liking for things Mexican, not only as tourists, businessmen and scientists but also as immigrants making Mexico their home. In legal matters too, it must not be forgotten, large areas of the United States were, at one time or another, parts of Mexico. This accounts for the fact that Spanish or Mexican law still governs many interests established before the change in sovereignty; and that civil law traditions still linger on as a permanent heritage in the south-western parts of this country.[1] Therefore, a study dedicated to the conflict of laws of the two countries, with emphasis on problems affecting their mutual relations, may be of more than mere academic interest.

[1] McKnight, The Spanish Legacy to Texas Law, 3 Am. J. Leg. Hist. 222 (1951); and The Spanish Influence on Texas Civil Procedure, 38 Texas L. Rev. 24 (1959); Dobkins, The Spanish Element in Texas Water Law (1959); Dart, Influence of the Ancient Laws of Spain in the Jurisprudence of Louisiana, 6 Tulane L. Rev. 83 (1931); Batiza, The Influence of Spanish Law in Louisiana, 33 Tulane L. Rev. 29 (1958).

The present study is primarily designed to present Mexican law of conflicts, international as well as interstate. American law, meaning the law in force in these United States, both federal and state, will be introduced only in most general terms, primarily through the presentation of American cases dealing with Mexican law.

Bibliographical data will be given in footnotes. On the American side recent authoritative treatises will be cited as well as a number of articles in legal periodicals. In regard to Mexican legal literature, a few bibliographical guides are available, among them De la Villa & Zambrano, *Bibliografia Sumaria de Derecho Mexicano* (1957) ; Vance, *A Guide to the Law and Legal Literature of Mexico* (1945) ; Clagett, *A Guide to the Law and Legal Literature of the Mexican States* (1947) , and in Bayitch, *Latin America and the Caribbean, a Bibliographical Guide to Works in English* (1967) .[2]

Mexican statutory law is published in various official gazettes. Federal enactments appear in the *Diario Oficial* (D.O.) while state legislation is available in the respective state publications. Useful digests are: Suinaga Lujan, *Veinte Años de Legislación Mexicana,* 1931-1950 (1951) , with supplement for 1951-1953 (1954) , and the *Repertorio Anual de Legislación Nacional Extranjera,* published by the Mexican Institute of Comparative Law (1960-) . Case law emanating from subordinate federal courts is available in *Anales de Jurisprudencia;* the opinions of the federal Supreme Court in the *Semanario Judicial de la Nación* (*Semanario*) ,[3] arranged by its four chambers (*salas*) : criminal, administrative, civil, and labor. An extensive digest of cases by Cajica, *Repertorio Alfabético de Jurisprudencia Mexicana* (1951-) is in the process of publication while a digest of cases appearing in the *Semanario* between 1917 and 1954 is available as *Jurisprudencia Definida de la Corte Suprema* (1955) . This digest was brought up to 1963 by Barrurieta Mayo, *Jurisprudencia y Tesis Sobresalientes de la Suprema Corte de Justicia de la Nación,* 1955-1963 (1964) , in five volumes.[4]

The Mexican legal literature is quite impressive. All branches of the law are discussed in treatises, monographs and in legal periodicals. A compact presentation of Mexican law is now available in *Panorama*

---

[2] A bibliography on comparative common and civil law is available in Bayitch, Common and Civil Law: a Bibliographical Essay, 4 Int.-Am. L. Rev. 349 (1962) (bilingual) .

[3] Pérez-Verdia, El Semanario Judicial de la Federación, (41) El Foro (4a ép.) 37 (1963) .

[4] Contains opinions of the chambers of the Supreme Court; hereinafter cited as Jurisprudencia (p.l) , i.e., pleno; (admin.) , i.e., administrativo; (civ.) , i.e. civil, and (lab.) . i.e. laboral.

del Derecho Mexicano published by the Mexican Institute of Comparative Law (1965). A brief introduction to Mexican law is included in Bernal Molina's *A Statement of the Laws of Mexico in Matters Affecting Business* (1955), published by the Pan American Union, and in the Department of Commerce publication entitled *Investment in Mexico: Conditions and Outlook for United States Businessmen* (1955).[5]

Finally, a few useful books dealing with general problems arising between Mexico and the United States may be mentioned: Brandenburg, *The Making of Mexico* (1964); Cline, *Mexico: Revolution to Evolution* (1962); James, *Mexico and the Americans* (1962), Wilgus (ed.), *The Caribbean: Mexico Today* (1964); and recently, Ewing (ed.), *Six Faces of Mexico* (1966).

[5] Translations of Mexican statutes have been published, among others, by the American Chamber of Commerce in Mexico, by Traducciones (Mexico), and by the Foreign Tax Law Association (St. Petersburg, Fla.). The quality of these translations vary considerably. Loose-leaf editions of Mexican laws are available from Andrade, S.A., Mexico, D.F.

PART ONE

1. THE MEXICAN LEGAL SYSTEM

Historical Background

The Mexican legal system belongs to the civil law family of nations. As New Spain, Mexico was for centuries a Spanish colony, subject to Spanish law in general and to Spanish colonial law in particular. Among Spanish legal sources the most important were the *Siete Partidas* (1265),[6] the *Leyes de Toro* (1505), the *Nueva Recopilación* (1567), and the *Novíssima Recopilación* (1805) while the colonial legislation was assembled in the *Recopilación de las Leyes del Reyno de Indias* (1681).[7]

After achieving independence from Spain in 1821, Mexico at first retained the legal system inherited from Spain,[8] with the exception of those matters that were irreconcilable with the newly acquired sovereignty. In this area sweeping constitutional and political legislation was needed, among others also in matters of nationality and

[6] Vance, The Old Spanish Code of Siete Partidas in Mexico, 14 A.B.A.J. 219 (1928); Lobinger, Las Siete Partidas: the Great Spanish Law Book, 6 Ann. Bull. Comp. L. Bureau 33 (1913), and The Forum Judicium: Fuero Juzgo, 8 Ill. L. Rev. 1 (1913). Nichols, Las Siete Partidas, 20 Cal. L. Rev. 260 (1932); translation by Scott, Las Siete Partidas (1931).

[7] Mexican legal history was traced in State v. Valmont Plantations, 346 S.W. 2d 853 (Tex. 1961), and others.

[8] Older sources are available in translation in Kimball, Laws and Decrees of the State of Coahila and Texas, in Spanish and English . . . (1839); White, A New Collection of Laws, Charters and Local Ordinances of the Government of Great Britain . . . together with the Laws of Mexico and Texas (1839); Schmidt, The Civil Law of Spain and Mexico Arranged on the Principle of a Modern Code . . . (1851); Rockwell, Compilation of Spanish and Mexican Law in Relation to Mines and Titles to Real Estate (1851); Reynolds, Spanish and Mexican Land Laws: New Spain and Mexico (1895); Hall, The Laws of Mexico: A Compilation and Treatise Relating to Real Property, Mines, Water Rights, Personal Rights, Contracts and Inheritances (1885). In general Vance, The Background of Hispanic American Law (1943).

alienage. In addition to basic provisions inserted in constitutions, the first Mexican legislation in this area, a law enacted in 1854, was copied closely from a Spanish model of 1851.[9] It contained elaborate conflicts provisions which, surprisingly, left no trace in subsequent legislation, enacted in 1886, or in any of the later laws.

Once the constitutional bases of the Republic became stabilized in the 1857 constitution,[10] Spanish law was eliminated gradually by a steadily growing body of domestic law. While in matters of constitutional law Mexico adopted guiding principles from the United States Constitution, in matters of private law it steadfastly remained a civil law system. In matters of civil (private) law generally, and of conflicts law in particular, Mexico closely followed European patterns, both in regard to choice-of-law and jurisdictional rules. The first enactment in the area of conflict law after the 1854 interlude was contained in the federal Civil Code of 1870, where conflict rules found their place among the preliminary provisions. This voluminous code, numbering no less than 4,126 articles, followed the Spanish draft for a civil code, prepared by García Goyena in 1851. From there the Mexican Code adopted the dominating statutist theory and enacted it in art. 13 to 19. When in 1884 a new, shorter version of the federal Civil Code,[11] borrowing from the Napoleonic (1804) and the Portugese Civil Code (1868), without abandoning the Goyena draft, was enacted, it introduced no changes in conflict provisions. The statutist theory was preserved and subsequently drifted into many civil codes enacted in the several states when they enacted the 1884 federal Civil Code as their local code. In some of the states, such civil codes are still in force.

The federal Civil Code of 1884 remained in force during the post-revolutionary period, surviving the 1917 Constitution[12] by more than one decade, until the victorious revolutionary tenets finally found expression in the innovations included in the third code, namely the

---

[9] Translation in 45 Brit. & For. State Papers 1038 (1865); also in Hamilton, Mexican Law: A Compilation of Mexican Legislation . . . 165 (1882). The Civil Code of Oaxaca (1829) contained conflicts provisions, (36) El Foro (4a ép.) 85 (1962).

[10] Translations in 2 Dodd, Modern Constitutions, a Collection . . . 37 (1909); 1 Rodríguez, American Constitutions 39 (1905); and 1 Wheless, Compendium of Mexican Law 1 (1910).

[11] Translation by Taylor, The Civil Code of the Mexican Federal District and Territories with an Appendix to the Civil Code of Various Mexican States (1904); summarized in Kerr, A Handbook of Mexican Law, Being an Abridgment of the Principal Mexican Codes 19 (1909).

Civil Code for the Federal District and Territories of 1928, in force since October 1, 1932.[13] These innovations, however, did not affect the statutist theory embalmed now in article 12 to 15. This Code, like its predecessor in force in the Federal District and Territories, has been enacted as local civil code in the majority of the Mexican states with only minor changes. Hence, both the federal Civil Code as well as the civil codes of the several states carry still the antiquated statutist principles adopted from Spain in the middle of the past century.

Advances, however, have been achieved in widely scattered provisions contained in enactments outside the civil codes, particularly in federal legislation dealing with matters of commerce, transportation, aliens, admiralty, and criminal law.

Constitutional Setting

The present Constitution of the United Mexican States, adopted in 1917, defines Mexico as a "federal, democratic and representative republic" (art. 40), composed of twenty-nine states (art. 43), all "free and independent in regard to their internal affairs" (art. 40), under a "popular, representative, republican system of government" (art. 115), and of a Federal District and two territories (art. 44, 45).

As in the United States legislative powers[14] delegated to the federal Congress are enumerated (art. 74) while powers not so delegated remain with the several states (art. 124). Legislative powers vested in the federal Congress are of two kinds: unlimited powers over the Federal District and Territories (art. 74, para. VI), and limited powers to be exercised for the entire Republic in matters delegated (art. 73). Among the latter powers the following are here of particular interest: hydrocarbons (petroleum), mining, the motion picture industry, commerce, credit institutions, electric power, labor (art. 73, para. X), maritime law (art. 73, para. XIII); "nationality, legal status of aliens, citizenship, naturalization, colonization, emigration and immigration" (art. 73, para. XVI); general means of communication

---

[12] Translated in Fitzgibbon, Constitutions of the Americas 498 (1948); 2 Peaslee, Constitutions of Nations 661 (1956); also by the Pan American Union (1958); Duncan, The Mexican Constitution of 1917: Its Political and Social Background, 5 Int.-Am. L. Rev. 277 (1963).

[13] Hereinafter referred to as: federal Civil Code. Translation by Schoenrich, The Civil Code for the Federal District and Territories of Mexico and the Mexican Law on Alien Land Ownership (1950), with supp. (1958).

[14] Burgoa, Breve Estudio sobre el Poder Legislativo 109 (Mexico, 1966).

(art. 73, para. XVIII) which include transportation by land, water, air, telegraph, telephone, and postal services (art. 73, para. XVII). The federal legislative powers also include copyright, patents and trademarks (art. 28). It must be kept in mind, however, that due to the overwhelming political influence exerted on the part of the federal government which, in many instances relies on a liberal inter- pretation of the necessary-and-proper clause (art. 73, para. XXX), the federal Congress has frequently expanded its legislative authority be- yond limits set up in the Constitution, without encountering serious objections.

It follows that the conflict law is within the federal legislative powers only insofar as it affects, (i) the Federal District and Territor- ies; (ii) matters within the federal legislative powers *ratione materiae,* such as commerce, labor, and communications; (iii) interstate con- flicts (art. 121), to be discussed later; and (iv) matters considered of "federal concern" (art. 1 of the federal Civil Code) which, in many instances, reach beyond those delegated to federal legislation *ratione materiae.* In all other matters, the states have retained their original powers to enact their own jurisdictional and choice-of-law rules (art. 124), subject, of course, to federal constitutional standards, treaties and federally established interstate conflict rules.

Judicial System

Following patterns developed by the northern neighbor, Mexico has adopted a dual system of the judiciary: federal and that of the several states.[15]

Federal judicial powers, vested in a Supreme Court of Justice,[16] with circuit and district courts as subordinate courts (art. 94 of the Constitution), take cognizance of two main group of cases: *amparo* proceedings as defined in article 104 of the Constitution, and other proceedings listed there. *Amparo* proceedings deal with controversies arising from (i) laws or acts of judicial or administrative authorities which allegedly violate individual constitutional guarantees; (ii) laws or acts of the same authorities which allegedly violate or restrict state sovereignty; and (iii) laws and similar acts of the states which allegedly

---

[15] Cabrera, History of the Mexican Judiciary, 11 Miami L.Q. 439 (1957); Riesenfeld, Federal Courts in Foreign Legal Systems, 13 L. & Cont. Pr. 29, 50 (1948).

[16] Castillo Flories, La Suprema Corte en México y en Estados Unidos, 9 (33–36) Revista de la Facultad de Derecho de México 139 (1959).

infringe upon federal powers. Furthermore, federal courts have exclusive jurisdiction in cases in admiralty, in cases where the federal government is a party; in cases arising between two or more states, or between a state and the federal government, and between the federal courts sitting in the federal district and territories and other federal or state courts; over cases arising between a state and one or more residents of another state of the Union[17] (*vecinos*); and over cases involving diplomatic or consular immunity. Federal courts exercise concurrent jurisdiction in cases involving the application of federal statutes, both civil and criminal, and treaties, allowing plaintiffs to take such cases to state court if they involve only private matters.

The powers vested in the federal judiciary are further defined in the Organic Law of the Federal Judicial Power of 1935, as amended in 1951.[18] In regard to federal district courts, this law distinguishes the following main areas of original federal jurisdiction: criminal cases, listed in article 51, para. I; extradition cases (ibid., para. II) ; *amparo* proceedings (ibid., para. III and IV) ; civil matters (art. 43) including *amparo* proceedings in such matters (art. 51, para. VI) ; and administrative matters (art. 42).

According to the Code of Civil Procedure for the Federal District and Territories,[19] the jurisdiction of its courts is determined by the subject matter of the case, by the amount involved (art. 157), by the hierarchical position of the court, and by the territory for which the courts have been established (art. 144). Only the territorial competence (venue) may be changed by parties' agreement (*prórroga*, art. 149), which may be express (art. 152) or implied (art. 153). Venue is determined, among others, by the place of performance; the location of the land involved; by the domicile of the defendant in matters involving movable property, personal action and status (art. 156). In matters involving inheritance, venue is determined by the last domicile of the deceased; in divorce proceedings by the marital domicile, or in case of abandonment, by the domicile of the abandoned spouse. Similar rules are contained in the Code of Civil Procedure for Federal Courts,[20]

[17] 69 Semanario (5a ép.) 3886 (1941).

[18] D.O. Jan. 19, 1936, implemented by the Organic Law for Courts of General Jurisdiction (*Tribunales Comunes*) of the Federal District and Territories of 1932, reprinted with amendments in D.O. Jan. 21 (1967).

[19] D.O. Sept. 1–21, 1932. Sodi, La Nueva Ley Procesal (Mexico, 1946), 2 vol.; Pallares Portillo, Historia del Derecho Procesal Civil Mexicano (Mexico, 1962).

[20] D.O. Febr. 24, 1943.

regulating jurisdiction over the subject matter (art. 18) and venue (art. 23 to 27). Similar rules obtain in the courts of the several states.

Labor disputes, individual as well as collective, are heard by the various boards for conciliation and arbitration established by the Federal Labor Law (art. 336 to 401).[21]

There are no commercial courts in Mexico.[22] Commercial matters in the sense of the federal Commercial Code[23] are within the concurrent jurisdiction of the federal and state courts. In commercial matters these courts apply, in addition to their own procedural rules, the rules contained in the Commercial Code (art. 1049 to 1414), including the provisions dealing with jurisdiction (art. 1090 to 1131) and service (art. 1068 to 1074), among them a special provision for service abroad (art. 1074).

All judicial powers not delegated to the federal judiciary remain with the several states (art. 124 of the federal Constitution). In the exercise of these powers, the states have established their own judicial systems by constitutions and by organic acts. The procedure in state courts, civil as well as criminal, is regulated by codes of civil and criminal procedures enacted by state legislatures since judicial rule-making power is unknown.

[21] D.O. Aug. 28, 1931, as amended. Castorena, La Jurisdicción Laboral: Su Competencia y Sus Organos, 13 Revista Mexicana del Trabajo (6a ép.) 97 (1966).

[22] Alcalá-Zamora, Examen del Enjuiciamiento Mercantil Mexicano y Conveniencia de su Reabsorción por el Civil, 7 Revista de la Facultad de Derecho de México 19 (1952); Ramirez Banos, Tratado de Juicios Mercantiles (Mexico, 1963).

[23] D.O. Oct. 7–13, 1889.

2. SOURCES OF
MEXICAN CONFLICT LAW

According to the federal system of government as adopted by the 1917 Constitution of the United Mexican States, conflict law originates from two main sources: federal law, including treaties, on the one hand, and state law on the other.[24] The existence as well as the hierarchy of these sources is expressed in the Mexican counterpart of our supremacy clause (art. 133 of the Constitution):

> This constitution, the laws of the Congress of the Union, made in pursuance thereof, and all treaties, in accordance with it, made or to be made by the President of the Republic with the approval of the Senate, shall be the supreme law of the entire Union: and the judges of every state shall comply with this constitution, laws, and treaties, anything in the constitutions or laws of the states to the contrary notwithstanding.

Federal Law

CONSTITUTION

In addition to the constitutional provisions allocating legislative powers as between the national government and that of the several states, the 1917 Constitution contains a few conflict rules, some international and others interstate. To the first group belong numerous provisions dealing with the status of aliens in Mexico generally (art. 33) and in regard to their holding land in particular (art. 27). Rules interstate in nature are contained in article 121 and deal with movables and immovables, acts of civil status and professional degress, combined with the Mexican equivalent of the full faith and credit clause.

Of course, some of the fundamental constitutional standards, such as due process (art. 14) play a decisive rule, particularly in *amparo* proceedings.

[24] Contreras Pliego, Fuentes del Derecho Internacional Privado Mexicano (Mexico, 1960). A collection of statutory materials in German and French translations is available in Makarow, Quellen des internationalen Privatrechts (1953—, 1.1.).

LEGISLATION

Among enactments originating in the national Congress,[25] the most significant are those implementing the federal Constitution (*leyes reglamentarias de la Constitución*). Among them, the following may be mentioned here: the Organic Law Regarding Paragraph I of Article 27 of the Constitution; the Regulatory Law Regarding Articles 4 and 5 of the Constitution, and the Regulatory Law of Article 27 of the Constitution in Matters of Petroleum,[26] to be discussed later.

In respect to matters delegated to the federal legislation *ratione materiae*, national Congress has unlimited legislative authority which enables it to enact legislation for the Federal District and Territories[27] including corresponding conflict rules. Among such enactments the following may be mentioned. The federal Civil Code contains choice-of-law rules (art. 12 to 16)[28] which apply primarily to situations arising within the territorial applicability of this Code, i.e., within the Federal District and Territories. In addition, they operate throughout the Republic in matters of federal concern (*asuntos del orden federal*, art. 1 of the Civil Code), a rule expressly repeated in some of the federal enactments, such as, for example, in article 9 of the Law Regulating Art. 27 of the Constitution in Matters of Petroleum (1958),[29] in article 4 of the Law on General Means of Communication of 1940[30] and in the Commercial Code (art. 2).

Among the federal procedural enactments, the most significant for conflict law are the two codes of federal civil procedure:[31] the Code of Civil Procedure for the Federal District and Territories of 1932, and the Federal Code of Civil Procedure of 1942, governing civil proceedings in the federal courts throughout the Republic. Additional jurisdictional rules are contained in the Organic Law of the Court of Justice of General Jurisdiction (*fuero comun*) of the Federal District and

---

[25] Burgoa, op. cit. n. 14 supra.   [26] To be discussed later n. 159.

[27] Fuentes Galindo, Organización Constitucional del Distrito Federal (1948); Gaxiola, El Distrito Federal, (8–9) El Foro (4a ép.) 17 (1955).

[28] Translated in Appendix I. Professor Rojina Villegas has prepared a draft reforming the federal civil code according to judicial rulings, in his Proyecto de Reformas al Código Civil . . . (Mexico, 1967), with conflict rules in art. 13 and 15 (at 59).

[29] D.O. Aug. 25, 1959.   [30] D.O. Feb. 19, 1940.

[31] Castillo Larranaga, El Código de Procedimientos Civiles Vigente, 13 Revista de la Facultad de Derecho de México 1 (1963).

Territories of 1932, and the overall federal judiciary act, the Organic Act of the Judicial Power of the Federation, enacted in 1935.[32]

Substantive as well as jurisdictional conflict rules are contained in the federal criminal legislation: the Criminal Code for the Federal District and Territories[33] and the dual procedural codes, namely the Code of Criminal Procedure for the Federal District and Territories[34] as well as the Federal Code of Criminal Procedure.[35]

TREATIES

Another source of Mexican conflict law is found in the treaties entered into with foreign countries by the President (art. 89, para. X of the Constitution), and ratified by Congress or, more precisely, by the Senate (art. 76, para. 1, and art. 133). As in the United States, the law emanating from treaties becomes the law of the land (art. 133), and the "judges of all states shall comply with . . . treaties," language which closely, though not exactly, follows the American model. Treaty law is, of course, subject to constitutional standards, since the Constitution expressly provides that no treaties may be entered into which would "change the guarantees and rights established in this constitution for individuals and citizens" (art. 15).[36] If, for example, a treaty should violate the due process clause of the Constitution (art. 14, para. 2), a federal court might in *amparo* proceeding find the treaty provision unconstitutional and, hence, of no effect in the particular case. This happened to provisions establishing a summary administrative procedure for the recovery of stolen property contained in the Convention for the Recovery and Return of Embezzled Motor Vehicles, Trailers, Air-

[32] D.O. Jan. 10, 1936.
[33] D.O. Aug. 14, 1931: hereinafter cited as: Federal Criminal Code. The complete title of the Code is: Criminal Code for the Federal District and Territories in Matters of General Jurisdiction, and for the whole Republic in Matters of Federal Concern (*Fuero Federal*).
[34] D.O. Aug. 29, 1931.   [35] D.O. Aug. 30, 1934.
[36] Treaty law is subject to constitutional guarantees, 19 Semanario (5a ép.) 1142 (1926); 31 Semanario (5a ép.) 349 (1931). Martínez Báez, La Constitución y los Tratados Internacionales, 8 (30) Revista de la Escuela Nacional de Jurisprudencia 167 (1946); Sepúlveda, La Situación de los Tratados en el Orden Legal Mexicano, in Comunicaciones Mexicanas al VI Congreso Internacional de Derecho Comparado, Hamburgo, 1962, at 203 (1962); and La Autoridad de los Tratados Internacionales en el Derecho Interno, 15 Boletín del Instituto de Derecho Comparado de México 511 (1962).

planes or Component Parts of Any of Them, concluded with the United States in 1936.[37]

Both countries are parties to a number of treaties, multilateral and bilateral, many of which contain important conflict rules.[38] Among the multilateral treaties, first universal convention to which both countries are parties should be listed, followed by inter-American treaties.[39]

Universal Conventions

Aviation

Convention for the Unification of Certain Rules Relating to International Transportation by Air, signed at Warsaw, October 12, 1929 (44 Stat. 3000) ;[40]

Convention on International Civil Aviation, signed at Chicago, December 7, 1944 (61 Stat. 1180) ; and

International Air Service Transit Agreement, signed the same day at Chicago (59 Stat. 1693).

Commodities

Sugar (London, 1958, 10 U.S.T. 2189) ; rice (Rome, 1961, 13 U.S.T. 2403) ; wheat (Washington, 1962, 13 U.S.T. 1571) ; coffee (New York, 1962, 14 U.S.T. 1911) ; and cotton (Washington, 1966, 17 U.S.T. 83).

---

[37] Evans, Treaty Enforcement and the Supreme Court of Mexico, 5 Am. J. Comp. L. 267 (1956).

[38] Bayitch, Conflict Law in United States Treaties: a Survey (1955); Wilson, United States Commercial Treaties and International Law (1960); also The International Law Standard in Treaties of the United States (1953).

[39] A compilation of treaties has been published by the Mexican Secretariat of Foreign Relations as Tratados y Convenciones Vigentes entre los Estados Unidos Mexicanos y Otros Países (1930–1938), 6 vol. A list of recent treaties is available in Briseño Sierra, Relación de los Tratados y Convenciones Debidamente Ratificados por la República Mexicana desde Jenero de 1955, con la Fecha de su Publicación en el Diario Oficial de la Federación, 14 Revista de la Facultad de Derecho de México 555 (1964), with a useful bibliography (564–582). On ratification procedures Evans, Treaty Practice in Chile, Argentina, and Mexico, Proceedings of the American Society of Int'l Law 302 (1959); and United Nations, Law and Practice Concerning Conclusion of Treaties . . . 87 (1955).

Treaties in force regarding the United States are listed in the annual publication of the Department of State entitled Treaties in Force.

[40] Bayitch, El Actual Derecho Convencional de la Aviación, 18 (54) Boletín del Instituto de Derecho Comparado de México 723 (1965). On recent developments regarding the Warsaw Convention, see infra n. 496.

Copyright

Universal Copyright Convention, signed at Geneva, September 6, 1952 (6 U.S.T. 2731) ; however, Mexico is not party to Protocol No. 1 and 3.

Finance

Articles of Agreement of the International Monetary Fund, formulated at the Bretton Woods Conference, July, 1944 (60 Stat. 1401) ;

Articles of Agreement of the International Bank for Reconstruction and Development, formulated July, 1944, at Bretton Woods (60 Stat. 1440) ;

Articles of Agreement of the International Finance Corporation, signed at Washington, May 25, 1955 (7 U.S.T. 2197) ;

Agreement Establishing the Inter-American Development Bank, signed at Washington, April 8, 1959 (10 U.S.T. 3029) ; and

Articles of Agreement of the International Development Association, signed at Washington, January 26, 1960 (11 U.S.T. 2284) .

Labor

Convention Concerning the Minimum Requirement of Professional Capacity for Masters and Officers on Board Merchant Ships, adopted at Geneva, October 24, 1936 (54 Stat. 1683) ;

Convention Concerning the Liability of the Shipowner in Case of Sickness, Injury or Death of Seamen, adopted at Geneva, October 24, 1936 (54 Stat. 1693) ; and

Convention Fixing the Minimum Age for the Admission of Children to Employment at Sea, adopted at Geneva, October 24, 1936 (54 Stat. 1705) .

Maritime Matters

Convention for the Unification of Certain Rules with Respect to Assistance and Salvage at Sea, signed at Brussels, September 23, 1910 (37 Stat. 1658) ;

Regulations for Preventing Collisions at Sea, approved at London, 1948 (4 U.S.T. 2956) ;

International Convention for the Prevention of Pollution of the Sea by Oil, signed at London, May 12, 1954 (12 U.S.T. 2989) ;

Convention on Safety of Life at Sea, signed at London, June 10, 1948 (3 U.S.T. 3450) ;

Convention on the Territorial Sea and the Contiguous Zone, signed at Geneva, April 29, 1958 (15 U.S.T. 1606) ;[41]

Convention on the High Seas, signed at Geneva, April 29, 1958 (13 U.S.T. 2312) ;[42]

Convention on the Continental Shelf, signed at Geneva, April 29, 1958 (15 U.S.T. 471);

Convention on Fishing and Conservation of Living Resources of the High Seas, signed at Geneva, April 29, 1958 (17 U.S.T. 138).

Patents

Convention for the Protection of Industrial Property, signed at Paris, 1883, as revised at London, June 2, 1934 (53 Stat. 1748).

Postal Matters

Universal Postal Convention, signed at Ottawa, October 3, 1957 (10 U.S.T. 314); and

Convention of the Postal Union of the Americas and Spain, signed at Buenos Aires, October 14, 1960 (12 U.S.T. 1449).

Inter-American Conventions

Among the inter-American conventions the following are in force between Mexico and the United States and contain conflict provisions:

Consuls

Convention Relating to the Duties, Rights, Prerogatives, and Immunities of Consular Agents, signed at Habana, February 20, 1928 (47 Stat. 1976).

---

[41] D.O. Oct. 5, 1966, with the following reservation:
The Government of Mexico considers that government owned vessels enjoy immunity regardless of their use and, therefore, makes reservations in regard to provisions contained in article 21 . . . insofar as it applies to para. 1, 2 and 3 of article 19, and para. 2 and 3 of art. 20.

[42] D.O. Oct. 19, 1966, with the following reservation:
The Government of Mexico makes an express reservation in regard to the contents of article 9, because it considers that government owned vessels enjoy immunity regardless of their use. . .

An agreement on traditional fishing in the exclusive fishery zones contiguous to the territorial seas of both countries has been signed on October 27, 1967, 57 Dep't State Bull. 685 (1967); text in 7 Int'l Leg. Mat. 312 (1968).

Copyrights

Convention on Literary and Artistic Copyrights, signed at Buenos Aires, August 11, 1910 (38 Stat. 1785).

Extradition

Convention on Extradition, signed at Montevideo, December 26, 1933 (49 Stat. 3111).

Nationality

Convention on the Nationality of Women, signed at Montevideo, December 26, 1933 (49 Stat. 2957).

Powers of Attorney

Protocol on Uniformity of Powers of Attorney Which Are to be Utilized Abroad, opened for signature in 1940 (56 Stat. 1377), adopted by Mexico with reservations (D.O. February 2, 1952, and December 3, 1953).

States, Rights and Duties

Convention on Rights and Duties of States, signed at Montevideo, December 26, 1933 (46 Stat. 2749).

Bilateral Conventions

A considerable number of bilateral conventions is in force between Mexico and the United States. Among them the following bear on conflict law.

Aviation

Air Transport Agreement, signed at Mexico, August 15, 1960 (12 U.S.T. 60), with extensions and amendments.

Boundaries

Treaty Relating to the Boundary Line, Transit of Persons, etc. (Gadsden Treaty), signed at Mexico, December 30, 1853 (10 Stat. 1031);[43]
Treaty Terminating Article VIII of the same, signed at Washington, April 13, 1937 (52 Stat. 1457).

[43] 6 Miller, Treaties and Other International Acts of the United States of America 293 (1942).

Convention for the Solution of the Problem of the Chamizal, signed at Mexico, August 29, 1963 (T.I.A.S. No. 5515), implemented by the American-Mexican Chamizal Convention Act of 1964 (78 Stat. 184).[44]

Boundary Waters

Convention Touching the International Boundary Line Where It Follows the Bed of the Rio Grande and the Rio Colorado, signed at Washington, November 12, 1884 (24 Stat. 1011);

Convention to Facilitate the Carrying out of Principles Contained in the Treaty of November 12, 1884, and to Avoid the Difficulties Occasioned by Reason of the Changes Which Take Place in the Beds of the Rio Grande and Colorado Rivers, signed at Washington, March 1, 1889 (26 Stat. 1512), extended indefinitely under article 2 of the treaty signed February 3, 1944 (59 Stat. 1219);

Convention for the Elimination of Bancos in the Rio Grande from the Effects of Article II of the Treaty of November 12, 1884, signed at Washington, March 20, 1905 (35 Stat. 1863);[45]

Convention for the Rectification of the Rio Grande in El Paso-Juarez Valley, signed at Mexico, February 1, 1933 (48 Stat. 1621);

Convention Providing for the Equitable Distribution of the Waters of the Rio Grande for Irrigation Purposes, signed at Washington, May 21, 1906 (34 Stat. 2953);

Treaty Relating to the Utilization of Waters of the Colorado and Tijuana Rivers and of the Rio Grande, with a supplementary protocol, signed at Washington, February 3, 1944 (59 Stat. 1219);[46]

Agreement to Proceed with the Construction of Amistad Dam on the Rio Grande, etc., signed at Ciudad Acuna, October 24, 1960 (11 U.S.T. 2396).

Consuls

Consular Convention, signed at Mexico, August 12, 1942 (57 Stat. 800).[47]

---

[44] Liss, A Century of Disagreement: the Chamizal Conflict, 1864–1964 (1965).

[45] For history, San Lorenzo Title & Improvement Co. v. Caples, 48 S.W. 2d 329 (Tex. 1932). Teclaff, United States River Treaties, 31 Fordham L. Rev. 697, 707 (1963).

[46] Hundley, Dividing the Waters: a Century of Controversy between the United States and Mexico (1966).

[47] See text in Appendix II.

Extradition

Extradition Treaty, signed at Mexico, February 22, 1899 (31 Stat. 1818), supplemented by conventions signed at Mexico, June 25, 1902 (T.S. No. 421), at Washington, December 23, 1925 (44 Stat. 2409), and at Mexico, August 16, 1939 (55 Stat. 1133).

Maritime Matters

Treaty for the Sending of Vessels for Purposes of Assistance and Salvage, signed at Mexico, June 13, 1935 (49 Stat. 3359).

Peace and Friendship

Treaty of Peace, Friendship, Limits and Settlement, signed at Guadalupe Hidalgo, February 2, 1848 (9 Stat. 922).[48]

Recovery of Stolen Property

Convention for the Recovery and Return of Stolen or Embezzled Motor Vehicles, Trailers, Airplanes, or Component Parts, signed at Mexico, October 6, 1936 (50 Stat. 1333), supplemented in Mexico by a decree of September 2, 1938.[49]

Taxation

Agreement on Relief from Double Taxation on Earnings from Operation of Ships and Aircraft, signed at Washington, August 7, 1964 (15 U.S.T. 1528).

To dispel possible doubts, the list of treaties just presented may be supplemented by a list of treaties which are not, or are no longer in force between Mexico and the United States but which might have had bearing on conflict law.

There is no general treaty of friendship and commerce presently in force between the two countries. The Treaty of Amity, Commerce and Navigation, signed on April 1, 1831 (8 Stat. 410), was terminated

[48] 5 Miller, Treaties and Other International Acts of the United States of America 207 (1937); Castillo Nájera, El Tratado de Guadalupe (Mexico, 1947).
[49] Decreto que Reglamenta los Art. 1 y 2 de la Convención . . . para la Recuperación de Vehículos, D.O. Sept. 2, 1948.

on November 30, 1881, by a notice on the part of Mexico, of intention to terminate the treaty.[50] In 1921 a draft convention of friendship and commerce was prepared by the United States and submitted to Mexico, but no action was ever taken.

The Convention Regarding the Status of Aliens in Their Respective Territories, adopted at the Sixth International Conference of American States in Havana (1928) was ratified both by Mexico and the United States.[51] However, the United States declined to accept the Mexican reservations and considers the Convention not to be in force in relation to Mexico. Another significant convention adopted by the same Conference, the Code of Private International Law (Codigo Bustamante) ,[52] was only signed by Mexico but never ratified.

The Inter-American Convention on the Rights of the Author in Literary, Scientific and Artistic Works, signed at Washington in 1946, was ratified by Mexico but not be the United States. On the contrary, the United States, but not Mexico, has ratified a number of inter-American conventions for the protection of inventions and patents (Buenos Aires, 1910) ,[53] and for the protection of trademarks.[54]

In the area of aviation law the Convention on the International Recognition of Rights in Aircraft, signed at Geneva in 1948, was ratified by both Mexico and the United States.[55] However, the Mexican reservations having been declined by the United States, the Convention

---

[50] [1888] Foreign Rel. U.S. 820 (1889), and [1935] 4 Foreign Rel. U.S. 800 (1953); also letter to the author from the Assistant Legal Advisor of the Department of State, dated Aug. 20, 1962.

[51] 46 Stat. 2753. Mexico expressed reservations to art. 5 of the Convention providing: States should extend to foreigners, domiciled or in transit through their territory, all individual guarantees extended to their own nationals, and the enjoyment of essential civil rights without detriment, as regards foreigners, to legal provisions governing the scope and usages for the exercise of said rights and guarantees. These reservations state that Mexico "interprets art. 5 in regard to subjecting the extent and the mode of the exercise of the essential civil rights to aliens to the limitations of the national law, as applicable to the civil capacity of aliens to acquire property in national territory." The United States expressed reservations to art. 3 and 4, dealing with military service and extraordinary contributions.

[52] Helguera, El Derecho Internacional Privado Mexicano y el Código Bustamante, in Comunicaciones Mexicanas al VI Congreso Internacional de Derecho Comparado, Hamburgo, 1962, at 29 (1962). Text in 1 Scott, The International Conferences of American States, 1889–1928, at 325 (1931), and in 4 Hudson, International Legislation 2283 (1921).

[53] 38 Stat. 1881.   [54] 30 Stat. 1675; 44 Stat. 2494; 46 Stat. 2907.

[55] 4 U.S.T. 1830. Bayitch, Aircraft Mortgage in the Americas 69 (1960).

is not in force in relation to Mexico.[56] In regard to the Warsaw Convention of 1929, it may be noted that Mexico has ratified both the Hague Protocol (1955) and the Guadalajara Convention (1961), but not the United States.

Finally it may be noted that Mexico did not ratify the multilateral Convention on the Settlement of Investment Disputes between States and Nationals of Other States, already ratified by the United States. (T.I.A.S. No. 6090). Nor did Mexico ratify the GATT complex of agreements (61 Stat. pt. 5 and 6).

EXECUTIVE REGULATIONS

A significant source of law-making in Mexico is the presidential power to issue administrative regulations under article 89, para. II of the federal Constitution providing that he may "promulgate and execute laws passed by the Congress of the Union, providing for their strict compliance within the administrative area *(esfera administrativa)* ."[57] Examples are the Regulation of Articles 47 and 48 of the Nationality and Naturalization Law (1940) [58] and the Regulation to the General Population Law (1962),[59] both dealing with the status of aliens.

CASE LAW

Legal rules applied by the Mexican courts in the process of disposing of individual litigation *(jurisprudencia)* have, as a matter of principle, no authority as rules of law (precedents). According to an express pro-

---

[56] Mexico deposited the instrument of ratification in 1950 with the following reservation:

> The Mexican Government expressly reserves the rights belonging to it to recognize the priorities granted by Mexican laws to fiscal claims and claims arising out of work contracts, over any other claim. Therefore, the priorities referred to in the Convention . . . shall be subject, within the national territory, to the priorities accorded by Mexican laws to fiscal claims and claims arising out of work contracts.

In a note to the ICAO dated July 1, 1950, the United States declared that it was unable to accept the reservations made by Mexico and will not regard the Convention as having entered into force in relation to Mexico. Letter from the Department of State, dated January 13, 1953.

[57] Baggett, Delegation of Legislative Power to the Executive under the Constitution of Mexico, 8 So. Cal. L. Rev. 114 (1935) ; Serra Rojas, Derecho Administrativo 318 (Mexico, 1961).

[58] See n. 117 infra.   [59] See n. 118 infra.

vision in the federal Civil Code (art. 19), the principle of *stare decisis* does not obtain since civil controversies "shall be decided in accordance with the text of the law *(letra de la ley)* or with its juristic interpretation *(interpretación jurídica)*."[60] This provision reflects the mandate of the federal Constitution that judgments shall be in accordance with the letter of the law or with the juristic interpretation thereof (art. 14, para. 4). This express provision, repeated in most of the state civil codes, is in accordance with the strictly applied doctrine of separation of powers (art. 49 of the federal Constitution) which makes the authoritative interpretation of statutory law an exclusive prerogative of the federal Congress (art. 72). Consequently, the authority of the courts of Mexico, both federal and state, is limited to the adjudication of the particular cases before them. Should there be a gap in the statutory scheme, the courts may develop the rule to be applied through analogy or by falling back on "general principles of law," as provided in article 14, para. IV of the federal Constitution and corresponding provisions contained in the several civil codes. This does not, however, preclude courts from being impressed by arguments contained on the opinions of other courts. But they are not bound by such precedents; hence, to use a term familiar to American lawyers, the effect of finding the controlling rule of law by a court has merely the effect of the law of the case.[61]

An exception is made, however, for the *amparo*[62] judgments, presently regulated by an amended provision of the federal Constitution (1950) and implemented by the Organic Act Regarding Articles 103

---

[60] On statutory interpretation generally, 111 Semanario (5a ép.) 2244 (1952).

[61] Case law must be proven, unless it is compiled; in case there is a compilation, it suffices to cite the compilation, 16 Semanario (6a ép.) 106 (1958); the burden of proof is on the party relying on it, 109 Semanario (5a ép.) 296 (1951).

[62] Burgoa, El Juicio de Amparo (1957); Palacios, Instituciones de Amparo (Puebla, 1963); Fix Zamudio, El Juicio de Amparo (Mexico, 1964); Clagett, The Mexican Suit of Amparo, 33 Geo. L. J. 418 (1945); Sanchez Mejorada, The Writ of Amparo, 243 Annals 107 (1946); Eder, Judicial Review in Latin America, 21 Ohio S. L. J. 570, 599, (1960); Cabrera & Headrick, Notes on Judicial Review in Mexico and the United States, 5 Int.-Am. L. Rev. 253 (1963); Karst, Latin American Legal Institutions: Problems for Comparative Study 614 (1966); Rangel y Vázquez, El Control de la Constitucionalidad de las Leyes y el Juicio de Amparo . . . , Mexico (1952), 3 vol.; Barberis, Verfassungsgerichtsbarkeit in Mexico, in Mosler (ed.), Verfassungsgerichtsbarkeit in der Gegenwart 392 (1962). Constitutionality of a statute may only be attacked by *amparo,* Informe Rendido a la Suprema Corte de Justicia de la Nación, 1946, at 116 (1942).

and 107 of the Constitution,[63] to the effect that a statute shall "determine conditions and situations where the opinions of the federal courts shall be binding, as well as requirements for their change" (art. 107, para. XIII) . "Binding" here means that the rule of the case might take effect beyond the particular litigation, notwithstanding the general principle that even in *amparo* proceedings the courts must limit themselves to the disposition of the particular case before them "without making a general pronouncement in regard to the law involved" (art. 107, para. II of the federal Constitution) . This constitutional provision was implemented by the Organic Act which repeats the constitutional rule of article 76, with a slight change in the language, and adds article 193, which reads as follows:

> Opinions (*jurisprudencia*) rendered by the Supreme Court of Justice sitting in banc in matters of interpretation of the constitution and federal laws or treaties entered into with foreign nations, is binding both upon the Supreme Court and on all chambers (*salas*) thereof, as well as on the circuit courts, both collegiate and one-judge, on district courts, state courts, courts of the federal district and territories, and labor boards of conciliation and arbitration. Opinions of the Supreme Court sitting in banc constitute precedents (*jurisprudencia*), providing such opinions have been followed in five consecutive cases and approved each time by at least fourteen justices.

It follows that even in *amparo* proceedings opinions of the Supreme Court are as a rule, binding only as the law of the case. Beyond this effect such opinions may become binding as general rules of law on the subordinate federal as well as on state courts only where strict requirements set out above have been met. However, in relation to administrative or legislative authorities such opinions may take on the effect of the law of the case but never that of a binding precedent.

State Law

Since in the Mexican federal system the powers of the national government are limited to those expressly delegated, states have the authority to create their own law in all areas not so delegated.

CONSTITUTIONS

Constitutions adopted by the several states[64] contain conflict provisions, among them rules dealing with aliens, in most cases repeating

---

[63] D.O. Jan. 10, 1936, reprinted with amendments in D.O. Feb. 4, 1963.
[64] De la Villa de Helguera, Constituciones Vigentes en la República Mexicana (1962) , 2 vol.

or adapting the corresponding provisions contained in the federal Constitution and in article 32 of the federal Law on Nationality and Naturalization of 1934, including the Calvo Clause. Furthermore, state constitutions are significant since they lay the jurisdictional and organizational foundations for the state judiciary.

LEGISLATION

From the limited extent to which legislative powers have been delegated to the federal legislature, it may be concluded that conflict law is mainly an area for legislative action by the several states.[65] As in the United States, conflict law is primarily state law. It is found mostly in the state civil codes which may be arranged in four groups:

(I) states with civil codes patterned after the federal Civil Code of 1928, including its conflict provisions, slightly adjusted to the different governmental level. In this group fall the great majority of states, namely: Aguascalientes (1947), Baja California (1959), Campeche (1942), Chiapas (1938), Chihauhua (1941), Coahuila (1941), Colima (1953), Durango (1947), Guerrero (1937), Hidalgo (1940), Jalisco (1935), Mexico (1956), Michoacan (1936), Nayarit (1937), Nuevo Leon (1935), Oaxaca (1943), Querétaro (1951), San Luis Potosí (1946), Sinaloa (1940), Tabasco (1950), and Veracruz (1932);

(II) states still following the 1884 federal civil code and its conflict rules, namely: Guanajuato (1894), Puebla (1901), and Zacatecas (1890);

(III) states which have adopted a combination of the federal civil codes of 1884 and 1928, namely: Tlaxcala (1928), and Yucatan (1941); and finally

(IV) states which have attempted original solutions: Morelos (1945), Sonora (1949), and Tamaulipas (1940). The Civil Code of Tamaulipas now superseded by the 1961 Code, may be used as an example. It provided that all acts which occur outside of the state, either in the Republic or abroad, shall have within the state the effect determined by its own laws (art. 8). With regard to both interstate and international conflict situations, article 9 provided as follows:

---

[65] Clagett, A Guide to the Law and Legal Literature of the Mexican States (1947); Aguilar Gutiérrez & Derbez Muro, Panorama de la Legislación Civil de México (1960); Sidou, Panorama Actual del Derecho Civil Mexicano, 11 Revista de la Facultad de Derecho de México 809 (1961). Handy editions of state codes are available at Editorial Cajica in Puebla.

(1) Acts which occur within the territory of the state are subject to the laws of this state, except as provided in the following sections.

(2) Controversies involving possession of land shall be solved according to the law of the place where the land is situated.

(3) Personal actions which do not involve possession of land shall be subject to the law of the place where the act occurred from which such actions originate.

The 1961 Code, however, fell pretty well in line with the federal model (art. 6, 13, and 14).

Far more complex is the state legislation in matters of civil procedure and jurisdictional rules contained therein.[66] Most of the state procedural codes follow the federal models. They are: Aguascalientes (1947), Baja California (1959), Chiapas (1938), Chihuahua (1941), Coahuila (1941), Colima (1954), Durango (1947), Guerrero (1937), Hidalgo (1940), Nayarit (1937), Oaxaca (1944), Querétaro (1950), Sinaloa (1940), Tabasco (1940), and Veracruz (1932). Modeled after the federal procedural code of 1884 are procedural codes of Tlaxcala (1928), and Zacatecas (1891). Both federal enactments are combined in the procedural codes of Nuevo León (1935), Michoacán (1936), Jalisco (1938), Yucatán (1941), and Campeche (1942). A combination of both present federal procedural codes is found in the civil procedure of Guanajuato (1934), followed closely by the procedural code of Mexico (1937). A combination of the procedural code for the federal district and that of Jalisco (1938) is the code of San Luis de Potosí (1937). Two state civil procedural codes are patterned after the draft for a new federal procedural code (1948), namely the codes of civil procedure for Morelos (1954), and Sonora (1949). Finally, the procedural codes of Puebla (1956), and Tamaulipas (1956) belong to a group apart from the others.

Other Sources

CUSTOMS

Even though of little significance for conflict problems, customs should be mentioned as a source of law, operative only where they are declared to be such by express statutory provision. The federal Civil Code makes, for example, specific references to customs[67] as does the

[66] Alcalá-Zamora, Unificación de Codigos Procesales Mexicanos, Tanto Civiles Como Penales, 10 (37–40) Revista de la Facultad de Derecho de México 265 (1960).

[67] Art. 777, 999, 1796, 1856.

Commercial Code[68] while the Law Regarding Documents of Credit refers to them in a general way.[69]

DOCTRINE

Doctrinal writing by recognized authorities must not be overlooked as a source of law, not only paralleling but by far outdistancing the books of authority in common law. Although excluded in criminal law, termed *"mayoría de razón"* in the federal Constitution (art. 14, para. 3), doctrinal writings domestic as well as foreign are of particular weight in conflict law, due not only to a lack of statutory provisions directly in point, but also because of the frequently intricate nature of many conflict situations. Learned writings are considered to be indicative of general principles of law, for example, in the Civil Code of Tamaulipas of 1940, where such writings are identified as "rules developed by legal doctrine;" they may be resorted to in order to "avoid moral injury to individuals or loss or unjust impairment of one's property" (art. 4).

The parties in their pleadings and the courts in their opinions rely frequently on writings, preferably by domestic authors. The extensive opinion in the Patiño case, for example, quotes at length from Mexican authors, among them Rojina Villegas, Gomis and Muñoz, and de Pina.[70]

FOREIGN LAW

Mexican courts are willing to apply foreign law whenever the conflict rules of the forum so order. The matter will be discussed in a later part of this study.[71]

LAST RESORT RULE

Since the courts are not permitted to refuse deciding a case because of the silence, obscurity, or insufficiency of the law (art. 18 of the federal Civil Code), additional stop-gap provisions must be supplied. Where even legal interpretation of the language of the statute fails and, at least in civil cases, analogy or "general principles of law" (art. 19 of

[68] Art. 304, 333, 726, 731, 750, 896.
[69] Art. 76, 113.   [70] 30 Semanario (6a ép.) 10, 102 (1959).
[71] Solarzano, Aplicación de Leyes Extranjeras, 6 Anales de Jurisprudencia 891 (1934); Trigueros, La Aplicación de las Leyes Extrañas: el Problema Fundamental, 6 (3) Jus 1 (1941).

the federal Civil Code) do not supply the needed rule, the federal Civil Code directs courts to decide the case so as to prevent damages to occur rather than benefit to accrue from their acts, with the additional directive that in cases where equal claims or claims of the same kind compete, the best available equality between litigants shall be attempted (art. 20), a rule repeated in many civil codes enacted in the several states.

KNOWLEDGE OF THE LAW

The time honored adage *iura novit curia* also obtains in Mexico.[72] Consequently, there is no need to prove domestic statutory law, including constitutions, both federal and state. This applies even to the law emanating from treaties, as stressed in the Patiño case. However, case law created in *amparo* proceedings must be proven by the party relying on it, as must be customs.

In regard to knowledge of law by parties, Mexican law adheres to the maxim that *ignorantia iuris nocet*. Civil codes, among them the federal (art. 21), provide expressly that lack of knowledge of the law does not absolve from the duty to comply with it. However, courts may, taking into consideration the backwardness, remoteness or the pitiful economic situation of the party involved, exempt, with the consent of the Attorney General (*Ministerio Público*), specific acts or omissions by such parties from the consequences imposed by the law or, if possible, grant such parties a period of grace to comply with the law, provided no laws are involved affecting directly what is termed public interest.

---

[72] Alcalá-Zamora, Iura novit curia, 11 (41-42) Revista de la Facultad de Derecho de México 388 (1961); also Clinica Procesal 225 (1963).

3. INTERSTATE AND INTERNATIONAL CONFLICTS

The dual system of government in Mexico has not only created a multiplicity of legal systems but also a dual system of the judiciary. Such governmental structure calls for conflict rules, both jurisdictional and choice-of-law, to solve the unavoidable interferences arising between them. Limiting the discussion at this point to choice-of-law questions, interstate conflict rules will first be explored. The basic answer is supplied by article 121 of the federal Constitution.[73] Its first part is an equivalent of the United States full faith and credit clause:

> In each State of the Federation full faith and credit *(entera fé y crédito)* shall be given to public acts, registers *(registros)*, and judicial proceedings of all the others, The Congress of the Union shall prescribe by general laws the manner to prove said acts, registers, and proceedings, and the effect thereof, in accordance with the following principles *(bases)* . . .

Like in the United States Constitution, it adds that the "Congress of the Union shall, by means of general laws, prescribe the manner in which acts, records and proceedings shall be proven, and the effect thereof." However, departing from its model, the Mexican counterpart has added a number of basic principles to guide Congress in enacting such supplementary legislation. These basic principles deal with full faith and credit in paragraphs III and IV, while others (para. I and II) provide choice-of-laws rules on the interstate level: the first paragraph proclaims the territorialistic principle in regard to state laws, and paragraph II adopts the same principle for movable and immovable property. The last paragraph V seems to be out of place: it deals with professional degrees.

The first question to be considered is whether or not these constitutional precepts are self-executing and applicable to conflict situations without the need of an intervening supplementary federal legislation. It seems that the former alternative has been adopted. The second

---

[73] Trigueros, El Articulo 121 de la Constitución, 1 Revista Mexicana de Derecho Público 180 (1946); Macías, Origen y Alcance del Art. 121 Constitucional, 17 Jus 159 (1946); Siqueiros, Los Conflictos de Leyes en el Sistema Constitucional Mexicano (Mexico, 1957); Stern, Full Faith and Credit: the Mexican Experience, 26 N.Y.U. L. Rev. 663 (1951).

question involves the scope of these principles: do they apply only to
interstate situations or to international conflict situations as well. It
seems clear that the first of these alternatives was envisaged by the
constitutional provision (art. 121) , not only because its first paragraph
sets the stage for the operation of the Mexican counterpart of the full
faith and credit clause, an inherently interstate institution, but also in
view of the fact that the express language of the added paragraphs I
through V expressly deals with interstate situations. Of course, this
does not prevent that one or the other of the choice-of-law-rules here
expressed might find application in an international conflict situation.

It may be added that Mexico, like the United States, is still waiting
for the implementing legislation promised in conjunction with the
full faith and credit clause. In Mexico, a draft was prepared by the
Mexican Bar, due to efforts of Professor Trigueros, but was never acted
upon.

In regard to international choice-of-law rules, the situation in
Mexico is strongly reminiscent of that in the United States. Since
article 121 of the Constitution deals with interstate conflicts, without
giving to the federal Congress needed additional legislative powers beyond those already vested *ratione materiae,* the primary source of these
rules remain the civil codes enacted in the several states and that in
force in the Federal District. However, it seems that the latter has a
prominent position, not only because its choice-of-law rules apply
throughout the Republic in matters of federal concern, but also because the Code reached beyond these boundaries by enacting in articles
12 and 13 as well as in the first sentence of article 15, conflict rules
nationwide in scope. They apply to all inhabitants of the Republic
(art. 12) and subject them to "Mexican laws" in a general manner
when dealing with foreign acts and contracts "to be performed in
the Republic" (art. 13) , and with formal requirements generally (art.
15) . Luckily, these trespasses into areas which, strictly speaking, remained in the legislative domain of the several states, created no
noticeable difficulties as most of the states have adopted in their civil
codes identical rules.

4. CHARACTERISTICS OF
MEXICAN CONFLICT LAW

Like any other system of private international law (*derecho internacional privado* as Mexicans call conflict law) Mexican law displays characteristics of its own.[74] The most pervasive feature is its adherence to the territorialistic doctrine. However, this attitude changes when acts abroad involve Mexican nationals. In such cases Mexican courts show a preference for the personal contact of nationality over the otherwise controlling contact of territoriality, thus bringing into operation Mexicans' own national law. The Mexican law thus applied, however, will not be any of the state laws with which a Mexican acting abroad may be connected through his domicile there, but federal law as his national law. This solution is supported by the argument that only the Union is a subject of international law while states do not exist in international relations, thus excluding state law from application to Mexicans in international choice-of-law situations.

A second significant feature of Mexican conflict law is the strong impact of public policy (*orden público, interés público*) under which it operates.[75] This doctrine eliminates otherwise applicable rules of foreign substantive law whenever they clash with segments of Mexican statutory law as represented in federal enactments which, in international choice-of-law situations, is frequently considered to be *ius cogens*, peremptory law.

A further characteristic is the increasingly discriminatory attitude toward aliens, including their own naturalized citizens. Insofar as this involves areas of sensitive economic interests, it must be understood as a defensive action taken by a developing nation rather than as an aggressive measure. However, the same attitude is frequently extended

[74] Gallardo Vásquez, Fundamentos Teoreticos y Filosóficos del Derecho Internacional Privado, in Pensamiento Jurídico de México en el Derecho Internacional 183 (Mexico, 1960) ; Carillo, Nuevas Tendencias Doctrinales en el Derecho Internacional Privado, 13 Revista de la Facultad de Derecho de México 855 (1963). For a critical evaluation, Siqueiros, La Crisis del Derecho Internacional Privado en México, (50) El Foro (4a ép.) 41 (1965).

[75] Magallon, El Orden Público como Sistema de Solución al Conflicto de Leyes, 15 Revista de la Facultad de Derecho de México 661 (1965). On the interstate level, 38 (1) Semanario (5a ép.) 427 (1936).

to foreign law when it happens to compete with the Mexican *lex fori*. In most cases the result has been the complete monopoly of Mexican law in regard to persons, acts and things within the Republic, even in situations where other legal systems might be willing to apply foreign law on the strength of nationality or domicile.

Comparing interstate conflicts problems in Mexico with their counterpart in the United States, it is surprising to find that in spite of an almost identical constitutional setting this class of conflicts, both jurisdictional and choice-of-law, is in Mexico of little consequence. This may be explained not only by lack of awareness, in many instances, of the very existence of a conflict problem, but also by the fact that the substantive civil as well as procedural law in force in the several states is, in most situations, uniform because it is patterned after federal models. This makes in many cases the question as to what state's civil code to apply, moot. In a recent case involving a conditional sale with retained title to land in Coahuila, litigated in a federal court in Mexico City due to a prorogation clause in the sales contract, the question whether the *lex rei sitae* or the *lex fori prorogati* applies, was answered by the Supreme Court in the sense that even if the prorogation should be interpreted as not including the substantive law of the chosen forum, it would make no difference if either law, the Civil Code of Coahuila or the federal Civil Code would apply because both contain identical provisions in the matter.[76] Finally, it should be taken into account that in many areas of potential interstate conflicts, such as commerce, labor, transportation, natural resources and others, uniform, i.e., nationwide federal substantive law prevails.

Finally, the Mexican statutory law regulating jurisdiction and procedure is characterized by its inconsistency with the prevailing dual system of government, federal and state, as adopted in Mexico. Most procedural codes dealing with judicial jurisdiction, adopted on the federal as well as on the state level, are closely patterned after foreign models, without taking into account that these codes are designed for unitarian governments with one judicial system and one system of laws. Of course, such procedural codes indiscriminately copied from Spain, France or Italy, provided no guidelines which would enable them to properly operate in a system of multiple co-existing and, in principle, equivalent judiciaries and legislatures. This lack of responsiveness of the imported statutory law to the Mexican federal system has caused

[76] 57 Semanario (6a ép.) 83, 110 (1962).

and will cause for some time to come serious difficulties, particularly in jurisdictional conflict both on the interstate and international level.[77]

[77] Trigueros, La Evolución Doctrinal del Derecho Internacional Privado (Mexico, 1938); Siqueiros, Breve Estudio Comparativo del Derecho Internacional Privado de México y de los Estados Unidos de Norteamérica, in El Pensamiento Jurídico de México en el Derecho Internacional 211 (Mexico, 1960).

For American law, see Ehrenzweig, Private International Law: a Comparative Treatise on American International Conflicts Law, Including the Law of Admiralty, General Part (1967).

5. MEXICAN LITERATURE ON CONFLICT LAW

For some time after Mexico has reached its independence, writers in the area of conflict law appear to have been more interested in discussing abstract problems and in engaging in academic disputes or in simply restating foreign developed, mainly European, doctrines than to face and explore questions particular to the Mexican scene, particularly those arising from the federal structure of the Republic. To this group of early writers belong, among others, Zavala with his *Elementos de Derecho Internacional Privado Civil, Commercial, de Procedimientos y Penal entre las Legislaciones de Diverso Países* (1866), followed by Verdugo's *Principios de Derecho Civil Mexicano* (1885–1890), Algara's *Lecciones de Derecho Internacional Privado* (1899), and Zavala's *Compendio de Derecho Internacional Privado* (1903). Even the work by Perez Verdia, *Tratado Elemental de Derecho Internacional Privado,* published as late as 1908, shows no signs of emancipation from foreign doctrines.

These mostly academic discussions resulted in a surprising lack of interest and understanding for domestic conflict problems, particularly since European authors without exception have developed their theories mainly along centralized, not federal governmental structures. After Avalo's study entitled *El Progreso Realizado en el Derecho Internacional Privado en la República* (1911), and following Cabrera Cosio's *Conflictos de Leyes en el Estado Federal Mexicano* (1943), a new period was initiated by the late Eduardo Trigueros. After having first put the past in proper perspective in his *La Evolución Doctrinal del Derecho Internacional Privado* (1938), he turned to some of the fundamental questions of Mexican conflict law as well as to much needed reforms. In a number of outstanding studies, among them *La Nacionalidad Mexicana: Notas para el Estudio del Derecho Internacional Privado* (1940), and *La Aplicación de las Leyes Extranjeras: el Problema Fundamental* (1941), Trigueros undertook numerous significant initiatives, among them one concerning the legislative implementation of article 121 of the federal Constitution (1946). A valuable historical study was contributed by Gallardo Vásquez in his *Derecho Internacional Privado,* as part of the extensive symposium on Mexican law entitled *Evolución de Derecho Mexicano* (1943). Though

still laboring under an uneasy burden of foreign dogmatic disputes
and of fortuitously gathered comparative materials, Arce's *Derecho
Internacional Privado* (1943, 1955) presents, nevertheless, an attempt
to discuss some of the conflict problems particular to the Mexican
constitutional setting. Similar in concept is also the section on conflict
law included in the extensive treatise on Mexican private law by
Rojina Villegas, entitled *Derecho Civil Mexicano* (1955–) .[78]

Only recently a new generation of Mexican lawyers began explor-
ing Mexican conflict law in depth and turning to foreign law and
doctrines only where a genuine link justifies such reference. Their
work, particularly by Helguera and Siqueiros,[79] will be referred to in
proper places.

---

[78] De La Villa & Zembrano, Bibliografía Sumaria de Derecho Mexicano
32 (Mexico, 1957) .
[79] For a survey, Siqueiros, Panorama del Derecho Mexicano: Síntesis
del Derecho Internacional Privado (Mexico, 1965) .

PART TWO

Nationality

6. MEXICAN NATIONALITY

Even though Mexican conflict law prefers territorialistic concepts, the contact of nationality remains of considerable consequence.[80] Moreover, following the European schemes of presenting this branch of law, a discussion of nationality is regularly included in Mexican treatises.

ACQUISITION

Article 30 of the federal Constitution, as amended in 1934, provides that Mexican nationality will be acquired by birth or by naturalization. Mexicans by birth are persons who:

(1) Are born in the territory of the Republic, regardless of the nationality of their parents;

(2) Are born abroad of Mexican parents, of a Mexican father and a foreigner-mother, or of a Mexican mother and an unknown father;

(3) Are born on board of Mexican vessels or aircraft, military, commercial.

It is apparent that Mexican law relies on both methods of acquiring original nationality: on *jus soli*[81] as well as on *jus sanguinis*.

Persons become Mexican nationals by naturalization:

[80] San Marín y Torres, Nacionalidad y Extranjeria, Estudios Migratorios, con Referencia a las Leyes Mexicanas (Mexico, 1954) ; Trigueros, La Nacionalidad Mexicana: Notas para el Estudio del Derecho Internacional Privado (Mexico, 1940) ; also Los Principios Fundamentales Referentes a la Determinación de la Nacionalidad, (6) El Foro (2a ép.) 189 (1949).

[81] 90 Semanario (5a ép.) 1026 (1947). Carillo, La Postura de la Constitución Mexicana Frente a los Problemas de Nacionalidad, 14 Revista de la Facultad de Derecho de México 389 (1964) ; Echanove Trujillo, La Nacionalidad de los Nacidos en México de Padres Extranjeros a Partir de 1857, 12 (45) Revista de la Escuela Nacional de Jurisprudencia 81 (1950).

(1) Who obtain from the Secretariat of Foreign Relations a certificate of naturalization (*carta de naturalización*) ; and
(2) Alien women who marry Mexicans and have established their domicile within the national territory.

These provisions are repeated in articles 1 and 2 of the Nationality and Naturalization Law, enacted in 1934,[82] except that the second paragraph is qualified by requiring such wife to apply personally to the Secretariat of Foreign Relation, renouncing her prior nationality, a rule which deprives the constitutional provision of its automatic effect.[83]

Proceedings leading to naturalization are of two kinds: regular and privileged.[84] Under the regular procedure the applicant must, after three years of residence in the Republic, prove in a federal district court, among other requirements, his legal residence, good behavior and health, knowledge of Spanish, and payment of taxes, at a hearing attended by the Attorney General (*Ministerio Público*) as well as a representative of the Secretariat of Foreign Relations. The certificate of naturalization is issued by the court and forwarded to the Secretariat of Foreign Relations which, provided the Secretariat considers it desirable (*conveniente*), will hand it over to the applicant, or withhold it in its administrative discretion.

Privileged naturalization proceedings dispense with judicial intervention. These exclusively administrative proceedings are available to (i) aliens who have established in Mexico an industry, enterprise or business advantageous to the country or of apparent social benefit; (ii) aliens who have legitimate children born in Mexico; (iii) aliens who have a Mexican national as a direct blood relative (*ascendiente*) ;

---

[82] D.O. Jan. 20, 1934. Koessler, The Reformed Mexican Nationality Law, 5 La. L. Rev. 420 (1943) ; United Nations, Laws Concerning Nationality 307 (1954) ; Espinosa, Protección de Mexicanos en el Extranjero, (14) Revista del ITAT 163 (1961).

[83] Ponce Lagos, Historia de las Reformas a los Artículos 34 y 115 Constitucionales que Conceden la Ciudadanía a la Mujer Mexicana (Mexico, 1954). In regard to dual nationality, art. 52 of the Mexican Nationality and Naturalization Law provides that a person who according to foreign law has two or more nationalities other than Mexican, will be considered for all effects accruing in Mexico as having one nationality, i.e., that of the country where he has his usual main residence, in case he has no residence in any of these countries then he will be considered to have the nationality of the country with which it appears, according to circumstances, to be "most intimately connected."

[84] Araujo, Veilla, Garau, Como Adquirir la Nacionalidad Mexicana (Mexico, 1950).

(iv) aliens married to a woman who is a Mexican national by birth; (v) colonists who settle in Mexico under the colonization laws; (vi) naturalized Mexicans who have lost their Mexican nationality because of residence in their country of origin, and (vii) Latin Americans and Spaniards by origin who have settled in Mexico.

Naturalized aliens must renounce their prior nationality, including their allegiance to foreign governments and their protection.[85]

LOSS

According to article 37 (A) of the Constitution, Mexican nationality is lost:

(1) By voluntary acquisition of foreign nationality;
(2) By acceptance or use of a title of nobility which implies submission to a foreign country;
(3) By a naturalized Mexican national who has resided in the country of origin for five consecutive years;
(4) By a naturalized Mexican who appears in a public document as an alien, or has obtained and used a foreign passport.

These constitutional provisions are repeated in article 3 of the Law of Nationality and Naturalization, except that this law qualified the rule contained in paragraph (1) to the effect that the rule does not apply where acquisition of foreign nationality took place (i) by operation of law, (ii) by mere residence, or (iii) as a condition to obtain work or keep it. The same article also provides that any loss of Mexican nationality does not affect other members of the family, particularly minor children and the wife who have acquired Mexican nationality through the naturalization of their father or husband. It may be added that a woman will not lose her Mexican nationality by marriage to an alien,[86] nor does adoption affect nationality.

---

[85] Under Mexican law naturalized Mexican nationals are subjected to considerable discrimination, which largely equates them to aliens. By contrast in Schneider v. Rusk, 377 U.S. 163 (1964), the Court stated in general terms that "the rights of citizenship of the native born and of the naturalized person are of the same dignity and are coextensive," the only difference being constitutional ineligibility to become President; consequently, the statutory provision denationalizing naturalized nationals because of their residence in the country of their birth was held unconstitutional.

[86] 117 Semanario (5a ép.) 115 (1964). Recently the United States Supreme Court held (Afroim v. Rusk, 87 S. Ct. 1660, 1967) that Congress has no power to enact a statute which would, in enumerated cases, deprive U.S. nationals of nationality.

CITIZENSHIP

The Mexican Constitution has introduced still another notion, that of citizenship, by providing in article 34:

> Citizens of the Republic are persons, male and female, who in addition of being Mexicans, meet the following requirements:
> (1) Are 18 years of age if married, or 21 years, if not, and
> (2) Lead an honest life.

The privileges conferred upon Mexican citizens are mainly political, such as the right to vote or to be elected to public office (art. 35) .

Mexican citizenship, a tie to the Republic as a whole rather to a particular state, may be lost in various ways: (i) by accepting or by using foreign titles of nobility; (ii) by voluntary rendering official services to a foreign government without permission from the federal Congress or its Permanent Commission; (iii) by accepting or using foreign decorations without a similar permission; (iv) by accepting from a foreign government titles and functions without such permission, except literary, scientific or humanitarian titles; (v) by aiding an alien or a foreign government against the Mexican nation in any diplomatic claim or before an international tribunal; and finally (vi) in a number of other cases specified by law.[87]

DUAL OR MULTIPLE NATIONALITY

The method best suited to the resolution of cases of dual or multiple nationality is that of option offering such persons an opportunity to elect the nationality they want. According to articles 53 and 54 of the Nationality and Naturalization Law this option may be exercised by renouncing Mexican nationality before the Secretariat of Foreign Relations or before a Mexican diplomatic or consular representative abroad. There are certain provisos, however: the person must be of age; the other country must grant nationality; and the person must be domiciled abroad. In case such person holds land in Mexico, he must agree to be treated henceforth as a Mexican and not to invoke the diplomatic protection of the foreign government in regard to such interests.

Option has been used in territorial and boundary settlements between Mexico and the United States and will be discussed later.

[87] For a survey of American law, Development in the Law: Immigration and Nationality, 66 Harv. L. Rev. 643 (1953) .

7. NATIONALITY OF LEGAL ENTITIES, VESSELS AND AIRCRAFT

Not only natural persons but also legal entities and even inanimate objects may share certain characteristics inherent in the notion of nationality.

LEGAL ENTITIES

As for legal entities, article 5 of the Nationality and Naturalization Law of 1934 provides:

> Legal entities (*personas morales*) of Mexican nationality are those which are constituted according to the laws of the Republic and maintain their domicile there.

By this provision Mexican law adopted the criterion of incorporation as determining nationality, in preference to that of control or of the place of its main activities. Nevertheless, the adopted criterion is a dual one: that of incorporation under domestic law and domicile in Mexico evidenced by maintaining there the seat of their administration (art. 33 of the federal Civil Code and the corresponding provisions of the state codes).[88]

VESSELS

Vessels have Mexican nationality provided they meet requirements established by article 275 of the Law of General Means of Communications of 1940 and article 90 of the Law of Maritime Navigation and Commerce of 1963[89]: (i) that they fly the Mexican flag in accordance with the law; (ii) that they are vessels abandoned in Mexican terri-

[88] Helguera Soine, La Nacionalidad de las Sociedades Mercantiles (1953); Villasenor, La Nacionalidad de las Sociedades y la Protección Diplomática de los Intereses Extranjeros en México (Mexico, 1930); Trigueros, La Nacionalidad Mexicana de las Personas Morales, 5 Revista General de Derecho y Jurisprudencia 529 (1934). Cf. The Nationality of International Corporations under Civil Law and Treaties, 74 Harv. L. Rev. 1429 (1961).

[89] D.O. Nov. 21, 1963. The Convention on the High Seas (Geneva, 1958) ratified by both countries requires in art. 5 that "there must exist a genuine link between the State [of the flag] and the ship; in particular, the State must effectively exercise its jurisdiction and control in administrative, technical and social matters over ships flying its flag."

torial water; (iii) that they have escheated to the Republic because of violation of Mexican laws; (iv) that they have been seized from the enemy and are considered as prize; or (v) that they have been built in the Republic for services there. In order to qualify for inscription in a Mexican register and fly the Mexican flag the vessel must be owned by a person of Mexican nationality, or in case of legal entities, by one established under Mexican laws, domiciled in Mexico, having as members Mexican nationals holding the majority of the capital and with members of its board of directors (consejo de administración) as well as its managers (gerente) Mexican nationals (art. 92 of the latter Law).

Vessels flying the Mexican flag are considered, when on the high seas, as Mexican territory, and their captains as representatives of the Mexican authorities charged, among other duties, with those of the officials of the public registers according to the federal Civil Code. It may be added that vessels acquired abroad must be registered in Mexico and must start flying the Mexican flag within one year since their arrival in a Mexican port. In the meantime such vessels may be granted the privilege to fly the Mexican flag provisionally by the Mexican consul in the foreign port of departure. They may operate with a foreign crew until their right to fly the Mexican flag becomes final (art. 93 and 94 of the Law on Maritime Navigation and Commerce).

AIRCRAFT

The Law of General Means of Communication as amended in 1949,[90] contains a number of provisions regarding the nationality of aircraft as well as their registration. In accordance with the Chicago Convention on International Civil Aviation (1944), aircraft registered in the Mexican register have Mexican nationality which is available only to aircraft owned by Mexican nationals or Mexican legal entities. Multiple nationality is prohibited; hence, aircraft registered in a foreign country qualify for registration in Mexico only after their foreign registration is first cancelled. Acquisition, change or cancellation of the mark of nationality or of the corresponding registration of a Mexican aircraft must meet requirements established by Mexican law.

Nationality of vessels and aircraft is significant both in regard to title and other interests in them as well as to acts occurring on board. Births on board Mexican vessels and aircraft are considered for purposes of nationality to be births within the national territory, regard-

[90] D.O. Jan. 29, 1950.

less of the then geographical position of the vessel or aircraft. It may be added that in regard to births and deaths on board of Mexican civil aircraft, provisions of the federal Civil Code regarding such events on board Mexican vessels apply.

8. ALIENS

less of the then geographical position of the vessel or aircraft. It may be added that in regard to births and deaths on board of Mexican civil aircraft, provisions of the federal Civil Code regarding such events on board Mexican vessels apply.

The treatment of aliens in Mexico and in the United States is a matter of constitutional and statutory law overshadowed by generally accepted principles of international law regarding minimum standards of treatment as well as treaties binding on both countries.

TREATIES

There is no bilateral treaty presently in force between Mexico and the United States concerned with the status of their nationals in the other country. As already indicated, the Convention of Amity, Commerce and Navigation of 1831, which contained a number of such provisions, was terminated by Mexico in 1881,[91] as was the Convention Regulating Citizenship of Emigrants signed in 1868 and terminated in 1882.[92] Equally of no avail is the inter-American Convention Regarding the Status of Aliens signed at Havana in 1928;[93] even though ratified by both countries, the Convention is considered by the United States as not in force in relation to Mexico. However, the Convention on the Rights and Duties of States signed at Montevideo in 1933[94] is binding on both countries. One of its provisions reads:

> Nationals and the foreigners are under the same protection of the law and the national authorities, and the foreigners may not claim rights other or more extensive than those of the nationals.

Equally in force is the Convention on the Nationality of Women adopted at the same conference,[95] it provides that:

[91] 15 Stat. 687; In re Rodríguez, 81 Fed. 337 (Tex. 1897).

[92] 46 Stat. 2753.

[93] Mexico expressed reservations to art. 5 and 6 of the Convention. Art 5 provides that "all individual guarantees" should be extended to aliens, as they are available to their own nationals, as well as the "enjoyment of essential civil rights without detriment, as regards aliens, to legal provisions governing the scope of and usages for the exercise of said rights and guarantees"; Mexico stated that it "interprets this principle of subjecting the extent and the mode of the exercise of the essential rights of aliens to the limitations of the National Law, as applicable also to the civil capacity of aliens to acquire property in national territory." In regard to art. 6 dealing with expulsion of aliens, Mexico declared that "said rights shall always be exercised by Mexico in the manner and to the extent established in her constitutional law," i.e., art. 33 of the federal Constitution.

[94] 49 Stat. 3097.   [95] 49 Stat. 2957.

There shall be no distinction based on sex as regards nationality in
their legislation or their practice.

The impact of territorial changes on the nationality has been the
subject of international conventions, permitting the affected residents
to exercise option for one or the other nationality. The Treaty of
Peace, Friendship, Limits, and Settlement signed at Guadalupe Hidalgo
in 1848 as well as the Gadsden Treaty of 1835 offer to Mexicans in the
territories affected by these treaties in article VIII, para. (2) the choice:

> Those who shall prefer to remain in the said territories may either retain
> the title and rights of Mexican citizens, or acquire those of citizens of
> the United States. But they shall be under the obligation to make their
> election within one year from the date of the exchange of ratifications of
> this treaty; and those who shall remain in the said territories after the
> expiration of that year, without having declared their intention to re-
> tain the character of Mexicans, shall be considered to have elected to
> become citizens of the United States.

Mexicans not opting for Mexico, article IX continues, shall be "incorporated in the Union of the United States and admitted . . . to the
enjoyment of all the rights of citizens of the United States" and "maintained and protected in the free enjoyment of their liberty and property, and secured in the free exercise of their religion without restriction."

An analogous provision is contained in the Convention for the
Elimination of Bancos (1905), providing in article IV, para. (1) that

> Those who prefer to remain on the eliminated *bancos* may either pre-
> serve the title and rights of citizenship of the country to which the said
> bancos formerly belonged, or acquire the nationality of the country to
> which they belong in the future.

On the contrary, no change of nationality was foreseen for persons
within the areas included in the Convention for the Solution of the
Problem of the Chamizal (1963).

HISTORICAL BACKGROUND

The historical development of Mexican law on the status of aliens
clearly falls into two periods. The first period includes the time from
independence to the Revolution and the second from the Revolution
and the 1917 Constitution to the present. The first period is characterized by a liberal policy toward aliens and their rights, including
economic opportunities, putting aliens, in most cases, on equal footing

with Mexicans. On the contrary, the second period is expressive of restrictive policies toward aliens. Particularly in economic matters recent enactments have given Mexicans priorities in the exploitation of natural resources as well as other economic opportunities in sensitive or important areas of the Mexican economy.

The first period was foreshadowed by the constitution of Apatzigan (1814).[96] It recognized as citizens also resident aliens of the Catholic faith, not opposed to the liberty of Mexico and as such entitled to the citizenship papers (*carta de naturaleza*). In the same vein, the Plan of Iguala (1821)[97] omitted any distinctions between nationals and aliens, granting the latter rights equal to those enjoyed by all inhabitants of the Mexican Empire with no other distinction than that of "merits and virtues." In pursuance of this policy, Congress issued two decrees, one dated May 16, 1823,[98] authorizing the executive branch of the government to issue citizenship papers to aliens who apply for them, and another, dated October 7, 1823, granting aliens the right to acquire mining concessions, a right withheld from them during the colonial period.

The Act Establishing the Federation (1824),[99] the political foundation of the constitution adopted the same year, granted aliens a most generous status by promising to protect human rights generally and rights of citizens in particular by wise and just laws (art. 30). Turning to specific problems, the legislature in 1824 enacted a decree on colonization, guaranteeing to aliens who settle in Mexico, personal and property rights.[100] A subsequent decree, dated March 12, 1828, promised aliens, legally settled in Mexico, protection and enjoyment of civil rights equal to Mexicans, except in the acquisition of farm land which may be held only by naturalized aliens.[101] This status of aliens remained unchanged in the six constitutional laws of 1836, granting them all "natural rights" as well as recognizing rights emanating from international conventions.[102] But these laws maintained the prohibition against aliens holding farm land, unless they are naturalized or married to a Mexican. Nevertheless, until 1842 resident aliens have been permitted to hold urban and farm land provided it

[96] Tena Ramírez, Leyes Fundamentales de México, 1808-1957, at 32 (1957).
[97] Ibid. 113.
[98] 1 Dublan & Lozano, Legislación Mexicana . . . 649, 681 (1876).
[99] 13 Brit. & For. State Papers 695 (1848); Tena Ramírez, op. cit. 167.
[100] 2 Dublan & Lozano, Legislación Mexicana . . . 712 (1876).
[101] 2 Dublan & Lozano, Legislación Mexicana . . . 64 (1876).
[102] 26 Brit. & For. State Papers 683 (1853); Tena Ramírez, op. cit. 204.

was acquired by purchase, judicial decision, *denuncia* or any legal title, even after President Santa Anna, by a decision of September 23, 1841, forbade aliens to engage in retail commerce.[103] So it happened that the Organic Bases of 1843 refrained from establishing a general rule for the status of aliens; instead they simply referred to the existing legislation and treaties.[104]

The first comprehensive law regarding alienage and nationality was enacted on January 30, 1854, modeled, as already indicated, after a Spanish enactment in the same matter.[105] Even though the binding effect of this law was doubtful in view of the fact that after the successful revolution of Ayutla all laws enacted during the Santa Anna regime were considered abrogated, nevertheless the law apparently was followed by administrative and judicial authorities, at least until 1886 when another law regulating the same matter took effect.[106]

In the meantime, the 1857 constitution was adopted, containing significant provisions regarding the status of aliens. It proclaimed in article 1 human rights as the basis as well as the aim of social institutions. It granted to aliens all constitutional guarantees as contained in title I, section (1), subject to the right of the government to expel dangerous aliens. In return, the constitution imposed upon aliens the duty to contribute to public expenses, to obey and respect institutions, laws and authorities of the Republic, and submit to the decisions of the courts, without recourse to other remedies than those available to Mexicans (art. 33), an early appearance of the Calvo Clause.

Following this constitution, a new law on alienage and nationality was enacted in 1886, known as the *Ley Vallarta,* in recognition to its author, a learned lawyer and president of the Supreme Court, Lic. Ignacio L. Vallarta. In articles 30 through 40 on rights and duties of aliens the law recognized the principle of equality with Mexican nationals in regard to constitutional rights and individual guarantees. This significant enactment remained in force until 1934 when the

[103] Translation in Hamilton, Mexican Law, a Compilation of Mexican Legislation . . . 157, 164 (1882).

[104] Ramírez, Código de los Extranjeros: Diccionario de Derecho Internacional Público y Privado de la República Mexicana . . . (Mexico, 1870); Azpinoz, Código de Extranjeria de los Estados Unidos Mexicanos: Ensayo de Codificación (Mexico, 1876).

[105] Translation in 2 Wheless, Compendium of the Laws of Mexico . . . 523 (1910). Law regarding acquisition of land by aliens (1856) in 1 Paula Ruanova, Lecciones de Derecho Civil 68 (Puebla, 1871).

[106] Rodríguez, La Condición Jurídica de los Extranjeros en México en la Administración del Sr. General Porfirio Diaz: Síntesis de Derecho Internacional Privado (Mexico, 1903).

present Nationality and Naturalization Law entered into force, following, to a considerable extent, the footsteps left by its predecessor.

FEDERAL OR STATE LAW

The question has arisen whether the status of aliens in Mexico is a matter within the powers delegated in article 73 of the federal Constitution to the federal Congress and, consequently, outside of the reach of state law, or whether it is a matter of concurrent legislative jurisdiction, except in regard to matters expressly delegated to Congress.[107] If the first position is to prevail, then the exclusive law governing the position of aliens in Mexico would be federal law. This would mean that contracts entered into by aliens in Mexico, or their marriages and divorces would be governed by the federal Civil Code, regardless of the law of the state which would control under its applicable conflict rules.

Starting the discussion with the federal Constitution, article 73, para. XVI has delegated to the federal Congress the power:

> To enact laws regarding nationality, the legal status (condición jurídica) of aliens, citizenship, naturalization, colonization and the health in the Republic.

It may be significant that the words "nationality, the legal status of aliens" were inserted by a constitutional amendment and that a few days later a new Nationality and Naturalization Law was enacted, containing in article 50 the following provision:

> Only a federal law may modify or restrict the civil rights (derechos civiles) enjoyed by aliens; consequently, the present law and the provisions of the Civil Code and the Code of Civil Procedure for the Federal District and Territories on this subject are federal in nature and shall be binding throughout the Union.

This provision drafted closely after article 32 of the Ley Vallarta of 1886, has been interpreted in an early case in the sense that it merely repeats the provision contained in its model. Considering a divorce involving aliens, the Supreme Court decided that the divorce granted by a state court under state law was unconstitutional.[108] The decision, subsequently not repeated, was widely criticized on the ground that

[107] Siqueiros, Ley Aplicable al Estado Civil de los Extranjeros en México, 15 (44) Boletín del Instituto de Derecho Comparado de México 345 (1962).
[108] 50 Semanario (5a ép.) 554 (1936).

the status of aliens mentioned in the Constitution would better be interpreted as delegating legislation regarding the status of aliens only in regard to particular problems arising from their alienage while legislation in matters of private nature (*derechos civiles*) , i.e., applicable to nationals and aliens indiscriminately, remains with the several states in pursuance of article 124 of the Constitution.[109]

When trying to reconcile the language used in the Constitution with that adopted by the statute, it must first of all be noticed that these provisions apparently do not deal with the same question. The term "status of aliens" as used in the Constitution is not necessarily identical with what the Nationality and Naturalization Law terms *derechos civiles*. The better way seems to be to interpret the term "status of aliens" as aiming at particular situations involving aliens only because of their alienage and without including provisions applicable, for example, under article 12 of the federal Civil Code equally to nationals and aliens. Accepting the premise that the statutory term *derechos civiles* is not identical with the constitutional term of *garantías individuales* as used in the Mexican Constitution in the sense of civil rights as understood in the United States, but having the meaning common to civil law jurisdictions, namely rights and obligations of private law under the civil and procedural codes as, for example the right of property, to contract, to marry, or to execute a will. Therefore, it appears only reasonable to suggest that the constitutional provision aims primarily at what may be called the immigration status and constitutional privileges, while the statute refers to aliens in regard to their enjoyment of rules of private law, as distinguished from public law. This analysis, then, would lead to the conclusion that article 50 establishes a minimum standard of treatment in private law matters, binding upon states. Consequently, private law matters would remain within the legislative powers of the several states which may grant in their laws a more favorable treatment to aliens than the minimum standards set by federal legislation. And, by the same token, states would be prevented to set lower standards of treatment accorded to aliens in private law matters than those set in corresponding federal

---

[109] The Mexican Supreme Court seems to consider the matter of the legal status of aliens to be "federalized," i.e., a matter of federal as opposed to state law, 25 Semanario (5a ép.) 1806 (1929) , 30 Semanario (5a ép.) 1806 (1929) ; even in matters of the applicable divorce law, both substantive and procedural, 50 Semanario (5a ép.) 554 (1936). Cf. 82 Journal de Droit International [Clunet] 412, 441 (1955) .

enactments since states cannot "modify or restrict" federally granted private rights.

The question of exclusive or concurrent legislative jurisdiction in private matters involving aliens arose in a case tried before the court of the state of Sonora. In its decision dealing with the recognition of an American divorce decree, the court applied its own Code of Civil Procedure. This ruling was attacked in *amparo* by pointing to an earlier case[110] decided by the Supreme Court where the Court in general terms stated that foreign judgments "pertain to international law and, therefore, are a matter of federal concern and governed by the Code of Civil Procedure for the Federal District and Territories." Without disavowing the underlying principle, the Supreme Court in this case[111] ruled that the provisions of the Code of Civil Procedure of Sonora applied by the judge below in determining the validity of an American divorce decree

> in no way amount to legislation on the legal position of aliens, nor do they affect their substantive civil rights [*derechos civiles*], and it is clear that they cannot be considered unconstitutional on the ground urged by the complainant, aside from the fact that these provisions are not specifically applicable to aliens, but apply to anybody who seeks to enforce in a state court a judgment rendered in a foreign country. Consequently, there can be no doubt that the Congress of Sonora had the power to enact legislation establishing requirements to be met if foreign judgments should take effect in the state.

This opinion, of course, decided only that the matter of recognition of foreign judgments is not a matter involving the legal status of aliens. Therefore, the basic problem of the degree to which the legal status of aliens in Mexico must be considered "federalized" remains open, except in those states which, as regards the status of aliens, in their civil codes simply refer to federal laws as, for example, Campeche, Colima, Chiapas, Hidalgo, Jalisco, and Sonora.

STATUS OF ALIENS

Even though the Mexican Constitution has no equivalent of the equal protection clause of the fourteenth amendment of the United States Constitution,[112] the Mexican Constitution provides in article 33 that aliens shall enjoy the personal constitutional guarantees set out in

---

110 1 Semanario (5a ép.) 554 (1918).
111 5 (4) Semanario (6a ép.) 121 (1957).
112 Bayitch, Aliens in Florida, 12 U. Miami L. Rev. 129, 136 (1958).

articles 1 though 20.[113] These individual guarantees include, among
others, personal freedom (art. 2) ; free education (art. 3) ; freedom of
work and profession (art. 4), and prohibition against compulsory
services (art. 5) ; freedom of expressing ideas (art. 6), to write and
publish (art. 7), as well as the right of petition (art. 8) and assembly
(art. 9) ; the right to possess arms (art. 10) and to travel (art. 11) ;
prohibition against special tribunals (art. 13) and against retroactive
laws as well as against deprivation of life, liberty, property, possession
or rights without a trial before a competent court, or in criminal cases
by analogy or on the strength of a prevailing opinion (art. 14), freedom from extradition for political offenses (art. 15), from unauthorized searches and arrests (art. 16), and from debtors' prison (art.
17) ; guarantees regarding detention and criminal trial (art. 19 and
20), penalties (art. 21 and 22), and freedom of religion (art. 24), of
correspondence, and, finally, from quartering of soldiers (art. 26).[114]

However, some of these guarantees have been taken away from
aliens by the same Constitution, for example, the right of petition (art.
8), of political activities (art. 9), and the unlimited right to work (art.
32). Other constitutional guarantees have been restricted by general
legislation as, for example, the right to free movement in and out of
the country, the right to possess arms, and others. Aliens are also prohibited by the Constitution from exercising in Mexico the vocation
of priests (art. 130). The most significant subsequent restrictions involve the right to work, to hold land, and to engage in business or
professions. They will be discussed later.

In return, aliens owe to the host country a number of self-evident
duties: they must pay both ordinary and extraordinary financial bur-
dens imposed by the proper authorities without discrimination, and
they must obey and respect local institutions, laws and authorities.
Aliens are exempt from military service, unless they are domiciled in

[113] Villa, Tendencias de la Legislación Mexicana Hacia la Igualdad
de Condición Juridica, 11 (32) Boletín del Instituto de Derecho Comparado
de México 35 (1958). For American law, see Gibson, Aliens and the Law
(1940) ; Hesse, The Constitutional Status of the Lawfully Admitted Permanent Resident Aliens, 68 Yale L. J. 1578 (1959).

[114] Echanove Trujillo, Manual del Extranjero (Mexico, 1965); Pina,
Estatuto Legal de los Extranjeros (Mexico, 1959); Pallares, El Extranjero
en México: Sus Derechos y Obligaciones (Mexico, 1934); Zavala Alvarez,
Status of Foreigners, 82 Journal de Droit International [Clunet] 413 (1956);
Dominguez, Let's Live in Mexico: a Manual of the Laws and Regulations
Concerning Aliens Taking up Residence in Mexico (1952); James, How
to Invest and Live in Mexico (1960).

Mexico and property and peace of their community is threatened. Aliens in the status of immigrants as well as nonimmigrants admitted as political refugees or students must register in the National Aliens Register (*Registro Nacional de Extranjeros*) [115] and inform the office in charge of the register of any change in their nationality, civil status, domicile or in their activities. In order to strengthen the enforcement of these rules, the same law has imposed on all public authorities, notaries, public accountants, and brokers, the duty to demand proof that the presence of aliens they are dealing with, is lawful.[116] The only exception permitted refers to urgent cases involving powers of attorney or wills; in every case the Secretariat of Government must be notified of such transactions.

The constitutions adopted by the several states treat the status of aliens within their borders in different ways. Some constitutions contain express provisions regarding aliens, their rights and duties. As for the rights, most state constitutions refer to the federal Constitution, for example, Baja California (art. 8, para. III), Coahuila (art. 25), Durango (art. 2), Sonora (art. 1), and Tabasco (art. 1). State constitutions which contain a chapter on individual guarantees, in most cases closely follow federal provisions and make these guarantees available to all "inhabitants" of the state, thus including aliens as well, for example, Durango (art. 2 to 26), Nuevo León (art. 1 to 27), and Oaxaca (art. 1 to 21). It may be added that the term inhabitants is one of the classes in which the population of a state is divided. The other, adopted in some states, is domiciliaries (*vecinos*), which class may also include aliens, or, in some instances, persons belonging to a particular state, for example, Chihuahuans (art. 18 of its constitution), or Pueblans (art. 11 of its constitution).

Some state constitutions include among individual guarantees also equality before law. In the constitution of Puebla, for example, equality is defined as equal treatment in the sense of "the strictest equality before law without any distinctions other than those resulting from the natural or legal positions of the persons"; and in that of Querétaro as the guarantee that "laws will be applied equally toward all individuals and legal entities, provided they find themselves in identical legal positions." The same idea found expression in the constitution of Oaxaca: "The law is the same for all and from the law emanate . . .

[115] Art. 24-27 of the General Population Law as amended in 1960, D.O. Dec. 30, 1960; Regulation, D.O. Feb. 25, 1932.
[116] Id. art. 71, para.2.

the rights and duties of the individuals of the human species," while the constitution of Chiapas simply proclaims equality before the law.

In regard to duties, state constitutions paraphrase the provisions of article 33 of the federal Constitution, stressing the duty imposed upon aliens to contribute toward public needs, to obey and respect local authorities, including judicial rulings. Some constitutions, for example, that of Baja California (art. 8, para. III), repeat the prohibition against political activities by aliens.

To summarize, it may be stated that the status of aliens in Mexico is regulated not only in the federal Constitution, but also in a number of regulatory laws, among them the Nationality and Naturalization Law of 1934,[117] with additional regulations; by the General Population Law of 1947, as amended in 1960,[118] with Regulations enacted in 1962,[119] replacing those issued in 1950. Further sources are mentioned in the following text.

IMMIGRANTS AND NON-IMMIGRANTS

The status of aliens in a foreign country is, to a considerable extent, particularly in administrative matters, determined by their immigration status, that is, by their belonging to one or another class of aliens arising from the kind of their admission. Under Mexican law aliens fall into two classes: one includes aliens who come to Mexico with the intent of settling there, called immigrants (*inmigrantes*), and the other, referring to aliens who enter Mexico for other reasons. This latter class encompasses tourists, transients, visitors, political asylees, and students.

The status of immigrant (*inmigrado*) is not acquired automatically by entry, but only after having resided, once legally admitted, for a period of five years. In addition to residence, honest and socially desirable, the immigrant must obtain from the Secretariat of Government a document declaring him to be an *inmigrado*. As such he acquires certain privileges in regard to travelling, investments, and work. Among the non-immigrants, most frequent are tourists; they may stay for no more than six months while transients are allowed only thirty days. The duration of stay of political asylees is determined from case to case by administrative authorities.

No alien may stay in Mexico in a dual capacity; but he may

[117] D.O. Jan. 20, 1934.
[118] D.O. Dec. 27, 1947; D.O. Dec. 30, 1960.
[119] D.O. May 5, 1962.

apply for a change of his status in accordance with articles 51 and 52 of the General Population Law.

Within the scope of the applicable provisions, the Secretariat of Government authorizes activities allowed to aliens, in addition to fixing the place of their residence. Violations of these limitations by aliens may result in fines, administrative detention, imprisonment or expulsion. Prior to the amendments to chapter V of the General Population Law in 1960, deportation was one of the sanctions. It is distinguished from expulsion by the fact that it presupposes some violation of immigration laws, while expulsion constitutes an extraordinary power granted to federal administrative authorities by the federal Constitution (art. 33) to force aliens to leave the country without delay and without the necessity of a previous legal action, whenever administrative authorities found their "presence . . . undesirable."

FOREIGN LEGAL ENTITIES

Alienage may affect not only the status of a person sojourning in a foreign country but also the status of legal entities making their presence in a foreign country felt through one or another kind of activities. While the physical existence of a human being as a legal subject is now recognized throughout the world, the recognition of the existence of foreign created legal entities remains subject to various requirements. Once their very existence in a foreign country is recognized, the particular problems arising out of their alienage affecting their activities must be explored. This task, however, is more complicated than that of individuals since a legal entity may consist, in whole or in part, of aliens or it may use foreign capital and serve foreign interests and, nevertheless, be constituted as a domestic legal entity. Consequently, in areas where alien exploitation of local resources and opportunities is unwanted, elaborate safeguards have been erected in order to prevent or minimize foreign economic penetration under the cloak of domestic legal entities, particularly commercial companies.[120]

[120] Rodríguez, Estatuto Jurídico y Fiscal de las Sociedades Extranjeras en México, 1 (2) Boletín del Instituto de Derecho Comparado de México 9 (1948) ; Siqueiros, Las Sociedades Extranjeras en México (Mexico, 1953), and Las Reclamaciones Internacionales por Intereses Extranjeros en Sociedades Mexicanas (Mexico, 1947). Foreign Corporation Law of Mexico, in Proceedings of the 9th Conference of the Inter-American Bar Association, Dallas, 1956, at 201; Cacho Méndez, Sociedad Extranjera ante la Legislación

There are in force, both in Mexico and in the United States, provisions applicable to individual aliens while others apply both to individuals and legal entities; there also is a number of provisions governing only legal entities, both foreign and domestic, restricting or preventing aliens from acquiring interests in land or in prohibited areas of the national economy by way of indirectly controlling natural resources or business through membership or other type of participation in business associations.

In regard to foreign created legal entities, Mexican law distinguishes between civil and commercial entities, the latter engaged in commercial activities as defined by the Commercial Code (art 3, para. I).

Foreign created civil legal entities may be active in the Federal District and Territories (art. 2737 of the Civil Code), provided they obtain from the Secretariat of Foreign Relations a permit (art. 2736) which will be issued if the foreign association is established "in accordance with the laws of its own country and its charter (*estatutos*) contains nothing contrary to the Mexican standards of public order," and has a representative "domiciled at the place of its operations, properly authorized to fulfill obligations undertaken by this legal entity" (art. 2737). Once such permit is issued, the legal entity will be inscribed in the register of charters of foreign associations and societies (art. 2738). However, such entities cannot hold or administer land or hold mortgages thereon, except buildings used directly for the purposes of the entity (art. 27, VI, of the federal Constitution).

As to state law in this matter, it may be generally assumed that civil codes in force in the several states stay close to the provisions enacted in the federal Civil Code. In addition to the permit from the Secretariat of Foreign Relations, foreign legal entities are required to inscribe in the local register of civil associations. In some codes they are admonished not to violate local laws.

Mexicana (Mexico, 1955); Gyves Goches, Estatuto Jurídico sobre las Sociedades Extranjeras en México (Mexico, 1952); Mantilla Molina, Capacidad de los Extranjeros para Ser Accionistas en Derecho Mexicano, 2 La Società per Azioni alla Metà del Secolo XX: Studi in Memoria de Angelo Sraffa 547 (Padova, 1961); Derbez Muro, El Control de la Constitución de las Sociedades Anónimas, in Comunicaciones Mexicanas al VI Congreso Internacional de Derecho Comparado 133 (1962); Miranda, Foreign Investment and Operations in Mexico, 2 Arizona L. Rev. 187 (1960); Sánchez Mejorada, Special Treatment by the Mexican Government of Foreign Owned Business and Investment, in San Antonio Bar Association, The Legal Aspects of Doing Business in Mexico 69 (1964).

For foreign commercial associations, the Commercial Code provides that "foreign associations or agencies and their subsidiaries which engage within the national territory in commercial acts" will be considered as merchants in the sense of the Commercial Code (art 3, para. III) and, consequently, will be subject to all rights and duties imposed on merchants by the same Code. Business associations "legally constituted abroad which settle in the Republic or maintain there an agency or subsidiary, are allowed to engage in commerce, thus subjecting themselves to this Code in regard to the setting up establishments (*establecimientos*) within the national territory, in regard to their commercial operations as well as in regard to the jurisdiction of the courts of the nation" (art. 15). However, before they may engage in business, they must be inscribed in the commercial register (art. 24),[121] kept in the offices of the public property registers. The inscription presupposes a permit from the Secretariat of Industry and Commerce (art. 251 of the General Law of Commercial Associations).

The question has arisen whether or not the recognition of foreign commercial associations depends on its inscription in the commercial register. In its earlier decisions the Mexican Supreme Court indicated that such inscription is necessary. In the case of Zardain Hnos (1929),[122] and in the well known Palmolive case (1929),[123] followed by the Ferrocarril Intercalifornia (1929),[124] the court denied *ius standi in judicio* to American corporations unless they comply with requirements of registration. In the Palmolive case, for example, the court stated that:

> In order for a foreign company to have legal existence in the Republic, it is necessary to comply with the requirements imposed by national law. It is not sufficient that it has been constituted in accordance with the laws of the country where it was organized. Without complying with their requirements [i.e., local registration], it cannot be properly assumed that the foreign company is a subject in regard to rights and obligations in Mexico.

However, the following year, a different solution was reached in

---

121 29 (1) Semanario (5a ép.) 1107 (1931); 46 (2) Semanario (5a ép.) 1460 (1937); 47 (1) Semanario (5a ép.) 746 (1937); 49 (1) Semanario (5a ép.) 1207 (1938).

122 27 Semanario (5a ép.) 387 (1929).

123 27 Semanario (5a ép.) 1294 (1929). 1929-1930 Annual Digest 261; also in Katz & Brewster, The Law of International Transactions and Relations 180 (1960).

124 29 Semanario (5a ép.) 1107 (1929).

the Chickering case (1930) .[125] There, the Supreme Court distinguished between the requirement of registration as condition for engaging in business and the right of a foreign corporation to bring *amparo,* made available under the then applicable Regulation (art. 6) to civil and commercial companies regardless of their nationality.

Enacted in 1934, the new General Law of Commercial Associations[126] replaced the pertinent provisions of the Commercial Code. It recognizes in general terms foreign commercial associations "lawfully constituted" as having "legal personality in the Republic" (art. 250) ,[127] and adds that such associations may engage in commerce only after their inscription in the commercial register (art. 251) .[128] An inscription will be allowed only upon an authorization from the Secretariat of National Economy, which will be granted (i) if the company proves that it has been established in accordance with the laws of its own country, by producing an authenticated copy of its charter (*contrato social*) and of other related documents as well as a certificate to the effect that the association has been lawfully established and authorized, issued by the diplomatic or consular representative of its country in Mexico; (ii) that the charter and other documents do not violate Mexican standards of public policy; and that (iii) the company settles in Mexico or establishes there an agency or a subsidiary (art. 251) .[129]

---

[125] 29 Semanario (5a ép.) 16 (1930). 3 Hackworth, Digest of International Law 713 (1942) ; Latty, International Standing in Court of Foreign Corporations, 28 Mich. L. Rev. 28 (1930) ; Schuster, The Judicial Status of Nonregistered Foreign Corporations: Mexico, 7 Tulane L. Rev. 341 (1933) ; Voekel, A Comparative Study of the Laws of Latin America Governing Foreign Business Corporations, 14 Tulane L. Rev. 42 (1939).

[126] D.O. Aug. 4, 1934.

[127] 49 (1) Semanario (5a ép.) 1062 (1938) ; 99 Semanario (5a ép.) 969 (1949).

[128] Inscription of a mortgage in favor of a foreign corporation does not replace registration; nevertheless, the corporation may appear in court, 43 (4) Semanario (5a ép.) 1312 (1935) ; 76 Semanario (5a ép.) 2077 (1944).

[129] Legal Status of Unregistered Foreign Business Organizations in Mexico, 51 Colum. L. Rev. 774 (1951). Cf. Recognition of the Legal Personality of Foreign Commercial Corporations, 22 Am. J. Int'l L. (supp.) 157 (1928).
Another type of business association, i.e., de facto, was recognized by an amendment of art. 2 of the Code (D.O. Feb. 2, 1943), providing that
> Associations not inscribed in the public commercial register which have acted as such (*exteriorizado*) in relation to third persons, have legal personality regardless of whether or not their existence is derived from a public document.
Cf. 105 Semanario (5a ép.) 2055 (1951) ; 125 Semanario (5a ép.) 1995 (1957).

In view of these changes the distinction between the recognition of the mere existence of a foreign business association, on the one hand, and its privilege to engage in commercial activities in Mexico, was definitively established.[130] The question of mere recognition of existence of a foreign corporation involving the right to appear in court in order to defend its title to land as well as initiate *amparo* proceedings against a judgment recovered by the State of Durango to escheat land under the Civil Code of the same state (art. 778), came before the Supreme Court in the case of United States Land & Lumber Company (1958).[131] Even though the plaintiff, a Delaware corporation, was not registered in accordance with article 251 of the General Law of Commercial Associations, the Supreme Court decided[132] that the legal existence of the foreign corporation must be recognized, quoting from the report (*exposición de motivos*) accompanying the General Law that:

> When a foreign association intends to establish in the Republic an agency or a subsidiary or to engage in commerce in a continuous manner, it has to comply with the formalities and assurances set up in article 251; but whenever a foreign association is faced with the task of defending before Mexican authorities rights created by legal acts validly effectuated within or without the national territory, then only the proof of having been lawfully established is required for the recognition of its existence.

The court found that the Delaware corporation has proven to have been legally established abroad by the documents accompanying the inscription of the litigated title to land, acquired in 1904. Consequently, the Court concluded, the corporation has a "legal personality in Mexico, even if it is not inscribed in the commercial register." In the opinion of the Court an inscription was not required since the act involved, namely that of acquiring and holding land in Mexico, did "not constitute a continuous exercise of commerce by the foreign corporation."[133]

In a later case involving the International Land and Investment Company, an American corporation suing a Mexican national for re-

130 57 Semanario (5a ép.) 856 (1938); 102 Semanario (5a ép.) 118 (1949).

131 7 Semanario (6a ép.) 53 (1958).

132 Changing its prior position in 76 Semanario (5a ép.) 2077 (1954), but referring to 99 Semanario (5a ép.) 969 (1949).

133 Foreign corporations acting in Mexico through agents may bring *amparo*, 130 Semanario (5a ép.) 400 (1965).

covery of land, the Court found that the plaintiff corporation did not comply with the requirements of article 250 of the General Law.[134] However, in the Court's opinion, this point was not properly raised by the Mexican defendant, nor did the attacked judgment "violate any provision of public order," since articles 27, paragraph (I) , and 33 of the federal Constitution deal with the capacity of foreign corporations to exercise rights inherent in ownership of land rather than with their capacity to appear in courts as parties plaintiff.

Of course, for the purpose of engaging in regular commercial activities, a full compliance with requirements contained in article 251 of the General Law of Commercial Associations is needed.[135]

EMPLOYMENT

Even though article 4 of the federal Constitution guarantees to everyone, including aliens (art. 33) , the right to work,[136] the right has

[134] Registration of a foreign corporation not required for bringing *amparo,* 102 Semanario (5a ép.) 118 (1950) ; 26 Semanario (6a ép.) 177 (1959) .

[135] 94 Semanario (5a ép.) 2152 (1948) ; 99 Semanario (5a ép.) 966, 1209 (1949) . For American law, see Wilson, U.S. Commercial Treaties and International Law 182 (1960) ; Drachsler, The Status of Aliens Corporations in the Law of the United States, 23 Fordham L. Rev. 49 (1954) ; Vries, Situación de las Sociedades Extranjeras en el Derecho de los Estados Unidos, (2) Cuadernos de Derecho Angloamericano 9 (1954) ; Menalco Solís, Creation and Enforcement of a Minimum Standard Treatment Applicable to Foreign and Domestic Juristic Persons, 37 Tulane L. Rev. 205 (1963) .

The Declaration, signed in Washington, June 25, 1936 (T.S. No. 973, also 7 Hudson, International Legislation 355, 1941) providing:

> Companies constituted in accordance with the laws of one of the Contracting States, and which have their seats in its territory, shall be able to exercise in the territories of the other Contracting States, notwithstanding that they do not have a permanent establishment, branch or agency in such territories, any commercial activity which is not contrary to the laws of such states and to enter all appearances in the courts as plaintiffs or defendants, provided they comply with the laws of the country in question.

was ratified by the United States with the following understanding: 1. It shall be understood that the companies described in the Declaration shall be permitted to sue or defend suits of any kind, without the requirement of registration or domestication; 2. It is further understood that the Government of the United States of America may terminate the obligations arising under the Declaration at any time after twelve months notice given in advance.

[136] Freedom to work for aliens, 119 Semanario (5a ép.) 3597 (1954) ; also 84 Semanario (5a ép.) 2849 (1946) . Cf. 94 Semanario (5a ép) 957 (1948) .

been eroded by far-reaching limitations. First of all, the Constitution itself proclaims the principle that Mexican nationals are entitled, under equal circumstances, to priority in all types of employment with the government whenever Mexican nationality is not required (art. 32). The same principle is imposed on private employers by article 111, paragraph I of the federal Labor Law of 1931, directing them to "give preference, under identical circumstances, to Mexicans over those who are not." The federal Constitution lists, furthermore, a number of jobs, both governmental and private, from which aliens are excluded. In regard to the former, the Constitution provides that aliens cannot serve in the army or police or security forces, at least in time of peace, nor may they be appointed to positions in the navy or air force for which Mexican nationality by birth is required;[137] the same rule applies to directors of seaports and airports as well as to customs officials. In regard to private employment, the Constitution in article 32 reserves to Mexican nationals employment as captains, pilots, masters, engineers and mechanics and, generally, all types of employment as members of crews on vessels or aircraft of Mexican nationality (art. 32, para. 2). In regard to seamen the General Law of Means of Communications repeats these restrictions by providing that all personnel employed in the Mexican merchant marine must be Mexican by birth (art. 286). In regard to employment in aviation, article 319, paragraph (3) of the same law refers to "respective regulations"; aliens may be employed only as instructors under a permit issued by the Secretariat of Communications (art. 320).

Employment of aliens[138] is further restricted by the Federal Labor Law of 1931. In any type of business with more than five workers, at least 90% of workers, skilled and unskilled, must be Mexican nationals; the percentage changes to 80% in businesses with less than five workers.[139] Exceptions may be allowed by the Conciliation and

---

[137] A naturalized American national expatriated himself by joining the Mexican police force from 1943-1947, Elizarraraz v. Brownell, 217 F.2d 829 (9th Cir. 1954). Cf. Fletes-Moro v. Rogers, 160 F.Supp. 215 (S. D. Cal. 1958); Prieto v. United States, 289 F.2d 12 (5th Cir. 1961); and Kennedy v. Mendoza-Martínez, 372 U.S. 144 (1963). But see Afroim v. Rusk cited in n. 86 supra overruling the Prieto and Mendoza cases.

[138] Not necessarily under an employment contract, 113 Semanario (5a ép.) 907 (1953).

[139] Limitation of aliens' employment by percentage not unconstitutional, 36 Semanario (5a ép.) 770 (1935); 43 Semanario (5a ép.) 339 (1935); adjustment of the number of alien workers, 41 Semanario (5a ép.) 913 (1936). Zavala Alvarez, Notes on Mexican Judicial Decisions, 82 Journal de Droit International [Clunet] 413, 419 (1955). In Truax v. Raich, 239

Arbitration Board *(Junta de Conciliación y Arbitraje)* for technical
personnel. However, the provision does not apply to managers, directors, administrators, superintendents and *jefes generales* (art. 9, para.
2) . Physicians employed in plants must be Mexicans (art. 10, para. 2) .
Railways may employ only Mexican nationals while aliens may be
hired only in executive positions whenever necessary, and for technical
or administrative posts provided no Mexicans are available (art. 175) .

In a general way it may be said in view of the Regulation Regarding the General Population Law that aliens may only engage in
activities under conditions expressly stated in the controlling legislative
enactments and by "their permit to enter the country, as well as those
subsequently imposed by the Secretariat of Government" (art. 65) .

To some extent employment of aliens who enter Mexico legally
and with the intent to settle there, is facilitated because they may
take on the "administration or other positions of responsibility and
trust in establishments *(empresas)* or in institutions established in
the Republic, provided that in the opinion of the Secretariat of Government there is no duplication and that the work deserves admission
into the country."[140] Immigrants also may be allowed to "perform
technical and specialized services which, in the opinion of the Secretariat of Government, cannot be performed by local residents."[141]

Non-immigrant aliens *(visitantes)* may devote themselves to "any
artistic, scientific or sportive activities and business [*negocios*], provided such activity is permitted and honest, even if remunerated, but
only if it is temporary." This provision is not applicable to tourists
who may not engage in "paid or lucrative activities, but may engage
only in sport as well as artistic, scientific and similar nonremunerated
activities."

PROFESSIONS

In regard to liberal professions this study will be limited to the law
in force in the Federal District and Territories. There the exercise
of professions is regulated by the federal Regulatory Law Regarding
Articles 4 and 5 of the Constitution Respecting Professions in the

---

U. S. 33 (1915), Arizona law limiting employment of aliens on a percentage
basis was held unconstitutional. Altug, The Right to Work of Aliens in the
United States, 12 Anales de la Faculté de Droit d'Istambul 269 (1962) ;
Wilson, U.S. Commercial Treaties and International Law 58 (1960) .

[140] Art. 47, V, of the General Population Law and art. 59 of Regulation.
[141] Art. 48, VI, of the General Population Law and art. 60 of the
Regulation.

Federal District and Territories enacted in 1944.[142] Generally, aliens are prohibited from exercising professions regulated by this law (art. 15) which includes: actuaries; architects; bacteriologists; biologists; dental surgeons; accountants; brokers (*corredores*) ; nurses, including midwives; various types of engineers; lawyers; economists; seamen; physicians; veterinarians; metallurgical engineers; notaries; pilots; professors of education; chemists, including pharmacists; and social workers. Aliens may be engaged in work as professors to teach subjects not taught (in Mexico) or are outstanding in their area, furthermore as consultants or instructors in institutions under development; or as technical directors engaged in exploitation of natural resources (art. 18). In all cases, such work must be temporary and subject to conditions imposed by federal administrative authorities (art. 19).[143]

In a number of cases courts have found such limitations to be unconstitutional.[144] However, as indicated before, administrative authorities will continue to impose them until necessary legislative changes respond to judicial attitudes. Recently, the question was again before the Supreme Court on *amparo*.[145] An American national born in Puerto Rico and graduated from the School of Medicine of the National University of Mexico, was denied the license to practice in the Federal District, the administrative authority relying on article 15 of the law just mentioned. The Supreme Court again held article 15 to

[142] D.O. May 26, 1945; Regulation, D.O. Oct. 1, 1945.

[143] Similar laws are enacted in several states. Veracruz, for example, requires (Law No. 101, 1963, G. O., Dec. 24, 1963) for all liberal professions listed in art. 2, among them attorneys, physicians, architects, accountants, pilots as well as faculty members in universities, to be Mexicans by origin or naturalization (art. 19). Registration of degrees granted in other states (art. 11), recognized in accordance with art. 121 of the federal Constitution, as well as awarded in foreign countries, is expressly regulated (art. 14), generally prohibiting aliens to exercise "technical and scientific" professions regulated by this law. An exception is available (art. 14, para. 2) to naturalized Mexicans, provided they have completed their higher education in Mexican institutions as provided by the same law (art. 8). Aliens with professional degrees referred to in this law may only engage in professional activities within the limits set out in art. 15.

[144] Tesis 825, 118 Semanario (app.) citing 97 Semanario (5a ép.) 1666 (1948); 94 Semanario (5a ép. 189) 478 (1947); 116 Semanario (5a ép.) 677 (1953); 119 Semanario (5a ép.) 3597 (1954); 127 Semanario (5a ép.) 608 (1956); 129 Semanario (5a ép.) 271 (1956); 60 Semanario (6a ép.) 159 (1962). The Zurhellen case (1951), 109 (2) Semanario (5a ép.) 1303 (1952), also 1 (3-4) Revista de la Facultad de Derecho de México 429 (1951). Buen Lozano, Las Garantías al Trabajo, in Comunicaciones Mexicanas al VI Congreso Internacional de Derecho Comparado, Hamburgo, 1962, at 143 (1962).

[145] 35 Semanario (6a ép.) 141 (1960).

be unconstitutional as violating article 4 of the federal Constitution which guarantees everyone present in the Republic the right to engage in work, which provision, according to article 33 of the Constitution, includes aliens as well. It is true, the Court added, that paragraph (2) of article 4 of the Constitution allows states, including the Federal District, to determine the needed degrees as well as other requirements; however, this must not amount to a simple denial of the right to work as was done in article 15 of the law mentioned above.[146]

LAND

In Mexico aliens are limited in regard to owning real,[147] but not personal property. The basic provisions on holding of land by aliens are contained in article 27, paragraph (7) (I) of the federal Constitution:[148]

> Only Mexicans by birth or naturalization and Mexican companies may acquire ownership of land, waters and their appurtenances, or obtain licenses to exploit mines or waters. The State may grant such right to aliens, provided they agree before the Secretariat of Foreign Relations to be considered with regard to these assets as nationals and not to invoke the protection of their governments in matters related to such

[146] As to the legal profession Martínez Báez, El Ejercicio Profesional de Abogados Extranjeros, (26-27) El Foro (4a ép.) 67 (1959). Cf. Matter of New York County Lawyers Association, 209 Misc. 698 139 N.Y. S.2d 417 (1955). Fees of foreign attorneys are regulated in art. 130 of the Code of Civil Procedure for the Federal District and Territories.

[147] According to para. 4 of art. 27 of the Constitution, as amended in 1960 (D.O. Jan. 20, 1960), the nation owns (*dominio directo*) also all natural resources in the continental shelf as well as in the airspace over the national territory "within limits and under conditions set by international law," Regulatory Law, D.O. Feb. 1, 1960. Similarly belong to the nation waters of the territorial sea "within limits and under conditions set by international law" (art. 27, para. 5 of the Constitution as amended in 1960, D.O. Jan. 20, 1960; Regulatory Law, D.O. Dec. 31, 1956). The ownership claimed under the para. 4 and 5 is declared to be "inalienable and imprescriptible" and their exploitation, use and appropriation subject to governmental concession, Art. 27, para. 6 of the Constitution as amended in 1960, D.O. Dec. 29, 1960.

[148] As amended in 1960, D.O. Jan. 20, 1960. Prior text translated in Schoenrich, The Civil Code for the Federal District and Territories of Mexico . . . 595 (1950). Cf. Karst, Latin American Legal Institutions: Problems for Comparative Study 460 (1966); Backus & Gallagher, Federal Zones in Mexican Law (1928). However, art. 27, sec. I, contains no absolute prohibition against alien holding of land, 80 Semanario (5a ép.) 577 (1944). Requirements of deed, 60 Semanario (5a ép.) 506 (1939).

assets, under the penalty of forfeiting in favor of the Nation assets acquired thereby if they breach the agreement. Under no circumstances may aliens acquire direct ownership of land and water within a zone of one hundred kilometers from the frontier and of fifty from the coast.

The strict constitutional policy against alien land holding had to be implemented so as to prevent various methods by which this prohibition may be avoided, particularly through the device of companies which, in turn, may hold interests in land otherwise out of reach to aliens. Furthermore, situations had to be considered where aliens would acquire interest in land by means other than purchase, mainly by inheritance or adjudication. Starting with the latter problem, the Organic Law Regarding Section I of Article 27 of the Constitution, adopted in 1925,[149] must be discussed. Enacted after an exchange of diplomatic notes with the United States, it provides in article 6 that whenever an alien is about to acquire, by inheritance or adjudication, an interest in land otherwise prohibited, the Secretariat of Foreign Affairs may issue a permit to allow the adjudication as well as the registration of the document, subject to the condition that the alien involved will transfer, within no more than five years from the date of the adjudication or from the date of the death of the predecessor, respectively, the interest thus acquired to a person legally qualified to hold it. This provision is further strengthened by article 1 of the Regulation to this law, issued in 1926,[150] ordering notaries, Mexican consuls abroad and all other officials to decline to legalize documents designed to transfer to aliens, including alien companies, direct ownership in land, waters and their appurtenances within the prohibited zone, or to transfer to aliens, including alien companies, any interest or participation in a Mexican company holding direct ownership in such lands or waters. These Regulations also require (art. 2) the same officials to include in any document establishing Mexican companies or societies, open to aliens and designed to acquire direct ownership in land, waters or their appurtenances outside of the prohibited zones, a declaration by aliens who may, in the constitutive act or subsequently acquire interest or any other type of participation in the association, to the effect that they consider themselves by this very declaration as Mexicans in regard to the interest or participation

[149] D.O. Jan. 21, 1926. Translated in Schoenrich, op. cit. 604. Reppy, Mexico's Laws against Foreign Land Ownership, 24 Current History 331 (1926); Suro, The Mexican Agrarian Code, 68 Bull. P.A.U. 599 (1934).

[150] A translation of the Regulation (D.O. March 29, 1926, as amended D.O. August 19, 1939) in Schoenrich, op. cit. 606.

in such association and that they will not invoke the protection of their governments under the penalty established in the Constitution. Of course, Mexican companies engaged in fibre, mining, oil or any other branch except agriculture, may acquire land within the prohibited zones insofar as necessary for their business; but federal as well as state administrative authorities shall determine in each case that no aliens, including legal entities, participate or own shares in the association. In case these prohibitions are violated, the acquisition of such interests will be considered null and void, and in consequence of these interests being without value, the capital of the company will be lowered to the extent of the value of such participation. To avoid such consequences, interested persons must apply to the Secretariat of Foreign Relations for a permit under section I of article 27 of the Constitution, authorizing them to establish such companies or to acquire this particular kind of land.[151]

[151] A prior permit from administrative authorities is always necessary, 110 Semanario (5a ép.) 1680 (1951). Permits are not subject to judicial review, 13 Semanario (5a ép.) 429 (1923). In an amparo against ejectment by military authorities from land held quietly by alien, protection was granted except for part of the land forming "maritime federal zone" according to sec. 24 of the Law of Federal Real Property, 1902, 59 (2) Semanario (5a ép.) 3948 (1939). Aliens may under no circumstances acquire land within the prohibited zone, 104 Semanario (5a ép.) 1348 (1950); 111 Semanario (5a ép.) 533 (1952); 117 Semanario (5a ép.) 115 (1964); 127 Semanario (5a ép.) 109, 115 (1956). Aliens may not acquire land by acquisitive prescription without previous permit by the Secretariat of Foreign Relations, 8 Boletín de Información Jurídica 251 (1952); Zavala Alvarez, Derechos de los Extranjeros para Adquirir Inmuebles por Prescripción, 4 (13) Revista de la Facultad de Derecho de México 229 (1954). As to trusts, Molina Pasquel, El Fideicomiso de Inmuebles en las Zonas Prohibidas en Favor de Extranjeros, (3) El Foro (4a ép.) 29 (1954); Zavala Alvarez, Status of Aliens, 82 Journal de Droit International [Clunet] 413, 425 (1955). Land acquired by aliens in violation of art. 27 of the federal Constitution escheats to the Nation; order by court to seller to execute a deed is without effect, Informe Rendido a la Corte Suprema de la Nación, 1945, at 39. Acquisition of land by aliens is held to be only voidable and not void, 61 Semanario (5a ép.) 3441 (1938); 81 Semanario (5a ép.) 4217 (1944); 104 Semanario (5a ép.) 1348 (1950); 111 Semanario (5a ép.) 17 (1953). Acquisition on judicial sale, 47 Semanario (5a ép.) 3269 (1937); 54 (3) Semanario (5a ép.) 2888 (1939); 85 Semanario (5a ép.) 2012 (1946); 92 Semanario (5a ép.) 128 (1948); by *datio in solutum,* 117 Semanario (5a ép.) 919 (1953); 119 Semanario (5a ép.) 1758 (1954). Generally, 49 (1) Semanario (5a ép.) 1047 (1938); 60 Semanario (5a ép.) 506 (1934); 61 Semanario (5a ép.) 3441 (1939); 67 Semanario (5a ép.) 2653 (1941); 77 Semanario (5a ép.) 7270 (1944); 80 Semanario (5a ép.) 577 (1945); 81 Semanario (5a ép.) 4217 (1945); 84 Semanario (5a ép.) 221 (1946).
Cusi, Is It Safe for a Resident of Texas to Own a Ranch in Mexico, in

It may be added that according to an amendment to the General Population Law of 1960, aliens may acquire land, shares or interests therein only subject to a prior permit by the Secretariat of Government and in accordance with further conditions established in the Regulations (art. 71, para. I). This provision was recently attacked as unconstitutional on the ground that the only administrative authority empowered to issue such permits is the Secretariat of Foreign Relations.[152]

A few cases brought before the Supreme Court on *amparo* may illustrate some of the questions involved. In an action against the New Sabinas Company, Ltd., an American corporation, the Court[153] found the acquisition in 1903 of land within the hundred kilometers zone to be invalid not only because the corporation failed to acquire title in accordance with the law then in force, i.e., the decree of March 11, 1842, and that of February 1, 1856, which remained in force even after the Ley Vallarta of 1886, but also because the predecessors in title have acquired land for colonization, which dedication was not wiped out by subsequent legislation. Finally, the corporation failed to comply with requirements imposed on foreign holders of titles to land acquired prior to the 1917 Constitution, as required by article 7 of the Organic Law implementing this constitutional provision.

Another interesting question arose in *amparo* brought in 1958 by a Delaware corporation, the United States Land & Lumber Company, against a judgment recovered by the State of Durango involving land owned by the corporation but to be escheated by the State under article 778 of its Civil Code as being vacant and abandoned.[154] Among other points the State urged that the foreign corporation cannot hold land under article 27 (I) of the Constitution, under the Organic Law and under article 18 of the respective Regulation. However, this position was not accepted by the Supreme Court on the ground that "the constitutional prohibition against foreign commercial associations to acquire, possess or administer farm land [*fincas rusticas*] is not abso-

---

San Antonio Bar Association, The Legal Aspects of Doing Business in Mexico 45 (1963); Garcia Cuellar, When and Under What Conditions Can a Non-Resident of Mexico Own Real Property in Mexico, ibid. 54 (1963).

152 Martínez Báez & Morineau, Algunas Consideraciones Acerca de la Constitucionalidad del Art. 71 Reformado de la Ley General de Población . . . , (33) El Foro (4a ép.) 13 (1961).

153 3 Semanario (6a ép.) 203 (1957).

154 7 Semanario (6a ép.) 53 (1958).

lute," pointing out that the Organic Law (art. 4, 5, and 7) allows aliens who have held prior to the enactment of this law fifty or more percent of the capital in any kind of companies holding title to farm land, to continue holding such interests until their death or, as in the present case involving a legal entity, for a term of ten years. The Court recognized that in order to take advantage of this exception, aliens had to make a declaration before the Secretariat of Foreign Relations, otherwise it would be assumed that the acquisition of land has happened subsequent to the enactment of this law. However, this latter provision was considered by the Court to amount to a retroactive application of a law and, consequently, prohibited by the federal Constitution (art. 14).

In a later *amparo* (1959),[155] the Supreme Court, citing the United States Land & Lumber Company case, decided that even the prohibition against holding of agricultural land by foreign corporations is not absolute and that such corporations may hold land acquired prior to the 1917 Constitution, provided they have complied with the requirements set out in article 5 of the Regulations.

Prohibitions against alien holding of interest include also waters owned by the Nation according to the Law of Waters in the National Domain, enacted in 1934.[156] The utilization of such *aguas nacionales* is, under article 3 of the law, reserved to Mexican nationals and to civil or commercial companies established under Mexican law (art. 9).[157]

Finally, it may be mentioned that the federal Constitution (art. 27, I, para. 2) allows foreign diplomatic and consular missions to acquire land at the permanent seat of federal authorities insofar as necessary for the direct use by foreign embassies or legations, subject to reciprocity.[158]

OIL AND MINING

While the enactments just discussed deal with land and interests therein of a general nature, two particularly sensitive areas are regulated by additional laws: oil and mining.

The Law Regulating Article 27 of the Constitution Regarding

---

[155] 26 Semanario (6a ép.) 177 (1959.   [156] D.O. Aug. 31, 1934.

[157] Cf. art. 27, para. 5 of the Constitution as amended in 1960, D.O. Jan. 20, 1960. Aliens may acquire no licences involving waters under federal control, 14 Semanario (5a ép.) 979 (1924).

[158] As amended in 1960, D.O. Jan. 20, 1960.

Petroleum, enacted in 1958,[159] proclaimed the principle that only the Nation may exploit these resources (art. 2) through *Petróleos Mexicanos* (art. 4), thus making the petroleum industry a matter of exclusive federal jurisdiction (art. 9). Additional rules are supplied by other federal enactments, i.e., the Commercial Code as well as the federal Civil Code. These rules are further implemented by the Regulation issued in 1959.[160]

Less exclusive are provisions regulating mining.[161] The new Law Regulating Article 27 of the Constitution in Regard to Exploitation and Utilization of Mining Resources, enacted in 1961,[162] provides for exploitation in three ways: by the public authority, by companies with public participation, and by individuals, persons or legal entities (art. 2). However, opportunities for participation by aliens are limited. In regard to exploitation with public participation, aliens may subscribe a certain percentage of shares type B and without limitations shares type C, except foreign sovereigns and governments (art. 5). In a general way the law provides that only Mexican nationals and Mexican companies with a majority of capital subscribed by Mexicans qualify for mining concessions. Mining interests once properly acquired cannot be transferred to foreign companies or governments or sovereigns, nor to Mexican companies wherein aliens own more than 49% of the capital (art. 15). In regard to special concessions involving mineral reserves, the law contains even more stringent restrictions authorizing the granting of such concessions only to Mexican nationals or Mexican companies with at least 66% Mexican capital (art. 76).[163]

[159] D.O. Nov. 29, 1958. Becerra Gonzáles, Principios de la Constitución Mexicana de 1917 Relacionados con el Subsuelo, Antecedentes Doctrinales y Legislativos, Principios Fundamentales Contenidos en la Constitución Original y Cambios Operados después de 1917 en el Mismo Texto Constitucional (Mexico, 1967).

[160] D.O. Aug. 25, 1959.

[161] Becerra, Derecho Minero de México 213 (1963); Gonzáles Guerier, La Nueva Ley Minera, (33) El Foro (4a ép.) 67 (1961); Browning, Historic Basis of Mexican Mining Law, 7 Int.-Am. L. Rev. 1, 26 (1965).

[162] D.O. Feb. 6, 1961, as amended D.O. Jan. 4, 1966, providing in art. 150: Rights to mining exploitation cannot be transferred, totally or in part, to foreign physical persons, societies, governments or sovereigns, nor to Mexican associations wherein aliens represent in the capital a larger percentage than that indicated in art. 14 and 76 of the Law.

[163] Regulation to the Reglamentary Law of Article 27 of the Constitution in Matters of Exploitation and Acquisition of Mineral Resources (D.O. Dec. 7, 1966) provides: In case somebody receives by succession or adjudication in payment of claims properly established in his favor, shares or parts thereof, the

Additional provisions are contained in the Regulation to the Regulatory Law of Article 27 of the Constitution in Matters of Exploitation and Acquisition of Mineral Resources issued in 1966, particularly in articles 24 through 32.

BUSINESS

Significant limitations are imposed upon aliens in regard to business activities.[164] The legal basis for these limitations is a presidential decree, dated June 29, 1944,[165] issued under the authority of a decree dated June 1, 1942,[166] approving war-time suspension of constitutional guarantees. The 1944 decree required aliens as well as Mexican and alien companies to apply for a permit to the Secretariat of Foreign Relations in order to establish businesses or to acquire control thereof, or, to have aliens as members in Mexican companies whenever such

---

property (*titularidad*) of which is prohibited in pursuance of the Law and this Regulation, the Secretariat of Natural Resources may, on application by the interested party, within 30 days from the date when the claim for transfer occurred, and after having ascertained the circumstances and after consultation with the Secretariat of Foreign Relations, authorize provisionally the registration of transfer, subject to the condition that the heir sells or transfers the shares in question within the period established in article 8 of the Law, to a person legally qualified to acquire them.

[164] Martínez de Escobar, How to Do Business in Mexico (1961); Brudno, Tax and Legal Aspects of Investment in Mexico, in S.W. Legal Foundation, Proceedings of the 1960 Institute on Private Investment Abroad 403 (1960); Siqueiros, Las Sociedades Extranjeras en México (1953); Ryan, Handbook for the Foreign Investor in Mexico (1960); Batiza, Current Attitudes on Mexico's Treatment of the Foreign Enterprise, 17 Rutgers L. Rev. 365 (1963); Miranda, Foreign Investment and Operations in Mexico, 2 Arizona L. Rev. 187 (1960); Hidalgo, Mexico, in Friedman (ed.), Legal Aspects of Foreign Investment 355 (1959); Ramon Beteta, What are the Businesses in Which Foreign Capital May be Invested in Mexico, in San Antonio Bar Association, The Law of Doing Business in Mexico 1 (1963); also Notas sobre las Inversiones Extranjeras en México, (39) El Foro (4a ép.) 25 (1962). Generally, Carrillo Castro, La Regulación Jurídica de las Inversiones Extranjeras en México (Mexico, 1965).

[165] D.O. July 7, 1944, and Oct. 29, 1945.

[166] D.O. June 2, 1942. Presently the list of activities affected contains: radio; production, distribution and display of movies; maritime, air, land, urban and interurban transportation; culture of fish and fishing; canning of sea products as well as of other foods; publishing and advertising; production, marketing and selling of carbonated and non-carbonated beverages, including concentrates; bottling of fruit juices and fruit; production and marketing of rubber products as well as basic chemical and petrochemical products; fertilizers and insecticides. Siquieros, Aspectos Jurídicos en Materia de Inversiones Extranjeras, (6) El Foro (5a ép.) 87, 96 (1967).

business involved industry, agriculture, cattle, timber, purchase and exploitation of land, agricultural or urban, including their subdivision or urbanization. A permit from the Secretariat was required also for the acquisition of land, mining concessions, water works and combustible minerals in general, including their leases for more than ten years, as well as trust arrangements (*contratos de fideicomiso*) whenever the beneficiary of the trust should be an alien. The same decree required also a prior permit for the establishment of business companies which have or may have aliens as members, particularly whenever Mexican members may be replaced by aliens, or the scope of the company may be changed. The decree vested the Secretariat with discretionary powers to deny such permits or impose specific restrictions. Furthermore, the decree required that aliens acting under such permits to maintain in Mexico their principal seat of business and use Mexico as the area of their investments, except in cases where land is inherited. In regard to farm land the decree emphasizes that in no case such land may exceed limitations established by the Agrarian Code.

When the state of war ended, individual constitutional guarantees were reestablished by an executive decree, dated September 28, 1945,[167] abrogating previous decrees issued under the extraordinary powers granted in 1942, except those authorizing intervention by the Republic in the economic life of the country (art. 6). Considering the decree dated June 29, 1944 as one affecting the economic life of the country, the Secretatiat of Foreign Relations has continued to exercise broad powers granted therein.[168] Subsequently, an interdepartmental agreement was published in 1947, [169] establishing the Mixed Interdepartmental Commission (*Comisión Mixta Intersecretarial*) charged with the task of coordinating the administration of laws controlling domestic and foreign investments. The administrative agencies involved, namely the Secretariat of Government, the Secretariat of Foreign Relations, the Secretariat of Treasury and Public Credit, as well as the Secretariat of Agriculture and Cattle Industry, shall cooperate in working out uniform solutions to problems of foreign investments, particularly in re-

---

[167] D.O. Dec. 28, 1945, and Jan. 21, 1946.

[168] Minvielle, Intervención de la Secretaria de Relaciones Exteriores en las Sociedades Mercantiles (Mexico, 1960); Derbez Munro, El Control de la Constitución de las Sociedades Anonimas, in Comunicaciones Mexicanas al VI Congreso Internacional de Derecho Comparado, Hamburgo, 1962, at 133 (1962).

[169] D.O. June 23, 1947.

gard to acquisition of assets by aliens as well as their participation in foreign and domestic business associations. This agreement remained in force although the Commission functioned, rather irregularly, until October 5, 1953, when it met for the last time. During its active period, the Commission produced a dozen general instructions (*normas*) .

Later, the Secretariat of Foreign Relations, partly on its own initiative, partly on urging from other administrative agencies, continued acting vigorously under the 1944 decree. Relying on article 3 of the 1944 decree the Secretariat gradually established a list of activities where 51% Mexican participation shall be required. This requirement applies, among others, to the following activities: radio stations; movies; transportation; fisheries and fish culture; canning; publishing; advertising; soft drinks; bottling of fruit juices; rubber products; basic chemical products; petroleum derivates; fertilizers; insecticides, agriculture and mining. Invoking art. 27 (IV) of the federal Constitution, the Secretariat denied permits to corporations to acquire, possess or administer farms, including timber land; it also denied permits to explore or exploit oil deposits, or to purchase, sell or do business in oil or its derivatives, including greases, fuels and lubricants and others. In spite of the prevailing opinion that the 1944 is unconstitutional or, at least presently, without force, parties affected did not, for obvious reasons, resort to *amparo*. Nevertheless, in 1962 such a case involving the Quimica Industrial de Monterrey, S.A. came before the Supreme Court. The Court found the control under article 1 and 2 of the 1944 decree only temporary and limited to the time for which the suspension of constitutional rights was in force; however, in view of art. 15 of the decree dated October 1, 1944, restoring these rights by abrogating the decree of 1944 in its entirety, the Court decided that the Secretariat of Foreign Relations had lost powers granted under the 1944 decree.[170]

[170] 66 Semanario (6a ép.) 25 (1964). For a full discussion, Laughran & Foster, Foreign Investment in Mexico: the Emergency Decree of 1944, 39 Tulane L. Rev. 538 (1965). The same position was taken by the Supreme Court in *amparo* brought by Playtex de Mexico, S.A. (September 7, 1964, amparo en revisión no. 3596/64). In order to prevent a binding rule to emerge, the Secretariat of Foreign Relations has shifted its statutory basis to art. 3, para. VII of the Law Regarding Secretariats and Departments of State (D.O. Dec. 24, 1958) which provides that the Secretariat is "authorized to grant to aliens licenses or authorizations required by law for the acquisition of land, waters and their appurtenances, to obtain concessions to exploit mines, waters or combustibles situated in the country; to participate (*intervenir*) in the exploitation of natural resources, to make investments specified in commercial or industrial enterprises, as well as participate in Mexican civil and commercial associations, and in regard to these to amend

Additional legislative enactments have further restricted alien participation in other areas of business. The Federal Law on Radio and Television of 1960 excluded aliens from any type of participation (art. 14) by limiting the issuance of permits to Mexicans and companies whose members are Mexicans and adding that in case these companies should be corporations, their shares must be nominative.[171] Foreign banking institutions[172] regulated by the General Law on Credit and Auxiliary Operations of 1941[173] may maintain subsidiaries or agencies in Mexico and engage in banking and credit activities listed in article 2. They must comply with the General Law Regarding Commercial Associations of 1934, particularly in regard to permits required by article 251, to be issued by the Secretariat of Economy. They also must maintain locally a minimum capital as prescribed by law and in the governmental permit. Such capital, including reserves, must be invested in domestic securities (art. 6, para. 2). These provisions apply also to agents, representatives and commission agents employed by foreign corporations (art. 6, para. 3). The required permit will only be issued provided applicants expressly promise to be liable "for transactions undertaken in the Republic with all their assets without limitations, not only with those located in the Mexican territory" (art. 7). Moreover, they must submit themselves to this law as well as to the jurisdiction of Mexican courts in all matters "related to business transacted in the national territory" (art. 7, para. 1), with the understanding that this submission shall be for the benefit of all persons who may have claims against or hold shares issued by the corporation, for transactions or business performed in the Republic or to be performed there (art. 7, para. 2). However, in 1965 far reaching limitations have been enacted to the effect that

> under no circumstances may, in any form, participate in these corporations foreign governments or their official agencies, foreign financial entities or groups of aliens, natural or legal, regardless of the kind of their formation, either directly or through nominees.

---

or change their charters and bylaws in order to accept aliens as members and acquire immovables or interests in them." Siqueiros, Aspectos Jurídicos en Materia de Inversiones Extranjeras, (6) El Foro (5a ép.) 87, 96 (1967).

[171] D.O. Jan. 19, 1960. Fernández, La Nueva Legislación Mexicana sobre Radio y Televisión, (28–29) El Foro (4a ép.) 107 (1960).

[172] Molina Pasquel, The Mexican Banking System, in U. Miami School of Law, Mexico: A Symposium on Law and Government 59 (1957); Myers, Mexico, in Beckhard (ed.), Banking Systems 573 (1954); 1 Hernández, Derecho Bancario 61 (Mexico, 1956); Rivera, Banking Across the Border and Back, in San Antonio Bar Association, op. cit. n. 151, at 33 (1963).

[173] D.O. March 31, 1941.

The official Bank of Mexico (*Banco de México*) is regulated by the Organic Law of 1941.[174] It imposes on branches and agencies of foreign banks the duty to subscribe a determined amount of the Bank's shares (art. 6, para. II), with the understanding that any alien who should "at any time acquire shares of the Bank, shall be considered by this very fact a Mexican with regard to his interest and participation, and shall be assumed to agree not to invoke the protection of his government, under the penalty of forfeiting his interests and participation for the benefit of the Nation. . . ." Like any other bank, investment banks must be licensed by the government according to article 3 of the Law of Investment Companies of 1955; they are prohibited from acquiring foreign issued shares and bonds, except those issued to finance basic production in Mexico (art. 12, IX).[175] Surety corporations (*instituciones de fianza*), regulated by the federal Law of Surety Institutions of 1950, must be Mexican corporations (art. 3).[176]

Different provisions apply to foreign insurance companies.[177] Their subsidiaries may enter the Mexican insurance market only through arrangements with domestic insurance companies, provided the latter are not prevented from doing so by law. Furthermore, such subsidiaries must secure a permit from the Secretariat of Treasury and Public Credit to be issued provided Mexican insurance companies are unable or unwilling to underwrite the particular kind of insurance. Subsidiaries must meet requirements set up by the General Law of Commercial Associations, among them to have the minimum capital required by article 20; to invest their capital, reserves and surplus in the way prescribed by the same law, and have the capital, reserves, negotiable instruments and other assets locally available. Moreover, they must obtain a permit from the federal government, by

[174] D.O. May 31, 1941. Translation in Aufright, Central Banking Legislation: a Collection of Central Banking Monetary and Banking Laws 857 (1961).

[175] Hill, Investment Companies in Mexico: a Study of Mexican Mutual Funds (Mexico, 1959); Salinas Martinez, Las Sociedades de Inversion en México, 8 (31–32) Revista de la Facultad de Derecho de México 233 (1958); Batiza, Mexico: New Law on Investment Companies, 5 Am. J. Comp. L. 625 (1956). A decree (D.O., December 30, 1965) prohibited participation in any form by foreign governments or their official agencies as well as foreign financial interests in whatever form; the decree also contains penalties and transitional provisions.

[176] D.O. Dec. 29, 1950 and Jan. 18, 1951. D.O., Dec. 30, 1965, p. 13, providing also for subsidiaries, penalties and transitional provisions.

[177] Crawford, Foreign Insurance Companies in Mexico, 18 Tulane L. Rev. 89 (1943).

proving to have been in business for five years as well as their qualification for the respective type of insurance business under the law of the
country of their incorporation. They also must have a local representative vested with unlimited powers of attorney (according to art. 2554 of
the federal Civil Code) and keeps books as provided by law. Such foreign subsidiaries may not distribute dividends not arising from local
business, nor advertise accounting data related to their parent organization (art. 6). Finally, foreign insurance companies authorized to do
business in Mexico must deliver insurance policies to the locally insured through their local subsidiaries (art. 5, III). It may be added that,
as in regard to banking and surety institutions, a recent enactment
(1965) forbids foreign governments or their official agencies or foreign
financial entities or groups in whatever form to participate in Mexican
insurance companies.[178]

Being a matter of federal legislation various types of transportation are regulated by the Law of General Means of Communication
of 1940. For activities not declared a government monopoly like, for
example, mails and telephone (art. 11), concessions may be issued only
to Mexican nationals or to companies established under Mexican law
(art. 12). In respect to the latter the law requires that in case they have
alien members, the charter (*escritura*) must provide that they will consider themselves in regard to the concession as Mexican nationals and
not invoke protection of their governments in this matter. If they
should break this promise, the law provides for escheat of the assets
acquired "for the construction, establishment, or exploitation" of the
particular means of communication as well as all other rights derived
from the concession (art. 12). In the same vein, the law prohibits any
cession or mortgage, direct or indirect, or any kind of encumbrance or
alienation of the concession, of rights conferred therewith, or of the
routes, buildings, stations, auxiliary services, dependencies or accessories in favor of any foreign government or state (art. 18). The admission of aliens as members of a licensed company is prohibited and any
transaction violating this prohibition is declared to be utterly null and
void (art. 18, para. 2); furthermore, the shares, obligations and bonds
issued by enterprises subject to this General Law lose all value to their
holder the moment they are acquired by a foreign government or state
(art. 19). Enterprises which have their board of directors or other administrative committees abroad, must have at the place of their seat

[178] D.O., Dec. 30, 1965, contains rules for subsidiaries of foreign insurance companies as well as for penalties and transitional provisions.

(*domicilio*) or at the place designated in the concession a local board of directors or administrative committee, corresponding to their organizational structure (art. 87).

In regard to maritime transportation, the General Law reserves in favor of Mexican vessels significant maritime business (art. 194), with only limited opportunities for foreign vessels (art. 197). Furthermore, the Law on Maritime Navigation and Commerce, enacted in 1963, grants the right to fly the Mexican flag only if the corporate owner of the vessel is constituted under Mexican law, has a domicile in Mexico, the majority of corporate capital is held by Mexicans, and members of the board of administration as well as the manager are Mexicans (art. 92).

Stringent limitations are imposed upon electrical power companies. The law regulating this industry, originally enacted in 1939, was drastically amended in 1960[179] making the industry a public monopoly:

> The production, transformation, distribution and supplying of electrical energy . . . belongs exclusively to the Nation. No concessions will be granted to individuals, and the Nation will utilize natural assets and resources necessary for these purposes.

The right to exploit fishing resources in national waters is reserved to Mexican nationals by birth and to companies established under Mexican law, as provided in the Fisheries Law of 1950.[180] Aliens may obtain licenses provided specific requirements of article 27 (I) of the federal Constitution and of the respective Organic Law and Regulation are met. Domestic licensees are forbidden to take as partners "foreign governments or sovereigns," or to assign in their favor any rights under their own licenses (art. 6, para. 3). Licensees must use vessels of Mexican registry both for fishing as well as for transportation of the catch to domestic ports (art. 29); an exception is allowed for the sport of fishing, for scientific purposes and in regard to foreign vessels having licenses in accordance with chapter V of the same law (art. 29).

Exploitation of timber resources is also reserved to Mexican nationals or to "associations of persons, also Mexicans, who in fact are the organizers in these exploitations." A transfer of permits is conditioned on the approval of the competent administrative authority (art. 87 of the Forestry Law of 1960).[181]

---

[179] D.O. Jan. 6, 1960 and Dec. 23, 1960; cf. art. 27, para. 6, in fine, of the federal Constitution as amended in 1960, D.O. Dec. 29, 1960.
[180] D.O. Jan. 16, 1950.   [181] D.O. Jan. 16, 1960.

Similar restriction are imposed on aliens in regard to radio and television under the Federal Law on Radio and Television enacted in 1960.[182] Concessions to operate commercial stations may be granted only to Mexican nationals or associations whose members are Mexicans (art. 14). Neither concessions nor installations or other accessories may be ceded or in any manner encumbered in favor of a foreign government or person, nor may they be admitted as members to licensed associations (art. 23). In case of violation of these prohibition the interests involved escheat to the Nation without any compensation (art. 24).

ACCESS TO COURTS

Aliens are guaranteed free access to courts, both in Mexico[183] and in the United States. In Mexico the guarantee is given in article 17 of the federal Constitution providing that "courts shall be open for the administration of justice at such times and under such conditions as the law may determine; their services shall be free and, consequently, all judicial costs are prohibited."

Free access to courts is available both to individuals and to legal entities. "Everyone who, according to the law, is in full possession of his civil rights, may appear in court," provides article 44 of the Code of Civil Procedure for the Federal District and Territories. This he may do personally or by an authorized representative (art. 46). Corresponding provisions appear in the codes of civil procedure in force for the several states. As has been discussed elsewhere in this study, foreign companies may appear in court without local registration, provided their litigation does not arise out of local business activities.

The same principles apply to *amparo* proceedings. *Amparo* may be brought by anybody affected by an act or law in violation of constitutional guarantees (art. 4 of the Law of Amparo), including legal entities which may appear through their authorized representatives (art. 8).

---

[182] D.O. Jan. 19, 1960. Immigrants may engage in commerce in accordance with art. 4 of the federal Constitution, 53 Semanario (5a ép.) 107 (1953). For American attitudes, see Vagts, The Corporate Alien: a Definitional Question in Federal Restraints on Foreign Enterprise, 74 Harv. L. Rev. 1489 (1961), and United States of America's Treatment of Foreign Investments, 17 Rutgers L. Rev. 375 (1963); also Wilson, U.S. Commercial Treaties and International Law 209 (1960).

[183] No alien is prohibited to bring an action to which he is entitled, in Mexican courts provided they have jurisdiction, 75 Semanario (6a ép.) 34 (1965). Cf. Alcalá-Zamora, Clínica Procesal 29 (1963).

In the United States jurisdiction may be denied, among others, because of lack of reciprocity required in § 2502 of the Judicial Code for actions by aliens in the Court of Claims.[184] Jurisdiction also may be declined on ground of the doctrine of *forum non conveniens.* On the international level, the doctrine will only be applied where there is an alternate court in the United States available to a domestic plaintiff. In the case of Burt v. Isthmus Development Company[185] the court held it inconsistent with the purpose of the doctrine to "allow a federal court to decline to hear a case and thereby in effect decree that a citizen must go to a foreign country to seek redress of an alleged wrong." In this case a New York citizen brought an action against a Texas corporation for recovery of money, equipment and damages in connection with drilling for oil in Mexico. The defendant corporation not only urged the application of the doctrine since all of its records, activities and all witnesses were in Mexico but also pointed out that the court is not "empowered to administer the laws of Mexico governing the transactions." In denying the motion, the court relied primarily on the lack of alternate court in the United States, adding that "the fact that success or failure [of the action] depends upon the law of Mexico does not, in itself, justify dismissal." Similarly unsuccessful was the reliance on the *forum non conveniens* doctrine in Root v. Superior Court.[186] In a prohibition proceeding, with the Nacional Financiera, S.A. of Mexico, as the real party in interest, the doctrine was held inapplicable in a situation where jurisdiction against the Mexican corporation was perfected *quasi in rem* under the controlling provision of the California Code of Civil Procedure, through attachment of bank accounts in California belonging to the Nacional Financiera. "To hold otherwise would be to provide a debt-free haven for nonresidents who desire to hold and maintain assets in California while not subjecting themselves to California jurisdiction, even as against claims of California residents. This is not the policy nor the law of this state. If it is convenient to hold and maintain property within the state, it should be convenient to defend that property within the state when the need arises. In such circumstances as are herein present," the court con-

[184] Jurisdiction of the Court of Claims: Foreign Plaintiffs and the Reciprocity Statute, 1962 Duke L.J. 145.

[185] 218 F.2d 353 (5th Cir. 1955), cert. denied, 349 U.S. 922 (1955); Latimer v. S.A. Industrias Reunidas F. Matarazzo, 175 F.2d 184 (2d Cir. 1949), cert. denied 338 U.S. 867 (1949). Cf. The Problem of the Inconvenient Forum, 15 U. Miami L. Rev. 273 (1961).

[186] 25 Cal. Rptr. 784 (1962).

cluded, "the fair and orderly administration of the laws fully justifies subjecting defendant to the jurisdiction of our courts to the extent of the property seized in this state."

A third kind of jurisdictional rules may affect aliens' actions in federal courts. These courts have "original jurisdiction of any civil action by an alien for a tort only, committed in violation of the law of nations or a treaty of the United States."[187] In Lopes v. Reederei Richard Schroeder,[188] both aliens, the Mexican plaintiff demanded damages caused by unseaworthiness and negligence. However, the court dismissed the action on the ground that both the doctrine of unseaworthiness and the alleged negligence are unconnected with the law of nations or treaties.

Finally, federal jurisdiction may be unavailable because of lack of diversity of citizenship, a requirement unknown to Mexican law. In Hernandez v. Lucas,[189] for example, the court held that:

> Although the children may have acquired the domicile of their deceased mother in Mexico, a citizen of the United States who acquires a domicile in another country is neither a citizen of any State nor an alien, and may not sue or be sued in federal courts on the basis of diversity of citizenship.

The same result was reached in Van der Schelling v. U.S. News & World Report, Inc.[190] discussed in the following section.

[187] 28 U.S.C.A. § 1350.   [188] 225 F. Supp. 292 (1963).

[189] 245 F. Supp. 901 (S.D. Tex. 1966). Diversity was found in Aguirre v. Nagel, 270 F. Supp. 535 (Mich. 1967).

[190] 213 F. Supp. 756, aff'd, 324 F. 2d 956 (3d Cir. 1963). Regarding sovereign immunity of government owned vessels, Mexico v. Hoffman, 324 U.S. 30 (1945). In regard to Pemex, however, the court took the position that its vessels "are not considered as being owned by the Republic of Mexico, but by an independent corporation engaged in a private commercial activity"; therefore, its vessels "may not only be seized to acquire jurisdiction but will have to respond for damages," with the alternative to "either post a bond for its release, which bond will be responsible for the damages found, or "allow the vessel to remain seized, and if damages are assessed against Petróleos Mexicanos, the vessel seized may be sold to satisfy the judgment." S. T. Tringali Co. v. Tug Pemex XV, 274 F. Supp. 227 (1967). Cf. United States v. Tug Pemex XV, 1960 A.M.C. 896.

In F. M. Stone Engineering Co. v. Petróleos Mexicanos, 352 Pa. 12, 42 A. 2d 57 (1945), Pemex was considered on suggestion from the Attorney General to be a governmental instrumentality and its deposit in an American bank immune from attachment. The subsequent change in policy evidenced by the Tate Letter (26 Dep't State Bull. 984, 1952) is discussed in Bayitch, International Law, 16 U. Miami L. Rev. 240, 266 (1961), and Florida and International Developments, 1962–1963, 18 U. Miami L. Rev. 321, 343 (1963).

9. DOMICILE

Aliens may, regardless of their nationality, acquire domicile in Mexico since the "acquisition, change or loss of domicile are governed by the laws of Mexico," according to article 35 of the Nationality and Naturalization Law, which laws include both federal and state laws applicable according to their respective coverage.[191]

The federal Civil Code and state codes following it distinguish three classes of domicile: natural, legal, and elective. The natural domicile is defined as the "place where a person resides with the intent to settle" (art. 28). In case there is no such place, then the place where the person has its business is regarded to be the domicile; and in case even such place cannot be found, the place where the person is present (art. 29). Since the required intent to settle is difficult to ascertain, the Code presumes such intent from the fact that a person has resided in one place for more than six months (art. 30). After the passing of six months, this presumption may be rebutted by notifying, within fifteen days, the municipal government of the former domicile as well as that of the new residence, that the new resident does not wish to abandon the former domicile or to acquire the new. Such notification, however, may not affect third persons to their detriment (art. 30). A special kind of domicile is the marital domicile, defined as the place where spouses are bound to live together (art. 163), subject to the power of the courts to exempt a spouse from this duty whenever the other spouse has transferred the domicile abroad, except in public or social service, or has settled in an unhealthy or improper place (art. 163). However, the scope of marital domicile has been interpreted restrictively in view of the fact that the wife's domicile, even if derived from her husband's, is not included in the notion of a legal domicile (art. 32).[192]

The legal domicile is defined as the place "where the law fixes one's residence for the enjoyment of rights and performance of duties,

[191] Art. 35 of the Nationality and Naturalization Law (1940).

[192] Semanario (5a ép.) 1560 (1937); 79 Semanario (5a ép.) 6373 (1944); Informe Rendido a la Suprema Corte de la Nación, 1948, at 135. Whether or not a Mexican national is domiciled in France is determined by Mexican law, i.e., art. 29 of the federal Civil Code, 51 (2) Semanario (5a ép.) 1609 (1938).

even though actually the person may not be there" (art. 31). The legal domicile of an unemancipated minor is that of the person to whose parental authority the minor is subject, or that of a guardian. The legal domicile of military personnel is the place where they are ordered to be; of public officials the place where they serve for more than six months; and of persons imprisoned for more than six months, the place of incarceration for all matters that have arisen after the judgment, and that of their former domicile for previously established relations (art. 32).

The domicile of a legal entity[193] is the place where its administration is located (art. 33). Entities having their administration outside of the Federal District or Territories are deemed to be domiciled where "the juridical acts have been executed, in regard to anything pertaining to these acts" (art. 33, para. 2). Branches operating in places different from the parent organization are domiciled at the same places with respect to performance of obligations incurred by them (art. 33, para. 3).

Finally, both persons and legal entities may designate an elective domicile, to be effective for the performance of obligations (art. 34 and 2082).

The fact that an alien is domiciled in Mexico in accordance with Mexican law may have significant legal consequences. Among others, domicile is a factor to be considered in connection with birth (art. 54 and 57 of the federal Civil Code), death (art. 126); marriage (art. 97); abandonment (art. 196); divorce by consent (art. 272, para. 1); adoption (art. 39); homestead (*patrimonio de familia,* art. 728); absence (art. 666, 674 and 705); place of performance (art. 2082, 2085 and 2387); and illicit societies (art. 2692, para. 3). Domicile may also determine jurisdiction in procedural situations, for example, in marital controversies, including annulment (art. 156, IX of the Code of Civil Procedure for the Federal District and Territories), divorce actions (art. 156, XII); and regarding venue (art. 156, IV).

The notion of citizenship, presupposing American nationality and domicile in one of the several states, is significant in the United States in determining diversity jurisdiction of federal courts. In Van der

---

[193] Informe Rendido a la Suprema Corte de Justicia de la Nación, 1942, at 27. Even when a corporation has changed its domicile but has omitted to inscribe it in the register, its former domicile under art. 34 of the federal Civil Code remained effective throughout the Republic, 126 Semanario (5a ép.) 405, 465 (1955).

Schelling v. U.S. News & World Report, Inc.,[194] the federal court dismissed a diversity action brought by plaintiff, an American national, living for more than ten years in Mexico as an immigrant. The court interpreted the statutory requirement of "citizens of a State, and foreign states or citizens or subjects thereof" in accordance with the *lex fori* and held that plaintiff, in spite of her domicile in Mexico and her immigration status under Mexican law, cannot be considered a "citizen or a subject" of Mexico. The characterization of these terms according to the *lex fori* seems justified, particularly since jurisdiction rather than choice-of-laws was involved.

[194] 213 F. Supp. 756, aff'd 324 F. 2d 956 (3rd Cir. 1963). Diversity existed in an action brought by a citizen of both Michigan and Mexico against a defendant, citizen of Michigan, Aguirre v. Nagel, 270 F. Supp. 535 (1967).

10. CALVO CLAUSE

Aliens who acquire interests or engage in activities in Mexico under administrative permits, are generally required to accept in regard to such interests or activities the Calvo Clause.[195] By so doing aliens agree to be treated as if they were Mexican nationals, i.e., accept the application of Mexican laws as they would apply in similar situations to Mexican nationals, as well as the jurisdiction of Mexican courts and, simultaneously, renounce the right to invoke diplomatic intervention on their behalf by their national governments.

Originally, the Calvo Clause appeared as a part of contractual arrangements between the Mexican government and aliens engaged in business in Mexico. This contractual basis was subsequently replaced by statutory schemes designed to bring the Clause into operation generally. There are three main types of such statutes. One consists of legislative enactments imposing upon Mexican authorities the duty to include the clause in permits issued to aliens for engaging in economic activities. Another method is the establishment of the presumption that aliens engaged in particular activities have impliedly submitted to the Clause. And finally, there is the straight legislative enactment nullifying any contrary arrangements. In certain instances legislation went even farther by declaring all interests acquired by aliens in violation of the Clause to escheat to the Republic. Examples of such provisions have already been mentioned.

[195] Shea, The Calvo Clause: a Problem of Interamerican and International Law and Diplomacy (1955); U.S. Department of State, The Calvo Clause in American Policy and Practice (1947); Feller, Some Observations on the Calvo Clause, 27 Am. J. Int'l. L. 461 (1938); Freeman, Recent Aspects of the Calvo Doctrine and the Challenge to International Law, 40 Am. J. Int'l. L. 121 (1946); Garcia-Mora, The Calvo Clause in Latin American Constitutions and International Law, 33 Marq. L. Rev. 204 (1950); Lipstein, The Place of the Calvo Clause in International Law, 22 Brit. Yb. Int'l L. 130 (1945); Summers, The Calvo Clause, 19 Va. L. Rev. 459 (1933), also 5 Hackworth, Digest of International Law 635 (1943). Mexican writings include, among others, García Robles, La Cláusula Calvo ante el Derecho Internacional (1939); Sepúlveda, La Responsibilidad Internacional del Estado y la Validez de la Cláusula Calvo (Mexico, 1944); and Las Reclamaciones Internacionales y la Cláusula Calvo, (11–12) El Foro (4a ép.) 197 (1956); Mantilla Molina, Capacidad de los Extranjeros para Ser Accionistas en Derecho Mejicano, in 2 La Società per Azioni alla Metà del Secolo XX: Studi in Memoria de Angelo Sraffa 547, 549 (Padova, 1962).

Presently, the Calvo Clause not only appears in the federal Constitution (art. 27, para. 7, I) but has also found expression in state constitutions. There it mostly aims at securing a complete effect to local judicial actions by denying aliens remedies against judicial decisions not available to Mexican nationals (e.g., Aguascalientes, art. 13, III; Baja California, art. 3, III; Coahuila, art. 25; Jalisco, art. 5, III; Michoacán, art. 4, II; and Nayarít, art. 14).

The Clause appears also in federal enactments, for example, in article 32 of the Nationality and Naturalization Law denying aliens and alien legal entities the right to use "remedies other than available under the laws to Mexicans. Nevertheless, diplomatic intervention is allowed "in cases of denial of justice or of intentional and patently malicious delay of its administration."[196]

In the United States a limited effect is granted to the Clause as expressed in the recent Restatement:[197]

(1) If an alien, as a condition of engaging in economic activity in the territory of a state, agrees with the state that he is to be treated as if he were a national in respect to such activity, and that his only remedy for injury in this respect is that available under the law of the state, such agreement, commonly called a "Calvo Clause," relieves the state

[196] Art. VI of the Consular Convention of 1942 provides that consular officers may "for the purpose of protecting" their nationals "in the enjoyment of rights accruing by treaty or otherwise" address local, state or national authorities, adding that "Complaint may be made for the infraction of those rights. Failure upon the part of the proper authorities to grant redress or to accord protection may justify interposition (*intervención*) through diplomatic channel." It may be added that the Pact of Bogotá (1948) ratified by Mexico, but only signed by the United States, provides in art. VII that the contracting countries "bind themselves not to make diplomatic representations in order to protect their nationals, or to refer a controversy to a court of international jurisdiction for that purpose, when the said nationals have had available means to place their case before competent domestic courts of the respective state," 1 Annals of the O.A.S. 91 (1949).
Article 32 of the Nationality and Naturalization Law provides:
Aliens and alien legal entities as well as Mexican associations which have or may have aliens as members, cannot obtain licenses (*concesiones*) nor can they execute contracts with municipalities, local governments or federal authorities without a prior permit from the Secretariat of Foreign Relations; such permit may be issued provided the interested parties agree before the Secretaria to consider themselves as Mexicans in regard to such contracts, and not to invoke, insofar as they are concerned, the protection of their governments, under the penalty determined from case to case by the Secretariat of Foreign Relations.
[197] Restatement (Second), Foreign Relations Law of the United States § 202 (1965).

of responsibility for injury to the economic interests of the alien in
respect to such activity, if

(a) the alien is in fact treated as favorable as if he were a national,

(b) the conduct of the state causing injury to the alien does
not constitute violation of an international agreement under the rule
stated in § 165 (1) (b), and

(c) the law of the state affords the alien a bona fide remedy for
such injury that satisfies the requirements of procedural justice stated
in §§ 180–182.

(2) A Calvo Clause does not relieve a state of responsibility for injury to an alien except as stated in Subsection (1).

Two remarks seem to be in order. First, that the Restatement deals
only with situations where the Clause is agreed upon by contract while
sidestepping the problems arising from statutory imposition of the
Clause. Secondly, the comment took the position that forfeiture of
interests in case of noncompliance with the Clause "is not effective . . .
in a case where the alien has exhausted whatever remedies are afforded
by the law of the taking state. In such situation, the forfeiture is an
unlawful taking."[198]

[198] The Calvo Clause is defined in the Interamerican Treaty on Pacific Settlement (Pact of Bogotà of 1948) ratified by Mexico but not by the
United States, 1 Annals of the O.A.S. 91 (1949), as an undertaking between
American Republics "not to make diplomatic representations in order to
protect their nationals, or to refer a controversy to a court of international
jurisdiction for the purpose, when the said nationals have had available
the means to place their case before competent domestic courts of the respective state" (art. VII). The United States declined to accept this provision, maintaining "the rules of diplomatic protection, including the rule
of exhaustion of local remedies by aliens, as provided by international law."

PART THREE

Choice-of-Law

11. PERSONS

Choice-of-law rules dealing with individuals determine the law which shall govern the existence of a legal subject personified in a human being and the law determining the capacity to create legal consequences, the latter understood in a general sense as well as in regard to the status, for example, filiation, adoption, and marriage.[199]

STATUS

In regard to physical persons Mexico has adopted a strict territorial principle, expressed in article 12 of the federal Civil Code,[200] in the following language:

> Mexican laws, including those regarding the status and capacity of persons, apply to all inhabitants of the Republic, be they nationals or aliens, domiciliaries or transients.

Compared with its predecessor in the Civil Codes of 1870 and 1884 providing that:

> Laws regarding the status and capacity of persons are binding on Mexicans of the Federal District and Territories of Lower California, even

---

[199] 1 Rojina Villegas, Derecho Civil Mexicano: Personas (Mexico, 1959).

[200] Civil status of aliens is controlled by art. 12 of the federal Civil Code to the exclusion of any foreign laws, 25 (2) Semanario (5a ép.) 1805 (1929); 39 (1) Semanario (5a ép.) 1549 (1936); 98 Semanario (5a ép.) 1623 (1948); 116 Semanario (5a ép.) 897 (1953). Art. 12 of the federal Civil Code appears in some state codes with considerable changes as, for example, in the Civil Code of San Luis Potosí (1946) where art. 8 reads:

> Laws regarding status and capacity of persons are binding on Mexicans of [this] State even when residing abroad, in regard to acts which shall be performed partially or completely within this State.

when they reside abroad, in regard to acts to be performed, wholly or partly, within the areas mentioned,

the present statute shows distinct differences: first, the substantive coverage of the present statute is expanded so as to include not only matters of personal status and capacity, but all acts within the Republic, of whatever nature they may be. The second difference is evidenced by the expanded scope of its application. While the old provisions limited the application of this rule to the Federal District and Territories, and to inhabitants thereof, the present article 12 claims nationwide application, both in regard to Mexican nationals and aliens. On the contrary, the extraterritorial application of the laws in force in the Federal District regulating status and capacity, to Mexican nationals "of the Federal District and Lower California" even when they are abroad, was omitted in the 1928 Code in favor of a consistent territorial limitation.

Starting the discussion with the notion of personal status, it must be stated that the articles just cited do not define the term. The meaning must be deduced from other provisions of the Code. From article 35 of the federal Civil Code it appears that civil status includes matters connected with the birth, recognition of children, adoption, marriage, divorce, guardianship, emancipation, death as well as absence, presumption of death and loss of legal capacity to administer one's patrimony (incompetency). Any juridical acts and transactions involving the status of persons present within Mexico, nationals as well as aliens, are governed by what the Code terms "Mexican laws." The question arises what is to be understood by this term, particularly since the Civil Code, at this point, has dispensed with the question of applicability *vel non* of this very Code and has, instead, enacted a rule addressed not only to inhabitants of the Federal District and Territories for which the Civil Code is intended (art. 1), but to all persons found within the Republic. However, it seems that no significant difficulties may arise since the laws so identified are not aimed at this particular Civil Code but Mexican laws generally. Therefore, it seems proper to assume that this provision is declaratory of the territorialistic principle generally, and in matters of personal status in particular, thus excluding foreign laws from being applied in Mexico in regard to the personal status of persons within Mexican territorial sovereignty. Instead, Mexican laws govern, i.e., those laws which control under the conflicts provisions in force under federal laws or under the laws enacted in the several states in matters of status as the case may be. The only difficulty still lingering on is the question of whether or not the status of aliens is exempt from this rule and reserved to exclusive federal legislative jurisdiction. This question has already been discussed in this study. There it was pointed out that some of the state civil codes refer to the federal Civil Code in all matters regarding aliens acting within the Republic and not only their status and capacity.

Acts affecting the civil status of persons present in Mexico, nationals as well as aliens, must be inscribed in the proper civil register, kept in the Federal District and in every state or political subdivision thereof. To use again as example the federal Civil Code, it provides in article 35 for the inscription of acts affecting the civil status of Mexicans and aliens, among them birth, recognition of paternity, adoption, marriage, divorce, guardianship, emancipation and death. In regard to aliens, article 70 of the Population Law orders these officials not to inscribe any such act unless the alien proves the legality of his presence in Mexico.

On the interstate level, the territorial scope of the laws is restated in section I of article 121 of the federal Constitution, in the sense that the laws of a state "shall have effect only in its own territory and, consequently, cannot be binding outside of it." In regard to acts affecting civil status, section IV of the same article reads that:

> IV. Acts of civil status in accordance with the laws of one State shall be valid in the others.

In view of the territorial principle pervading Mexican law, this provision is best interpreted in the sense that acts affecting the civil status (e.g., marriage, adoption) performed in one Mexican state (or within the Federal District or one of the Territories) in accordance with its controlling law, i.e., conflict as well as substantive, will be recognized in any other state or within the Federal District or Territories. This means that a marriage entered into in one state, the civil code of which declares the *lex loci celebrationis* to be determinative of impediments, will be recognized in all other jurisdictions. Of course, difficulties may arise from public policy interpreted differently in different jurisdictions. As a consequence, attack in one state on recognition of a marriage celebrated in another state on grounds of public policy prevailing in the second state must be foreseen. Finally, acts creating or affecting personal status may properly be perfected in one jurisdiction and then claim recognition in another where such status does not exist. For example, must adoption properly executed in one Mexican state be recognized in another in spite of the fact that the latter state has no adoption at all? In one case, the Mexican Supreme Court has ruled in favor of recognition.

As already stated, the great majority of the state civil codes have adopted the federal Civil Code as their local enactments with only a few necessary adjustments; the term "Mexican laws" in article 12 of the federal Code is changed so as to refer to the laws of the particular state. However, some of the state codes still retain the language of the 1870 or 1884 federal civil codes. The Civil Code of Puebla of 1901, for example, provides in article 10 that laws regarding personal status and capacity apply to all Pueblans "even if they reside outside of the State whenever acts involved are to be performed, wholly or partly, within that State." This provision appears to be unconstitutional in interstate situations because it cannot be reconciled with article 121, IV, of the federal Constitution. On the contrary, in international situations this constitutional principle does not prevail and, consequently, the provision may not be objectionable.

This brings the discussion to the final question as to what law governs the status of Mexican nationals abroad insofar as Mexican courts are concerned. There is no express statutory provision available, and answers vary. One would allow an equivalent of the Mexican territorial principle apply in favor of the law in force in the foreign jurisdictions and suggest the *lex loci celebrationis*. Such solution may find support in article 12 of the federal Civil Code which limits in regard to status the application of what it terms "Mexican laws" to Mexican nationals present within the national territory, an argument strengthened by a comparison with the 1870 and 1884 versions of the same provision granting a limited extraterritorial effect to Mexican laws in regard to Mexican nationals.

The only statutory provision regarding acts of status involving Mexican nationals abroad deals with one aspect of the problem, namely with the registration in Mexico of such foreign status creating acts.[201] In order to "establish the civil status acquired by Mexicans outside the Republic" article 51 of the federal Civil Code declares sufficient the respective foreign documents, provided they are registered in the

---

[201] Since art. 12 and 13 of the federal Civil Code provide that Mexican laws apply to all inhabitants within the Republic, nationals as well as aliens, and to acts and contracts entered into abroad and to be performed in the Republic, formalities regarding registration in the civil register do not apply to acts celebrated abroad (art. 15 of the same Code), unless they shall take effect within the Republic; to hold otherwise would amount to claiming for Mexican laws extraterritorial effect, 98 Semanario (5a ép.) 1623 (1948).

proper civil status register in Mexico. In regard to marriages by Mexicans abroad, the proper register is that of the marital domicile of the couple in Mexico (art. 161). The significance of these provisions becomes clear by taking into consideration the strict rule contained in article 30 of the same Code that personal civil status can only be proven by the inscriptions in the civil status register and that no other evidence may be admitted, except where the law so permits as, for example, in case of adoption (art. 85). The lack of such registration will be discussed elsewhere in this study.[202] It may be added that acts by Mexican nationals abroad resulting in changes of their personal status may involve consular services under the Consular Convention of 1942. "In pursuance of the laws of their respective countries" (art. VII) consular officers may, among other functions, "authenticate . . . transcripts of civil registry of the nationals of the State which has appointed the consular officer," i.e., of the sending country. However, under this Convention consular officers may not act as officers of the civil status register nor perform functions which are, under Mexican laws, entrusted to officials of the civil register (art. 35 to 138 of the federal Civil Code).

Jurisdiction in matters of personal status (*estado civil*) which includes questions involving birth, death, marriage or its nullity, filiation, recognition, emancipation, guardianship, adoption, divorce, absence, and attacks on rulings by the civil registrar (article 24 of the Federal Code of Civil Procedure) is vested, within the federal judiciary and in states which have adopted federal procedural codes, in the court of defendant's domicile (art. 156, IV, of the Code of Civil Procedure for the Federal District and Territories).

In conclusion, it may be pointed out that article 12 of the federal Civil Code adopted also in the great majority of the states civil codes mentions status and capacity only as two areas not to be excluded from the scope of this provision. Thus it makes Mexican laws applicable to "all inhabitants of the Republic." This general conflict rule embracing not only the status and capacity but also any acts of persons present within the national territory without any limitations makes article 12 and its counterparts in the civil codes of the states one of the most pervasive provisions of the Mexican conflict law.

There are only few American cases dealing with status related to Mexican law, outside of those arising from marriage or filiation to be discussed later. In Banco de Sonora v. Bankers' Mutual Casualty Com-

---

[202] See infra under Marriage.

pany[203] the question arose whether or not persons handling insured articles sent by mail in Sonora, at the seat of the insured, were adults, as required by the insurance policy. The court looked to the *lex loci actus,* i.e., Sonora, and found it to be not a common law type, but one of the "civil or Justinian law." Since this controlling law was not properly proven in the court below, the appellate court reversed.

CAPACITY

Capacity *(capacidad)* means legal ability in the sense of existence as well as acting so as to create legal consequences. According to article 22 of the federal Civil Code capacity starts with the birth and ceases with the death, with the addition that a *nasciturus* is considered to be under the protection of the law, and even to be born in regard to "effects established in the Code." A person of age has full capacity and may "dispose freely of one's person and its assets, within the limits set by law" (art. 24), while minors and incompetents are granted only limited capacity to act (art. 23).[204]

According to article 12 of the federal Civil Code and the corresponding provisions in the codes of a majority of the states, capacity is a matter governed by the *lex loci actus* whenever the person acts within the Republic, regardless of its nationality or domicile. However, in states still maintaining the language of the 1884 federal Civil Code (Puebla, San Luis Potosí, Tlaxcala and Guanajuato) the law regarding capacity in force in the respective state also applies to Mexicans "even when they reside abroad, in regard to acts to be performed, wholly or partially" within these states.

The *lex loci actus* prevails generally in regard to the capacity on the part of aliens to issue *titulos* or to perform of any acts related to them. This rule applies equally to their capacity for such acts when performed in the Republic or abroad (art. 252 of the General Law on Credit Titles and Operations).

[203] 124 Iowa 576, 100 N.W. 532 (1904).

[204] Cf. art. 33 of the Nationality and Naturalization Law, providing that aliens, alien legal entities *(personas morales)* as well as Mexican associations which have or may have aliens as members, cannot enter into contracts with municipal or local governments nor with federal authorities without a permit from the Secretariat of Foreign Relations.

Suretyship by alien not null because of his non-compliance with art. 92, 183, and 206 of the General Population Law, 72 Semanario (5a ép.) 4657 (1942).

MARRIAGE

Mexican law considers marriage to be a civil contract (art. 130, para. 3 of the Constitution). Consequently, marriage and all other acts affecting the marital status are within the exclusive jurisdiction of secular authorities as distinguished from ecclesiastical. In regard to marriage, this principle is expressed by making the act of marriage an administrative matter (art. 146 of the federal Civil Code) and divorce as well as annulment a matter within the exclusive jurisdiction of civil courts.

Like all civil (private) law, family law is a matter within the legislative powers of the several states and of the federal Congress in regard to the Federal District and Territories. Therefore, the respective conflict and jurisdictional rules must be consulted. Using the federal Civil Code as example, it may be pointed out that a marriage ceremony is performed by the official of the civil registry office (art. 101) of the domicile of at least one of the parties (art. 97), provided parties have supplied the necessary documents (art. 98) and there is no impediment (art. 156). The marriage is inscribed in the civil register (art. 103), which constitutes the only proof (art. 39).[205]

Mexico considers marriage not only a civil act but also a formal act to be officiated by a competent public official.[206] Consequently, it is not surprising to find that the institution of common law marriage is not recognized. Even a statutory common law marriage recognized, for example, by the Civil Code of Tamaulipas (art. 70), now repealed, was ruled by the Supreme Court to be void as violating article 130, para. (3) of the federal Constitution.[207] The only *de facto* cohabitation recognized by Mexican law is concubinage which need not meet requirements for a common law marriage under American law and creates only limited consequences. It establishes presumption as to children (art. 383 of the federal Civil Code) and gives the female

---

[205] Carillo, Matrimonio y Divorcio en México a la Luz del Derecho Internacional Privado, 14 Revista de la Facultad de Derecho de México 923 (1964). German translations of statutory materials are available in Bergmann, Internationales Ehe-und Kindschaftsrecht (1963–, 1.1.).

[206] American consular officers cannot perform marriages, Parry, A Conflicts Myth: The American Consular Marriage, 67 Harv. L. Rev. 1187 (1954); Mexican diplomatic and consular officers only where there is treaty authority, e.g., with France, 1908 (102 Brit. & For. State Papers 645, 1913), and Italy, 1910 (103 Brit. & For. State Papers 560, 1914).

[207] 121 Semanario (5a ép.) 38 (1951).

partner limited rights of inheritance (art. 1635), but does not establish a marital status between the parties comparable to common law marriages. In regard to common law marriages between aliens established in accordance with the foreign *lex loci,* Mexican courts would probably follow such law. However, it is rather doubtful that a common law marriage abroad between Mexican nationals would be recognized, if for no other reason than for lack of a document to be registered in the civil register in accordance with article 161 of the same Civil Code.

These provisions apply to all inhabitants of the Federal District and Territories, both Mexican nationals and aliens.[208] In case their marriages are celebrated in one of the states, the corresponding provision of state civil codes apply. It may be added that for marriages between aliens and Mexican nationals in Mexico a permit must first be obtained from the Secretariat of Government as well as the legality of their presence in Mexico evidenced (art. 70 of the General Population Law).[209] An alien who marries a Mexican by birth or has children born in Mexico, may obtain the status of immigrant or retain the present immigration status. In case of the first alternative, the alien will lose his status of immigrant if the marriage is divorced or the alien has defaulted on duty of support as "prescribed by the civil legislation in matters of support" (art. 49 of the General Population Law as amended in 1960).

Marriages performed in one Mexican state between nationals or aliens will be recognized in another state and in the Federal District and Territories (art. 121, IV of the Constitution).[210] Such recognition does not depend on local registration of the marriage in a state other than that of the *locus celebrationis.* Article 97 of the Civil Code of Veracruz (1932) requiring additional registration in Veracruz of marriages celebrated in a sister-state has been held unconstitutional[210a] on the ground that the matter of recognition of a status act is within the exclusive jurisdiction of the federal Congress. Consequently, the

[208] Alien's marriage in Mexico, lack of interpreter of no effect, 108 (3) Semanario (5a ép.) 2112 (1952).

[209] Marriage of an alien woman in violations of these administrative requirements makes the act of marriage punishable but not void, 123 (2) Semanario (5a ép.) 1062 (1951). Mexican law applies to matrimonial matters of an alien domiciled in Jalisco under art. 12 of the federal Civil Code, Jurisprudencia (civ.) 632 (1964).

[210] On interstate recognition of marriage, Informe Rendido a la Corte Suprema de la Nación, 1944, at 39 (two cases).

[210a] 15 Semanario (6a ép.) 225 (1958).

provision of article 121, IV, of the federal Constitution cannot be modified by state legislation. However, this rule does not apply to international situations, namely where marriages are celebrated abroad.

As to marriages of Mexican nationals abroad, the former federal Civil Code (1884) contained an express provision in article 175:

> A marriage celebrated abroad between Mexicans, or between a Mexican national and an alien woman, or an alien national and a Mexican woman, will have civil effects in the national territory, provided it is found that it was celebrated in accordance with the formalities and requirements established by the laws of the place of celebration, and provided that the Mexican [male] has not violated provisions of this Code regarding impediments, capacity to marry and the consent of parents (*ascendientes*).

This provision, however, was not carried over into the present Civil Code. Nevertheless, it appears that, in substance, courts still follow its precepts. Of course, the provision is in force in those states whose civil codes remained addicted to the 1884 Code. This is, for example, the case in Puebla (art. 169 of the Civil Code). Unqualified recognition seems to be granted to foreign marriages in the Civil Code of Veracruz (art. 97).[211]

In any case, the civil effects (*efectos civiles*) in Mexico of a marriage of Mexicans who marry abroad, is dependent on its inscription in the civil register kept at the "place where the spouses establish their domicile" (art. 161, para. 1 of the federal Civil Code). What these civil effects are, is not clear since the Code only mentions them when providing that they will be retroactive to the day of marriage if the inscription is performed within three months, and effective from

---

[211] In case of marriage abroad, registration thereof is necessary to give effects within the Republic, regardless of whether or not the wife has acquired Mexican nationality, 33 Semanario (5a ép.) 636 (1931); marital domicile in the Republic will be determined by the place where foreign marriage was registered, 54 Semanario (5a ép.) 1560 (1937). Martínez Negrete, El Matrimonio de Mexicanos en el Extranjero, aun Cuando no se Inscribe en el Registro no es Concubinato, 15 Revista de la Facultad de Derecho de México 413 (1965).

The requirement of registration was recognized by an American court in an action by a Mexican national against the administator of his wife's estate, Logan v. Forster, 250 P. 2d 730 (1952). There, plaintiff attempted to prove community property, pointing out that this regime would apply to the property of spouses in Mexico. However, he did not succeed because of failure to register his marriage celebrated in Texas with the deceased, an American national, in the civil register in Mexico. In the opinion of the court, this "obviated the need for applying the Mexican system of community property to subsequent acquisitions."

the day of inscription if it is delayed longer (art. 161, para. 2). Even though the Code establishes no sanctions for lack of inscription, it may be assumed that lack of registration will deprive a marriage concluded abroad of its specific local effects regarding, for example, the marital property regime. However, it appears that the very existence of such marriage will not be affected.[212]

In regard to marriages celebrated abroad doubts may arise in cases where the ceremony was performed not before a civil, but before an ecclesiastical authority according to the rules of the respective religious law and valid under the *lex loci celebrationis.* Difficulty may stem from the principle proclaimed by the federal Constitution (art. 130, para. 3) that marriage is a civil act and, therefore, marriages celebrated by Mexicans abroad in religious forms may be in violation of the public policy of their home country. These difficulties may arise both in regard to religious marriages celebrated in countries where there is a free choice between civil and religious marriage forms, as, for example, in the United States, or where religious marriage is the only available form as, for example, for Catholics in Spain and Italy.

It would appear that religious marriages between non-Mexicans abroad will be recognized. Still paying lip-service to the principle that

---

[212] As to consequences of lack of domestic registration art. 180 of the federal Civil Code of 1884 provided that "Lack of such registration (*transcripción*) does not invalidate the marriage; however, the contract of marriage will have no civil effects [*efectos civiles*] if such registration is not made." The Mexican Supreme Court, 33 Semanario (5a ép.) 636 (1933), interpreted this provision to mean that lack of registration will affect "primarily the recognition of its existence in the Republic, in order to make it amenable to dissolution, including consequences for the guilty party arising from a divorce judgment as, for example, guardianship and alimony," and concluded that a non-registered foreign marriage cannot be divorced by Mexican courts since they may exercise jurisdiction only in regard to "juridical relations between individuals arising from acts or contracts performed in accordance with the laws of the land, or, even if performed abroad, such acts and contracts meet both requirements of foreign law as well as of our laws in order to create legal effects in the national territory, and thus parties have submitted themselves to the laws of the land in regard to acts which should be enforceable in the Republic." It is to be kept in mind, however, that the corresponding article 161 of the present federal Civil Code contains no express sanction for noncompliance with the requirement of domestic registration.

A foreign, non-registered marriage is basis for bigamy, 119 Semanario (5a ép.) 407 (1954); effects of inscription of a marriage in Germany by a Mexican, 119 Semanario (5a ép.) 2398 (1954); foreign marriage cannot be dissolved without proper judicial proceedings, 95 Semanario (5a ép.) 144 (1948).

"canon law marriages have no legal effect at all", but admitting the fact that such marriages create "effects similar to civil marriages, and that they, as long as they exist, constitute for those united by the canonical *vinculum,* an impediment against a civil marriage with a different person," the Mexican Supreme Court decided that all this does not prevent Mexican courts "following international obligations, from giving marriages of any other kind but civil, performed in other countries, the same validity and legal effects as they have according to their own laws,"[213] i.e., according to the *lex loci celebrationis.* The Court appears to be willing to give to a religious marriage in Spain all civil effects it has under the *lex loci celebrationis* by agreeing with the way the law was applied by the lower court, namely article 5 of the Hague Convention as well as article 15 of the federal Civil Code. Faced with the question whether or not a foreign religious marriage between aliens is to be considered an impediment in Mexico, the Supreme Court decided that such effect is "based on an act performed in Spain and governed by its laws; and that according to these laws, the canon law marriage has legal effects similar to those connected with the civil marriage, even though under Mexican law such impediment would not be recognized since a canon law marriage produces no effects." Nevertheless, this did not prevent the Court from recognizing the validity and effects of a foreign non-civil marriage as they are given to such marriages under the *lex loci celebrationis,* provided such effects are properly proven (art. 284 of the Code of Civil Procedure for Federal District and Territories).

With the exception of the unsuccessful statutory common law marriage in Tamaulipas, already discussed, Mexico has no institution identical with the American common law marriage.[214] However, stabilized extramatrimonial relations are granted certain well defined effects. While the federal Civil Code and the codes patterned after it are reluctant to give to a companion more than a share of the estate of the male consort in cases of intestacy (art. 1635) and privileges to their children (art. 383), some state civil codes go much further. The female companion may inherit in Hidalgo, Morelos, San Luis de Potosí, and Veracruz, but in Campeche, Jalisco, and Tamaulipas

---

[213] 36 Semanario (6a ép.) 45 (1960).

[214] Ortiz & Urquidi, Matrimonio por Comportamiento (1955); Menéndez, El Concubinato Legal, 8 (31) Revista de la Escuela Nacional de Jurisprudencia 33 (1946); Ochua, Derecho de Concubina, (11-12) Revista Mexicana del Trabajo 32 (1954); Arraras, Concubinage in Latin America, 3 J. Fam. L. 330 (1963).

she has not even rights granted in the federal Civil Code. In some states the female partner has the right to alimony (e.g., Morelos, art. 403; Sonora, art. 467), in the latter state against the estate if she has "lived with the deceased as if he were her husband, during the last five years immediately preceding his death or had children with him, provided both remained free of matrimonial ties during the concubinage" (art. 1443, V).

The question what effect, if any, is to be given in a Texas court to a concubinage established in Mexico was litigated in Nevarez v. Bailon.[215] The plaintiff claimed rights which would be granted in Texas to a common law wife against the estate of her consort. The court denied the claim even though it admitted concubinage to be "an institution recognized by the law of Mexico." But because "the relationship between appellant and the deceased was entered into and existed wholly within the state of Chihuahua, it must be regulated and defined by the code law of that state which defines appellant as a concubine, and grants her certain rights of inheritance as such, but does not recognize her relationship as a valid provable marriage." The court concluded that it must "recognize her as do the courts of her residence, viz., as a concubine," adding that "there is no provision in the Texas law for her to inherit as such," because she cannot claim "as a common law wife in Texas, for such relationship is nonexistent in the jurisdiction of her residence."

PROXY MARRIAGES

The Mexican federal Civil Code and state codes patterned after it expressly allow marriages by proxy (art. 44 and 102 of the federal Civil Code). However, no special conflict rules have evolved as to foreign executed powers to marry by proxy, involving nationals or aliens. Nevertheless, it may be concluded from art. 13 of the same Code that the effects in Mexico of a foreign executed power to marry in Mexico will be governed by Mexican law. Furthermore, it follows from art. 44 of the same Code that the Mexican *lex loci celebrationis* will prevail, since it requires a special power for the particular act, i.e., marriage, in the form of a public document, e.g., notarial act, or a private document signed by the principal and two witnesses, authenticated by a public notary and a judge. The statutory condition that marriage by proxy may only be had if the "interested parties cannot appear per-

---

[215] Nevarez v. Bailon, 287 S.W. 2d 521 (Tex. 1956).

sonally" has no sanction, nor is it required that such impossibility be established in the proxy document or otherwise. It follows that the law of the place where the power was executed, or nationality or domicile of the prospective spouses will not be considered by Mexican courts as determining the question of validity of a proxy marriage between nonresident aliens to be performed in Mexico. The same rule, it may be assumed, will prevail when a Mexican court would have to decide the validity of a proxy marriage performed in the United States, provided it meets the requirements of the *lex loci celebrationis.*[216]

As to the United States,[217] in most jurisdictions domestic as well as foreign proxy marriages are recognized on the ground that they do not contravene a strong public policy nor are they deemed repugnant to natural law. Particularly in jurisdictions were the institution of the common law marriage still obtains, courts rationalize the recognition of proxy marriages by pointing out that such marriages comply with requirements of local law for common law marriages, i.e., capacity and consent, while factual cohabitation is held in some jurisdictions not to be essential. Nevertheless, a noticeable reluctance is shown by courts which go to great pains to show that the *lex fori* or *domicilii* has no express provision demanding the presence of both parties at the marriage and that the consent to marry is the only essential requirement. In jurisdictions requiring that the consent to marry be given *in praesenti* during the marriage ceremony, the recognition of proxy marriages abroad of their domiciliaries is rationalized by interpreting the *lex fori* (or *domicilii*) as limited in application to marriages performed within the same jurisdiction, provided there is a proper reason for the resort to a foreign *locus celebrationis* thus excluding a possible *fraus legis*. The latter factor, namely proper reason for a proxy marriage abroad, moves, in most instances, courts to recognize proxy marriages even if they are not available under the *lex fori* or *domicilii*. Thus, interests to be protected by such recognition are

---

216 However, Mexican administrative authorities took the opposite position. The Secretariat of Government issued in January 1959 a circular to all governors to the effect that the Secretaria will not authenticate certificates of marriages where both parties were represented by proxies. Siqueiros, *Síntesis del Derecho Internacional Privado* 65 (Mexico, 1965).

217 Lorenzen, Marriage by Proxy and the Conflict of Laws, 32 Harv. L. Rev. 473 (1919); Stern, Marriage by Proxy in Mexico, 19 So. Cal. L. Rev. 109 (1945), also Matrimonios por Poder en México, 8 (31) Revista de la Escuela Nacional de Jurisprudencia 213 (1946); Howery, Marriages by Proxy Marriage and the Conflict of Laws, 1 Drake L. Rev. 43 (1952).

given preference over a strict interpretation of the ceremonial requirements contained in the *lex fori* which, in most cases, happens also to
be the *lex domicilii* of the spouses married by proxy. These particular
reasons include absence in military service, insurance claims of the
widow arising from military insurance, legitimacy of children and
immigration cases.

Courts have constantly held the proxy aspect of the act to be a
formal requirement and therefore controlled by the *lex loci celebrationis*. This rule was clearly stated in Hardin v. Davis[218] involving
a proxy marriage in Mexico and its subsequent recognition in Ohio:

> Under the ordinary rules governing the conflict of laws a marriage is
> valid as regards the mode of celebration if it conforms to the law of the
> place of celebration. The law of the place of celebration, therefore, will
> decide whether or not a marriage by proxy is valid. If the *lex loci
> celebrationis* allows this mode of celebration, it will determine all ques-
> tions relating to the powers of attorney and all formalities concerning
> the marriage ceremony. Since the question whether a marriage may be
> entered into by proxy relates to the formalities of a marriage, a marriage
> so celebrated in conformity with the local law will be recognized,
> notwithstanding any evasion of the law pertaining to marriage cere-
> monies of the state in which the parties are domiciled.

It appears that the laws of the place where the proxy was executed or
that of the domicile of the parties about to marry or of their intended
marital domicile are never considered.

There are only a few reported American cases dealing with proxy
marriages in Mexico. In the just cited case Hardin v. Davis neither
party appeared before the officiating registrar in Juarez, where the
marriage was celebrated by proxies appointed by both parties in compliance with the *lex loci celebrationis,* i.e., of Chihuahua. The court
found that the reason for the proxy marriage, not available under
the *lex fori* and *domicilii* of the parties (Ohio), were "sound and com-
mendable," namely to legitimate a child. Interpreting the laws of Ohio
requiring a formal ceremony *in presenti,* the court held that this requirement applies only to marriages celebrated in Ohio and has no
extraterritorial effect. It may be added that defendant attempted to
show that in view of the easy method to dissolve marriages in Chihuahua ("parties there may abrogate a marriage in accordance with
their wills without the consent of the state") such marriage does not
qualify as marriage under the *lex fori.* The court declined this argu-

218 30 Ohio Op. 524, 526 (1945).

ment by distinguishing the status of marriage which is, under Mexican law, established equally by proxy and non-proxy marriages, from incidents of a marital status, among others, the question of divorce. Even if there exists such great difference in respect to incidents of marriage between the laws of the forum and those of Mexico, the court concluded, "such difference does not invalidate in Ohio a marriage legally performed under the laws of Mexico."

In two other cases Mexican proxy marriages played but a subordinate role. In Re Crawford's Estate[219] both parties went to Mexico, appeared in some office and later received papers by mail showing "proxy marriage in Juarez, based upon the appearance of the parties and their nomination of proxies." Subsequently, they lived together for some months and separated shortly before husband's death. The family allowance granted to the widow was upheld as being a matter within the discretion of the trial court. In another case involving rights of the surviving spouse in community property created by a putative marriage[220] proxy marriage in Tijuana was alleged, but not established.

MARITAL PROPERTY

The federal Civil Code and the majority of state civil codes have no specific conflict rules regarding the marital property regime. Consequently, applicable conflict rules must be deducted from the broad provisions contained in articles 12 through 15 of the federal Civil Code and the corresponding provisions of civil codes in force in the several states.

Summarizing by way of introduction Mexican law of marital property regimes, it may be stated that the prevailing regime is the one established in the federal Civil Code and adopted also in Baja California, Coahuila, Chihuahua, Durango, Guerrero, Mexico, Morelos, Nayarit, Nuevo León, Querétaro, Sinaloa, and Tabasco. In these states as in the Federal District and Territories spouses are directed to select their matrimonial property regime from two regimes (art. 178) available to them in the civil code: matrimonial community (*sociedad conyugal*, art. 183 and 189) or separate property (*separación de bienes*), which may refer only to the spouses' present property or include future acquisitions as well (art. 207). A few states provide for a supplementary property regime in case spouses did not select one as required. These states are: Campeche, Michoacan, San Luis Potosí,

[219] 160 P. 2d 65 (Cal. 1945).
[220] Sutton v. Sutton, 303 P. 2d 21 (Cal. 1956).

Tamaulipas,[221] and Tlaxcala. Finally, a considerable number of states offer a triple choice: voluntary community (*sociedad voluntaria*), separate property regime, and in case parties have not selected either, the regime of legal community (*sociedad legal*) according to the federal Civil Code of 1884. These states are: Aguascalientes, Chiapas, Guanajuato, Hidalgo, Jalisco, Oaxaca, Puebla, Sonora, Yucatán. and Zacatecas.

In states which require spouses to choose at their marriage one of the two property regimes available, their choice will be inscribed in the civil register as part of the marriage documentation (art. 98, V, and 103, VII, of the federal Civil Code). Thus, the marital property regime is, normally, ascertainable from the civil register of the jurisdiction where the marriage was celebrated. In case parties made no choice or their choice is invalid, the courts are inclined to uphold the marriage in spite of lack of one of its basic requirements.[222]

As already mentioned, civil effects of a marriage by Mexicans abroad are secured by the inscription of the foreign marriage certificate in the civil register of the place of the spouses' domicile (art. 161 of the federal Civil Code). Lack of such inscription deprives, it seems, the marriage of its collateral local effects, among them to bring into operation the marital property regime in force at such domicile. For aliens, the 1917 Law of Family Relations, still in force in a few states, reads in article 1 of its miscellaneous provisions:

> Married aliens residing in the country or who subsequently came to settle there or who there entered into a legal marriage, shall be subject to this law in regard to property which they possess in the Republic as well as in regard to effects which their marriage shall effectuate therein.

Difficulties arising in regard of matrimonial property regimes established abroad but not subsequently registered in Mexico, were solved by the Mexican Supreme Court in the sense that the effects in Mexico of a marital property regime agreed upon by the spouses or

---

[221] Art. 182 of the new Civil Code of Tamaulipas provides that spouses are under no duty to enter into a marital property agreement; if none is concluded, the property regime follows art. 182 to 217 of the Code. Generally, López Monroy, Régimen Económico Matrimonial, 16 Revista de la Facultad de Derecho de México 791 (1966) ; Aguilar Gutiérrez, Mexique, in Rouast, Herzog & Zajtay (ed.), Le Régime Matrimonial Légal dans les Législations Contemporaines 249 (Paris, 1957).

[222] 25 Semanario (6a ép.) 253 (1959) ; cf. 42 (4) Semanario (5a ép.) 2910 (1936). Matrimonial regime of aliens under the Law of Family Relations (1917), art. 1 misc. prov., 45 (2) Semanario (5a ép.) 1365 (1937).

to be presumed under the *lex loci celebrationis* as, in this case,[223] in France, depends on two factors: that the marriage, including its accompanying marital property regime, has been registered in Mexico in accordance with article 161 of the federal Civil Code, and second, that sufficient proof is submitted to the court in case the substantive rules of the foreign property regime are disputed. The question arose as a consequence of a marriage in France between a Mexican and a French national who later than three months after their return to Mexico registered there their French marriage certificate. Dismissing the question as to the time when the French wife acquired Mexican nationality as immaterial, the Supreme Court in *amparo* proceedings brought by the wife against a judgment obtained by the referee in bankruptcy of her husband in regard to property acquired before the registration in Mexico of the French marriage certificate, was faced with the position taken by the court below that article 161 applies only to marriages abroad between Mexican nationals. The Supreme Court compared the present language of article 161 with that of the corresponding article 175 of the 1884 federal Civil Code and found that the latter included also mixed marriages while the former refers only to "Mexicans who marry abroad." Without deciding this very point, the Supreme Court held that to extend the "penalty that the marriage will not take effect until registered" imposed upon spouses whose duty it is to register their marriage, so as to affect third parties, would mean not only a right to keep their marriage secret but also would amount to fraud. As a consequence, the Supreme Court found that the court below did not violate "to the detriment of the claimant [the provision contained in] article 161, by not accepting that effects [of the registration of the foreign marriage] set in only after the date of registration."

Two Mexican states have specific conflict provisions in matters of marital property patterned after the 1884 federal Civil Code. The Civil Code of Puebla (art. 1848) considers a marriage celebrated abroad by persons who later become domiciliaries of Puebla: their property arrangements are governed by the *lex loci celebrationis*, subject to article 11 (*lex rei sitae*) and article 15 (*lex voluntatis* in regard to movables) of the same Code. The Civil Code of Sonora (Art. 311) provides that the property and its administration by spouses, whether domiciliaries or not, whose marriage was concluded outside of the state (which includes both in another Mexican state and a foreign

[223] 124 Semanario (5a ép.) 357 (1954).

country), together with a property agreement, will be governed by such agreement; if there is only a presumed property regime, the property as well as the administration of assets acquired by the spouses in Sonora will both be governed by the law of this state (art. 312).[224]

It may be safely stated that the decisions of the Supreme Court of Mexico in matters of marital property regime are far from consistent.[225] Some decisions rely on the *lex loci celebrationis* as decisive of the marital property regime which will thus be determined once and for all. Other opinions, by contrast, decline the law of the place where marriage was celebrated, and prefer, in accordance with article 121, II, of the federal Constitution, the *lex rei sitae*.[226] In an interstate situation the former position was adopted by the Supreme Court in an *amparo* case involving, in the opinion of the court, interrelations between *statutum personale* and *statutum reale*,[227] namely between the matrimonial regime of separate property established in consequence of a marriage between Mexican nationals domiciled in the Federal District on the one hand, and the right to assign a credit secured by a mortgage on land situated in the state of Jalisco. The Supreme Court started from the then valid Civil Code of Jalisco (1887, art. 12), patterned after article 12 of the federal Civil Code of 1884, as the *lex fori*, providing that "laws regarding status and capacity . . . bind Mexicans in regard to acts to be performed even when they reside abroad" and decided that this law gives to the *lex loci celebrationis et domicilii*, i.e., to the Law of Family Relations for the Federal District (enacted in 1917 and abrogated by the Civil Code of 1928), as the

---

[224] Mexican law applies to matrimonial matters of an alien domiciled in Jalisco according to art. 12 of the federal Civil Code, Jurisprudencia (civ.) 632 (1964); interstate situation, 114 Semanario (5a ép.) 191 (1953).

[225] The regime of matrimonial property and its liquidation are not governed by the territorial principle, thus eliminating the application of art. 121, sec. III of the federal Constitution; matrimonial property is governed by the *lex loci celebrationis* of the marriage, 53 Semanario (5a ép.) 2272 (1937); marital property interests of aliens married in the Republic or settling there, already married, will be governed by the *lex rei sitae*, 41 Semanario (5a ép.) 2765 (1934). Mexican laws regulating marital property interest do not apply to assets situated abroad, 35 Semanario (5a ép.) 775 (1932). Marital property regime under sec. 1 of misc. provisions of the Law of Family Relations (1917), 41 Semanario (5a ép.) 2765 (1936).

[226] Mexican laws do not apply to matrimonial assets situated abroad; consequently, such assets cannot be included in the dissolution of the community property regime under Mexican law, 35 Semanario (5a ép.) 775 (1932).

[227] 9 Boletín de Información Judicial 80 (1953).

statutum personale, extraterritorial effect, thus making it applicable also in Jalisco. Apparently, the Court considered questions of status, including those created by marriage in regard to the marital property regime, to be part of the *statutum personale,* and as such controlling the litigated assignment of the secured credit. The fact that the credit assigned by one of the spouses was secured by a mortgage on land did not affect the marital regime of separate property since the *statutum reale, i.e.,* the *lex rei sitae,* would, in the opinion of the court, apply only to the security aspect of the credit and not to the rights of the spouses *inter sese* to dispose by assignment of the credit so secured.

International conflict problems have been discussed in the Patiño case.[228] In view of the rather scarce case materials as well as paucity of writings in the matter, the position taken here by the Supreme Court seems of particular interest. In the opinion of the Mexican Supreme Court the matrimonial property regime as established by Mexican laws, in this case in the federal Civil Code, being the *lex fori* as well as the present *lex domicilii* of the plaintiff husband, is the only regime which may be given effect by Mexican courts (art. 178, 179, and 180). Of the two property regimes available under the same law, either may be chosen by parties, but none will apply by operation of law in case parties have not made the choice or their choice is ineffective for any of the reasons making contracts invalid. The parties in this case have entered in Spain into an agreement establishing the system of separate marital property, one of the regimes available under Spanish law. However, this agreement has been declared null by the Supreme Court of Spain, on the grounds that the wife was a minor. Thus, Mexican courts faced the question what matrimonial property regime to assume in connection with the subsequent Mexican divorce decree. The Supreme Court started its reasoning from the general rule that the contents of contracts are derived from two sources: from the freedom of contracting available to parties, and from cogent laws *(lex imperativa)*. Within the scope of freedom of contract, other (dispositive) legal rules play only a supplementary role whenever parties have not covered all the facets of the agreement. In the present case, however, the Supreme Court was unwilling to consider the use of such supplementary legal rules because the agreement between parties was found not incomplete, but null. In order to determine to what extent the property agreement between parties

[228] 30 Semanario (6a ép.) 12 (1959).

may be valid in Mexico, after it has been found invalid by the Spanish courts, the Court turned to the identification of cogent rules in Mexican law which may make the agreement as concluded by the parties invalid also in Mexico. In this respect, the Court was unable to find in the *lex fori* rules which would oppose the agreement, concluded in Spain. Turning at this point to the judgment of the Spanish courts, the Mexican Supreme Court decided that the question of the effect in Mexico of such a judgment may only be determined by the cogent law of the forum, i.e., the laws of Mexico. The personal law of the contracting parties, in the opinion of the Court, cannot affect cogent legal rules of the forum, effective against any person, against parties' freedom of contracting as well as against judicial acts of foreign courts since the very existence of these rules is designed to protect the community by disallowing individual interests involved since such rules secure the necessary order, fixed and invariable, and are not subject to the will of parties (art. 8 of the federal Civil Code). At this point, the Supreme Court reached the crucial question as to what law applies in a case where a foreign marital property agreement is declared null by the courts of the foreign country where it was concluded. The answer the court gives is that there is no special statutory provision in Mexican law. Instead, the general rule must be applied (art. 2239) namely, that the annulment of a juridical act imposes upon parties to it the duty of restitution. It is not the same thing, the court continues, to marry without a property agreement, or to marry and enter into an invalid agreement. In the first instance, Spanish law would assume the spouses have accepted the property regime provided by the Spanish law in case parties did not agree upon another regime. In the second instance, Mexican law cannot replace the will of the parties since it would be improper to assume that they have intended to accept the subsidiary community property regime available according to Spanish law when one of the parties at least has rejected it and has, instead, chosen the regime of separate property. In conclusion, the Supreme Court held that the decision of the Supreme Court of Spain imposing, in accordance with its substantive law, upon parties the community property system as the subsidiary alternative cannot be accepted in Mexico for two reasons: it would establish a community of acquests (*sociedad legítima de ganancias*) which does not exist under Mexican law; and because it would give to a null and inexisting agreement consequences contrary to Mexican public order as declared in article 2239 of the federal Civil Code, demanding that each party regain its own property through restitution.[229]

American cases dealing with the matrimonial property regimes under Mexican law are rare. In Racouillat v. Sansevain[230] the court applied Mexican law and held a nonresident alien wife entitled to half interest in the property acquired by her husband in Los Angeles as against the escheat to the state, in absence of a proceeding in the nature of an inquest of office. In Mexican Gulf Oil Co. v. Compañía Transcontinental de Petróleo S. A.[231] the question was whether or not a husband after an ecclesiastical marriage, but before the obligatory civil marriage, had the right to convey land in Veracruz without his wife joining in the deed, under the *lex rei sitae,* i.e., the Civil Code of Veracruz (art. 1876, 1878, and art. 43, para. 3 of the Veracruz Law Regarding Community Property and Civil Status).[232]

FILIATION

The civil status of a child born in Mexico, legitimate, illegitimate, or there adopted, will be determined by Mexican law, regardless of the nationality or domicile of its parents (art. 12 of the federal Civil Code and corresponding provisions of state codes). Moreover, the status acquired in one of the Mexican states or within the Federal District and Territories according to the controlling law will be recognized in

[229] Faced with the same situation French courts held (Court of Appeals, Paris, July 1, 1959, 86 Journal de Droit International [Clunet] 428, 1960) the effect of an invalid matrimonial property agreement to be controlled by the national law of the minor party while the subsequent change of nationality in consequence of marriage is immaterial; the void contract will be governed by the law chosen by the parties, i.e., Bolivian law. The Court of Cassation, May 15, 1963 (90 Journal de Droit International [Clunet] 506, 1964), ruled that the national law of the minor at the time of the property agreement concluded one day before marriage, i.e., Spanish law, will control, regardless of the parties' agreement on Bolivian law as the *lex voluntatis,* as well as regardless of the subsequent change of wife's nationality to Bolivian.

[230] 32 Cal. 376 (1867).

[231] 281 Fed. 148 (1922), aff'd, 292 Fed. 846 (2d Cir. 1923).

[232] In order to determine the marital property interest in Mexican utility company in the light of the requirement of registration of a marriage between a Mexican and an American, the proof of Mexican law was held necessary, Logan v. Forster, 114 Cal. App. 2d 587, 250 P. 2d 730 (1952); community property system under Spanish and Mexican law was involved in Sneed v. Commissioner of Internal Revenue, 220 F.2d 313 (5th Cir. 1955).

all other states (art. 121, IV, of the federal Constitution). In international situations Mexican courts will probably apply the same territorial principle. However, no reported cases support this assumption.

There are interesting American cases related to Mexico, involving the status of a child born in concubinage; of an illegitimate but recognized child; of an adopted child; and finally, guardianship.

The question of benefits due to an illegitimate child born in Durango as lineal descendant of her father under the Wisconsin Workmen's Compensation Act was litigated in Waunakee Canning Corp. v. Industrial Commission.[233] The court upheld the claim, holding the child born to a concubinage in Durango to be a lineal descendent, both under Mexican law and under the Workmen's Compensation Act, on the ground that "it appears that under the provisions of the law of Mexico the child . . . was a lineal descendent and is considered heir under the Wisconsin statute."

The status of an illegitimate child, recognized in accordance with Mexican law was involved in an action to determine its rights to succession to chattels located in New York.[234] The illegitimate father, a Mexican national, died in Oaxaca, but his will was probated in New York in regard to movable property left there. The child claimed a share in this estate, but was denied. The court found that the child was born out of wedlock in Oaxaca but in 1937 "recognized as the natural child of the deceased" according to the law of Oaxaca. Following the *lex fori* that the status of a person is to be determined by the law of its domicile, the court accepted the status as it was created under Oaxaca law, but no more, in spite of the fact that Oaxaca law would grant an acknowledged illegitimate child certain rights of support and inheritance against its father's estate. Nevertheless, for the purposes of the New York proceedings the child was held only to be a recognized illegitimate daughter of the deceased and as such, under the substantive rule of the *lex fori,* not entitled to a share in the estate. A different result was reached in another common law jurisdiction, namely in Ontario, Canada. A daughter born out of wedlock to deceased's grandson claimed a share in her great-grandfather's estate. Being an illegitimate child, even though acknowledged according to the law of her domicile (art. 318 of the Civil Code of Michoacan), her claim was opposed on the ground that she remains an illegitimate

233 268 Wis. 518, 68 N.W. 2d 25 (1955).
234 In re Tomacelli-Filomarino Estate, 189 Misc. 410, 73 N.Y.S. 2d 297 (1947).

child and as such is not entitled to the share under the substantive
lex fori. The Ontario court took notice of the fact that claimant had,
under the Civil Code of Michoacan (art. 344, III), the right to claim
a share in her father's estate and, considering her right to inherit as
an incident of her status which the court found to be closely akin to
that of a child born in a lawful wedlock in Ontario, treated her as
such.[235] A similar case was litigated in Pilgrim v. Griffin.[236] There,
plaintiff claimed a share in a lot situated in Texas against his father's
divorced wife, alleging that he is a legitimized son from deceased
father's second wife, a Mexican, by the name of Guadelupe. It appears
that plaintiff's father, an American national employed in Mexico,
started to live with Guadelupe in 1921 and that plaintiff was born to
them in Mexico City in 1924. In 1928 plaintiff's father obtained from
his first wife a divorce in Cuernavaca and subsequently married Guadelupe in Mexico City, thus making plaintiff a legitimized son, even
though before this he was a meretricious child. The court accepted
plaintiff's legitimized status on two grounds. First, it held that since
the plaintiff as well as his parents were domiciled in Mexico, Mexican
law controls (art. 354 of the federal Civil Code), making plaintiff
a son by subsequent marriage, thereby relying on the domicile as the
contact decisive under the *lex fori.* A second ground the court adopted
in the alternative, namely that even if parties involved would not
have been domiciled in Mexico, the law of Texas would apply as the
lex rei sitae as well as *lex fori,* and being substantially the same as
Mexican law, the same conclusion would be reached.

The recognition of an adoption in Tamaulipas in 1851 was at
issue in Martínez v. Gutiérrez[237] as a preliminary question to the decision whether or not this adoption has established a status which
would, under Texas law as the *lex rei sitae,* entitle plaintiff to inherit
land. The court declined to give any significance to the alleged
differences between adoption procedures in Tamaulipas and Texas
on the ground that such procedures are a matter of legislative authorities which may make the ceremony simple, like in Texas, or a formal
judicial matter, like in Tamaulipas. A more serious question, however,
involved the consequences of adoption in face of the allegation that
inheritance rights given by Mexican law to adopted children are more
restricted than those under Texas law. The court decided this issue
by carefully distinguishing between two things: between the status

---

[235] Re MacDonald, 34 D.L.R. 2d 14 (1962).
[236] 237 S.W. 2d 448 (Tex. 1950).   [237] 66 S.W. 2d 678 (Tex. 1933).

created by adoption on the one hand, and its incidental consequences, the right to inherit land, on the other, and held that the first issue is governed by the law of Mexico where the status was created, while the second is governed according to the *lex rei sitae*. Thus, the Texas court recognized the status of an adopted child created in accordance with the law of the foreign country on the basis of comity, without carrying over what it called incidental capacity arising from the law under which the status of adoption was created.

The case involving guardianship arose in New York. A minor, national and resident of Mexico, had a guardian appointed by a New York court[238] which also retained jurisdiction. Subsequently, the application for an order to terminate this guardianship and to turn trust assets over to a Mexican guardian, i.e., the Bank of Mexico, was held proper since the domicile of an infant is the most appropriate place for the appointment of a guardian of his person and property, although for protection of either, a guardian may be appointed in any country where the ward or his property is found. The court also added that, ordinarily, the powers of a guardian are determined by the law of the jurisdiction in which he has been appointed; but in absence of contrary statutory provisions, the court held that the law of the domicile of the ward will control the management and investment of ward's assets.

DIVORCE

Characterized as a civil contract, marriage may be dissolved by divorce in all Mexican states as well as in the Federal District and Territories, provided one or another ground for divorce listed in the *lex fori* is established in judicial proceedings.[239] Even though these grounds vary

[238] Central Hanover Bank & Trust Co. v. de la Vega, 205 Misc. 684, 128 N.Y.S. 2d 297 (1954).

[239] Alvarez, The Divorce Laws of Mexico, in Albrecht (ed.), Divorce in Liberal Jurisdictions 25 (1955); Stern, Mexican Divorces: The Mexican Law, 7 (5) Pract. Law. 78 (1961); Mexican Marriage and Divorces, 20 Cal. S.B.A.J. 53 (1945), Developments in the Law of Mexican Marriages and Divorces, 24 Cal. S.B.A.J. 305 (1949), and Mexican Marriage and Divorce (1952); Galíndez, El Divorcio en el Derecho Comparado de América, 2 (6) Boletín del Instituto de Derecho Comparado de México 10, 38 (1949); Ireland, Divorce in the Americas 192 (1947); Cartwright, Yucatan Divorces, 18 A.B.A.J. 307 (1932); Dámaso Melgarejo, Divorce Law of Sonora, Mexico (1929); Fortul, Mexican Marriage and Divorce Laws . . . (1926); Haberman, The Divorce Laws of Mexico (1930); Randolph, Divorce Law of Sonora

from jurisdiction to jurisdiction, in the great majority of the states they are patterned after the federal Civil Code, while a few states (e.g., Chihuahua, Morelos, and Tlaxcala) display a more liberal attitude. It may be added that in all Mexican jurisdictions divorce by consent also is available.

This liberality offers aliens from jurisdictions with stricter divorce laws the opportunity to voyage to Mexico and shed there their matrimonial ties. Constant streams of weary spouses seeking to regain their marital freedom as refugees from their own laws, resulted in a system of organized, highly profitable abuses, unwelcome to both countries.[240] Courts as well as legislative[241] and administrative authorities attempted to stem the flow, but with little success.

In deciding divorce suits, Mexican courts follow the *lex fori* in regard both to jurisdiction[242] and to choice-of-law. In order to elucidate jurisdictional problems involved, the law applicable in federal courts shall be considered. The Code of Civil Procedure for the Federal District and Territories vests divorce jurisdiction in the courts of marital domicile; where there is no longer any marital domicile, the court of the domicile of the abandoned spouse will have jurisdiction (art. 156,

---

(1929); Summers, Divorce Law of Mexico, 2 L. & Cont. Pr. 310 (1935); Vance, Divorce Laws of Yucatan, 13 Geo. L. J. 227 (1925); Yankwich, Marriage and Divorce . . . with Extracts from Mexican Law on the Subject (1937); Zavala, Divorce Code: State of Campeche (1926); Carillo, Matrimonio y Divorcio en Mexico a la Luz del Derecho Internacional Privado, 14 Revista de la Facultad de Derecho de México 923 (1964); also Gallardo, La Solution des Conflits de Lois dans les Pays de l'Amérique Latine, Divorce . . . 190 (Paris, 1956).

[240] Mason, Mexico's Cash and Carry Divorce for Americans, 88 Scribner's 360 (1930); Bergeson, The Divorce Mill Advertizes, 2 Law & Contemp. Pr. 348 (1935). For vivid descriptions of the routine, see How to Get a Quickie Divorce, 59 (2) Esquire 94 (1962); Samuels, To Juarez on the Divorce Run, N.Y. Times Mag. 18 (Sept. 12, 1965); and Shearer, Instant Divorce: a Speciality of Juarez, Parade 4 (March 19, 1967).

[241] Congress attempted to prevent these abuses by enacting in 1939 a statute (18 U.S.C.A. §1714) making nonmailable matter "Every written or printed card, circular, letter, . . . giving or offering to give information concerning where or how or through whom a divorce may be secured in a foreign country, and designed to solicit business in connection . . . thereof . . . " punishable by no more than $500 or one year in prison. Cf. In re Anonimus, 80 N.Y.S. 2d 75 (1948). In Adams & Adams, Ethical Problems in Advising Migratory Divorce, 16 Hastings L. J. 60 (1964), the statement that "mail order divorce are proper under most Mexican laws" (at 74) is erroneous.

[242] Siqueiros, Competencia Jurisdiccional en Materia de Divorcios Extranjeros, (15) Lecturas Jurídicas 3 (1963), also (45) El Foro (4a ép.) 9 (1964).

XII) .[243] The same rule appears in the Federal Code of Civil Procedure (art. 27, para. 2) . The question of domicile of the abandoned spouse was litigated in the Patiño case,[244] already mentioned. The Supreme Court decided that the domicile of an alien is determined by the federal Civil Code and not by the General Population Law. This latter law established, in the opinion of the Court, only a general population register for both nationals and aliens, imposing upon aliens the additional duty to register in a special register (registro de extranjeros) upon entering Mexico as immigrants but not in other capacities, like that of plaintiff who entered on a diplomatic passport. Thus, the abandoned husband-plaintiff was capable to establish his domicile in Mexico, to be determined according to Mexican laws for purposes of determining his marital status. The Court also rejected the argument that a person with a diplomatic passport who settles in Mexico, cannot be subject to local jurisdiction (art. 56, 57 and 69 of the General Population Law) , on the ground that this law only deals with "demographic questions." However, in regard to the diplomatic passport the court found that entering Mexico on such passport did not give plaintiff diplomatic status.

The federal jurisdictional rules are adopted in the great majority of state procedural codes.[245] Only the procedural codes of Morelos and Sonora vest divorce jurisdiction in cases of abandonment in the court of defendant's domicile (art. 88, XI, and art. 109, XI, respectively). In

[243] 113 Semanario (5a ép.) 1172 (1952); unless parties did not subject themselves to the jurisdiction by prorogation, 52 Semanario (5a ép.) 1649, 2755 (1937); 57 Semanario (5a ép.) 66, 2135 (1938); 63 Semanario (5a ép.) 1283 (1940); 118 Semanario (5a ép.) tesis 377 (appendix). Summons of alien in divorce action, 46 (5) Semanario (5a ép.) 3581 (1937).

[244] 30 Semanario (6a ép.) 10 (1960). For criticism, Carillo, El Caso Patiño-Borbon ante el Derecho Internacional Privado, (33) El Foro (4a ép.) 51 (1961).

[245] 113 Semanario (5a ép.) 1172 (1952); 46 Semanario (5a ép.) 3581 (1935); 54 Semanario (5a ép.) 1560 (1937); 76 Semanario (5a ép.) 6464 (1943); 108 Semanario (5a ép.) 1422 (1951). Abandonment involving aliens is effective only if such change is registered with local authorities; a factual change without such notification of local authorities will not affect the properly registered marital domicile since the domicile in compliance with registration requirement is tantamount to a legal domicile under art. 31 of the federal Civil Code; in consequence, the abandoned spouse will be considered to have been abandoned at such domicile, art. 27 and 33 of the same Code, Informe Rendido a la Suprema Corte de la Nación, 1952, at 66. Change of domicile by aliens, 113 Semanario (5a ép.) 1172 (1953).

Divorce action on the interstate level, 33 Semanario (5a ép.) 977 (1933); 50 Semanario (5a ép.) 822 (1938).

Zacatecas where local law is still that of the federal code of 1884, jurisdiction is vested in the court of husband's domicile (art. 196).

In most states statutory jurisdiction may be changed by agreement
of the parties (*prórroga*).[246] Both federal procedural codes provide
that parties may submit to another court, provided such prorogation
affects only territorial competence (venue; art. 23 and 149, respectively). An exception seems to exist in Morelos due to the 1954 amendment of article 75 of its Code of Civil Procedure to the effect that in
"all cases involving personal status, territorial competence cannot be
prorogated."

In spite of these and similar statutory provisions, the degree of
defendant's participation in divorce proceedings in Mexican courts
seem not to be clearly defined. There is some judicial authority to
the effect that *ex parte* divorces may be vulnerable on jurisdictional
grounds since the courts consider the presence of both parties, at least
through properly authorized attorneys, mandatory. Consequently, mail-
order divorces are considered open to attack by *amparo* on the ground
that they violate article 14, paragraph (2) of the federal Constitution.
Defendant's participation in divorce proceedings was at issue, for
example, in the Patiño case.[247] Admitting the interstate scope of article
121, III, of the federal Constitution and relying on article 12 of the
federal Civil Code, the defendant-wife urged that she never was a
domiciliary or even a transient in Mexico and, consequently, was not
amenable to Mexican judicial sovereignty nor to Mexican laws. However, the Mexican Supreme Court rejected these arguments, pointing
out that the defendant has participated fully in the judicial proceedings through her attorney, after having been personally served abroad,
thus leaving open the question whether or not a mere service of process
without appearance would suffice.[248]

[246] 54 Semanario (6a ép.) 189 (1961). Not available for actions involving civil status (incl. divorce), for example, in Morelos (art. 75 of its Code
of Civil Procedure).

[247] See supra n. 244.

[248] Party residing outside of the jurisdiction will be summoned in accordance with the *lex loci actus,* i.e., the law of the place of the intended
service; in divorce actions service must comply with the law of such residence,
18 Semanario (5a ép.) 631, 1926; 33 Semanario (5a ép.) 977 (1933), whenever the residence is known, 47 Semanario (5a ép.) 3581 (1936). Service
by publication is insufficient, 29 Semanario (5a ép.) 1000 (1930); 42 Semanario (5a ép.) 160 and 3596 (1934); 46 Semanario (5a ép.) 3581 (1937);
53 Semanario (5a ép.) 2700 (1937); 62 Semanario (5a ép.) 1610 (1939),
particularly if plaintiff knew defendant's residence, Informe Rendido a la
Suprema Corte de la Nación, 1944, at 35. This rule applies also in respect

The so-called liberal states, particularly Chihuahua, are well known for their even laxer jurisdictional requirements. The Divorce Law of this state, enacted in 1932, provides in article 22 that a contested divorce is within the jurisdiction of the court of the place where plaintiff resides, and a divorce by mutual consent at the place where either of the spouses resides, which residence may be proven "by the appropriate certificates of the municipal register" of the respective locality (art. 24). Furthermore, jurisdiction may also be established by submission expressed by the parties' renunciation of the courts which would otherwise have jurisdiction, or implied by the "fact that plaintiff has filed his action or that the defendant, having been summoned in proper form, fails timely to raise the lack of jurisdiction or, having raised it, desists" (art. 23). Guerrero is another state with similar jurisdictional rules. Under its Divorce Law of 1938, jurisdiction in cases of divorce by agreement is perfected by the mere appearance of both parties (art. 6). In cases of contested divorces jurisdiction is established by express or implied submission of parties to the court (art. 5). Express submission requires a declaration by the parties that they "renounce the court which the law would make available to them, and indicate precisely the judge to whom they submit"; implied submission requires that plaintiff has filed the action and defendant has not contested it (art. 7). It may be added that the same law regulates summons by providing that the "first notification shall be personal" (art. 34).[249] In case defendant is domiciled in the Republic but outside of the jurisdiction of the court (*luego de juicio*), he shall be notified by an *exhorto;* if he resides abroad, he "shall be notified in accordance with the law of the country where he lives" (art. 34).

The federal administrative authorities in Mexico have attempted, particularly in view of undesirable practices in Chihuahua, to stop the flow of improper divorce decrees granted to thousands of Americans, by declining to authenticate signatures of state officials on such decrees, on the ground that article 12 of the federal Civil Code allows the application of Mexican laws only to persons at least present (*habitantes*) in Mexico upon compliance with the federal laws governing admission of aliens for one or another type of stay in the

to aliens, 46 Semanario (6a ép.) 3581 (1961); 47 Semanario (5a ép.) 1821 (1936). Alcala Zamora, Clinica Procesal 455 (1963). Lack of intervention by the Attorney General (*Ministerio Publico*) in a divorce action between spouses with children resulted in nullity, Supreme Court, 1955, in 5 (17-18) Revista de la Facultad de Derecho de México 358 (1955).

[249] 65 Semanario (5a ép.) 1558 (1940).

country. However, the Mexican Supreme Court has taken a dim view of such administrative well intentioned action. In a recent case the Court ruled that a divorce rendered by a competent court may not be made ineffective by administrative authorities, regardless of its undesirability, unless the decree violates legal procedures and such violation is found by competent judicial authorities.[250]

The jurisdictional issue may be raised in a Mexican court in two ways: by the *declinatoria* brought in the court where the case is pending, or by the *inhibitoria* in the court considered by the complaining party to have jurisdiction (e.g., art. 163 of the Code of Civil Procedure for the Federal District and Territories). A jurisdictional conflict may arise between the courts of different states or between a state and a federal court, or between federal courts in cases where two or more claim jurisdiction over the same litigation. Such conflicts are resolved by the federal Supreme Court.

Choice-of-law aspects of divorce cases are determined in Mexico by the *lex fori*. This means that divorce grounds listed in the *lex fori* will be available regardless of whether or not they are recognized at the place where they should have occurred. These grounds apply regardless of the domicile of the defendant, provided the alien-plaintiff has been abandoned and has subsequently established domicile in Mexico. Once such domicile has been established, the Supreme Court reasoned in the Patiño case, Mexican laws apply to his personal status according to article 12 of the federal Civil Code.

Recognition of divorce decrees rendered in Mexico and in the United States is discussed in another part of this study.

ANNULMENT

A marriage performed in violation of an impediment (art. 156), or contrary to provisions regarding formalities prescribed in articles 97, 98, 100, and 103, or because of an *error in persona,* may be annulled (art. 235 of the federal Civil Code and corresponding provisions of state civil codes). Jurisdiction is vested in the court of defendant's domicile (art. 156, IV, of the Code of Civil Procedure for the Federal District and Territories). Analogous provisions are found in most of the state procedural codes.

[250] 120 Semanario (5a ép.) 542 (1953).

12. THINGS

Conflict rules regarding corporeal assets and interests in them vary depending mainly on their immovable or movable nature. The *lex rei sitae* reigns supreme as to immovable property while vestiges of the earlier statutist doctrines relying in respect to movables on personal contacts still linger on.

TREATY LAW

Treaties in force between the two countries deal both with immovable as well as movable property.[251]

Treaty rules regarding interests in land have arisen from territorial changes between the two countries. Subsequent to such changes, significant questions involving titles to land, particularly their previous validity and their post-treaty changes unavoidably arise. Moreover, the boundary line along the Rio Grande has created a number of problems, not only caused by changes in the flow of the river but also due to the *bancos* appearing in it.

In regard to territories affected by the treaty of Guadalupe Hidalgo (1848, art. VIII), and the subsequent Gadsden treaty (1853, art. V), the United States undertook in regard to Mexicans remaining in these territories as well as those not established there, the obligation to allow the former to retain their property possessed there, or to dispose thereof, "without being subjected, on this account, to any contribution, tax, or charge whatever." Mexican nationals not established in these territories shall have their "property of every kind . . . inviolably respected. The present owners, the heirs of those, and all Mexicans who may hereafter acquire said property by contract, shall enjoy with respect to it guarantees equally ample as if the same belonged to citizens of the United States," or, in other words, enjoy with regard to their property rights the equal (national) treatment. Subsequent to the deletion of article X from the treaty of 1848, the question was clarified in the second paragraph of the Querétaro Protocol (1848)[252] in the sense that grants made by Mexico in the ceded territories

[251] Bayitch, Conflict Law in United States Treaties: a Survey, 69 (1955); Wilson, U.S. Commercial Treaties and International law 95 (1960).
[252] Subsequent conventions between the two countries dealing with

preserve the legal value which they may possess; and the grantees may cause their legitimate titles to be acknowledged before the American tribunals. Conformably to the law of the United States, legitimate titles to every description of property, personal and real, existing in the ceded territories, are those which were legitimate titles under the Mexican law in California and New Mexico up to the 13th day of May, 1846, and in Texas up to the 2nd day of March, 1836.

The obligations undertaken by the United States were defined by the United States Supreme Court[253] as arising "under the principles of international law by reason of annexation, and by its treaty obligations." While the treaty provided for the acknowledgment of Mexican land titles "before American tribunals," the treaty remained "silent as to the mode of selection or creation of such tribunals." Considering itself free in this respect, the United States could delegate the adjudication of such claims to its ordinary courts, or set up an administrative tribunal, as it was done by congressional acts, among them the one for California (1851). However, there was no doubt that the validity of Mexican titles had to be determined in accordance with Mexican law as the *lex rei sitae,* insofar as in force and applicable before the date stated in the treaties.[254]

---

distribution of waters were involved in various litigations. The 1906 convention was discussed, for example, in State of New Mexico v. Backer, 199 F. Supp. 426 (1952), and Hudspeth County Conservation and Reclamation District No. 1 v. Robbins, 213 F. 2d 425 (5th Cir. 1954). The 1944 convention was involved in United States v. 85-237 Acres of Land, etc., 157 F. Supp. 150 (1957); the 1945 convention in Martínez v. Maverick County Water Control and Improvement District No. 1, 219 F.2d 666 (5th Cir. 1955), and in Hidalgo County Water Control and Improvement District No. 7 v. Hedrick, 226 F.2d 1 (5th Cir. 1955), cert. denied, 350 U.S. 983 (1955).

[253] United States v. O'Donnell, 303 U.S. 501 (1938).

[254] "All right of any validity before the cession was equally valid afterwards," United States v. Moreno, 68 U.S. 400 (1863); Gonzáles v. Ross, 120 U.S. 605 (1887); Interstate Land Co v. Maxwell Land Co., 139 U.S. 569 (1891); Sonoita Grant, 171 U.S. 220 (1898); Ainsa v. New Mexico & Arizona Railroad, 175 U.S. 76 (1899); Richardson v. Ainsa 218 U.S. 289 (1910).

As stated recently in Martínez v. Rivera, 196 F. 2d 192 (10th Cir. 1952), cert. denied, 344 U.S. 828 (1952), on the authority of Tameling v. United States Freehold & Immigration Co., 93 U.S. 644 (1876), Astiazaran v. Santa Rita Mining Co., 148 U.S. 80 (1893), and Yeast v. Pru, 292 F. 598 (1923), the duty to provide the "mode for securing and establishing claims to Spanish and Mexican land titles and fulfilling the treaty of Guadalupe Hidalgo devolved on the political department of the Government. Congress could either discharge that duty itself or delegate it to the judicial department." Such congressional action was "conclusive as to the validity and the character or nature of the grant, and was not subject to review of the Supreme Court of the United States or any other tribunal" (ibid.). Cf. Maxwell Land-Grant Case, 121 U.S. 325 (1887), reh. denied, 122 U.S. 365 (1887); Reilly v. Ship-

Omitting a discussion of the work of the commissions charged under various congressional as well as state laws with the confirmation of Mexican land titles, a few cases may be mentioned which arose in courts involving Mexican land titles within the scope of the Guadalupe Hidalgo treaty.

Plaintiff's attempt to eliminate the effects of the statute of limitations against him as a violation of the treaty guarantee was denied by the court in Amaya et al. v. Stanolind Oil & Gas Co.[255] The court interpreted the treaty in the sense that acquired property rights will be respected which obligation, however, does not exempt such property from the "valid, and non-discriminatory property laws of the State of Texas," nor does it "guarantee that those Mexicans would never lose their title to persons by foreclosure, sales under execution, trespasses, adverse possession or other non-governmental acts." The same position was taken in regard to a non-discriminatory taxation *ad valorem* of such property.[256] However, it was held in Grant v. Jaramillo[257] that treaty guarantees do not include inchoate claims, such as uninterrupted possession since 1825, or acquisitive prescription in accordance with Mexican law in force in 1848. Being inchoate,[258] such claims were reserved to Congress for determination by the political department of the American government or by tribunals set up by Congress. Grants by the former sovereign are presumed to be within its authority[259] and, consequently, qualify for protection under the treaty. Land not actually alloted to settlers under the Law of the Indies, remained property of the King, to be disposed by him; claimants with no better claim had no right to demand title from the Mexican government and,

---

man, 266 F. 825 (1920); Flores v. Bruesselbach, 149 F. 2d 616 (10th Cir. 1945); Chávez v. Chávez de Sánchez, 7 N. M. 58, 32 P. 137 (1893); Catron v. Laughlin, 11 N.M. 604, 72 P. 26 (1903). In Sánchez v. Taylor, 377 F.2d 733 (10th Cir. 1967), the court held that plaintiffs "as a matter of law, have no rights in [defendant's] land under Mexican law or the original grant. Any conflicting rights prior to the confirmatory Act of 1860 [12 Stat. 71] which might have arisen or existed by reason of the original grant from Mexico, considered in the light of Mexican law and the Treaty of Guadalupe-Hidalgo, were thereby extinguished." As to conflict between confirmation and treaty, Barker v. Harvey, 181 U.S. 481 (1900), and H.N.D. Land Co. v. Suazo, 44 N.M. 547, 105 P. 2d 744 (1940).

[255] 158 F.2d 554 (5th Cir. 1946); cert. denied 331 U.S. 808 (1947), reh. denied 331 U.S. 867 (1947).

[256] Chadwick v. Campbell, 115 F. 2d 401 (10th Cir. 1940).

[257] 28 P. 508 (Cal. 1892).   [258] Burges v. Gray, 16 How. 48 (1853).

[259] Clark v. Hiles, 2 S.W. 356 (1886); State v. Gallardo, 166 S.W. 369 (1914).

consequently, not under the treaty.[260] However, the treaty does not affect restrictions imposed in a Mexican grant of 1839. When plaintiff attacked the devise of the land by his father for a public park as void, pointing out that the restriction was valid under Mexican law and that the change of sovereignty did not destroy its application to the land in question, defendants maintained that the mortmain is to be understood as a condition subsequent and void under section 711 of the California Civil Code. The court[261] adopted this latter viewpoint, adding that the validity of the title is guaranteed by the Guadalupe Hidalgo treaty, as evidenced by the subsequent approval (1855) and confirmation (1875) of the title. However, any question as to "restraint or restrictions upon the use of property, acquired prior to the conquest, is to be determined by American law. There is no provision in the treaty that the United States would continue restrictions on the use of property owned by Mexicans prior to conquest, or that the United States would preserve for Mexico or any citizen of Mexico the rights of forfeiture or any remedy based upon the mortmain provision." The court held that the mortmain provision in the Mexican grant is "superseded by the cession of the property by Mexico to the United States, and by the patent of the United States to the heirs of the grantee in the Mexican grant. The mortmain provision in the grant, the court concluded, is void under section 711 of the Civil Code" and "inconsistent with American law and public policy."

A Mexican grant, even if limited to agricultural uses and under Spanish and Mexican law not including mineral rights, may presently have them included under the intervening patent issued by the United States.[262] However, the treaty does not apply to land which prior to the treaty was already public domain in the independent Texas Republic,[263] nor does it apply to Mexican grants executed after the signature of the treaty.[264] Finally, a case may be mentioned where a Mexican national about to be deported unsuccessfully applied for habeas corpus in an attempt to prevent deportation by invoking article VIII of the treaty, insisting that he as a Mexican national cannot be pre-

[260] United States v. Santa Fé, 165 U.S. 675 (1897); United States v. Sandoval, 167 U.S. 278 (1896).

[261] Hart v. Gould, 259 P. 2d 49 (1953).

[262] Blue v. McKay, 136 F. Supp. 315 (D.C. 1955), aff'd 232 F. 2d 688, cert. denied, 352 U.S. 846 (1956).

[263] McKinney v. Saviego, 59 U.S. 235 (1856); Texas Mexican Ry. v. Locke, 12 S.W. 80 (1889).

[264] Kennedy Pasture Co. v. State, 231 S.W. 683 (1921), cert. denied, 258 U.S. 617 (1921).

vented from enjoying the land he owns in the United States.[265]

Difficult problems related to changes in territorial sovereignty[266] arose from the fact that the agreed upon boundary river, Rio Grande, changes from time to time its main stream. As a consequence, the so-called *bancos* appeared, i.e., parts of land which, due to the changes in the flow of the river, accrued to another sovereignty. In order to prevent complications arising from article V of the Boundary Convention of 1884, which provided that these *bancos* retain their original sovereignty, the subsequent Convention for the Elimination of the Bancos from the Article II of the 1884 Convention (1905), allocated the existing *bancos* to one or the other contracting country and in regard to those not so allocated as well as to future *bancos* adopted in article IV the following rule:

> The citizens of either of the two contracting countries who, by virtue of the stipulations in this convention, shall in the future be located on the land of the other may remain thereon or remove at any time to whatever place may suit them, and either keep the property which they possess in said territory or dispose of it . . . Property of all kinds situated on said bancos shall be inviolably respected, and its present owners, their heirs, and those who may subsequently acquire the property legally, shall enjoy as complete security with respect thereto as if it belonged to citizens of the country where it is situated.

Title to land which by avulsion from Mexico in 1926 became part of the territory of the United States was litigated in Shapleigh v. Mier.[267] The land, part of a latifundium, was in accordance with the *lex rei sitae* (Chihuahua) taken over by the state, thus divesting the American plaintiff of his title. The title acquired subsequently by defendant, a Mexican national, from the state of Chihuahua was held to be protected under the 1905 treaty. The court held that the change in sovereignty did not affect ownership acquired prior to the avulsion. A different situation was involved in San Lorenzo Title & Improvement Co. v. Caples.[268] There the land in question separated from Chihuahua by avulsion in 1898 was claimed by plaintiff in an action for trespass to try title under a title obtained by plaintiff's prede-

---

[265] Application of Galvan, 127 F. Supp. 392 (1953), aff'd, 201 F. 2d 302 (5th Cir. 1953); 346 U.S. 812 (1953).

[266] Similar questions arose under the Gadsden Treaty (1853). Ainsa v. New Mexico & Arizona Railroad, 175 U.S. 76 (1899); Richardson v. Ainsa, 218 U.S. 289 (1910); Ely Real Estate & Investment Co. v. Watts, 262 Fed. 721 (1920).

[267] 83 F. 2d 673 (5th Cir. 1936), aff'd, 299 U.S. 468 (1936).

[268] 48 S.W. 2d 329 (1932), aff'd, 73 S.W. 516 (1934).

cessor from the State of Chihuahua in 1926. After an extensive discussion of boundary treaties with Mexico since 1828, the court held that:

> If the right of dominion and sovereignty was transferred by the action of the river when the banco was cut off, or, as in the present case, at the date on which the treaty [of 1905] was effective, then the sovereignty retained by . . . Mexico . . . was such a sovereignty as might be necessary for the government of the territory and police protection, but could not extend to the granting of titles or to any act which might prejudice the right of the United States of America in the territory thus acquired by it.

Consequently, the court found the proceedings in Chihuahua in 1926 to be not only outside of the authority of Mexico (art. 1 of the 1905 treaty), but also void because of noncompliance with the procedural *lex fori,* i.e., Chihuahua.[269]

It is significant that the most recent treaty between the two countries involving changes in territorial sovereignty, the Convention for the Solution of the Problem of Chamizal (1963), avoided the vexing problems of land titles by agreeing in article 4 that:

> The lands that, upon relocation of the international boundary, pass from one country to the other shall pass to the respective Governments in absolute ownership, free of any private titles or encumbrances of any kind.

In order to make this possible, the United States undertook to acquire, in accordance with the *lex rei sitae,* the lands to be transferred to Mexico as well as those needed for the new river channel within the territory of the United States (art. 6).

Movable property is the object of the Convention Providing for the Recovery and Return of Stolen or Embezzled Motor-Vehicles, Trailers, Airplanes or Component Parts of Any of Them, signed in 1936. Either government may request the office in charge of foreign affairs of the other country to "use every proper means to bring about the detention of alleged stolen or embezzled" chattels as listed in article 1, paragraph II of the Convention. Such requests shall be accompanied by "documents legally valid in the [requesting country] supporting the claim of the person or persons interested in the property the

---

[269] See also Willis v. First Real Estate & Investment Co., 68 F.2d 671 (5th Cir., 1934), and Fragoso v. Cisneros, 154 S.W. 2d 991 (Tex. 1941). Black, Ownership of Minerals in the Bancos along the Rio Grande, in San Antonio Bar Association, The Legal Aspects of Doing Business in Mexico 115 (1964).

return of which is requested." After such property has been detained and "in the absence of evidence conclusively controverting the proof just before mentioned, it will be delivered to the person or persons designated for such purpose" by the embassy of the requesting country (art. I and II).[270]

While there has been no judicial test of this treaty in American courts, a number of cases have arisen in Mexico. The Supreme Court adopted the view that an exclusively administrative procedure implementing the Convention's "proper means" to seize chattels is in violation of article 14 of the federal Constitution which allows dispossession only by judicial decision. Since neither the Convention nor the implementing decree issued in Mexico in 1938, gives an opportunity for a judicial test of the "detention," the Supreme Court in *amparo* found the purely administrative procedure to be unconstitutional, invoking specifically article 133 of the federal Constitution which gives treaties the authority of the law of the land only if they are "in accordance therewith," namely with the Constitution.

It has been already pointed out that the Convention on the International Recognition of Rights of Aircraft (Geneva, 1948) has been ratified by both countries but is considered by the United States not to be in force in relation to Mexico.

MEXICAN LAW

Interests in immovable as well as movable property are generally governed by the *lex rei sitae,* a rule which agrees with the territorial attitude prevailing in Mexican conflict law.

On the interstate level, the rule has found expression in section II of article 121 of the federal Constitution:

> Movable and immovable property are governed by the law of the place where it is situated.

The same rule is reiterated for both kinds of property situated in the Federal District and Territories in article 14 of the federal Civil Code and has been repeated in the civil codes of the several states. The rule applies also in respect to assets subject to a trust (*fideicomiso*), ac-

---

[270] Evans, Treaty Enforcement and the Supreme Court of Mexico, 5 Am. J. Comp. L. 267 (1956).

For the work of various Claims Commissions established to settle claims by nationals of one country against the government of the other, see Feller, The Mexican Claims Commissions, 1923–1934: a Study in the Law and Procedure of International Tribunals (1935).

cording to article 353 of the General Law of Credit Titles and Operations (1932), as well as under article 124, paragraph (2) of the General Law of Credit Institutions and Auxiliary Operations (1941) in respect to mortgaged assets.

In international situations the same rule applies by analogy. Transactions creating interests in things situated in Mexico are, in regard to formalities, governed by the *lex loci actus* (art. 15 of the federal Civil Code), while their substantive effects are controlled by the law of the *situs*. In any case, in order to take effect in Mexico, such interests must be registered in accordance with the *lex rei sitae* as prescribed by article 3005 of the federal Civil Code and corresponding provisions of the state civil codes as well as federal or state regulations regarding such registers.[271]

Limitations upon holding of land in Mexico by aliens result in corresponding limitations on the contractual freedom to establish interests prohibited under the *lex rei sitae*.[272] Contracts in violation of such prohibitions are invalid. Even long term leases (over ten years) involving aliens are considered by article 49 of the Nationality and Naturalization Law and article 8 of the Organic Law of Article 27, I, of the Constitution, to be equivalent to alienation and, consequently, subject to the same limitations as outright titles to land. Such leases

[271] Villalon Igartua, The Public Registry of Property in Mexico, in U. Miami School of Law, Mexico: A Symposium on Law and Government 40 (1957); Castro Marroquín, Derecho de Registro; su Reorganización y Unificación (Mexico, 1962).

Additional provisions are contained in state law. The Regulations of the Public Property Register of 1956, as amended in 1966, of the State of Mexico (101 Gaceta de Gobierno, March 23, 1966), for example, provides in article 42:

> Acts executed and contracts made in another federal entity will be inscribed only if they meet the formalities required by the laws of the place of making and, furthermore, if they qualify for inscription (*inscribibles*) under the Civil Code of [this] State and of this Regulation.
>
> Acts executed and contracts made abroad will be inscribed only if they meet the requirements of art. 2858 of the Civil Code in force, and, furthermore, if the signatures of the officials authorizing them, are authenticated by the proper authorities of the country where they have been issued, and these authentications are legalized by the Secretariat of Foreign Relations.

[272] Contracts involving immovables are subject in regard to form to the *lex loci actus* as well as the *lex rei sitae*, these laws being the *statutum reale* controlling all questions pertaining to substantive interests in land, 33 Semanario (5a ép.) 2524 (1931). Art. 12 of the Civil Code of Oaxaca provides that "whenever owners should be aliens, provisions of federal law in the matter shall be considered."

in favor of aliens are void unless approved by the Secretariat of Foreign Relations. The nullity, however, is not automatic, but must be declared by a federal court as provided in article 16 of the Regulations to the Organic Act of Article 27, I, of the Constitution, and a party to such a lease may not avail itself of the nullity unless it recovers a judgment to this effect.[273]

In regard to interests in aircraft, article 23 of the Regulation Regarding the Mexican Aviation Register of 1951[274] provides that the "acts executed, contracts entered into and judicial decisions rendered in a foreign country will be inscribed in the Mexican aviation register, provided they meet requirements contained in article 3005 of the Civil Code for the Federal District and Territories" and are accompanied by an authorized Spanish translation. However, there is no corresponding international choice-of-law rule governing these transactions. By contrast, an interstate conflict rule contained in the same Regulation (art. 24) reads:

> The acts executed or contracts entered into in another federal entity, will be inscribed only if they meet both the formal requirements as set up by the law of the place of making as well as qualify for inscription under the provisions of the Civil Code for the Federal District and Territories, the Law of General Means of Communication and the present Regulations.

When a whole aviation enterprise is involved, the arrangement must meet requirements established in article 124 of the General Law of Credit Institutions and Auxiliary Organizations, including their pro-

---

[273] Alien creditors may enforce their judgment claims against land without a permit from the Secretariat of Foreign Affairs since they do not intend to acquire title to such land but only payment from the land, 32 Semanario, (5a ép.) 13 (1931).

[274] D.O. Oct. 25, 1951. Translation in Bayitch, Aircraft Mortgage in the Americas . . . 110 (1960). The American conflict rule is now contained in sec. 506 of the Federal Aviation Act, as amended in 1964 (49 U.S.C.A. § 1406):
> The validity of any instrument the recording of which is provided by section 503 of this Act shall be governed by the laws of the State, District of Columbia or territory or possession of the United States in which such instrument is delivered, irrespective of the location or the place of delivery of the property which is the subject of such instrument. Where the place of intended delivery of such instrument is specified therein, it shall constitute presumptive evidence that such instrument was delivered at the place so specified.

A saving clause is added for the Convention on the International Recognition of Rights in Aircraft (1948).

visions as to inscription, as well as those contained in article 214 of the General Law on Credit Titles and Operations, the latter whenever obligations are issued.

Generally, transportation enterprises may be subject to mortgages and other security devices for a time of nine-tenths of the duration of their license (art. 92 of the Law of General Means of Communication), with limitations stated in article 95. Security arrangements may encumber the enterprise as a whole, i.e., the license, routes, fixed and movable materials as well as capital and cash (art. 93), unless the security interest is limited, by contract, to specific assets (art. 93). Applicable choice-of-law rules must be gleaned from general rules contained in the federal Civil Code, which control since transportation is a matter of federal concern within the meaning of article 1 of the federal Civil Code.

AMERICAN LAW

American courts resort frequently to the Spanish or Mexican law or both whenever such law was the *lex rei sitae* at the time when interests in land have been acquired or modified.[275] This is understandable in

[275] Mexican law remained in force, American Ins. Co. v. Canter, 1 Pet. 511 (1848); Ainsa v. New Mexico & Arizona Railroad, 175 U.S. 76 (1899); First Nat'l Bank v. Kinnen, 1 Utah 100 (1873); Haynes v. State, 100 Tex. 426, 100 S.W. 912 (1907); State v. Gallardo, 106 Tex. 274, 166 S.W. 369 (1914); State v. Grubstake Investment Asso., 117 Tex. 53, 297 S.W. 202 (1927); Miller v. Letzerich, 121 Tex. 248, 49 S.W. 2d 404 (1932); Manry v. Robinson, 122 Tex. 213, 56 S.W. 2d 438 (1932); State v. Balli, 173 S.W. 2d 522, aff'd 190 S.W. 2d 71 (1945); Luttes v. State, 159 Tex. 500, 324 S.W. 2d 167 (1958). Rockwell, A Compilation of Spanish and Mexican Law in Relation to Mines and Titles to Real Estate in Force in . . . Mexico (1851); Sayles, Early Laws of Texas . . . Laws and Decrees of Spain Relating to Land in Mexico . . . (1891): Reynolds, Spanish and Mexican Land Laws . . . (1895); 2 Wheless, Compendium of the Laws of Mexico . . . 545 (1910); McKitrick, The Public Land System of Texas, 1823–1910 (1918); Little, The Land Laws of Mexico (1921); Brown, Mexican Land Laws, 20 Am. J. Int'l. L. 519 (1926); Baker, Mexican Land Grants in California, 9 (3) Historical Association of Southern California Annual 236 (1914); Ferris, Land Titles Difficulties in Mexico, 24 Business Historical Soc'ty Bull. 13 (1950); Hill, Spanish and Mexican Grants between Nueces and Rio Grande, 5 So. Texas L. J. 47 (1960); Fernandez y Fernandez, Land Tenure in Mexico, 25 J. Land Econ. 219 (1943); McBride, The Land System of Mexico (1923); Lamar, Land Policy in the Spanish Southwest: a Study in Contrasts, 22 J. Econ. Hist. 498 (1962); West, Validity of Certain Spanish Land Grants in Texas, 2 Texas L. Rev. 435 (1924).

For a recent incident, see Napier, The Tragicomedy of Spanish Land Grants, 6 (24) The National Observer 5 (June 12, 1967).

118   CONFLICT OF LAWS: MEXICO AND THE UNITED STATES

view of the fact that Texas, New Mexico, Arizona, California, Nevada and Utah as well as parts of Colorado, Kansas, Oklahoma, and Wyoming have been, at one time or another, parts of New Spain and Mexico.[276] Among other questions, cases involve: different types of Mexican land grants;[277] land grants to villages (*pueblos*) ;[278] grants for public parks;[279] grants in connection with colonization;[280] deeds under Mexican law, some perfected too late, some imperfect;[281] confiscation of land as punishment for treason;[282] questions of inheritance

[276] "The United States have directed their tribunals, in passing upon the rights of the inhabitants, to be governed by the stipulation of the treaty, the law of nature, the laws, usages, and customs of the formed government, the principles of equity, and the decisions of the Supreme Court so far as they are applicable," United States v. Auguisola, 68 U.S. 352, 385 (1863).

[277] Henshaw v. Bissell, 85 U.S. 255 (1873); United States v. San Pedro Canon del Agua, 17 P. 337 (1888); United States v. Cameron, 21 P. 177 (Ariz. 1889); Sheldon v. Milmo, 90 Tex. 1, 36 S.W. 413 (1896); Sullival v. Solis, 52 Tex. Civ. App. 464, 114 S.W. 456 (1908); State v. Balli, 114 Tex. 195, 190 S.W. 2d 71 (1945); City of Weslaco v. Turner, 236 S.W. 2d 635 (1951); Armijo v. Town of Artisco, 239 P. 2d 535 (1951).

[278] Brownsville v. Cavazos, 100 U.S. 138 (1879); San Francisco City & County v. LeRoy, 138 U.S. 656 (1890); Kemper v. Town of Victoria, 3 Tex. 135 (1848); City of Victoria v. Victoria County, 100 Tex. 438, 101 S.W. 190 (1907); Ditmar v. Dignowity, 78 Tex. 22, 14 S.W. 268 (1890); Corporation of San Felipe de Austin v. State, 111 Tex. 108, 229 S.W. 845 (1921); Texas Mexican Ry. Co. v. Jarvis, 69 Tex. 527, 7 S.W. 210 (1888); Downing v. Diaz, 80 Tex. 436, 16 S.W. 49 (1891); State v. Gallardo, 136 S. W. 664, 166 S.W. 369 (1914); Sullivan v. Solis, 114 S.W. 456 (1908); Alexander v. García, 168 S.W. 376 (1914); Mitchell v. Town of Refugio, 265 S.W. 2d 261 (1954). Hart v. Burnell, 15 Cal. 530 (1860); Vernon Irrigation Co. v. City of Los Angeles, 39 P. 762 (1895); City of San Diego v. Cuyamaca Water Co., 287 P. 475 (1930). Jones, Local Government in the Spanish Colonies as Provided by the Recopilación de Leyes de los Reinos de las Indias, 19 SW. Hist. Q. 65 (1915); Norwell, A Primer of Spanish Towns in Southwest United States, 37 Notre Dame Law. 630 (1962).

[279] Hart v. Gould 259 P. 2d 49 (Cal 1953).

[280] Texas-Mexican Ry. Co. v. Locke, 12 S.W. 80 (1889); Haynes v. State, 100 S.W. 912 (1907).

[281] United States v. Perot, 98 U.S. 428 (1878); Brownsville v. Cavazos, 100 U.S. 138 (1870); Chaves v. United States, 168 U.S. 177 (1897); Crespin v. United States, 168 U.S. 208 (1897); Jones v. Borden, 5 Tex. 410 (1849); State v. Palacios, 150 S.W. 229 (1912); State v. Bustamente, 47 Tex. 320 (1877).

[282] In consequence of insurrection in Bexar in 1811, Spanish officials seized land for treason, ordered subsequent sale and conveyed land, reciting these facts in the deed: the court held that this raises no presumption, under the law of any civilized country, that any judicial proceedings have been instituted against the owners of such lands, to find him guilty or to confiscate property for such offence, Sabariego v. Maverick, 124 U.S. 261 (1888).

prohibited because of alienage, resulting in escheat;[283] proof of titles;[284] also water rights;[285] riparian rights;[286] and claims to submerged lands.[287]

From a large number of American cases dealing with Mexican law as the present *lex rei sitae,* a few may be briefly mentioned. In cases dealing with escheat of titles to land to the state, on the ground that the alien claiming title was ineligible under the *lex rei sitae* because of alienage, courts found escheat to be governed by the *lex rei*

[283] Middleton v. McGrew, 64 U.S. 45 (1859); Glover v. McFaddin, 205 F.2d 1 (1953); People v. Folsom, 5 Cal. 373 (1855); Webb's Heirs v. Kirby Lumber Co., 107 S.W. 581 (1908).

[284] State v. Cardinas, 47 Tex. 250 (1877); State v. Cuellar, 47 Tex. 295 (1877); State v. Sais, 47 Tex. 307 (1877).

[285] Vernon Irrigation Co. v. City of Los Angeles, 39 P. 762 (1895); Miller v. Letzerich, 121 Tex. 248, 49 S.W. 2d 404 (1932); State v. Valmont Plantations, 346 S.W. 2d 853 (Tex. 1961). Dobkins, The Spanish Element in Texas Water Law (1959); Davenport, Development of the Texas Law of Waters, 21 Vernon's Annot. Stat. XIII (1925); Wiel, Water Rights in the Western States (1908); and Origin and Comparative Development of the Law of Watercourses in the Common and Civil Law, 6 Cal. L. Rev. 245 (1918); Davenport & Canales, The Texas Law of Flowing Waters with Special Reference to Irrigation from the Lower Rio Grande, 8 Baylor L. Rev. 138 (1956); Hawkins, Water Rights in Texas Interstate and Boundary Streams, 9 Texas L. Rev. 501 (1931). Mineral rights, Cox v. Robison, 105 Tex. 426, 150 S.W. 1149 (1912).

[286] Lux v. Haggin, 10 P. 674 (1886); Boquillas Land & Cattle Co. v. Curtis, 213 U.S. 339 (1909); Motl v. Boyd, 286 S.W. 458 (1926); San Antonio River Authority v. Lewis, 363 S.W. 2d 444 (1962). Pomeroy, A Treatise on the Law of Riparian Rights 193 (1887); Hildebrand, The Rights of Riparian Owners at Common Law in Texas, 6 Texas L. Rev. 19 (1927); Trelease, Coordination of Riparian and Appropriative Rights to the Use of Water, 33 Texas L. Rev. 24 (1954).

[287] Shoreline: State v. Balli, 173 S.W. 2d 522 (1943), aff'd 190 S.W. 2d 71 (1944), cert. denied, 328 U.S. 852 (1945); Giles v. Ponder, 275 S.W. 2d 509 (1955), aff'd 293 S.W. 2d 736 (1956); Luttes v. State, 324 S.W. 2d 167 (1958), noted in 5 So. Texas L. J. 213 (1960); Petersen v. United States, 327 F. 2d 219 (9th Cir. 1964).

Navigable waters: Manry v. Robinson, 122 Tex. 213, 56 S.W. 2d 438 (1932); Heard v. Town of Refugio, 103 S.W. 2d 728 (1937); Humble Oil & Refining Co. v. Sun Oil Co., 190 F. 2d 191 (1951), 191 F. 2d 705 (5th Cir. 1951), cert. denied, 342 U.S. 920 (1952).

Riverbed: State v. Grubstake Investment Assoc., 297 S.W. 202 (1927); Manry v. Robinson, 56 S.W. 2d 438 (1932); McCurdy v. Morgan, 265 S.W. 2d 269 (1954).

Irrigation: Motl v. Boyd, 116 Tex. 82 (1926); State v. Valmont Plantations, 346 S.W. 2d 853 (1961). Davenport, The Texas Law of Flowing Waters with Special Reference to Irrigation from the Lower Rio Grande, 8 Baylor L. Rev. 138 (1956).

Generally, Dobkins, The Spanish Element in Texas Water Law (1959).

sitae, and requiring a formal procedure (office found) , in many states regulated by statute while in others the time-honored common law principles still obtain. Until such procedure is completed, an alien grantee's executed lease remains valid.[288] American courts even looked to analogous proceedings in Mexico and discussed escheat in civil law.[289]

Titles to land situated in Mexico are always tested against the *lex rei sitae.*[290] An expropriation under Mexican law of land which at that time was within Mexico, will be recognized in the United States after the land has become American territory through avulsion.[291] In an action in New York for damages to real estate in Veracruz, recording was held unnecessary under the *lex rei sitae* (art. 3057, 3081 of the Veracruz Civil Code) since the land had a value of less than 200 pesos; nevertheless, such unrecorded deed was held good against third parties with knowledge (art. 3057, 3081) . In another case, the court granted damages for oil taken out of land in Mexico beyond the rights granted.[292] On appeal, the court affirmed[293] characterizing the action as one in conversion and, therefore, *in personam.* Equally *in personam* was held an action to cancel a mortgage on land in Mexico[294] because under the *lex fori* such action is in equity, with the defendant alien residing within the jurisdiction. Another action for conversion of oil in Mexico was litigated in Riley v. Pierce Oil Company.[295] There the court held that Mexican law controls the claim, including collateral issues involved, i.e. the defendant's alleged capacity as undisclosed principal as well as that of the holder of complete control over the Mexican subsidiary.

In the majority of the American states aliens, including alien or alien controlled domestic corporations, are allowed to acquire interests in real property.[296] By way of a brief summary, it may be stated that

[288] Ramirez v. Kent, Bartell & Co., 2 Cal. 558 (1852) .

[289] Phillips v. Moore, 100 U.S. 208 (1879) .

[290] Booth v. Scott, 205 S.W. 633 (1918) , jurisdiction denied, 253 U.S. 475 (1919) .

[291] Shapleigh v. Mier, 83 F. 2d 673 (5th Cir. 1936) , 299 U.S. 468 (1936) .

[292] Mexican Gulf Oil Co. v. Compañía Transcontinental de Petróleos, 281 F. 148 (1922) .

[293] 292 F. 846 (1923) .

[294] Frontera Transportation Co. v. Abaunza, 271 F. 199 (1921) .

[295] 245 N.Y. 152, 156 N.E. 647 (1927) .

[296] Validity of State Restraints on Alien Ownership of Land, 51 Mich. L. Rev. 1053 (1953) ; Property Rights of Aliens under Iowa and Federal Law, 47 Iowa L. Rev. 105 (1961) ; The Alien Land Laws: a Re-evaluation, 36 Temple L.Q. 15 (1962) .

in Alabama, Delaware, Colorado, Florida, Maine, Massachusetts, Michigan, Nevada, North and South Dakota, New York, Ohio, Rhode Island, Tennessee, Vermont, and West Virginia there is no discrimination against alien land holding. In a few states, Connecticut, Iowa, Mississippi, New Hampshire, North Carolina, Oklahoma, Wisconsin, the District of Columbia and the territories, nonresident aliens may not acquire land. Other states, Arizona, California, Idaho, Kansas (in regard to acquisition through inheritance), Louisiana, Montana, New Mexico, Oregon, Washington, and Wyoming, require eligibility under federal law to become nationals. In California, Montana and Oregon, this statutory provision was found to be unconstitutional; in any case, disabilities for naturalization based on race have been abandoned in the Naturalization and Nationality Act of 1952,[297] while other disabilities seem to be insignificant. The requirement of eligibility for citizenship was interpreted in Hughes v. Kerfoot[298] in the sense that it must be distinguished from being eligible to naturalization. "The former refers to a broad class of aliens who are capable of becoming citizens upon full compliance with federal naturalization laws and regulations. The latter refers to those aliens who not only are eligible for citizenship, but who also have already established their eligibility to naturalization by compliance with federal rules . . . As a practical matter, an alien might be eligible to citizenship, and at the same time ineligible for naturalization, due to his moral background or political beliefs." It must be mentioned that the opinion antedates the 1952 Immigration and Nationality Act. Finally in Georgia, Maryland, New Jersey, New York and Virginia only enemy aliens are prohibited from holding land, while in the remaining states: Illinois, Indiana, Kansas, Kentucky, Mississippi, Nebraska, South Carolina, Texas, and Utah, various partial disabilities are in force.

A closer look shall be taken at the statutes in force in the states bordering on Mexico. These statutes not only contain significant limitations upon holding of land by aliens but also corresponding prohibitions against foreign or foreign controlled corporations, with exemptions of particular interest to Mexicans.

California's constitution grants in art. I, paragraph 17, resident aliens eligible to citizenship equal national treatment in regard to holding land. The limitation was held unconstitutional in Sei Fujii v. State of California,[299] as violating the equal protection clause of

---

[297] 8 U.S.C.A. § 1422 (1952).   [298] 263 P. 2d 226 (Kan. 1953).
[299] 217 P. 2d 481 (1950), reh. denied, 218 P. 2d 585; rev'd 242 P. 2d 617 (1952).

the federal constitution by discriminating against aliens not of white or African descent, at that time not eligible for naturalization. The right to own property is expressed in article 671 of the California Civil Code: "Any person, whether citizen or alien, may take, hold, and dispose of property, real or personal," which rule is qualified in regard to inheritance by the requirement of reciprocity (Probate Code, art. 259).

Arizona[300] allows "aliens eligible to citizenship under the laws of the United States [to] acquire, possess, enjoy, transmit and inherit real property or any interest therein, the same as citizens of the United States, except as otherwise expressly provided by law," or by treaties (sec. 33–1201, para. (2)). In respect of foreign corporation, Arizona has enacted in 1958 (sec. 10–484) a complete prohibition against their holding land in the state:

> D. No corporation organized under any jurisdiction other than the United States, or any political subdivision or possession thereof, shall own or hold land within this state,

a provision applicable regardless of whether or not such foreign corporation has complied with the requirements for doing business in the state (sec. 10–481). This amendment seems to be inconsistent with section 33–1202, enacted in 1921, at least in regard to corporations organized under the "laws of . . . any other . . . nation . . . but not having a majority of the members aliens ineligible to citizenship, or in which a majority of the issued capital stock is owned by such aliens." It may be assumed that the subsequent enactment of 1958 abrogated this exception. However, it would appear that other types of foreign associations, not corporations, may still take advantage of this provision, provided the majority of their members are eligible for United States nationality, or in case of nonincorporated associations with capital, that the majority of capital is owned by aliens eligible for United States nationality. It must be added, however, that these statutes have not yet been judicially interpreted. Additional statutory provisions deal with aliens or alien corporations as guardians (sec. 33–1203); trusts for aliens (sec. 33–1204); sale in probate (sec. 33–1205); escheat (sec. 33–1206); invalidity of conveyances (sec. 33–1207), including penalties (sec. 33–1208) and enforcement (sec. 33–1209); and actions by aliens to enforce their rights (sec. 33–1210).

Like Arizona, New Mexico allows aliens eligible for United States

[300] Rev. Stat. sec. 33-1201 (1956).

nationality to acquire land in article II, paragraph 22 of the constitution, as amended in 1921, but excludes any "corporation, co-partnership or association, a majority of the stock or interest in which is owned or held by such aliens," meaning aliens ineligible to become American nationals.[301] Other aliens have

> (F)ull power and authority to acquire or hold real estate by deed, will, inheritance, or otherwise, when the same may be acquired in good faith and in due form of law, and also to alienate, sell, assign and transfer the same to their heirs or other persons, whether such heirs or other persons be, or not, citizens of the United States; and when a foreigner having title or interest in any lands or estate dies, such lands or estate shall descend and vest in the same manner as if such foreigner were a citizen of the United States, and such circumstance shall not be an impediment to any person holding an interest in said estate, although not a citizen of the United States, for all such persons shall have the same rights and resources and shall, in all respects, be treated on the same footing as native citizens of the United States with respect to the personal estate of a foreigner dying intestate, and all persons interested in said estate, under the law of this state, whether foreigners or not.

Finally, Texas has a most elaborate scheme of statutory law in the matter.[302] This statute starts out with the general rule that "no alien or alien corporation shall acquire any interest, right or title, either legal or equitable, in or to any lands in the State of Texas" (art. 166), but admits significant exceptions in articles 167 and 174. Among these exceptions, the following are significant in regard to Mexicans: aliens eligible to acquire American nationality, being *bona fide* residents of Texas and having declared "their intention to become citizens of the United States"; aliens "natural born citizens of nations which have a common boundary with the United States" which includes Mexico; and aliens citizens of a "nation which now permits citizens of this State [i.e., Texas] to own land in fee in such country," i.e., by reciprocity.

Similar provisions apply in Texas to corporations. As a general rule, no corporation in which the majority of capital stock is legally or equitably owned by aliens who are prohibited by law to hold land in Texas, may acquire title or any other interest in Texas lands. Exemptions are provided for corporations "the majority of the capital

---

[301] N.M. Stat. Annot. 70-1-24 (1953).

[302] Tex. Rev. Stat. tit. 5, art. 166-177 (1959) ; Branhan v. Minear, 199 S.W. 2d 841 (Tex. 1947).

stock of which is legally or equitably owned by citizens of the United States, if any such stock is so owned, and by

(a) Aliens, either individual or corporate, who are citizens or subjects of, or in the case of corporation incorporated under the laws of, any nation, country, province or state which has a common boundary with the United States; or

(b) Aliens, either individual or corporate, who are citizens or subjects of, or in the case of a corporation incorporated under the laws of any nation . . . or state which permits citizens of this state to own land in fee in such nation . . . or state; and any such corporation shall not be, or be deemed to be, an alien corporation for the purposes of this Title 5.

The only limitation is that restricting the extent of land allowed to be owned by corporations generally (art. 174, as amended in 1961). From further provisions of this title 5 of Texas Statutes, only article 175 shall be mentioned, prohibiting that land be held in trust by aliens or by nationals of the United States for the benefit of aliens or any corporation prohibited from owning land in Texas. Other statutory provisions deal with the time to alienate (art. 168); liens, loans and debts (art. 169); term of title (art. 170); escheat (art. 171, 172); guardianship (art. 173); report of alien ownership (art. 176, 176 A, B); and personal property (art. 177).

TRUSTS

Trusts were introduced to Mexico by way of statutes.[303] They are limited in scope since the function of a trustee may only be conferred upon banking institutions expressly authorized (art. 350 of the former and art. 44 of the latter law). Trusts may be established by an act *inter vivos* or by will, always in writing in accordance with the "requirements of general laws [*legislación común*] regarding the transfer of rights or conveyance of property in the things which are given in trust" (art. 352 of the General Law of Credit Titles and Operations).

[303] General Law of Credit Titles and Operations, art. 346-359 (1932); General Law of Credit Institutions and Auxiliary Organizations, art. 44-46 and 136-138 (1941). Batiza, El Fideicomiso: Teoría y Práctica (Mexico, 1958); also The Evolution of the Fideicomiso (Trust) under Mexican Law, in U. Miami School of Law, Mexico: a Symposium on Law and Government 67 (1957); and Trusts in Mexico, in Yiannopoulos (ed.), Civil Law in the Modern World 128 (1965); Molina Pasquel, Conferencias sobre Fideicomiso, Trust and Equity, 5 (20) Revista de La Facultad de Derecho de México 51 (1955); Barrera Graf, Dos Estudios Sobre Fideicomisos, in his Estudios de Derecho Mercantil 312 (Mexico, 1958).

In case the *corpus* of the trust is immovable property, the trust must be inscribed in the public property register of the *locus rei sitae* and takes effect in regard to third persons from the date of registration (art. 353 of the same law). If movables are involved, the trust takes effect in relation to third persons from the moment the corporeal thing is handed over to the institutional trustee (art. 354, III); in case of a chose in action, from the moment the debtor is notified (ibid., I); and from the moment that a nominative title is endorsed to the institutional trustee and this is noted in the books kept by the issuer (ibid., II).

Since trust arrangements are strictly tied to specifically authorized Mexican banking institutions and are a matter of federal law, it is not surprising that no conflict law has developed in this matter.[304]

Among American cases there is but one reported case dealing with trusts related to Mexico. In Equitable Trust Co. v. Pratt[305] the settlor executed a trust agreement in Mexico, acknowledged its execution before the American consul in Mexico City, and mailed it to the trustee in New York. The court refused to apply the *lex loci actus* under which the trust would be invalid. Instead, it applied the law of New York as that of settlor's domicile, on the ground that the settlor did not abandon his New York domicile when he executed the trust in Mexico.

[304] Foreign banks in Mexico may not engage in trust operations, art. 6 of the General Law of Credit Institutions and Auxiliary Organizations.

[305] 193 N.Y. Supp. 152 (1922), aff'd, 199 N.Y. Supp. 921 (1923).

13. COPYRIGHTS, PATENTS
AND TRADEMARKS

In conflict of laws the status of incorporeal assets is a matter of wide disagreement. In view of the paucity of case materials, the present discussion is limited mainly to treaties[306] and statutory materials.

Copyrights

TREATY LAW

At present, there are two multilateral copyright conventions binding both on Mexico and the United States: the Inter-American Convention on Literary and Artistic Copyright, signed at Buenos Aires in 1910, the Universal Copyright Convention signed at Geneva in 1952. The conflicts provisions of the 1910 Convention may be summarized by pointing out that under article 3 copyrights obtained in one member country "in conformity with its laws" shall have full effect in all others "without the necessity of complying with any other formality, provided always there shall appear in the work a statement that indicates the reservation of property right." Authors of protected works may bring suits for infringement and such suits "shall be admitted by the courts of the Signatory States" (art. 5). Publications infringing a copyright may be confiscated in the signatory countries "in which the original work had the right to be legally protected, without prejudice to indemnities or penalties which the counterfeiters may have incurred according to the laws of the country in which the fraud may have been committed" (art. 14).

The Universal Copyright Convention of 1952[307] grants, in principle, equal national treatment to nationals of all contracting countries for their published works as well as to works first published in these countries, regardless of the nationality of the author. If a con-

---

[306] Bogsch, The Law of Copyright under the Universal Convention (1964); UNESCO, Copyright Laws and Treaties of the World (Paris, 1955-, I.I.); Ladas, Interamerican Copyrights, 7 U. Pitt. L. Rev. 283 (1941).

[307] Dubin, The Universal Copyright Conventions, 42 Cal. L. Rev. 89 (1954); Warner, The UNESCO Universal Copyright Convention, 1952 Wisc. L. Rev. 493.

tracting country has in its domestic law assimilated domiciliaries to its own nationals, such equality will also take effect in regard to the Convention (art. II, para. 3). The duration of the copyright protection is governed by the *lex fori*, i.e., "by the law of the Contracting State in which protection is claimed" (art IV, para. 1), but cannot be less than a uniform minimum period established by the Convention (art. IV, para. 2). Nevertheless, the contracting countries are not bound to grant protection for a period longer "than that fixed for the class of works to which the work in question belongs, in case of unpublished works by the law of the Contracting State of which the author is a national, and in the case of published works by the law of the Contracting State in which the work has been first published" (art. IV, para. 4). In case a work of a national of a contracting country was first published in a non-contracting country, the duration of his copyright will be determined by the law of the country of which the author is a national (art. IV, para. 5). Upon compliance with municipal law regarding formalities of registration, deposit, and others (art. III, para. 1), actions for infringement of copyright must meet "procedural requirements, such as that the complainant must appear through domestic counsel or that the complainant must deposit with the court or an administrative office, or both, a copy of the work involved in the litigation" (art. III, para. 3); however, failure to comply with these requirements "shall not affect the validity of the copyright, nor shall any such requirement be imposed upon a national of another Contracting State if such requirement is not imposed on nationals of the State in which protection is claimed" (ibid.).

MEXICAN LAW

Copyright is presently regulated by the Federal Law of Authors' Rights as amended in 1963.[308] The law grants "aliens living there permanently, temporarily or as transients in the Republic of Mexico" in regard to their works the same rights as enjoyed by Mexican authors (art. 29). If the home country of an alien has a treaty with Mexico regarding copyrights, such aliens will "enjoy the protection provided in this law

[308] D.O. Dec. 21, 1963. Devaux, Copyright in Mexico, the Federal Law ... 1956, 16 Revue Internationale de Droit d'Auteur 34 (1957); 11 UNESCO Copright Bull. 40 (1958); Pinner, World Copyright: an Encyclopedia (1953-1960), 5 vol.; Plaisant, The Exploitation of the Copyright and the Conflict of Laws, (35) Revue Internationale du Droit d'Auteur 62 (1962).

insofar as this is not incompatible" with treaties (art. 30). In regard to alien authors with whose home countries Mexico has no treaty in this matter, or in case their work has been published for the first time in a country without such a treaty with Mexico, article 28 grants such authors a protection of only six years from the date of the first publication, always subject to reciprocity; if after the expiration of these six years the work is not registered with the *Dirección del Derecho de Autor*, anybody may publish the work provided he obtains a permission from the Secretariat of Public Education. However, if after the expiration of this period the author has registered his work, it will receive complete protection, except editions authorized by the Ministry of Public Education prior to registration (art. 28, para. 2).

AMERICAN LAW

Both the treatment of alien authors as well as the impact of the Universal Copyright Convention on American law are discussed elsewhere.[309] Here, it should only be noted that according to the Copyright Law[310] aliens are accorded equal national treatment, provided they are domiciled in the United States at the time of the first publication of their work, or their own country "grants either by treaty, convention, agreement, or law" American nationals substantially the same protection and the compliance with this requirement is established by a Presidential Proclamation. In relation to Mexico, such proclamations have been issued.[311]

In the United States the Universal Copyright Convention was implemented by an amendment to the Copyright Act.[312] It provides that certain requirements under the act will not apply to nationals of other contracting countries or in which their work was first published (art. 9 c).

---

[309] Sherman, The Universal Copyright Convention: Its Effect on United States Law, 55 Colum. L. Rev. 1137 (1955); International Copyright Convention and the United States: the Impact of the UNESCO Universal Copyright Convention on Existing Law, 62 Yale L.J. 1065 (1953); Hoffman, The Position of the United States in Relation to International Copyright Protection of Literary Works, 22 U. Cinc. L. Rev. 415 (1953); Shulman, International Copyright in the United States: a Critical Analysis, 19 L. & Cont. Pr. 141 (1954); Bogsch, The Law of Copyright under the Universal Convention 558 (1964).

[310] 17 U.S.C.A. §§ 1-217 (1966).   [311] 29 Stat. 877; 36 Stat. 2685.

[312] 17 U.S.C.A. § 9, 68 Stat. 1030.

Patents

TREATY LAW

The only convention in force between Mexico and the United States is the Convention for the Protection of Industrial Property, signed first in Paris in 1883, later revised at London in 1934.[313]

The basic conflict provision applicable to patents is contained in article 2 of the Convention. It grants to nationals of countries—members to the Convention

> the advantages that their respective laws now grant, or may hereafter grant, to their own nationals, without prejudice to the rights specially provided by the present Convention. Consequently, they shall have the same protection as the latter, and the same legal remedy against any infringement of their rights, provided they observe the conditions and formalities imposed upon nationals.

Thus, the Convention guarantees equal national treatment, but where the Convention would grant a more favorable treatment than municipal law, the provisions of the Convention prevail. Moreover, such equal national treatment is granted regardless of the alien's domicile or establishment outside of the country where the protection of patent under the Convention is sought (art. 2, para. 2).

MEXICAN LAW

The Law of Industrial Property enacted in 1942[314] distinguishes patents of invention, improvement patents, and patents on industrial models and designs. Applications for patents already filed in the United States may be filed in Mexico within one year, and within six months for industrial models and designs. In these cases the effect of the Mexican grant of patent will be retroactive from the day of the original filing. However, a patent will be denied if the application is filed in Mexico later than six months after publication or use elsewhere.

[313] Ladas, The International Protection of Industrial Property (1930); Ebb, International Business: Regulation and Protection 496 (1964); Harris & Siegel, Industrial Property in Latin American Development, 6 Pat. TM. & Cop. J. of Res. & Educ. 327 (1962); Sepúlveda, El Derecho Internacional Convencional en Materia de Prioridad de Patentes, 9 (25) Boletín del Instituto de Derecho Comparado de México 11 (1956). Cf. Ortman v. Stanray Corporation, 371 F. 2d 154 (7th Cir. 1967).
[314] D.O. Dec. 31, 1942. Translation in 33 Trade-Mark Rep. 21 (1943).

Trademarks

TREATY LAW

As already stated, both Mexico and the United States are members to
the Convention for the Protection of Industrial Property signed in
London in 1934. In addition to provisions regarding patents, discussed
previously, the Convention contains conflict rules applicable to trade-
marks.[315]

During the period of applicability of the previous version of the
convention, namely that signed at Washington in 1911, guaranteeing
to nationals of all contracting countries with regard to trademarks the
"advantage which their respective laws now grant or may hereafter
grant to the citizens of that country" (art. II), the Supreme Court of
Mexico denied protection to the trademark "Palmolive" on the ground
that the plaintiff, a Delaware corporation, has not complied with the
requirements contained in article 24 of the Mexican Commercial Code
and, consequently, has no legal existence in Mexico to claim any remedy
in local courts. The decision brought about a flurry of diplomatic activities, and when one year later the Chickering case came before the
Supreme Court in *amparo,* the Court, relying on article 6 of the Regulatory Law on Amparo, decided that a foreign corporation has standing in a Mexican court regardless of its noncompliance with the requirements of local registration.

MEXICAN LAW

The Mexican Law on Industrial Property enacted in 1942,[316] deals
also with trademarks. Among others, the law provides that an application for registration of a trademark filed within six months after the

[315] Ladas, The International Protection of Trade-Marks by the American
Republics (1929); Federico, Treaties between the United States and Other
Countries Relating to Trade-Marks, 39 Trade-Mark Rep. (supp.) (1949);
Halliday, Interamerican Conventions for the Protection of Trade-Marks, 28
Can. B. Rev. 609 (1950); Bogsch, Design Laws and Treaties of the World
(1960-, 1.1.).
[316] Rangel Medina, Tratado de Derecho Marcario: las Marcas Indus-
triales y Comerciales en México (Mexico, 1960); Solórzano, Registration of
Foreign Trade-Marks in Mexico, 42 Trade-Mark Rep. 615 (1952); Protection
of Registered Trade-Marks in Mexico, 40 Trade-Mark Rep. 16 (1950); Sierra,
Trademarks in Mexico: Registration, Maintenance and Renewal, 45 J. Pat.
Off. Soc'ty 779 (1963). 70 Semanario (5a ép.) 1280, 5252 (1941), also Jurisprudencia Definida, 118 Semanario (5a ép.) tesis 736; and 53 Semanario (6a
ép.) 15 (1961).

application was made in a foreign country, it will be assumed that the application was filed in Mexico on the same date, provided there is reciprocity. Trade names are protected without registration: however, the publication in the Industrial Property Gazette affords the owner the right to prosecute infringements by a criminal action.

AMERICAN LAW

International aspects of trademarks outside of the scope of applicable treaty law are governed by the Lanham Trade-Mark Act,[317] making actionable deceptive use of marks in all "commerce within the control of Congress," which includes also the commerce with foreign nations.[318]

This act was tested in two cases involving trade with Mexico. The import from Mexico into the United States of watches bearing the Bulova trademark, affixed in Mexico by an American national in his business conducted in Mexico City, was considered sufficient to give American courts jurisdiction and bring the infringement within the scope of the Lanham Act, in spite of the fact that the trademark has been registered in Mexico by defendant since 1939.[319] The court pointed out that defendant's "operations and their effects were not confined within the territorial limits of a foreign country," and declined as decisive the fact that defendant has affixed the trademark in Mexico City or that his purchases in the United States "when viewed in isolation do not violate any of our laws. They were essential steps in the course of business consummated abroad; acts in themselves legal lose that character when they become part of an unlawful scheme . . . In sum, we do not think that [defendant] by so simple a device can evade the thrust of the laws of the United States in a privileged sanctuary beyond our borders."[320]

The same Lanham Act was applied to conspirators in a scheme to use the American registered trademark "Las Palmas" in Mexico.[321]

[317] 15 U.S.C.A. § 1053-1127 (1963) ; § 1126 deals with resident aliens.

[318] Rappeport, Trade-Mark and Unfair Competition in International Conflict of Laws: An Analysis of the Choice of Law Problem, 20 U. Pitt. L. Rev. 1 (1958); Durham & Vassil, Marcas de Estados Unidos Solicitadas y Registradas por Extranjeros, 5 (9) Revista Mexicana de la Propriedad Industrial y Artística (1967).

[319] Steele v. Bulova Watch Co., 344 U.S. 280 (1952).

[320] Noted 47 N.W.U. L. Rev. 677 (1952) ; 70 Harv. L. Rev. 743 (1957). Ebb, International Business: Regulation and Protection 371 (1964).

[321] Ramirez & Feraud Chili Co. v. Las Palmas Food Company, 146 F. Supp. 594, aff'd, per curiam, 245 F. 2d 874 (9th Cir. 1957), cert. denied, 355 U.S. 927 (1958).

In order to take advantage of the trademark well established since 1922, the defendants caused the trademark to be registered in 1953 in Mexico by a straw-man from Tiajuana, to be later assigned to one of the defendants; whether or not this assignment was accompanied with the transfer of the establishment using it in accordance with article 6 (quater) of the International Convention for the Protection of Industrial Property (1934), was not explored. Subsequently, the defendant California corporation and others started using on products canned in Mexico the trademark which was printed in California and identical in design and color with that used by plaintiffs. Following the statutory interpretation in the Steele case, the court was faced with a different trademark situation. While the Bulova trademark registration was cancelled in Mexico before the case reached the United States Supreme Court, in this case plaintiffs only started cancellation proceedings in Mexico. A defense urging this fact was declined by the court by pointing out that "defendants' Mexican registration of plaintiffs' mark can have no greater effect than to confer upon defendants a license or permission to use the mark in Mexico." The court added that "there could be no affront to Mexican sovereignty or Mexican law if, as between parties, this court should declare that defendants may not use their license under Mexican law as to injure plaintiff's foreign commerce conducted from the United States," and repeated from the Steele case that "where, as here, there can be no interference with the sovereignty of another nation, the [court below] in exercising its equity powers may command persons properly before it to cease to perform acts outside its territorial jurisdiction."[322]

[322] Ebb, International Business: Regulation and Protection 382 (1964).

14. CONTRACTS

In the area of choice-of-law dealing with contracts two positions clash: one, advocating freedom of contracting including the freedom of choosing the controlling legal system to govern the contract; and another, urging legal limitations on such freedom both in regard to the contents of the contract and the choice of the law to control it. Such limitations may arise from the fact that either rules are expressly designated or interpreted as being peremptory (*ius cogents*) and, consequently, beyond the parties' reach.[323]

While the law in force in the United States, by and large, considers both substantive and conflict law of contract to be pliable (*ius dispositivum*), Mexican courts tend to a stricter position and consider not only the substantive law of the forum, at least in international conflict situations, to be rigid because of its public policy character, but also choice-of-law rules.

TREATY LAW

Between Mexico and the United States there are only three areas where conflict rules may be derived from treaties. One area is that of international air transportation contracts within the scope of the Warsaw Convention (1929), to be discussed later. Another involves provisions contained in the Article of Agreement of the International Monetary Fund (1944) dealing with exchange contracts in article VIII (2) (6):[324]

> Exchange contracts which involve the currency of any member and which are contrary to the exchange control regulations of that member maintained or imposed consistently with this Agreement, shall be unenforceable in the territory of any member.

[323] Bayitch, Connecting Agreement: A Study in Comparative Conflict Law, 7 Miami L.Q. 293 (1953); also La Autonomía de las Partes en la Elección del Derecho Aplicable . . . , (7) Boletín del Instituto de Derecho Comparado de México 41 (1954).

[324] Bayitch, Florida and International Legal Developments, 18 U. Miami L. Rev. 321, 348 (1963); additional bibliography ibid., note 144.

For the work of Claim Commissions for the settlement of claims of nationals of one country against the government of the other, see Feller, The Mexican Claims Commissions, 1923-1934: a Study in the Law and Procedure of International Tribunals (1935).

At the present time, however, this provision is of no practical significance since both countries favor free monetary transfers.

The third area deals with powers of attorney[325] and is regulated by the Protocol on Uniformity of Powers of Attorney (1940). In order to provide the needed background, it may be pointed out that in Mexican law the relationship between principal and agent is considered to be contractual in nature (*mandato*), as defined in article 2546 of the federal Civil Code as a "contract by which the agent (*mandatario*) promises to perform for the principal (*mandante*) juridical acts with which the former has charged the latter." The identification of the controlling conflict rule may bring into play two contacts: the law of the place where the power has been executed, or the law of the place where the power is to be used, in most cases, the *lex fori*. Of course, there may also be combinations of both. The Protocol provides mainly uniform substantive rules, thus, to the same extent, dispenses with corresponding conflict rules. The substantive provisions deal with the principal (art. I) and the interrelations between special and general powers (art. IV). General powers for lawsuits (art. IV, para. 3) are deemed to have been granted without limitations "when so worded as to indicate that they confer all general powers as, according to the law, ordinarily require a special clause," a provision far from clear. In a general sense, the Protocol provides that powers granted in any member country "executed in conformity with the rules of this Protocol, shall be given full faith and credit (*serán válidos legalmente*), provided, however, that they are legalized in accordance with the special rules governing legalization " (art. V.), again without disclosing what law governs legalization. In regard to local registration or protocolization of powers granted in the other country, article VII of the Protocol provides in general terms that such local acts are not necessary, adding a rather mysterious proviso that "this rule will not prevail when the registration or protocolization of such instrument is required by the law as a special formality in specific cases." There is also a provision dealing with the *negotiorum gestor*[326] (agent without authority) appearing in

[325] Eder, Inter-American Protocol on Powers of Attorney, 2 Am. J. Comp. L. 69 (1953); also Powers of Attorney in International Practice, 98 U. Pa. L. Rev. 840 (1950); Maigrel, Formulas Internacionales de la Procuración, 5 Revista Internacional del Notariado 321 (1953); Rigaux, La Forma del Poder en Derecho Internacional Privado, (755) Revista Notarial 816 (B.A., 1964); Barrera Graf, Notas sobre la Representación en el Derecho Privado Mexicano, 13 Revista de la Facultad de Derecho de México 289 (1963).

[326] Dawson, Negotiorum gestio: the Altruistic Intermedler, 74 Harv. L. Rev. 817 (1961). See art. 1896-1909 of the federal Civil Code.

judicial or administrative proceedings on behalf of a principal without his actual authorization (art. VIII). If such acting is permitted under the *lex fori,* then the volunteer, as the *negotiorum gestor* is called in the English text (and *gestor* in the Spanish), shall "furnish the necessary legal authority in writing," or post bond "at the discretion of the competent tribunal or administrative authority, to respond for costs or damages which his action may occasion" (art. VIII). In case powers are contained in foreign notarial acts, article IX establishes in favor of the foreign notary the presumption of authority equal to that granted to local notaries "by the laws and regulations . . . without prejudice, however, to the necessity of protocolization in the case referred to in article VIII" (art. IX). This rule is extended in article X to include authorities or officials who exercise notarial functions "under the laws of their respective countries." This applies, for example, to judicial or consular officers who, in many cases, have authority to authenticate signatures or verify copies of documents.

MEXICAN LAW

In matters of contracts Mexican choice-of-laws rules are contained a few provisions of the federal Civil Code and repeated in most of the civil codes in force in the several states. Essentially, these rules provide that in regard to formalities the *lex loci actus* controls (art. 15), and alternatively, that Mexican nationals and aliens residing outside of the Federal District and Territories may agree that the formalities prescribed by the federal Civil Code shall apply, provided the contract is to be performed in the area of the Code.[327] Generally speaking, the effects of contracts entered into abroad will be governed by the *lex loci solutionis* whenever this is within the Republic (art. 13). Mexican laws, including those governing the capacity of contracting parties, apply to contracts entered into in Mexico by virtue of article 12 of the federal Civil Code and corresponding provisions of the civil codes of the several states.[328]

[327] Contracts executed by aliens, 110 (2) Semanario (5a ép.) 907 (1952). Population Law grants no power to declare aliens' transactions null, 88 Semanario (5a ép.) 694 (1947). See also art. 32 of the Nationality and Naturalization Law, supra n. 196. Abarca, Condición de los Contratos de los Extranjeros, (32) El Foro (4a ép.) 135 (1961); also in 14 Revista Internacional del Notariado 107 (1962).

[328] 29 Semanario (5a ép.) 625 (1931). 33 Semanario (5a ép.) 2524 (1931); 98 Semanario (5a ép.) 1623 (1948). Damages for breach of a travel agreement with a travel agency to visit among others, a specific locality in

Compared with American courts, Mexican courts seem to be reluctant to permit parties to choose the controlling legal system. This attitude, however, seems not to be supported by statutory law, past or present. A liberal attitude is evident, for example, in the federal Civil Code of 1884, which allowed an alien testator to choose between his *lex nationalis* or Mexican law in regard to chattels (art. 17). The present Code allows a choice of law in article 15, with the only limitation that the law so chosen is that of the same Code. The General Law of Titles of Credit and Credit Operations allows in article 254 a similar choice, even though it seems to be limited to formalities and does not affect substance. Similar favorable attitudes appear in the civil codes of the states, for example, in the Civil Code of Puebla (art. 15), patterned after the federal Civil Code of 1884. These attitudes are reflected in a recent interstate conflict case where the Supreme Court decided that the prorogation of the courts of Mexico City not only conferred jurisdiction on the federal courts there, but also resulted in making the substantive law of this forum, i.e., the federal Civil Code, applicable to a conditional sales contract involving land situated in Coahuila.[329]

Of course, the cogent or dispositive nature of the conflict rules is not the only decisive criterion in determining the effect of parties' choice of the applicable legal system. A free choice may be affected, first of all, by the forum's public policy. In a general sense, parties' freedom to act is always subject to the law which will withhold from parties' contractual dispositions matters of public interest and those prejudicial to interests of third parties (art. 6 of the federal Civil Code).[330] Moreover, the compatibility of the substantive law of a legal system applicable only because of parties' choice, with the substantive law of the forum, may also be decisive. In this respect, it appears that when in doubt Mexican courts prefer to consider substantive rules of the *lex fori* to be cogent and as such cannot be excluded by parties' choice of another legal system. This seems to be the case in international conflict situations as evidenced in the Patiño case considering the marital property regime of the *lex fori* as expressive of public

---

Europe, decided under federal Civil Code (art. 2110), 72 Semanario (6a ép.) 13 (1965). Shannon, Export Sales to Mexico, 4 Texas Int'l L. Forum 116 (1968).

[329] 57 Semanario (6a ép.) 83, 108 (1960).

[330] Flores Barroeta, La Voluntad Contractual en el Derecho Mexicano, 16 Boletín del Instituto de Derecho Comparado de México 699 (1965).

policy. The Mexican Supreme Court[331] explained its position as follows:

> If the autonomy of parties in regard to contractual obligations were complete, manifestly unacceptable results might be reached in respect to public policy [*orden publico*]. Therefore it must be pointed out that there are imperative or prohibitive statutes in Mexican law in regard to a marriage contract when it is to be determined how valid is an agreement establishing a separate property regime between the parties after it was found invalid by Spanish courts.

Contracts in foreign currency are regulated by the Monetary Law of the United Mexican States, enacted in 1931.[332] It denies to foreign currency the quality of legal tender in the Republic, except where the law provides otherwise. Generally, obligations contracted within or without the Republic and to be performed within the Republic in foreign currency, must be paid in national currency at the current rate of exchange at the place and time of payment (art. 8). This provision cannot be waived and any agreement to the contrary is null and void (art. 9). However, the rule established in article 8 for obligations contracted in the Republic, does not apply if the debtor shows, in the case of a loan, that the currency he received from the creditor was any kind of domestic currency; or, in cases of other transactions, if he proves that the currency in which the original transaction was contracted, was domestic currency of whatever kind. In both cases, the obligation will be paid in domestic currency in accordance with articles 4 and 5, establishing tender for various types of currency, i.e., at the rate parties had in mind for such conversion at the time when the transaction took place. In case this is impossible to ascertain, the obligation must be paid at legal parity (art. 4 of transitory provisions).

Substantially the same provisions apply to commercial transactions falling under the Commercial Code (art. 635 to 639). The Mexican peso is the "basis of the mercantile currency" for all exchange operations with foreign countries (art. 635). The same currency shall be used in contracts entered into abroad, to be performed within the Re-

[331] 30 Semanario (6a ép.) 67 (1955).
[332] D.O. July 27, 1931, as amended, D.O. Dec. 29, 1938, Dec. 20, 1950, Sept. 13, 1955, and Dec. 31, 1956. Translated in Aufricht, Central Banking Legislation, a Collection of Central Bank, Monetary and Banking Laws 883 (1961). The value of an obligation in foreign currency in the sense of art. 8 of the Monetary Law is determined according to the time when payment is made, not when it should have been made, 128 Semanario (52 ép.) 57 (1956); 129 Semanario (5a ép.) 16 (1956). Cf. Conversion Date of Foreign Monetary Obligations, 65 Colum. L. Rev. 490 (1965).

public (art. 636). There the only legal tender is Mexican currency, and nobody is bound to accept foreign money (art. 638), which has no more value in the Republic than it has on the open market (art. 637).

AMERICAN LAW

Whenever parties have chosen, expressly or impliedly, the legal system they want to control their contract, such choice will be given effect subject to the public policy of the forum, except in jurisdiction where also a close relation between the law so chosen and the contract is required. Outside of such choice, contracts are controlled in matters related to the making by the *lex loci actus,* and in matters of performance, including breach, by the *lex loci solutionis,* or both. In some jurisdictions, the doctrine of center-of-gravity has been adopted considering also other contacts between the contract and the legal system.

From American cases involving Mexican law, a few may be selected. In a general way, the court in Parrot v. Mexican Central Railway[333] assumed in regard to a contract entered into in Mexico that a written contract enjoys there "all the sanctity and attendant rights as it does in this country." In a similar vein, the court sidestepped the determination of the *lex loci actus,* i.e., Mexico, by assuming that a simple contract "creates a liability in all countries, which presumption is sufficient to entitle the plaintiff to recover [for reasonable expenses incurred in the preparation of a travel guide prepared for defendant], if no evidence is introduced of the law of the place where the contract was made . . . We treat this . . . as a presumption that all countries, in their courts of justice, will give effect to universally recognized fundamental principles of right and wrong."[334]

The freedom of contract may be affected by prohibitions in the *lex loci actus* as well as in the *lex fori.* In contracts involving restrictions as to ownership of land contained in the *lex situs* also may apply. In Losson v. Blodgett[335] prohibitions established by the Mexican *lex rei sitae* have been recognized. The court held a contract to convey land within the prohibited Mexican border zone to be unenforceable in the United States. By contrast, in a case involving movables the

---

[333] 207 Mass. 184, 93 N.E. 590 (1911).

[334] In Loiza v. Superior Court, 24 P. 707 (1890), the court assumed Mexican law of contracts, including rescission, to be identical with the law in force in California, i.e., *lex fori.*

[335] 36 P. 2d 147 (Cal. 1934).

master of a vessel was held not to be justified to decline the delivery of Mexican currency in the United States in pursuance of his contract, even though the shipment was in violation of Mexican tax laws.[336] Similarly, defendant was not justified to decline payment to plaintiff for liquor sold to him in Mexico as being against the Volstead Act then in force as the *lex fori*.[337] Illegality of a contract in Mexico because of lack on part of plaintiff of proper entry permit as well as of compliance with the statute of frauds were pressed as defenses in Glasband v. Hussong;[338] however, the court declined to rule unless the pertinent provisions of Mexican law are proven.

The illegality under the *lex fori* of an agreement to share winnings in the Mexican National Lottery was pressed by defendant in Castilleja v. Camero[338a] on the ground that the agreement was made in Texas where any kind of lottery violates a well established public policy. Nevertheless, the court held that the contract was not illegal since it did not violate nor aid

> in the violation of any gaming statute of Texas. The only other jurisdiction involved was Mexico. In Mexico the purpose of the contract had the express approval of the Mexican government in that the Mexican government has a revenue interest in the lottery. Thus the agreement was to do a lawful thing: participate in the National Lottery, in a lawful manner, by going to Mexico. This means that the partnership, in the form of one or more members, had to go to Mexico, buy tickets in Mexico, and collect the proceeds, if any, in Mexico. At this point, collection from the lottery, that [plaintiff's] right and title to the money arose, and at this point Texas had not been involved in any matter other than as the place where the agreement was made.

The dissenting opinion, however, considered it

> unfortunate that the court has applied the law and policy of Mexico in a case in which Mexico is not the forum, none of the parties is or was citizens of Mexico, and the case does not concern a contract made in Mexico. The Mexican National Lottery and Mexico have no concern or interest in this dispute. It is unfortunate that Texas courts are required to apply the law of another jurisdiction to a dispute between its own citizens. It is unfortunate that in doing so Texas holds that its own policy is inferior to that of a foreign jurisdiction. In my opinion,

---

[336] Kohn v. Schooner Renaissance, 5 La. Ann. 25 (1850).
[337] Veytia v. Alvarez, 247 P. 117 (1926).
[338] 304 P. 2d 225 (1956).
[338a] 414 S.W. 2d 424 (Tex. 1967). In Garza v. Richmond, 249 S.W. 889 (Tex. 1923), a check issued in Mexico for gambling debts incurred there, was held unenforceable.

Texas is the only jurisdiction which now has interest in this dispute, and its own public policy should apply.

The Texas supreme court affirmed the decision of both subordinate courts holding that plaintiff has "ownership of and a lawful right to $17,000 of the specific fund deposited" in a bank in Reynosa, Mexico, and that "ownership right is enforceable in the courts of Texas."

The statute of frauds was litigated in a few cases. With American jurisdictions split on the question whether the statute is substantive or procedural and, consequently, to be determined by the *lex causae* or *lex fori,* it was held in Briscoe v. Bronaugh[339] that an oral agreement of sale accompanied by delivery of the goods is sufficient under the *lex loci actus,* i.e., Mexico.[340] In a more recent case[341] the sale brought about by phone and telegraph between a New York seller and a Mexican importer was considered to be controlled by Mexican law which does not require writing. The federal court reached this conclusion by applying, under the Erie-Klaxon rule, the New York center-of-gravity doctrine.[342] In so doing, the court considered the following factors: (1) where is the center-of-gravity under the facts of the case; (2) which jurisdiction has the "most significant contacts with the matter in dispute"; (3) which jurisdiction is the "most intimately concerned with the outcome of the litigation"; and (4) whether one law or the other, i.e., that of Mexico or of New York, "produce the best result," and found in favor of Mexican law and upheld the contract.

The question of unilateral mistake on the part of two Mexican corporations from Yucatán was raised in their action against the denial by the trustee for a Kansas bankrupt firm to rescind the contract. Since twine import was under control of the Mexican Secretary of Industry and Commerce, both the Mexican exporters as well as the American importers had to be registered with the *Cordeleros de Mexico,* a limited liability firm of public interest.[343] A Nebraska corporation, properly registered as an importer, sold the trademark under which it operated as well as "all the rights of the corporation as importer of twine . . . from Mexico" to the now bankrupt Kansas firm to which the Mexican corporations supplied twine without knowing that they are dealing with a different customer. Without suspecting a choice-of-law problem,

[339] 1 Texas 326, 46 Am. Dec. 108 (1846).
[340] Contra, Hoen v. Simmons, 1 Cal. 119, 52 Am. Dec. 291 (1850).
[341] Global Commerce Corporation v. Clark-Babbitt Industries, 239 F. 2d 716 (2d Cir. 1956).
[342] Auten v. Auten, 308 N.Y. 155, 124 N.E. 2d 99 (1954).
[343] According to the respective law, D.O. Aug. 11, 1934.

the court simply applied common law, found a unilateral mistake going to the heart of the transaction "because it directly affected their right and power to sell," and allowed rescision.[344]

In a case of breach the court applied the *lex loci solutionis* in Rauton v. Pullman Co.[345] Plaintiff alleged that the defendant company assumed the obligation to provide him with a berth sold to him by the round-trip ticket to Mexico City, and breached it when a less comfortable berth was substituted for the return trip. Relying on Article 2108 of the federal Civil Code, the court was unable to find any actual damages and denied the claim. In Parrot v. Mexican Central Railway Co.[346] the action was brought on an oral contract entered into in Mexico, to prepare a travel guide. The court declined to presume the *lex loci actus* to be identical with the *lex fori*. Instead, it relied on the presumption that all countries "will give effect to universally recognized fundamental principles of right and wrong," and decided the question of consideration under the *lex fori*, without reference to Mexican law. Expenses in reliance on a contract giving plaintiff the right to cut timber in Mexico were litigated in E. M. Fleischman Lumber Corp. v. Resources Corp. International.[347] In an action by a Mexican firm against the manufacturer as well as the dealer for damages because of misrepresentations as to the performance of a diesel engine,[348] the court applied as decisive the privity rule of the forum. Damages for breach of a contract of sale entered into in Mexico and to be performed there, with the purchase price stated only in Mexican pesos, were determined in pesos but converted in the judgment to American dollars at the rate of exchange at the time of the judgment[349] on the authority of Deutsche Bank Filiale Nürnberg v. Humphrey.[350] In any case, there is a well established rule that American courts may not render judgments but in this country's own currency.[351]

[344] Potucek v. Cordeleria Lourdes, 310 F. 2d 527 (10th Cir. 1962), cert. denied, 372 U.S. 930 (1963).

[345] 191 S.E. 416 (1937).   [346] 207 Mass. 184, 93 N.E. 590 (1911).

[347] 211 F. 2d 204 (3d Cir. 1954), affirming 114 F. Supp. 843 (1954); cf. 105 F. Supp. 681 (1953).

[348] Industrias Velasco, S.A. v. Applied Power Equipment & Manufacturing Co., 227 F. Supp. 937 (1964).

[349] Paris v. Central Chiclera, S.R.L., 193 F. 2d 960 (5th Cir. 1952).

[350] 272 U.S. 517 (1926); but cf. Zimmermann v. Sutherland, 274 U.S. 253 (1927).

[351] Frontera Transportation Co. v. Abaunza, 271 F. 199 (1921). Damages for breach of contract to be performed in Mexico and therefore governed by Mexican law, expressed in Mexican pesos, will be converted into dollars at the exchange rate on the day of the judgment, Paris v. Central Chiclera, 193 F. 2d 960 (5th Cir. 1952).

Subsequent impossibility of performance due to embargo imposed by the Mexican government on export of meat was decided in Wagner v. Derecktor[352] without recourse to Mexican law. This point was brought out only when the judgment was reversed.[353] The court held that defendant's fault in connection with the Mexican embargo may be decisive and overruled the trial judge's ruling that these matters are not a defense. Instead, the appellate court found that the embargo did prevent defendant's performance, and reversed so that it could be properly established whether or not there was actually an embargo under Mexican law.

Among particular contractual transactions sales, distribution agreements, insurance contracts, and powers of attorney have been litigated. In Motores de Mexicali, S.A., v. Bank of American National Trust & Savings Association[354] the plaintiff Mexican corporation sold to a California corporation a number of cars delivered in Mexico to an agent of the latter who drew nonnegotiable drafts payable through the defendant Bank against the documents of title. However, no documents of title accompanied the drafts which, subsequently, were dishonored. The issue arose whether or not the Bank acquired a lien on the cars for subsequent loans granted by the Bank to the corporation. The court found the lien to exist stating that the transaction took place in Mexico, but declined to pass on the question whether the conclusion was correct under the applicable law. A distribution agreement involving powdered milk was at issue in Maple Island Farm, Inc. v. Bitterling;[355] plaintiff's demand for compensation for his services performed in Mexico was denied on factual grounds, without resort to Mexican law. The same happened in Refrigeradora del Noroeste, S.A. v. Appelbaum.[356] In Pearson International v. Congeladora de Mazatlán, S.A.,[357] the plaintiff Delaware corporation entered into a written agreement with defendant, appointing plaintiff exclusive distributors of frozen shrimp packed by defendant. Plaintiff's demand for damages for breach of contract and for the cost of containers again was decided without resort to Mexican law.

The validity and scope of powers of attorney, executed in Mexico for acts to be performed there, were determined by the Mexican *lex*

---

[352] 116 N.Y.S. 2d 480 (1952), aff'd, 120 N.Y. 2d 926 (1953).
[353] 306 N.Y. 386, 118 N.E. 2d 570 (1954).
[354] 227 F. 2d 643 (9th Cir. 1955).
[355] 209 F. 2d 867 (8th Cir. 1954).   [356] 138 F. Supp. 354 (1956).
[357] 141 N.Y. S. 2d 221 (1955).

loci actus in Merinos Viesca y Compania v. Pan American P. & T. Co.[358]

Among cases involving insurance contracts the following three may be mentioned. In Zuckerman v. Underwriters at Lloyd's, London,[359] the accident arose from exposure during fishing in Mexican waters; the court applied simply California law. In Líneas Aéreas Colombianas Expresas v. Travelers Fire Insurance Company[360] an "All Risk Hull Policy" insured an airplane of Colombian registry only when flown by insured's regular pilots with licenses issued from Colombian or United States authorities but not for illegal flights. Nevertheless, the insured made the airplane available to a coadventurer to be used for thirty days on intra-Mexican flights, knowing that such flights are illegal under Mexican law. The court held that for the time of such use the coverage was suspended.

As restated recently in Bostrom v. Seguros Tepeyac, S.A.,[361] a contract of insurance[362] is "governed, as to its nature, validity and construction, by the law of the place where it was made, unless the parties appear to have intended the law of a different place to govern." Interpreting a liability insurance contract entered into by an American tourist in Mexico for a motor-car trip through Mexico, the court considered the statutory provisions of Mexican law ("all of the federal statutes," quoted in the opinion, i.e., articles 25, 59, 78, 79, 145 to 150 of the Law on Insurance Contracts), but not article 1796 of the federal Civil Code because "it has long been recognized that in some instances the general law of contracts does not apply to insurance policies."[363] Then the court, reading article 147 of the Mexican Law on Insurance Contracts "into the . . . insurance policy," found plaintiff to be "in privity to the insurance company so as to entitle him to sue the defendant insurance company," article 147 providing that

> Liability insurance grants the right to the indemnity directly to the damaged third person, who shall be considered as beneficiary of the insurance from the moment of the loss.

[358] 49 F. 2d 352 (N.Y. 1931).
[359] 250 P. 2d 653, aff'd, 267 P. 2d 777 (Cal. 1954).
[360] 257 F. 2d 150 (5th Cir. 1958). [361] 225 F. Supp. 222 (1963).
[362] McLauglin, Mexican Insurance Law Applicable to Automotive Tourists, 1 Comp. L. Ser. 391 (1938); Aguilar, Civil Liability Arising out of Traffic Accidents in Mexico, in U. Miami School of Law, Mexico; a Symposium on Law and Government 53 (1958); Mossa, Estudio sobre el Seguro de Responsibilidad en el Derecho Mexicano, (22-23) El Foro (4a ép.) 139 (1958).
[363] Not correct in view of art. 1 of the federal Civil Code.

The court held this provision of Mexican law to be "consistent with the generally accepted practice in Texas" and concluded that the provisions of the policy "in connection with the applicable statutes of Mexico, are adequate to create the status recognized by courts in G. A. Stowers Furniture Co. v. American Indemnity Co.[364] and Fidelity & Casualty Co. of New York v. Robb."[365] Here, the court switched from Mexican law to the *lex fori*, i.e., to Texas law, and found that "there is no credible proof on the Mexican law relative to the status created by the policy read with the governing statutes of that country." It presumed that the latter law and that of Texas are the same, and, as a consequence, resorted to the Stowers doctrine that "where an automobile public liability policy surrenders to the insurance company the control of settlement of claims within its coverage, the company assumes the responsibility to act as the exclusive agent of the accused in the matter of settlement." Finding this rule of Texas law to be one of liability for negligence, the court, relying on a special jury verdict, held the defendant insurer liable for the amount of the judgment recovered in a Texas court by a guest passenger against the insured owner and driver of the car.[366] However, on appeal the court[367] affirmed the judgment as to the face amount of the policy of $10,000—and reversed as to the excess. In view of the fact that the insurance contract was "executed in Mexico; the insurer was a Mexican company; [and] the parties anticipated public liability coverage for accidents taking place in Mexico," the appellate court agreed with the trial judge "that Mexican law controls the meaning of the contract. Article 147 of the Mexican law governing insurance therefore must be read into the policy. This article, consistent with the civil law generally, specifically recognizes that the injured party is a third party beneficiary of the insurance contracts." Since the policy was a liability policy, the court concluded that "under Texas law as well as Mexican law the plaintiff had standing, as third party beneficiary to the contract, to sue for the amount of the policy." In regard of the excess amount of $265,000—the court took a different approach. Faced with the lower court's holding that Mexican law was not proven and, consequently, assuming to be the same as the law of Texas which then was applied, the appellate court relegated the problem to a footnote and held that,

[364] 15 S.W. 2d 544 (Tex. 1929).   [365] 267 F. 2d 473 (5th Cir. 1959).
[366] Noted 11 U.C.L.A. L. Rev. 382 (1964).
[367] 347 F. 2d 168 (5th Cir. 1965). Cf. Marmon v. Mustang Aviation, Inc., 416 S.W. 2d 58 (Tex. 1967).

even though insured's tort liability was governed by the *lex loci delicti,* i.e., Mexico, the "insurer's liability to the insured for negligence in a Stowers situation, the place of the accident is irrelevant and certainly is not determinative as to whether foreign law or the law of the forum should control." In this respect the court found that insurer's liability to a Texas assured is at stake and, therefore, "Texas has a more significant relationship to the determination of liability than Mexico." Furthermore, "Bostrom's offer to settle was made to [the insured] in Texas; suit was filed in the federal court in Texas against a Texas defendant; the insurer's misconduct—failure to initiate and bring about a settlement and failure to defend the suit—took place in Texas; the insurer qualified to do business in Texas; Texas has an interest in protecting its citizens when there is a breach of the insurer's duty to an insured Texan." Accepting the center-of-gravity doctrine in favor of the "local law of the state which has the most significant relationship with the occurrence and with the parties," as expressed in § 379 of the Restatement, Second, Tentative Draft No. 9, the court reached the same conclusion as did the trial court, namely that this phase of the events is governed by Texas law, "without passing on the effect of [the lower court's] ruling that the defendant's expert failed to prove the pertinent Mexican law and without our having to make the violent assumption that in a Stowers situation[368] the law of Mexico is the same as the law of Texas." Applying Texas substantive law, the appellate court held that the injured claimant had no standing to sue the insurer for the excess over the policy limits for latter's alleged breach of duty to defend or settle, where insured had not paid all or part of the judgment for such excess.

[368] Kronzer, The Present Status of the Stower Doctrine, 1 So. Texas L.J. 167 (1954); Keeton, Liability Insurance and the Responsibility for Settlement, 67 Harv. L. Rev. 1136 (1954); Wymore, Safeguarding against Claims in Excess of Policy Limits, 28 Insurance Counsel 44 (1961).

15. TORTS

The *lex loci delicti* stood for a long time like a rock in the ever moving sea of conflict law. Only recently the time-honored rule began desintegrating under the weight of complex situations arising from novel transportation risks. This is the case in the United States while in Mexico no similar changes may be noticed.

TREATY LAW

As already indicated, there is a summary method to recover stolen vehicles and other means of transportation available under a bilateral convention signed in 1936.[369]

The Convention on the High Seas, signed at Geneva in 1958, has established substantive claims in favor to the country of the flag for any loss or damage caused by an unwarranted seizure of a vessel on the high seas on suspicion of piracy (art. 20) ; in favor of a vessel boarded on the high seas on unfounded suspicion of piracy, slave trade, or because of a suspicious flag (art. 22, para. 3) ; also for any loss or damage sustained by stoppage or arrest on the high seas in "circumstances which do not justify the exercise of the right of hot pursuit" (art. 23, para. 7) . In regard to damages to cables and pipe lines under the high seas, the Convention only imposes upon member-countries the duty to provide for necessary legislative measures (art. 27 to 29) , with a saving clause for treaties already in force (art. 30) .[370]

MEXICAN LAW

For practical reasons a summary of Mexican substantive law of torts,[371]

[369] Art. 11 (d) of the Convention for the Solution of the Problem of the Chamizal (1963) provides that the transfer of territory resulting therefrom "shall not affect in any way . . . (d) [T]he law or laws applicable to the acts or omissions referred to in paragraph (c) ", i.e., "acts or omissions occurring within or with respect to the said portions of territory prior to their transfer."

[370] Mexico is not a party to the Convention for the Protection of Submarine Cables, signed at Paris, 1884 (24 Stat. 989) .

[371] 5 (2) Rojina Villegas, Derecho Civil Mexicano: Obligaciones 393 (Mexico, 1953) ; Gutiérrez y Gonzáles, Derecho de las Obligaciones 549 (Puebla, 1961) ; Ellis, Civil Liability in Mexico, 13 (3) Federation of Insurance Counsel 9 (1963) .

according to civil law classification, one of the three kinds of obligations will precede the discussion of pertinent conflict rules.

Mexican law imposes liability for damages arising out of "illicit acts or acts contrary to good customs" (art. 1910 of the federal Civil Code), unless the damage is caused by the fault (*culpa*) or inexcusable[372] negligence of the victim. Absolute liability (*responsibilidad objetiva*) is imposed upon those who operate dangerous instrumentalities, as defined in article 1913 of the same Code, with the same proviso. The amount of damages for bodily injuries is determined in the federal Civil Code by schedules used for workmen's compensation claims (art. 1915), a provision repeated in the state civil codes which follow the federal code, namely, Baja California, Colima, Durango, Jalisco, Mexico, Neuvo León, Querétaro, and Sinaloa, and with some modifications in Morelos, Sonora, and Tamaulipas. Other states have adopted no such limitations on liability (Aguascalientes, Campeche, Coahuila, Chiapas, Chihuahua, Hidalgo, Michoacán, Nayarit, Oaxaca, San Luis Potosí, Tabasco, Veracruz, and Yucatán). The old-fashioned states, adhering to the 1884 federal Civil Code (Guanajuato, Puebla, Tlaxcala, and Zacatecas) have not adopted absolute liability for damages arising from the operation of dangerous instrumentalities and maintain the traditional principle of liability for fault to be proven by the plaintiff.[373]

Mexican courts find the rule of *lex loci delicti* expressed in article 12 of the federal Civil Code and the respective articles in the civil codes of the several states. This rule, applied to tort situations, would submit to Mexican laws any acts done or omissions committed by any person within the territorial limits of the Republic, nationals and aliens alike. This complete domination of Mexican law over all happenings within Mexico brings torts safely within the rule of the *locus delicti*. Of course, the question may arise whether this law is that of the place where the tortfeasor was acting or of the place where he failed to act, or the law of the place where the injury occurred. However, this question cannot be answered from available Mexican authorities.

On the interstate level, article 121, I, of the federal Constitution may be interpreted in support of the territorial rule of the *lex loci delicti*.

[372] Translation in Schoenrich, op. cit. at 374, of *inexcusable* with inexplicable is wrong.

[373] On adjudication of civil damages in criminal proceedings, Briseño Sierra, Acción Privada y Acción Publica en Proceso Penal de los Países Americanos, 10 Revista de la Facultad de Derecho de México 775 (1960).

It may be assumed that in international conflict situations Mexican courts also would apply the *lex loci delicti*. To what extent would limitations on liability established in the *lex fori* affect foreign tort claims arising in jurisdictions with no comparable limitations, cannot be predicted because of lack of reported cases as well as lack of Mexican writings in this matter. It may be that Mexican courts would deny a claim arising under a foreign *lex loci delicti* in cases where the act was not recognized as the basis for tort liability under the Mexican substantive *lex fori,* invoking the argument of public policy.

The law applicable to tortious acts on board vessel and aircraft is discussed elsewhere in this study.

AMERICAN LAW

Interpreting the *lex loci delicti,* the prevailing rule was recently re-stated in Bostrom v. Seguros Tepeyac, S.A.,[374] close to that appearing in the Restatement:

> The rules which fix the *locus delicti,* the place of the wrong, as the jurisdiction whose law determines the actionable character of the tort, makes necessary the determination of the place where the wrong was committed. No particular difficulty is encountered until the act or omission complained of and the injury done occur in different places. In such case it is usually announced as the general rule that the place of wrong, the *locus delicti,* is the place where the injury sustained was suffered rather than the place where the last event necessary to make an actor liable for an alleged tort takes place.

The *lex loci delicti* still prevails, except in some jurisdictions where in view of the accidental nature of the place of injury, combined with other significant contacts pointing toward the *lex fori,* the latter is applied to some aspects of foreign tort claims.[375]

An instructive case was litigated before a California court[376] and decided under the traditional conflict rule. Two American owned and registered cars collided in Baja California, due to the negligence on the part of the drivers of both cars. Plaintiff, who was riding in one of the cars as guest, claimed damages from both drivers as well as from the owner of the other car, who at the time of the accident was

[374] 225 F. Supp. 222 (1963).

[375] Kilberg v. Northeast Airlines, Inc., 9 N.Y. 2d 34, 172 N.E. 2d 526 (1961); Pearson v. Northeast Airlines, Inc., 307 F.2d 131 (2d Cir. 1962) and 309 F.2d 553 (1962), cert. denied, 372 U.S. 912 (1963); Babcock v. Jackson, 12 N.Y. 2d 473, 191 N.E. 2d 279, 240 N.Y.S. 2d 743 (1963).

[376] Victor v. Sperry, 329 P. 2d 728 (Cal. 1958).

in the car but was not driving. In regard to the first claim, the court applied the *lex loci delicti*,[377] and finding negligence on the part of both drivers, applied article 1910 of the Civil Code of Baja California, enacted in 1949 and identical with that of the federal Civil Code. Applying the *lex loci delicti* fully, the court reduced in accordance with article 1915 of the Code[378] the demand from $40,462.05 to $6,135.59, which amount included also punitive damages (*reparación moral*) in the sense of article 1916, i.e., one-third of factual damages.[379] On appeal, the court held that under California precedents the *lex loci delicti* determines the basis as well as the amount of damages and affirmed, adding that "the limitation upon the amount of damages imposed by the laws of Mexico is not contrary to the public policy of California or injurious to the people thereof." Plaintiff's attack against the ruling of the court below that the provision establishing absolute liability (art. 1913)[380] is "in substantial conflict with the public policy of California" was equally unsuccessful. The court held that "since no right of action exist in California for damages for liability without fault under the circumstances set forth therein and in article 1913 of the [Mexican] Civil Code . . . , the trial court . . . properly concluded that this article should not be enforced against [defendant] as the owner of one of the automobiles involved."[381] The court apparently overlooked that the action under article 1913 lies only against the

---

[377] Aguilar Gutiérrez, Civil Liability Arising out of Traffic Accidents in Mexico, in U. Miami School of Law, Mexico: a Symposium on Law and Government 53 (1957), also 6 (22-24) Revista de la Escuela Nacional de Jurisprudencia 363 (1944); Gual Vidal, Responsibilidad Civil Derivada del Uso de las Cosas Peligrosas, 2 Revista de la Escuela Nacional de Jurisprudencia 275 (1940); Cuevas Mantecón, Ensayo Crítico sobre el Problema de la Limitación de la Indemnización Debida a los Daños y Perjuicios según el art. 1915 del Código Civil, 2 Revista de la Escuela Nacional de Jurisprudencia 197 (1940).

[378] Interpretation of art. 1915, Jurisprudencia (civ.) 357 (1965); of art. 1913, 117 Semanario (5a ép.) 463 (1953); 119 Semanario (5a ép.) 855 (1954); 84 Semanario (6a ép.) 84 (1965). In Richter v. Impulsora de Revolcadero, S.A., 278 F. Supp. 169 (N.Y. 1967), the court held that lower standards of recovery under Mexican law do not affect the jurisdictional issue.

[379] 30 Semanario (6a ép.) 152 (1959). *Reparación moral* may only be awarded where there is some degree of fault on defendant's part, not absolute liability, Jurisprudencia (civ.) 796 (1964).

[380] Borja Soriano, Teoría General de las Obligaciones 437 (1953); Valenzuela, La Responsibilidad Civil Objectiva en el Derecho Mexicano, (38) El Foro (4a ép.) 115 (1962).

[381] Carpenter, Conflicts: Concurrent Legislative Jurisdiction in Determining Tort Liability, 45 Marq. L. Rev. 1, 19 (1961).

person who "uses the mechanisms . . ." which excludes mere owners of such instrumentalities, and that particular cases of vicarious liability are listed in the following articles 1919 to 1933. These articles, however, include only owners of expressly listed things through which damages have been caused, namely animals (art. 1929), buildings (art. 1932) and special chattels listed in article 1932. The last article might have supplied a legal basis for absolute liability of the mere owner of machines for damages caused by their weight or movement (art. 1932, VI).

In simple tort cases, the *lex loci delicti* rule prevails. In Greyhound Corporation v. Gonzáles de Avilés[382] the court applied the tort law of Oklahoma in an action by the deceased's widow alleging negligence on the part of the defendant for the death of her husband, a Mexican from Jalisco, shot when traveling as a paying passenger on one of defendant's buses.

While American jurisdictions follow the generally accepted rules of conflict law, Texas has developed a doctrine all of its own.

TEXAS DOCTRINE

Compared with other jurisdictions in the United States which generally adhere to the *lex loci delicti* and decline its application only if it should be incompatible with the public policy of the forum or fortuituous as compared with contacts pointing to the forum, Texas has developed a different conflict rule for cases where the *lex loci delicti* happens to be the law of Mexico.[383]

Starting with cases involving interstate situations, Texas courts declined to adjudicate foreign created tort claims where the rule of the *lex loci delicti* was unknown to common law or dissimilar when compared with the *lex fori*. In Mexican National Railway v. Jackson[384] the court denied recovery for damages arising out of an accident in Mexico, not only because of substantial differences between the *lex fori* and *lex loci delicti*, but also because of difficulties in ascertaining Mexican law and, furthermore, because of Mexico's interest in its railroads, because of availability to plaintiff of courts in Mexico, and because of the danger that such actions would crowd Texan courts.

[382] 391 P. 2d 273 (Okla. 1964).
[383] Stumberg, Conflict of Laws: Torts, Texas Decisions, 9 Texas L. Rev. 21 (1930); and The Place of Wrong: Torts and the Conflict of Laws, 34 Wash. L. Rev. 388 (1959); Paulsen, Foreign Law in Texas Courts, 33 Texas L. Rev. 437 (1955).
[384] 89 Tex. 107, 33 S.W. 857 (1896).

This position was maintained in spite of the fact that both parties were Americans, the defendant an American corporation operating railways in Mexico. The argument of "radical dissimilarity" was used in Mexican Central Railway v. Mitten[385] to justify the court's position that it simply cannot enforce the *lex loci delicti,* i.e., the law of Mexico. Before the dissimilarity finally became a plain presumption without the court even comparing the applicable rules of Mexican law with those of Texas, courts still felt that such comparison was necessary. In Mexican Central Railway Co. v. Olmstead[386] the appellate court reversed a judgment of dismissal which relied simply on the dissimilarity rule, reminding the court below that a dissimilarity cannot be established without determining first what Mexican law is.

It is well to notice that federal courts sitting in Texas have consistently granted damages arising from accidents in Mexico.[387] However, when such a case came before the United States Supreme Court in Slater v. Mexican National Railways,[388] the traditional rule followed by federal courts sitting in Texas was abandoned on the ground that a federal court has no "power to grant remedy" as provided by the *lex loci delicti,* i.e., in articles 318 and 319 of the Mexican Criminal Code,[389] on the ground that "Texas courts would deem the dissimilarity between local law and that of Mexico too great to permit an action in the Texas state courts." Admitting that the "method of arriving at and distributing the damages [pertains] to procedure or remedy . . . regulated by the laws of the forum. . . . ," the dissenting justices were satisfied that the "act complained of here was wrongful by both the law of Texas and the law of Mexico, and in such a case the action lies in Texas, except where the cause of action is not transitory." In regard to alleged dissimilarity the dissent dismissed Texas cases emphasizing, in accordance with the Swift v. Tyson doctrine, that the "question is one of general law, and we are not bound by that [i.e., Texas] ruling." The dissent concludes that the

[385] 36 S.W. 282 (1896).   [386] 60 S.W. 267 (1900).

[387] Every v. Mexican Central Railway, 81 F. 294, cert. denied, 167 U.S. 746 (1896); Mexican Central Railways v. Marshall, 91 F. 933 (1899); Mexican Central Railways v. Jones, 107 F. 64 (1901).

[388] 194 U.S. 120 (1904), affirming 115 F. 593 (1904). In Tramontana v. S. A. Empresa de Viacao Aerea Rio Grandense, 350 F. 2d 460, 468 (D.C. 1965) the court remarked that the Supreme Court in Richards v. United States (369 U.S. 1, 1962) and "in many earlier cases has recognized the inadequacies of the theoretical underpinnings of Slater and its progeny."

[389] Translation of the 1871 Code in 2 Wheless, Compendium of the Laws of Mexico . . . 671 (1910).

legal relations of Slater with the United States and Texas were not destroyed by crossing the Rio Grande to work in the railroad yard. This Colorado corporation [i.e., defendant] was domiciled in Texas, as Slater was. The laws of Texas protected them alike. The injury was inflicted in Mexico and resulted fatally in Texas. The wrongful act was actionable in Texas and in Mexico. The jurisdiction of the Circuit Court over the person and subject matter was unquestionable, and I cannot accept the conclusion that the form in which the law of Mexico provides for reparation to its own citizens constitutes a bar to recovery in Texas in litigation between citizens of this country.

It must be recognized that the Slater case never was considered good law, nor did it improve with the passing of time, particularly after the abolition of forms of action and the dualism of law and equity. In 1917 a statute was enacted in Texas[390] providing:

> Whenever the death or personal injury of a citizen of this State or of the United States, or of any foreign country having equal treaty rights with the United States on behalf of its citizens, has been or may be caused by the wrongful act, neglect or default of another in any foreign state or country for which a right to maintain an action and recover damages thereof is given by the statute or law of such foreign State or country, such right of action may be enforced in the courts of the State within the time prescribed for the commencement of such actions by the statutes of this State. The law of the forum shall control in the prosecution and maintenance of such action in the courts of this State in all matters pertaining to the procedure.

Reading this clear statute it would seem that the unusual attitude taken by Texas courts in regard to foreign created tort claims will change. Alas, the established case law survived under the pretext of two arguments: one, that the statute does not impose on Texas courts jurisdiction in cases involving Mexican tort situations;[391] and the other, that the 1917 statute is only declaratory of the existing law and, consequently, changes nothing.[392] So, El Paso & Juarez Traction Co. v. Carruth still remains the leading case. There, a Texan brought an action against a Texas corporation for damages suffered in Chihuahua. The court dismissed the action finding lack of jurisdiction, stating that

---

[390] Originally art. 7730½, Vernon's Complete Statutes (1920) ; presently art. 4678 Vernon's Ann. Tex. Civ. Stat. For a recent discussion, see Marmon v. Mustang Aviation, Inc., 416 S.W. 2d 58 (Tex. 1967). For a similar statute in Maryland, see Debbis v. Hertz Corporation, 269 F. Supp. 671 (Md. 1967).

[391] El Paso & Juarez Tranction Co. v. Carruth, 255 S.W. 159 (1923), reversing 208 S.W. 984 (1919).

[392] Wells v. Irwin, 43 F. Supp. 212, aff'd, 132 F. 2d 316 (5th Cir. 1942).

(I) n all cases for wrongful death or personal injuries in . . . Mexico, in which the laws of that Republic have been alleged and proven, the courts of this state have consistently refused to entertain a suit for the recovery of damages for such death or injury, because the laws of Mexico giving the cause of action and providing for its enforcement are so materially different from the laws of our state relating to torts that the courts of Texas cannot undertake to adjudicate the rights of the parties. . . . This has become the settled policy of the courts of this state, and we are of the opinion that, when the pleadings and evidence disclose that the laws of Mexico pertaining to such actions are now substantially what they have been heretofore, the court should dismiss the case for lack of jurisdiction.

Recently, this holding was followed with approval in Carter v. Tillery.[393] The action arose between two Americans for damages arising out of an airplane accident in Chihuahua. Relying on the assurance by a Mexican expert that the Mexican system in regard to tort actions "has been the same from the year 1870 down to the present time and that such was true as to the rights of parties to maintain an action for tort," the court, quoting article 4678, but not discussing its applicability in the case, nor any rule of the new Civil Code of Chihuahua, enacted in 1942, decided that it has no jurisdiction over the subject matter and dismissed the action.

Contrary to these cases, Texas courts took jurisdiction and granted remedies in cases involving conversion of American-owned property by Mexicans in Mexico. In Banco Minero v. Ross & Masterson[394] relief was granted for conversion of money deposited by plaintiff in the Mexican bank by the latter paying it over wrongfully.[395] Equally successful was an action for conversion by a Mexican of plaintiff's cattle by selling it in Mexico[396]; the court applied Texas law under the presumption that the controlling *lex loci delicti*, i.e., Mexican law, is identical with that of Texas, and this in spite of defendant's reliance on the dissimilarity doctrine, resulting in lack of jurisdiction. The court took into consideration the revolutionary conditions in Mexico, adding that "under such circumstances when a party [i.e., defendant] who has been in this country, disregarded the rights of our citizens and appropriated their property, he should be held responsible in our courts for such wrongs." However, the dissimilarity rule appeared in Banco de Mexico, etc. v. Da Camara.[397] The action was brought against

[393] 257 S.W. 2d 465 (1953) .   [394] 138 S.W. 224 (Tex. 1911) .
[395] Cf. Banco Minero v. Ross, 172 S.W. 711 (Tex. 1915) .
[396] Mendiola v. Gonzáles, 185 S.W. 389 (1916) .
[397] 55 S.W. 2d 631 (Tex. 1932) .

a Mexican corporation in Tamaulipas for the conversion of an automobile sold by plaintiff to a third person who subsequently removed it to Mexico and sold it to the defendant bank, in violation of the mortgage in favor of plaintiff for the unpaid purchase price. The court reached back to the Jackson case, found that Mexican law which would apply since all acts complained of, including conversion, took place in Mexico, was "materially different," and dismissed because of lack of jurisdiction.

16. DECEDENTS' ESTATES

Succession upon death, by will or by law, presents difficult conflict problems, jurisdictional, procedural as well as substantive. These difficulties increase where relations arise between two different legal systems, one of the civil and the other of the common law type.

TREATY LAW

The Consular Convention between Mexico and the United States signed in 1942,[398] imposes, first of all, a duty upon the competent local authorities at once to inform the "nearest consular officer of the State of which the deceased is a national, of the fact of his death" (art. VIII, para. 1). In case such national died in the territory of the other country "without will or testament whereby he has appointed testamentary executors," the consular officer within whose district the deceased "made his home at the time of death, shall, so far as the laws of the country permit and pending the appointment of an administrator and until letters of administration have been granted," take charge of the assets of the estate, "for the preservation and protection" thereof (art. VIII, para. 2). The consular officer also may request to be "appointed as administrator within the discretion of the court or other agency controlling the administration of the estates, provided the laws of the place where the estate is administered so permit" (art. VIII, para. 3). A consular officer who undertakes such duties "subjects himself in that capacity to the jurisdiction of the court or other agency making the appointment for all necessary purposes to the same extent as if he were a national of the State by which he has been received" (art. VIII, para. 3).

The question of eligibility of a Mexican consul for appointment as a provisional administrator was litigated in Evans v. Cano del Castillo.[399] An Arkansas probate court appointed the Mexican consul administrator of the estate of a Mexican national who died there leaving only a cause of action for wrongful death. This order was attacked by creditors of the estate on the ground that the consul was ineligible since he was not a local resident as required by Arkansas law. The state supreme court held in a split decision that the appointment amounted in fact to that of a "special administrator" for which

[398] See Appendix II.
[399] Evans v. Cano del Castillo, 220 Ark. 350, 247 S.W. 2d 947 (1952).

the statutory requirement of local residence does not apply. Holding
the order not to be appealable under the applicable Arkansas statute,
the court did not reach the question of reservation in favor of local
law[400] established in the Consular Convention.[401]

In addition to acting as administrators of their nationals' estates,
consular officers of either country may intervene in probate proceedings[402] in two capacities: first, they may represent their nonresident
nationals in "all matters concerning the administration and distribution of the estate" unless "such heirs or legatees have appeared, either
in person or by authorized representatives" (art. IX, para. 1) ; and
second, they may on behalf of their nonresident nationals "collect
and receipt for their distributive shares derived from estates in process
of probate or accruing under the provisions of the so-called Workmen's
Compensation Laws or other like statutes, for transmission through
channels prescribed" by their own governments (art. IX, para. 2).
The court or other agency in charge of probate may "require [the
consular officer] to furnish reasonable evidence of the remission of
the funds to the distributees."[403]

Consular officers of both countries also may act as notaries in con-
nections with matters involving succession. Article VII of the Convention authorizes consular officers to perform, within the receiving
country, notarial functions in accordance with the laws of their own,
i.e., sending country. This means that a Mexican consular officer may
perform notarial functions in this country in accordance with the
Notarial Law enacted for the Federal District and Territories and the
federal Civil Code.[404] These rules apply also to wills which will have
in both countries the authority of a notarial act "as if drawn up before

[400] Bayitch, Conflict Law in United States Treaties: a Survey 19 (1955).

[401] For complete text, see Appendix II.

[402] Lee, Consular Law and Practice 135 (1961) ; Puente, Consular Pro-
tection of the Estates of Deceased Nationals, 23 Ill. L. Rev. 635 (1929) ; Boyd,
Constitutional, Treaty, and Statutory Requirements of Probate Notice to
Consuls and Aliens, 47 Iowa L. Rev. 29 (1961) ; and Treaties Governing the
Succession to Real Property by Aliens, 51 Mich. L. Rev. 1001 (1953).

[403] Mexican consul's action on behalf of dependents was decided under
sec. 102.19 Wisconsin Stat. (1945), disregarding the Consular Convention,
Waunakee Canning Corp. v. Industrial Commission, 208 Wis. 518, 68 N.W.
2d 25 (Wis. 1955).

[404] Law regarding notaries, not being a matter delegated to the federal
legislature, remains a matter of state law. However, the Notarial Law for
the Federal District and Territories (D.O. Feb. 23, 1946) is applied in con-
junctions with matters considered to be of federal concern. Law of Foreign
Service, D.O. 31 Jan. 1934; Regulation, D.O. May 12, 1934. But note Ley
Orgánica del Servicio Exterior Mexicano, D.O. March 4, 1967.

a notary public or other public officer duly authorized" (art. VII, para. 2) of the sending country. However, the Convention contains a saving clause in favor of the law of the country where such acts "are designed to take effect." This means that in case a Mexican national should appear before his consular officer in Florida in order to dispose of real property located there, such testament will be valid in Florida only if it is executed in accordance with the *lex rei sitae,* in this case § 731.07 Fla. Stat. (1967).

MEXICAN LAW

Generally speaking, Mexican law adheres in regard to succession[405] to traditional civil law principles. Through succession upon death heirs take all assets of the deceased, including obligations, except those which do not survive, but not beyond the value of the estate. The estate is immediately vested in the heirs designated by will or, if there is no will, in those designated as heirs by law. In both instances the heirs acquire title to the estate as property in common, until partition is made. They may dispose of their interest in the estate but not of the estate itself or of particular assets. Not only the title but also the right to possession of the estate is immediately transmitted to the heirs, or to executors (*ejecutores*), except where there is a surviving spouse who may continue in possession and administration until the time of partition.

Wills may be public and open, or public but sealed, both executed before a notary public with three witnesses present (art. 1511 and 1521 of the federal Civil Code). Special provisions in the Code take care of testators who do not know Spanish (art. 1503 and 1518). Public wills may also be executed before consular officers who are authorized to "draw up, attest, certify and authenticate . . . testamentary dispositions," following in this respect the applicable law of their countries (art. VII of the Consular Convention). There are additional forms of wills available under particular circumstances: private oral (art. 1565 of the federal Civil Code), requiring five witnesses of whom one reduces

[405] 4 Rojina Villegas, Derecho Civil Mexicano: Sucesiones (Mexico, 1958); also Los Conceptos Jurídicos Fundamentales del Derecho Hereditario, (6) El Foro (2a ép.) 93 (1949); Uribe, Sucesiones en el Derecho Mexicano (Mexico, 1962); Wren, Problems in Probating and Using Foreign Representatives, in San Antonio Bar Association, The Legal Aspects of Doing Business in Mexico 69 (1963); Garza, Drafting a Will under Mexican Law, in San Antonio Bar Association, The Legal Aspects of Doing Business in Mexico 18 (1964); Succession in Mexico, 16 Syracuse L. Rev. 622 (1965).

the will to writing (art. 1567); military (art. 1569); maritime (art. 1583), available when the testator is on board a Mexican vessel on the high seas; and, finally, the so-called foreign will (art. 1593).

Formalities required for a will executed in Mexico are governed by Mexican law (art. 12 and 15 of the federal Civil Code and respective articles of state civil codes), regardless of the nationality or domicile or sojourn of the testator. In case the testator does not understand Spanish and wants to execute a public will, two interpreters selected by the testator take part in the act and co-sign the will (art. 1503). In a holographic will, the testator may use his "own language" (art. 1551, para. 2). In regard to the form of wills executed abroad, the federal Civil Code contains, in addition to the general rule of article 15, namely that the formal requirements of juridical acts are governed by the law of the place where they are executed, the specific provision that "wills executed in a foreign country will be given effect in the Federal District and Territories, provided they have been made in the form as required by the law of the country where executed" (art. 1594).[406] The same provision is adopted in the civil codes of the several states, for example, Morelos (art. 1601), and Tamaulipas (art. 1939).

The second sentence of article 15 of the federal Civil Code permits Mexicans as well as aliens residing outside the Federal District and Territories, to "subject themselves to forms prescribed by this Code when the act is to be executed within the said areas." In other words, the *lex loci actus* applies to domestic (art. 12) wills, regardless of the nationality[407] or domicile of the testator, with the additional alternatives, one for both Mexicans and aliens under article 15, and the other for Mexicans to use the facilities of their diplomatic and consular services abroad for notarial functions, provided "testamentary dispositions should take effect in the Federal District and Territories" (art. 1594). This latter limitation seems to have been eliminated, in relation to the United States, by article VII of the Consular Convention. It may be added that the Mexican diplomatic or consular official

---

[406] 131 Semanario (5a ép.) 604 (1965). See also art. 891 and 892 of the Code of Civil Procedure for the Federal District and Territories. Some of the state civil codes have analogous provisions, e.g., § 1468 of the Civil Code of Oaxaca (1944), providing that "A maritime will and a will executed abroad shall be valid in the State, provided that they comply with the federal statutes as well as the statutes of the State."

[407] Will executed by alien is governed by the *lex situs* of movable and immovable property to be disposed of (art. 121, II of the Constitution), 36 Semanario (5a ép.) 436 (1935).

involved will transmit authenticated copies of the will to the Secretariat of Foreign Relations which will announce in the press the death of the testator in order to give interested parties an opportunity to have the will probated (art. 1595). An additional provision is found in the Civil Code of Puebla (art. 3399) that maritime as well as foreign wills take effect in Puebla, provided they meet requirements set both by federal as well as the law of Puebla.

Civil law jurisdictions generally, and Latin American countries in particular, have adopted the institution of forced heirship (*legitima*), whereby a defined portion of the estate must devolve to close relatives, in spite of a will to the contrary. However, it cannot be said that Mexico adopted the other extreme, namely that of complete freedom of testation, familiar to most of the common-law jurisdictions. Under Mexican law a testator is bound to provide for the support of certain close relatives, among others, sons under twenty-one years of age or older but unable to work; daughters unable to work and living an honest life; the surviving spouse and even the concubine (art. 1368 of the federal Civil Code). The support imposed upon the estate consists of providing such persons with their needs in kind, namely with food, clothing, lodging and assistance. Wills not providing for such support are considered ineffective (*inoficiosos*), insofar as they impair needed support (art. 1374).

The general rule that capacity is governed by the *lex loci actus,* whenever the locus is within Mexico (art. 12), applies also to testamentary capacity (art. 12 and 1305 of the federal Civil Code). Consequently, the testamentary capacity (*capacidad para testar*) of aliens executing wills in Mexico will depend upon Mexican law, regardless of reciprocity. In international situations, however, capacity to execute a will might be controlled by the national law if the testator is a Mexican national. This rule was recently stated by the Supreme Court[408] as follows:

> It is a general principle of law that the capacity to will is part of the personal statute [*estatuto personal*], in other words, it is governed by the national laws of the testator, even more so since in the present case the act testament was executed in Spain and not in the place of death; neither can the Mexican nationality of the testatrix be disregarded who, according to articles 1283 and 1305 of the Civil Code, would have freely disposed of her assets.

Wills executed in Mexico as well as wills executed abroad will be

[408] 131 Semanario (5a ép.) 623 (1965).

given effect in Mexico only subject to Mexican laws (art. 13 of the
federal Civil Code), since "juridical effects of acts and contracts made
abroad to be performed in the territory of the Republic, shall be governed by the provisions of this Code."[409]

Intestate succession is regulated in Mexican law by classes of
heirs called to succession in this order: descendents, spouse, ascendents,
collaterals, and concubine.[410] In case none of these classes inherits, the
estate escheats to public charity (art. 1602).

In order to inherit either under a will or *ab intestato*, the heir
must have the capacity to inherit (*capacidad para heredar*). Taking
again the federal Civil Code as example, aliens may inherit provided
they meet general requirements (art. 1313) as well as special conditions imposed upon aliens. These later limitations arise, first, from
constitutional provisions prohibiting them to hold interests in land
or in corporations, and others already discussed (art. 1327). Second,
they may be prevented from inheriting under Mexican law because of
lack of reciprocity (art. 1313, IV, and 1328), namely that they "under
the laws of their country, are unable to will in favor of Mexicans or
Mexicans are unable to inherit *ab intestato*."[411] However, in regard to

---

[409] In regard to a will executed in a foreign country (France), the
Supreme Court, 131 Semanario (5a ép.) 604 (1965), stated the rule in the
following syllabus: If a will executed abroad has not been attacked and as
long as there is no judicial decision declaring it invalid or ineffective, it will
have full legal effect in Mexico, particularly if it has been probated in the
country where executed. Then it is no longer possible to question the power
of a Mexican court to decide an issue arising out of such a will if the probate
proceedings have been already unsuccessfully attacked in the country where
the will was executed. And since these probate proceedings involved also
the question of the domicile of the deceased, this question is closed. Without
passing judgment as to the justice of such foreign adjudication, it must
be pointed out that if in such foreign adjudication nothing was decided
regarding the validity or efficacy of the will, the validity of the will cannot
be affected by the fact that the presumptive heir has submitted his claim,
with or without objection, to the jurisdiction of a foreign court, because
the consequences of such submission can only affect those assets which were
not litigated in the present case.

[410] 36 Semanario (5a ép.) 436 (1932); 131 Semanario (5a ép.) 669 (1965).

[411] 75 Semanario (6a ép.) 34 (1965). García Villalobos, Trabajos Pre-
sentados por la Delegación Mexicana a la Asamblea de la International Bar
Association . . . , Colonia, 1958, (22-23) El Foro (4a ép.) 75 (1958). Application to the Secretariat of Foreign Affairs, Jurisprudencia (civ.) 556 (1964).
The Civil Code of Oaxaca (1944) contains a slightly different provision in
§ 123 that because of lack of reciprocity are "incapacitated to inherit by
will or intestate, from inhabitants (*habitantes*) those aliens who, under the
laws of their country, cannot will or leave by intestate succession their assets
to Mexicans."

constitutional limitations, the Secretariat of Foreign Affairs may, whenever an alien is about to inherit land, unavailable to him, permit
probate proceedings to be concluded and title to be registered in
the name of the alien heir, subject to the condition that such interests
will be conveyed within five years since the death of the *de cujus* to a
person eligible to hold such interests. The period may be extended in
cases of protracted litigation (art. 6 of the Organic Law to Section I
of Article 27 of the Constitution).[412]

A choice of the substantive law controlling succession is given to
aliens and Mexicans in the Civil Code of Puebla (art. 3127), provided
they are not Pueblans, although present in the state. They may choose
between their national law or the laws of Puebla to govern the contents
of their will (*solemnidad interna*); however, they must comply with
the law of Puebla in regard to form.

Jurisdiction for probate, under Mexican procedural law exercised
as *juicios sucesorios,* is vested in the court of the last domicile of the
deceased (art. 156 of the Code of Civil Procedure for the Federal District and Territories).[413] In case there is no such domicile, jurisdiction
is vested in the court within whose district immovable assets belonging to the estate are situated. If immovables are situated in more than
one district, jurisdiction vests in the court that has first opened proceedings. In case there is no domicile nor immovable property, the
court of the place where the deceased died will be competent (art. 156,
IV). The same court has jurisdiction over actions involving the
succession (art. 156, VI).

As in all matters of civil procedure, the procedural rules governing probate are contained not only in the two federal codes of civil
procedure but also in the procedural codes of the several states. Again
limiting the discussion to the federal law, it may be pointed out that

[412] On the local effect of foreign acts on status affecting succession, 98
Semanario (5a ép.) 1623 (1948).

[413] Informe Rendido a la Corte Suprema de la Nación, 1949, at 89. In
126 Semanario (5a ép.) 605 (1955) the Supreme Court decided that "since
both the Civil Code of Tlaxcala and that of Puebla contain identical provisions in regard to the domicile (art. 17 and 25, respectively), and since
codes of civil procedures in force in both states (art. 1548, par. IV, and 145,
par. 5, respectively) provide that the court of the last domicile of the deceased
has jurisdiction, the Tlaxcala court was held to be competent in view of
the evidence presented."

On non-contentious procedure generally, Alcalá-Zamora y Castillo, El
Procedimiento Civil no Contencioso en México, in Comunicaciones Mexicanas al VII Congreso Internacional de Derecho Comparado, Upsala, 1966,
35 (Mexico, 1966).

in regard to estates left by aliens, "consuls and consular agents will intervene in accordance with the law" (art. 777), a provision interpreted as meaning: in accordance with the treaty, if any. In cases where there is a will, the court will summon all interested parties to a hearing (art. 790). Heirs with no known domicile or residing outside of the seat of the court will be notified by publication at the seat of the court, at the last domicile of the deceased and at place of his birth (art. 792). The Attorney General (*Ministerio Público*) will also be notified and will represent the heirs whose whereabouts are unknown as well as those who have been summoned but did not appear (art. 795). In case of intestate succession, the provisions of articles 799 through 815 apply.

Whenever all the heirs instituted in a public testament are of age, proceedings may be conducted by a notary public (art. 872). This may also apply in cases of intestate succession, provided all heirs are of age and their respective rights have been established by courts (art. 876).

AMERICAN LAW

The American choice-of-law rule may be stated in a simple way: succession, including formalities of wills, is governed in regard to movables by the law of the last domicile of the deceased while succession in regard to immovables is determined by the *lex rei sitae*. Consequently, the *lex loci actus* of the will is immaterial. This was clearly shown in Re Brace's Estate,[414] involving the validity of a holographic codicil executed in Mexico by the testator, subsequently to a will. Even though the testator died in Guadalajara, the court held that the finding in the probate proceedings that he was domiciled in California was *res judicata*. Consequently, his codicil not valid under the *lex loci actus* (Mexico), was held valid under the law of testator's last domicile (California) since the estate consisted only of movable property. In another case, a bequest in Mexican pesos worded as "to my daughter the sum of twelve thousand Mexican pesos," was litigated.[415] The trial court held this provision ambiguous, but was overruled on appeal on the ground that the will is to be construed so as to mean "Mexican pesos, gold or silver, at the executor's option either in silver or gold pieces or their equivalent in United States money at the rate of exchange prevailing when payment is due."

---

[414] 4 Cal. Rptr. 683 (1960).
[415] Volpe v. Benavides, 214 S.W. 593 (Tex. 1919).

American courts have frequently resorted to Mexican law because it was in force in their jurisdictions at the time when acts decisive for the present adjudication took place. The validity of a will executed in 1846 by a Mexican citizen in California was determined by the Spanish and Mexican law as the *lex loci actus*.[416] In a suit in trespass to try title[417] the court found that claimants as collateral heirs to the American grantee from the State of Coahuila in 1835 could have acquired no interest in the lands because of the Mexican *lex rei sitae* in force at that time making aliens ineligible to take real property by inheritance and because the subsequent constitution and statute of Texas, removing such discrimination, were but prospective in operation.[418]

Most jurisdictions in the United States do not discriminate against aliens in regard to acquiring land through succession from deceased American nationals nor do they impose discriminatory restrictions on taking or sharing in the estates of aliens, Mexican or others, left in the United States. Nevertheless, in some states the requirement of reciprocity prevails, mostly limited to non-resident aliens who, in order to qualify for succession, must prove that their countries grant reciprocity. Reciprocity in one form or another is adopted, for example, in California,[419] and North Carolina.[420] The discrimination against non-resident aliens was held not to be unconstitutional;[421] but it must yield to a treaty.[422] Arizona, for example, does not discriminate against aliens acquiring title to land by descent; however, only aliens eligible for American nationality will inherit by will and keep the title provided they become nationals within five years; they also may sell such land within this period to avoid forfeiting the land to the state (sec. 14–212). An outright prohibition against aliens inheriting land, still

[416] Panaud v. Jones, 1 Cal. 488 (1851).

[417] Glover v. McFaddin, 205 F. 2d 6 (5th Cir. 1953), affirming 99 F. Supp. 385.

[418] Relying on the Mexican decree of March 12, 1828, art. 6, making aliens ineligible to take by inheritance; as a consequence, property escheated to the Republic of Mexico, Middleton v. McGrew, 64 U.S. 45 (1859); Webb's Heirs v. Kirby Lumber Co., 107 S.W. 581 (1908). The contention that the subsequent Texas constitution of 1836 removed this discrimination was unsuccessful, the constitutional provision held prospective in operation, Holliman v. Peebles, 1 Texas 673 (1848); Yates v. Iams, 10 Tex. 168 (1853); Blythe v. Easterly, 20 Texas 565 (1857); McGaham v. Baylor, 32 Tex. 789 (1870); Douthit v. Southern, 155 S.W. 315 (1913).

[419] Probate Code, sec. 259 (1959). [420] N.C.S. sec. 1208 (1959).

[421] In re Bevilacqua's Estate, 191 P. 2d 752 (Cal. 1948).

[422] Kolovrat v. Oregon, 366 U.S. 187 (1961).

on the books in some states, was held in some of the states to be unconstitutional, for example in Oregon.[423]

[423] Kenji Namba v. McCourt & Neuner, 204 P. 2d 569 (Ore. 1949), explained in Krachler's Estate, 263 P. 2d 769, 773 (1953). Wrenn, Problems in Probating Foreign Wills and Using Foreign Personal Representatives, 17 S.W. L. J. 55 (1963), discussing problems involving Texas and Mexico. García León, Aspects of Mexican Probate Law of Interest to the North American Lawyer, in San Antonio Bar Association, The Legal Aspects of Doing Business in Mexico 82 (1964).

The Laws of Pedro Murillo Velarde regarding the execution and probating of wills (1790) and the Kearney Code (1846) are discussed in Bent v. Thompson, 5 N.M. 408, 23 P. 234 (1890).

17. LABOR LAW

In the area of labor law the conflict rules in force between both countries originate mainly from treaties. They cover two principal types of employment: maritime and agricultural.

TREATY LAW

Seamen

Conventions sponsored by the International Labor Organization establish uniform law in the countries where they have been ratified and apply regardless of whether or not the employers or employees are nationals of the country or aliens.

Mexico has ratified a considerable number of these conventions, while the United States has ratified but a few, namely No. 53, 55, 58, and 74, the last not ratified by Mexico. Convention No. 53 provides that masters and officers must be qualified under a certificate issued or approved by the "public authority of the territory where the vessel is registered" (art. 3), i.e., in accordance with the law of the flag. Of greater practical significance would appear to be convention No. 55, regulating the liability of shipowners for sickness, injury or death, and repatriation; it establishes uniform substantive rules, with some leeway for national legislation.[424] From a conflict law viewpoint, the anti-discriminatory provision of article 11 deserves to be quoted in full:

> The Convention and national laws or regulations relating to benefits under this Convention shall be so interpreted and enforced as to ensure equality of treatment to all seamen irrespective of nationality, domicile or race.

Convention No. 58 regarding the minimum age for employment at sea forbids, in principle, maritime work to children under fifteen years of age (art. 2). Insofar as Mexico is concerned, this provision seems to have eliminated doubts created by the apparent contradiction between articles 136 and 231 of the Federal Labor Law, stating that

---

[424] O'Donnell v. Great Lakes Dredge & Dock Co., 318 U.S. 36, 42 (1943); Aguilar v. Standard Oil Co. of New Jersey, 318 U.S. 724, 737 (1943); Farrell v. United States, 336 U.S. 511, 517 (1949); Warren v. United States, 340 U.S. 523 (1951), reversing 179 F.2d 919 (1950); Smith v. United States, 167 F.2d 550 (4th Cir. 1948); Robinson v. United States, F.2d 582 (5th Cir. 1949); Desmond v. United States, 217 F.2d 948 (2d Cir. 1954); Travis v. Motor Vessel Rapids Cities, 315 F.2d 805 (8th Cir. 1963).

persons below sixteen years of age "residing abroad or transients there, and lacking parents or guardians" may be allowed by the Mexican consul to accept maritime employment, with the proviso that the right of their legal representatives to ratify such employment remains unimpaired (art. 136), while article 231 prohibits maritime apprenticeship to persons under sixteen years of age. Finally, Convention No. 74, in force only in the United States, provides for the qualification for employment as able seamen to perform duties as a member of the deck crew, this qualification to be subject to the "national laws or regulations" (art. 1), apparently to the law of the flag.

The settlement of labor disputes on board ship constitutes a traditional prerogative of consular officers. As between Mexico and the United States, matters are regulated by the Consular Convention of 1942 in regard both to the "internal order on private vessels of [their] country", i.e., on board ship having the nationality of the sending country, as well as to disputes concerning the "adjustment of wages and the execution of labor contracts of the crews" (art. X, para. 1). In regard to the first class of disputes consular officers have "exclusive jurisdiction over controversies arising out of the internal order of private vessels of [their] country, and shall alone exercise jurisdiction in situations wherever arising, between officers and crews, pertaining to the enforcement of discipline on board, provided the vessel and the persons charged with wrongdoing shall have entered territorial waters or a port within his consular district" (art. X, para. 1). Insofar as such controversies amount to disorders, Mexican port authorities may intervene whenever "the peace of the port is disturbed, if a Mexican is involved, or at the request of the captain."[425] Furthermore, consular officers are given under the Convention (art. X, para. 3) the right to demand such intervention and "invoke the assistance of the local police authorities in any matter pertaining to the maintenance of internal order on board a vessel" flying the flag of the sending state. In controversies involving wages and labor contracts of the crew, by contrast, the powers of consular officers are limited. They are conciliatory in character and do not include authority to decide such disputes. Hence, this power will not "exclude the jurisdiction conferred on the respective local authorities under existing or future laws of the place" (art. X, para. 1).[426]

Where seamen who are nationals of the sending state appear in

[425] Law of General Means of Communication, art. 272.
[426] Bayitch, Conflict Law in United States Treaties: a Survey 35 (1955).

courts of the receiving state, their consular officers have, under article X, paragraph 4, of the Convention, the privilege to appear "for the purpose of observing proceedings or rendering assistance as an interpreter or agent."[427]

Migratory Workers

The fact that more than a quarter of a million Mexican agricultural workers used to be employed in the United States annually, mainly in Texas and California, accounts for treaties as well as a considerable amount of domestic law in both countries dealing with Mexican migratory workers.

The basic agreement was signed in 1951 and has since then been repeatedly amended, extended, supplemented and finally terminated.[428] Limiting this discussion to conflict rules, a few provisions may be pointed out. The employment of legally admitted workers was "governed by the terms of this Agreement, including the Work Contract which is . . . made a part of the Agreement," and by the joint interpretations provided for in article 37. "Neither the Mexican worker nor the employer may individually or jointly change the Work Contract without the consent of the two Governments" (art. 11), thus making the conditions of employment of the three sources just mentioned, *ius cogens*. Mexican workers shall not have been assigned work in localities where "Mexicans are discriminated against because of their nationality or ancestry" (art. 8, para. 1). The status of Mexican workers during a strike also was clarified (art. 22). Generally, no

---

[427] For American law, see Gilmore & Black, The Law of Admiralty 386 (1957); Jenkins, Applicability of United States Laws to Foreign Seamen on Foreign Flag Vessels, in Interamerican Bar Association, 12th Conference Proceedings, Bogotà, 1961, at 144 (1963); Kleinman, Admiralty Suits Involving Foreigners, 31 Texas L. Rev. 889 (1953).

[428] 2 U.S.T. 1940; 5 U.S.T. 1793; 6 U.S.T. 1017; 13 U.S.T. 2022; 14 U.S.T. 307. Coalson, Mexican Contractual Labor in American Agriculture, 33 S.W. Soc. Scie. Rev. 228 (1952); Goot, Employment of Foreign Workers in United States Agriculture, 21 Dep't State Bull. 43 (1949); Hawley, The Politics of the Mexican Labor Issue, 1950-1965, 40 Agric. Hist. 157 (1966); Scruggs, Evolution of the Mexican Farm Labor Agreement of 1942, 34 Agric. History 140 (1960); and The United States, Mexico and the Wetbacks, 1942-1947, 30 Pac. Hist. Rev. 149 (1961); Spradlin, The Mexican Farm Labor Importation Program: Review and Reform, 30 Geo. Wash. L. Rev. 84, 311 (1961). Cf. Massa Gill, Bibliografía sobre Migración de Trabajadores Mexicanos a los Estados Unidos (Mexico, 1959). For a definition of *braceros*, 121 Semanario (5a ép.) 2877 (1955). Padilla de Alba, La Protección del Trabajador Mexicano en el Extranjero (Mexico, 1960).

discrimination was permitted against Mexican workers in regard to the prevailing wage (art. 15), or in comparison with the rate specified by the United States Secretary of Labor, which rate was binding on both the American employer as well as on the Mexican worker (ibid.). In regard to social insurance, both the Agreement (art. 19) and the Standard Work Contract (art. 3) provided that in the absence of a state workmen's compensation law covering agricultural workers, the employer had to obtain an insurance policy covering at least risks listed. The Government of the United States undertook to guarantee to Mexican workers the performance on the part of their respective employers (art. 32), and in a general sense to "exercise special vigilance and its moral influence with state and local authorities to the end that Mexican workers may enjoy impartially and expeditiously the rights which the laws of the United States grant to them" (art. 35).

A number of American cases deal with questions affecting Mexican migratory workers arising from these treaties as well as from domestic statutory law.[429] An action for injunctive relief against the enforcement of an order by the Secretary of Labor related to wages of Mexican workers was denied in Johnson v. Kirkland.[430] Equally unsuccessful remained an injunctive suit against the revocation of a permit to employ Mexican labor.[431] Prevailing wages set by the Secretary of Labor cannot be enjoined unless it is shown that they are arbitrary, unlawful, erroneous or unauthorized.[432] The recovery of money paid to Mexican worker by the Government for a defaulting American employer was litigated in United States v. Morris.[433] A certification by the Secretary of Labor that admission of alien (i.e., Mexican) workers to the United States during a strike in Texas will "adversely affect wages and working conditions of workers in the

---

[429] 7 U.S.C.A. § 1461-1468 (1966). Williams, Recent Legislation Affecting the Mexican Labor Program, 29 (1) Employment Security Review 29 (1962). According to an amendment enacted in 1963 (77 Stat. 363) no workers are available under this title for employment after December 31, 1964. Creagan, Public Law 78: a Tangle of Domestic and International Relations, 7 J. Int.-Am. Studies 541 (1965). Cf. Braude v. Wirtz, 350 F.2d 702 (9th Cir. 1965).

[430] 290 F. 2d 440 (5th Cir. 1961), cert. denied, 368 U.S. 889 (1961).

[431] Rio Hondo Harvesting Association v. Johnson, 290 F. 2d 471 (5th Cir. 1961); McBride Farms Marketing Association v. Johnson, 290 F.2d 474 (5th Cir. 1961).

[432] Dona Ana County Farm & Livestock Bureau v. Goldberg, 200 F. Supp. 210 (1961); also Limonera Company v. Wirtz, 225 F. Supp. 961 (1963).

[433] 252 F. 2d 643 (5th Cir. 1958).

United States similarly employed" was considered not to include workers commuting from Mexico.[434]

In this connection, three criminal cases may be briefly mentioned. In one it was decided that the removal of Mexican workers from one area where they have been admitted to another does not constitute a federal offense under the Immigration and Nationality Act.[435] Chasing Mexican workers during a strike toward the gate of the labor camp and dragging them did not constitute kidnapping.[436] The third case involved a prosecution under the federal involuntary servitude statute[437] against a farmer who hired in Mexico two Mexican families for work on his farm in Connecticut. The indictment under the statute which originated from "An Act to abolish and forever prohibit the System of Peonage in the Territory of New Mexico and other Parts of the United States"[438] was dismissed, the court finding no "law or force [which] compels performance or a continuation of the service,"[439] even though defendant's conduct was found "highly reprehensible."[440]

MEXICAN LAW

Employment Contracts

While legislative powers in matters of labor law are delegated to the Congress under article 73, X, of the Mexican federal Constitution, the administration of these laws "pertains to the authorities of the states within their respective jurisdictions." Nevertheless, federal authorities have been granted exclusive administrative powers in labor problems arising in enumerated economic areas as, for example, in the textile, electrical, movie, coal, sugar, mining, oil, and other industries.[441]

[434] Amalgamated Meat Cutters & Butcher Workmen v. Rogers, 186 F. Supp. 114 (1960). Haltigan, A Federal Court Looks at the Mexican Program, 29 (5) Employment Security Rev. 19 (1962).

[435] United States v. Orejel-Tejeda, 194 F. Supp. 140 (1961).

[436] Cotton v. Superior Court, 364 P. 2d 241, 15 Cal. Rptr. 65 (1961).

[437] 18 U.S.C.A. § 1584.   [438] 14 Stat. 546 (1867).

[439] Clyatt v. United States, 197 U.S. 207 (1905).

[440] United States v. Shackney, 333 F. 2d 475 (Cir. 1964).

Mexican cases involving unauthorized introduction of migratory workers into the United States: 22 (1) Semanario (5a ép.) 38 (1953); 23 (1) Semanario (5a ép.) 186 (1954); 24 (1) Semanario (5a ép.) 601 (1954). Fraudulent promise to secure employment in the United States is not a federal offense, regardless of the treaty of 1951, 11 (101) Boletín de Información Jurídica 11 (1956).

[441] Art. 123, XXXI, of the Constitution as amended in 1962, D.O. Nov. 21, 1962.

Generally speaking, employment contracts[442] entered into in Mexico or to be performed in Mexico will be, regardless of the nationality or domicile of the parties, governed by Mexican law (art. 12 and 13 of the federal Civil Code), labor being matter of federal concern in the sense of art. 1. Employment contracts must be in writing, with some exceptions, for example, contracts for domestic or temporary employment. Contracts for services by Mexican nationals to be performed abroad also must be in writing. Nevertheless, the fact that such formal requirements have not been met does not deprive the employee of the rights granted by federal law since such omission is considered to be a fault on the part of the employer.[443]

The Federal Labor Law contains particular provisions for conflict situations involving two classes of employees, namely seamen and aviation personnel. In regard to the former the law provides that it applies to services performed on board Mexican vessels and other floating objects (art. 132). Whenever seamen's contracts call for services by Mexican nationals on board foreign vessels, these contracts must be in writing (art. 141) and must contain terms specified in art. 29. In case a Mexican vessel is transferred to foreign registry, seamen's contracts are terminated, without prejudice to their right to be repatriated and to claim wages up to the time of disembarking as well as three months severance pay (art. 143). Under certain conditions, Mexican seamen may demand wages in foreign currency (art. 151).

As to aviation personnel, the Federal Labor Law as amended in 1959,[444] provides that the employment of members of flight crews which include the captain, the co-pilot, the navigation officer, the flight mechanic or engineer, the radio operator, as well as the stewards and

---

[442] De la Cueva, Derecho Mexicano del Trabajo (Mexico, 1964); U.S. Department of Commerce, Labor Law and Practice in Mexico (1963); Cormack, Operation of the Mexican Labor Law, 7 S.W. L. J. 301 (1953); Cepeda Villareal, Aspects of Mexican Labor Law, Especially as They Affect Foreign Owned Business, in San Antonio Bar Association, The Legal Aspects of Doing Business in Mexico 54 (1964). Employment with the Mexican-American for the Eradication . . . , Jurisprudencia (pl.) 154 (1964). Form of an employment contract to be performed abroad in Climent Beltran, Formulario de Derecho del Trabajo 44 (Mexico, 1961).

[443] The federal Constitution prohibits in art. 123, VII, discrimination in wages because of nationality of the worker.

[444] D.O. Dec. 31, 1959; Regulations for Licenses to Technical Aeronautical Personnel, D.O. Dec. 28, 1957 (requirement of Mexican nationality, art. 15,I, and 16,I).

Employment contracts in commerce are listed as one of the commercial acts (art. 75, XXII of the Commercial Code) and, therefore, subject to the Code.

stewardesses (art. 133 bis) on Mexican civil aircraft (art. 132 bis), shall be governed by Mexican laws "regardless of the place where they journey in performance of their services" (art. 135 bis). Ground crews, on the other hand, are subject to general rules of the Federal Labor Law, since they are employed in enterprises operated under a federal permit (art. 123, XXXI of the federal Constitution). Wages of the flying personnel are paid in national currency, unless otherwise agreed (art. 151, bis, para. 2).

Conflict rules for the area of labor law in force in the United States are discussed elsewhere.[445] Nevertheless, a case may be mentioned here. A Mexican soccer player brought an action for breach of the contract of employment for one year, concluded by correspondence, the employer, a sport club in Chicago, having signed it there and mailed to Mexico. The court found the contract void under the then existing federal immigration statute prohibiting employment contracts prior to immigration.[446]

Social Insurance

There are no treaty provisions in force between Mexico and the United States dealing with various types of social insurance.

In Mexico a comprehensive scheme is established under the nation-wide Law on Social Insurance, enacted in 1943 and amended in 1949 and 1959, supplementing the corresponding provisions of the Federal Labor Law (art. 284–333).[447] Its coverage provisions subject in terms of literal universality to the insurance scheme all "persons found to be bound to others by an employment contract, regardless of the legal or economic nature of the employer" (art. 3, I). In the United States, on the contrary, coverage provisions of the Social Security Act[448] expressly disregards the citizenship or residence of both

[445] For conflict rules in force in the United States, Rothman, Conflict of Law in Labor Matters in the United States, 12 Vand. L. Rev. 997 (1959), also in Acts of the Second International Congress on Labour Law, Geneva, 1957, at 425 (1961). Sec. 703 of the Civil Rights Act of 1963, 78 Stat. 255, 42 U.S.C. § 2000(e) (2) (a), guarantees equal employment opportunities by prohibiting discrimination because of "race, color, religion, sex, or national origin."

[446] Valdez v. Viking Athletic Ass'n, 347 Ill. App. 376, 110 N.E. 2d 680 (1953).

[447] Law on Social Insurance, D.O. Jan. 19, 1943, as amended D.O. Feb. 28, 1949, and Dec. 31, 1959. Note also art. 204 of the Law of General Means of Communication.

[448] 42 U.S.C.A. § 410 (1966).

parties to the employment contract, provided such employment is "within the United States," or "on or in connection with an American vessel or American aircraft under a contract of service which is entered into within the United States or during the performance of which and while the employee is employed on the vessel or aircraft as it touches a port in the United States, if the employee is employed on or in connection with such vessel or aircraft when outside the United States." In other cases American nationality is required.[449]

In regard to benefits Mexican statutory law displays no discrimination against aliens or nonresident beneficiaries. On the contrary, the Social Security Act orders a suspension of benefits to aliens while outside the United States. And under a number of state workmen's compensation acts nonresident beneficiaries are denied benefits or allowed only in reduced amounts or lump sums.[450]

Jurisdiction

In Mexico individual as well as collective labor disputes are outside of the jurisdiction of regular courts, state and federal, and entrusted to conciliation and arbitration boards (art. 342 of the Federal Labor Law), insofar as arising from enterprises listed in article 123, XXXI of the federal Constitution. There also is a federal board sitting in Mexico City (art. 358). Jurisdiction is based on two factors: the branch of the economy involved (art. 359), and the place where the enterprise functions, namely "in the federal zones and territorial waters, in cases where conflicts involve two or more federal entities and affect collective agreements declared binding for more than one federal entity" (art. 361). The jurisdiction of other boards is determined in article 429 of the same law.

Labor Unions

It may be noted that aliens may be members of labor unions but are ineligible to serve as officers (art. 240).

[449] Alien's old-age benefits, Flemming v. Nestor, 363 U.S. 603 (1960).

[450] Andrews, Discrimination Against Non-resident Dependents, 13 Am. Lab. Leg. Rev. 232 (1925); Hyde & Watson, The Equities of Nonresident Alien Dependents under Workmen's Compensation Laws, 7 Ill. L. Rev. 414 (1931). In Serrano v. Cudahy Packing Co., 190 N.W. 132 (Iowa, 1922), the nonresident Mexican parents were unable to prove dependency on the deceased Mexican worker. In Waunakee Canning Corp. v. Industrial Commission, 68 N.W. 2d 25 (Wis. 1955) child from invalid marriage between Mexican nationals was held dependent within the Wisconsin Workmen's Compensation Act.

18. COMMERCIAL LAW

There is a basic difference between the Mexican and the American approach to commercial law. While in the United States—regardless of the so-called Uniform Commercial Code—the term includes legal rules applicable to business activities, in Mexico as in most civil law countries commercial law has the specific connotation of a separate body of law, endowed with its own substantive and procedural rules which exist and operate, in principle, apart from rules applicable as general law *(derecho común)*.[451]

MEXICAN COMMERCIAL CODE

At the outset it may be well to remember that according to the Mexican Constitution commercial law is a matter of federal legislation and, consequently, uniform for the entire Republic.[452]

The Commercial Code enacted in 1889, still in force despite continual attempts to substitute a modern code, applies to the transactions listed in article 75 of the Code. Among such commercial acts[453] appear, for example, speculative buying and selling,[454] both of chattels and

[451] Register, The Dual System of Civil and Commercial Law, 61 U. Pa. L. Rev. 240 (1912); Schlesinger, The Uniform Commercial Code in the Light of Comparative Law, 1 Int.-Am. L. Rev. 11 (1959).

[452] Clagett, The Sources of the Commercial Law in Mexico, 18 Tulane L. Rev. 437 (1944). Translation of the commercial code in Foreign Tax Law Association, Commercial Code of Mexico (1.1., n.d.), and Taylor, The Commercial Code of Mexico (1908). Gaither, Handbook of Mexican Mercantile Law (1948); Karst, Latin American Legal Institutions: Problems for Comparative Study 313 (1966); Barrera Graf, Derecho Mercantil (Mexico, 1957); Mantilla Molina, Derecho Mercantil (Mexico, 1963); Piña Vara, Elementos de Derecho Mercantil Mexicano (Mexico, 1958); Rodríguez y Rodríguez, Curso de Derecho Mercantil Mexicano (Mexico, 1964), 2 vol.

[453] Barker & Cormack, The Mercantile Act: a Study in Mexican Legal Approach, 6 So. Cal. L. Rev. 1 (1932); Mantilla Molina, Sobre la Definición de Acto de Comercio, 5 (18-20) Revista de la Escuela Nacional de Jurisprudencia 71 (1943); Barrera Graf, El Acto de Comercio: Análisis del Art. 75 del Código de Comercio, 5 (20) Revista de la Facultad de Derecho de México 103 (1955), and El Contenido del Derecho Mercantil Mexicano, in his Estudios de Derecho Mercantil 223 (Mexico, 1958).

[454] Warren, Mexican Retail Installment Sales Law: a Comparative Study, 10 U.C.L.A. L. Rev. 15 (1962).

Like other Latin American commercial codes, the Mexican Code or its supplements, deal extensively even though not exclusively, with the following activities: business associations, brokers and factors, mortgages, loans, sales, insurance, negotiable instruments, transportation by land and on rivers, maritime law, bankruptcy, and commercial courts and procedure.

land as well as of corporate shares (art. 75, I, II, III). Such transactions are subject to the Commercial Code while non-speculative transactions of the same kind are governed by the civil codes, federal or state. This dualism makes it necessary to determine the commercial or non-commercial nature not only of sales contracts, but also of all other transactions listed in article 75, regardless of the particular commercial-speculative motive involved. Once it is determined that a transaction falls within those listed in article 75, it will be governed first by the Commercial Code, supplemented, if necessary, by the federal Civil Code as *derecho común* in the sense of article 2 of the Commercial Code and in accordance with article 1 of the federal Civil Code, commercial law being a matter of federal concern. It follows that conflict rules applicable to commercial transactions are contained, first, in the Commercial Code as well as in the enactments supplementing it, for example, in the laws regulating negotiable instruments or business associations. Where there is no relevant provision in the Commercial Code, then according to its article 2 conflict rules of the general law (*derecho común*) apply, namely conflict rules contained in the federal Civil Code.[455]

The Commercial Code has but few conflict rules.[456] They provide that alien merchants may engage in business on the basis of treaties and in accordance with the laws regulating their rights and duties (art. 13), particularly the Code as well as other laws in force in the Republic (art. 14). As to the form of commercial acts, the Code dispenses with formalities of any type, including that of writing (art. 78), except where contracts have been concluded abroad. These contracts must comply with the formal requirements of the *lex loci actus* even though such formality is not required by Mexican law (art. 79, II). Whenever foreign currency is involved in a commercial transaction (art. 635 to 639), both the Commercial Code and the Monetary Law of 1931 apply.

It may be added that transportation of all kinds, except by air, is listed as a commercial transaction (art. 75, VIII). This rule is repeated in the Law of General Means of Communication of 1939, which refers to the Commercial Code in particular situations, for example, in regard to liability for loss or average (art. 80), and generally in article 4 (III). In such situations the Commercial Code

[455] The federal Civil Code is the supplementary source to the Commercial Code, Informe Rendido a la Suprema Corte de la Nación, 1943, at 43.

[456] Moreno Cora, Tratado de Derecho Mercantil Mexicano Seguido de Unas Breves Nociones de Derecho Internacional Privado Mercantil 463 (Mexico, 1905).

precedes the federal Civil Code as a subsidiary source, thus making the former, in this particular situation, applicable also to aviation. However, there are direct references to the federal Civil Code (art. 347 and 355 of the Law on General Means of Communication), by-passing the Commercial Code. In regard to shipments from abroad, regardless of whether or not the Mexican transportation enterprise is the ultimate or intermediate shipper, as well as in regard to shipments destined for a foreign country and, finally, in regard to transit shipment, the Law on General Means of Communication contains detailed provisions (art. 77 to 79).

Conflict rules of the American Uniform Commercial Code are discussed elsewhere.[457]

BUSINESS ASSOCIATIONS

It may be briefly mentioned that the General Law of Commercial Associations (*sociedades mercantiles*), enacted in 1934 as an amendment to the Commercial Code, distinguishes six types of associations:[458] partnerships (*sociedad en nombre colectivo*, art. 25); limited partnership (*sociedad en comandita simple*, art. 51), with some partners liable only to the extent of their contributions (*aportaciones*); limited liability firms (*sociedad de responsibilidad limitada*, art. 58);[459] corporations (*sociedad anónima*, art. 87); comandit company with shares (*sociedad en comandita por acciones*, art. 207);[460] and cooperatives

---

[457] Bayitch, Florida: Conflict of Laws, 1964-1966, 20 U. Miami L. Rev. 495, 498 (1966); Tuchler, Boundaries to Party Autonomy in the Uniform Commercial Code: a Radical View, 11 St. Louis U. L. J. 180 (1967).

[458] Rodríguez y Rodríguez, Tratado de Sociedades Mercantiles (Mexico, 1947); Cormack & Barker, Mexican Law of Business Organizations, 6 So. Cal. L. Rev. 181 (1933); and Mexican Mercantile Organizations under the New Law, 8 So. Cal. L. Rev. 187 (1935); Inman, Legal and Economic Aspects of Incorporation in Mexico, (1) Studies in Law & Economic Development 86 (1966). Cf. Ramos Flores, La *Corporation* en el Derecho Norteamericano, 19 Boletín del Instituto de Derecho Comparado de México 337 (1966).

For a survey, see Barnhill, Mexican Business Associations, 4 Texas Int'l L. Forum 79 (1968).

[459] Crawford, The Mexican Limited Liability Company, 13 Tulane L. Rev. 258 (1939).

[460] Crawford, The Use of Mexican Corporate Shares, 27 Tulane L. Rev. 383 (1953); and The Capital Structure of Mexican Corporations, 28 Tulane L. Rev. 45 (1953); Dillenbach, The Shareholder's Suit in Mexico, 9 Am. J. Comp. L. 78 (1960); Carillo, Control Estatal de la Venta Publica de Valores en México, 15 Revista de la Facultad de Derecho de México 335 (1965); Gómez, A Survey of the Law of Latin American Business Associations, 14 SW. L. Rev. 169 (1960); Hannon, Choice of Business Organization for Latin

(art. 212 and General Law of Cooperative Societies enacted in 1938).[461] The Code also regulates the *asociación en participación* (art. 252) comparable to joint venture. All types of these associations are for the purposes of the Commercial Code considered merchants by operation of law (art. 3, II)). They must be constituted by a notarial acts (art. 5 and 6) as well as inscribed in the public commercial register by an order of the competent court (art. 260 to 262).

Questions related to foreign business associations, particularly corporations, have been already discussed in another part of this study.

NEGOTIABLE INSTRUMENTS

Neither Mexico nor the United States has ratified the Geneva Convention of 1930 and 1931 on conflict of laws regarding bills of exchange, promissory notes and checks. The same applies to the Montevideo Conventions of 1889 and 1940, as well as to the Bustamante Code signed at Havana in 1928. The only treaty provisions related to negotiable instruments presently binding on both countries are found in the Agreement Relative to Money Orders and Final Protocol of the Postal Union of the Americas and Spain (1960).[462] A general rule concerning applicability of member countries' domestic law is contained in article 27, providing that such law "shall apply in all matters not expressly provided for by the Acts of the Union or in the Universal Postal legislation," and, of course, where the convention expressly refers to domestic law. Conflict rules proper, contained in the Convention, deal with money orders exchanged, i.e., transmitted from one country to another, such money orders are "subject, insofar as their issue and payment is concerned, to the provisions applicable to domestic money orders" in force in the countries of their origins and destination, respectively (art. 14). Another provision makes the *lex loci actus* applicable to endorsements (art. 7), by permitting endorsement of such foreign money orders "in accordance with their domestic legislation," i.e., with the

---

American Operations, 34 Tulane L. Rev. 733 (1960); Domínguez, What is Necessary to be Done in Forming a Corporation in Mexico, in San Antonio Bar Association, The Legal Aspects of Doing Business in Mexico 9 (1963); Gaither, The Necessary Steps to Take in Forming a Mexican Corporation, in San Antonio Bar Association, The Legal Aspects of Doing Business in Mexico 1 (1964); Cusi, Appropriate Use of Corporations and Other Types of Business Organizations Available under Mexican Law, ibid. 61.

[461] General Law of Cooperative Societies, D.O. Feb. 15, 1938.

[462] 12 U.S.T. 1604. Note also art. 76-89 of the Regulation of the Service of Telegraphic National and International Money Orders, D.O. Jan. 4, 1962.

law of the country where the money order originated. Finally, the Agreement provides that the payment of money orders be in the "currency of the country of destination . . . or in any other agreed upon, in accordance with the regulations in force in each country for the payment of international money orders" (art. 17).

The General Law of Negotiable Instruments and Credit Transactions (*Ley General de Títulos y Operaciones de Crédito,* 1932)[463] applies to what it terms "commercial things" (*cosas mercantiles*), namely documents (*títulos*) "necessary for the exercise of rights written therein (art. 5). These documents include: bills of exchange (*letras de cambio,* art. 76); promissory notes (*pagaré,* art. 170), and checks (*cheques,* art. 175). Furthermore, the statute regulates various kinds of obligations and certificates (art. 210, 228a, and 229). These statutory provisions will be supplemented, if necessary, first by "general commercial legislation" (art. 2, II); then by banking and commercial usages (art. 2, III); and lastly, by the general law (*derecho común*), here expressly identified as the federal Civil Code (art. 2, IV). The same sources supply also the controlling choice-of-law rules.

Omitting a discussion of conflict rules derived from subsidiary sources, the discussion will turn to the particular statutory provisions contained in the General Law. In the chapter entitled "Application of Foreign Laws" (art. 252 to 258) the General Law deals not only with the application of foreign laws regarding *títulos* but also with the application of domestic law and with some general conflict problems. A variety of contacts are relied on, among others the *lex loci actus* (art. 252, 253, and 254); the *lex loci solutionis* (art. 253, para. 2, 256 and

---

[463] D.O. Aug. 27, 1932. Translation in 2 Foreign Tax Law Association, Commercial Laws of Mexico 151 (n.d.); Barrera Graf, Some Principles of the Negotiable Instruments Legislation in Mexico, 34 Texas L. Rev. 426 (1956); Ahumada, Estudio Comparativo de los Sistemas Cambiarias Mexicano y Norte-Americano, 6 (27) Revista de la Facultad de Derecho de Buenos Aires 1670 (1951); Gaxiola, El Cheque y la Letra de Cambio en el Derecho Norteamericano y Mexicano, 4 (10) Boletín del Instituto de Derecho Comparado de México 31 (1951); López de Goicoechea, La Letra de Cambio (Mexico, 1964); Tena, Títulos de Crédito 355 (Mexico, 1956), also in his Derecho Mercantil Mexicano 580 (Mexico, 1967); Almanza, Los Conflictos Internacionales de Leyes en Materia de Títulos de Crédito (Mexico, 1940); Gordillo, Aplicación de las Reglas del Estatuto Formal al Otorgamiento de Documentos Mercantiles en Países Extranjeros Respecto de Actos que Hayan de Ejecutarse en México, 1 Revista de Legislación y Jurisprudencia 210 (1889). On letters of credit Kozolchyk, Commercial Letters of Credit in the Americas: a Comparative Study of Contemporary Commercial Transactions 59 (1966). Cf. Marine Midland Grace Trust Company of New York v. Banco del Pais, 261 F. Supp. 884 (1966).

257) ; the *lex rei sitae* (art. 255) ; the *lex loci delicti* (art. 257) ; the *lex fori* (art. 258) including its public policy (art. 254) ; and, to some extent, the *lex voluntatis* (art. 254), the law chosen by parties themselves.

Capacity to issue a *título* or to undertake any act included therein is considered by the General Law in two situations: one, as regards the law determining such capacity for acts to be performed abroad, both by Mexicans and aliens; and the other, the law to control the issuance of *títulos* or the performing of any acts include therein, by aliens in Mexico, leaving the other alternative, namely the performance of such acts by Mexicans within Mexico to be regulated by article 12 of the federal Civil Code. In the situations within the first two alternatives, the *lex loci actus* applies (art. 252), domestic (art. 252, para. 2) or foreign (art. 252, art. 1). At any rate, it is not the *lex nationalis* or *domicilii*. In consequence, a bill of exchange issued by a Mexican or alien abroad and void under the law of the place where issued, because of age or other disabilities of the issuer under that law, will be denied effect in Mexico even if, under Mexican law, such a bill of exchange might have been valid if issued by the same drawer in Mexico. Of course, the question of *renvoi* may appear whenever the *lex loci* should refer to the *lex nationalis* of the issuer.[464]

All essential requirements of a foreign issued *título* as defined by the General Law specifically for each kind, are governed by the law of the place "where the *título* was issued or the act took place" (art. 253, para. 2) ; the same rule applies where the place is within Mexico under art. 12 of the federal Civil Code. However, whenever the *título* is payable in Mexico, then the *título* as well as any act connected with it, e.g., endorsement or protest, will be valid, provided it meets the essential requirements for validity as prescribed by Mexican law, regardless of the fact that under the otherwise applicable *lex loci actus* the *título* or the act would be void. Thus, in this situation, the *lex loci solutionis* will prevail over the *lex loci actus*.

The use of foreign currency in negotiable instruments raises not only the question of their enforcement in Mexico but also their very validity. As has been already explained, the legal tender in Mexico is the national currency. Therefore, courts will render judgments only in such currency. However, in regard to bills of exchange a different re-

---

[464] Trigueros, El Reenvío en la Aplicación del Art. 252 de la Ley General sobre Títulos y Operaciones de Crédito, 5 Revista General de Derecho y Jurisprudencia 41 (1934).

sult may be reached in view of the fact that the General Law (art. 76) requires as one of the essential elements an "unconditional order to the drawee to pay a determined sum of money *(dinero)* ." In cases where the sum was in American dollars, the Mexican Supreme Court has decided repeatedly that the term 'money" means any kind of currency and that an unconditional order to pay a determined sum in foreign currency meets the statutory requirement, observing that this interpretation is not contrary to article 8 of the Monetary Law, since the term "money" includes both national and foreign currency.[465]

In situations where the General Law identifies foreign law as controlling, a further possible limitation must be taken into consideration, namely public policy *(leyes mexicanas de orden público,* art. 254) :

> In case parties have not expressly agreed that the act be governed by Mexican law, then obligations and rights arising from the issuance of the *título* abroad or from an act included therein, provided the *título* shall be paid fully or partially in the Republic, will be governed by the law of the place of execution *(otorgamiento)* , provided this law does not contravene Mexican laws of public policy.

This stautory provision contains two qualifications: one regarding the *lex voluntatis,* and the other, that the *título* is payable in Mexico. These two qualifications allow for six alternatives: three in regard to the *lex voluntatis,* and three in regard to the *lex solutionis.* Considering, for the sake of discussion, only the first qualification, parties may have (i) not chosen any applicable law at all; (ii) chosen the law of Mexico; or (iii) chosen a law other than that of Mexico. The only alternative regulated by the General Law is the one where parties have not chosen Mexican law, a situation which may be brought about by either of the alternatives (i) or (iii) . Of course, it may be reasoned that the provision of this article starting with "In case parties have not expressly agreed that the act be governed by Mexican law . . ." only attempts to express the positive side of the alternative, namely that parties have agreed upon Mexican law and that, in consequence, such choice would eliminate any need for further determination of the controlling law, in view of the fact that it is Mexican. However, the disturbing second proviso must not be overlooked, namely that the *título* is payable fully or partially within Mexico. This qualification regard-

[465] 128 Semanario (5a ép.) 57 (1964) ; 41 Semanario (6a ép.) 131 (1960) ; 44 Semanario (6a ép.) 133 (1961) ; 48 Semanario (6a ép.) 182 (1962) ; 56 Semanario (6a ép.) 75, 77 (1962) ; 61 Semanario (6a ép.) 159 (1964) .

ing the place of payment adds new difficulties, since it introduces three possible alternatives: (i) that the place of payment is in Mexico, in accordance with Mexican law; (ii) that the place of payment is in Mexico in accordance with the law chosen by parties' agreement though not that of Mexico; and (iii) that the place of payment is in Mexico according to Mexican law as chosen by parties. The unfortunate complexity of the provision will be even more patent if combinations of the two sets of alternatives are considered.

Article 256 of the General Law further provides that "terms and formalities regarding the presentation, payment and the protest of the *titulo* shall be governed by the law of the place where such acts must be performed." Articles 254 and 256 combined would give the following answer: in case the *titulo* is payable in Mexico, then claims arising out of the *titulo* would be determined by the law of the place of its issuance whenever such place is in a foreign country (art. 254), while the periods and formalities for presentation as well as for payment would be subject to the law where such acts are performed (art. 256).

If a *titulo* is secured by an interest in real property situated in Mexico, all questions concerning the security aspects of the transaction, i.e., capacity, formalities, inscription and enforcement, are subject to Mexican law as the *lex rei sitae* (art. 255), a rule following the principle adopted in article 14 of the federal Civil Code. The General Law also deals with the question of embezzlement or theft of a *titulo*. Whenever the *titulo* is payable in Mexico, interested parties will not be relieved from taking necessary steps according to Mexican laws by their mere reliance on the remedies available under the law of the place where these delicts have occurred (art. 257).

Finally, the General Law deals with the statute of limitations (*prescripción*) as well as with preclusion (*caducidad*). While prescription is open to tolling and to other grounds of extension or interruption of the period stated in the statute, preclusion remains a strict limitation on the very existence of the right so qualified. As a consequence, the mere running of the period of preclusion extinguishes the right finally and unconditionally. The solution adopted by the General Law (art. 258) is, in principle, identical with the American rule of the prevailing *lex fori:*

> Mexican laws regarding limitation and preclusion of actions arising from a *titulo* shall apply even if the *titulo* was issued abroad, whenever the action is submitted to Mexican courts for adjudication.

There are only a few American cases[466] dealing with negotiable instruments related in one way or another to Mexican law. In Hunter v. West[467] an action was brought on a bill of exchange executed in Mexico in Spanish and later endorsed in Texas, with the "place of destination" Mexico City. Appellant contended that both liability upon endorsement and the time to bring suit are controlled by Mexican law "in the form of a written code." Since the code was not produced in accordance with article 3718 of the Texas Statutes, the court considered Mexican law on this point to be the same as that of the forum and gave judgment for plaintiff-endorsee. In another case,[468] an attorney brought a suit for payment of his services against a Mexican client made by a draft for Mexican pesos, accepted and delivered by the client in Mexico. Giving judgment for defendant, the trial judge granted a new trial and was upheld on appeal. It appears that the expert on Mexican law referred to the Mexican commercial code as the applicable statute, but since the court had no satisfactory evidence of Mexican law in regard to execution and delivery of the draft, it assumed, in accordance with the California rule, Mexican law to be identical with that of the forum.[469]

BANKRUPTCY

In both countries bankruptcy is a matter of federal legislation: in Mexico because bankruptcy is a matter of commercial law, and in the United States under an express constitutional provision.

In Mexico two kinds of bankruptcy must be distinguished: civil (e.g., art. 2964 to 2998 of the federal Civil Code; art. 738 to 768 of the Code of Civil Procedure for the Federal District and Territories),[470]

[466] Stumberg, Commercial Paper and the Conflict of Laws, 6 Vand. L. Rev. 489 (1953).

[467] 293 S.W. 2d 686 (1956).

[468] Henderson v. Drake, 258 P. 2d 879 (Cal. 1953).

[469] Action on a note payable in Mexican pesos, carrying the inference that Mexican law controls, was considered insufficient due to lack of allegation of applicable Mexican law in Luckett v. Cohen, 145 F.Supp. 155 (1956). In Nacional Financiera, S.A. v. Banco de Ponce, 120 N.Y. S. 2d 373 (1953), an action for money had and received (unjust enrichment) brought by a Mexican bank against a Puerto Rican bank to which the former issued a letter of credit, was decided without resort to Mexican law. A check in dollars executed and delivered in Mexico City, payable by a New York bank was held invalid under Mexican law as the place of delivery in Hennenlotter v. De Orvananos, 186 N.Y.S. 488 (1921).

[470] Dorantes-Jamayo, La Procedure du *Concurso Civil* en Droit Mexicain, 10 Revue Internationale de Droit Comparé 753 (1958).

and commercial,[471] regulated by the Law on Bankruptcy and Suspension of Payments, enacted in 1943.[472] Commercial bankruptcies involving individual merchants are handled by the court of the place of the main enterprise or, if there shall be none, of the place of bankrupt's domicile (art. 13) .[473] In cases of bankruptcies involving business associations, the "social domicile" is decisive, except where such domicile may be fictitious; then the place of the main seat of the business becomes decisive (art. 13, para. 2) .

In regard to foreign "enterprises" the law provides that their subsidiaries may be declared bankrupt in Mexico, regardless of jurisdiction vested in foreign courts (art. 13, para. 3) . In these cases bankruptcy affects assets situated in the Republic and is available to creditors for the enforcement of claims arising out of transactions entered into with the subsidiary.

As a general rule, foreign bankruptcy decrees are not recognized in Mexico, unless their formal correctness as well as their compliance with the requirements for bankruptcy under Mexican law are established (art. 14, para. 1) . The effects of a foreign bankruptcy decree are determined not by the law of the respective foreign country (*lex fori concursus*) , but by Mexican law (art. 14, para. 2) .

Conflict rules applicable under American law, are discussed elsewhere.[474]

MONOPOLIES

In Mexico the scope of anti-monopoly legislation is set by article 28 of the federal Constitution, implemented by the Organic Law of Article 28 of the Constitution, enacted in 1934. In regard to foreign trade,

[471] Sánchez Mejorada, Bankruptcy Law of Mexico, 5 J. Nat. Asso. Ref. Bankr. 109 (1931) ; Hansen & Young, Bankruptcy in Mexico, 4 Texas Int'l L. Forum 140 (1968) .

[472] D.O. April 20, 1943.   [473] 52 Semanario (6a ép.) 90 (1961).

[474] Nadelmann, The National Bankruptcy Act and the Conflict of Laws, 59 Harv. L. Rev. 1025 (1946) ; and Revision of Conflicts Provisions in the American Bankruptcy Act, 1 Int'l & Comp. L. Q. 484 (1952) ; The American Bankruptcy Act and Conflicting Administrations, 12 Int'l & Comp. L.Q. 684 (1963) ; Legal Treatment of Foreign and Domestic Creditors, 11 Law & Contemp. Pr. 696 (1946). The same author has published a number of valuable studies in Spanish: La Quiebra en el Derecho Norteamericano, 12 (45) Revista de la Facultad de Derecho de México 257, 284 (1962) ; Revisión de las Reglas sobre Conflictos de Leyes en la Ley Norteamericana de Quiebras, 2 (8) Revista de la Facultad de Derecho de México 85 (1952) ; and La Ley Norteamericana sobre Quiebras y el Conflicto de Jurisdicciones, 13 (49) Revista de la Facultad de Derecho de México 137 (1963) .

article 28, paragraph 4, of the Constitution exempts from anti-monopoly laws "cooperative associations or societies (*asociaciones o sociedades cooperativas*) which, in defense of their interests or of the general interest, sell directly to foreign markets national or industrial products which are the main source of wealth of the region where they are produced, without being article of prime necessity," provided the associations involved are government controlled and have obtained the necessary permits.[475]

In the United States the Sherman Act[476] was applied to trade with Mexico in connection with sisal production in Yucatán. In *United States v. Sisal Sales Corporation*[477] the Supreme Court found that American banks, the importing corporations as well as the Comision Exportadora de Yucatán have "by constant manipulation of the markets, acquired complete dominion over them, destroyed competition, obtained power to advance and arbitrarily to fix excessive prices, and have made unreasonable exactions." Since the contracts in restraint of trade have been made within the United States by parties subject to its jurisdiction, the Court held the fact that the conspiracy was "aided by discriminating legislation" enacted in Mexico, was immaterial since the conspirators had, by their "own deliberate acts here and elsewhere, . . . brought about forbidden results within the United States," and therefore the conduct fell within the scope of the Sherman Act.[478]

FAIR TRADE PRACTICES

Certain aspects of fair trade practices are covered by treaties, among them by the Convention for the Protection of Industrial Property, signed at London in 1934. The substantive Mexican law on this matter has been well presented by a recognized Mexican writer else-

[475] Browning, A Comparative Glance at the Antimonopoly Laws of the United States and Mexico, 42 Texas L. Rev. 577 (1964); Goldstein, Sistema Actual del Derecho Antitrust, 14 Revista de la Facultad de Derecho de México 1035 (1964).

[476] E.g., Fugate, Foreign Commerce and Anti-Trust Laws (1958); Brewster, Antitrust and American Business Abroad (1958); Haight, International Law and Extraterritorial Application of Antitrust Laws, 63 Yale L.J. 639 (1954); Reynolds, Extraterritorial Application of Federal Antitrust Laws: Delimiting the Reach of Substantive Law under the Sherman Act, 20 Vand. L. Rev. 1030 (1967).

[477] 274 U.S. 268 (1927).

[478] Aftermath of the controversy was a consent decree issued by the Federal Trade Commission, Matter of Cordage Importers Association, Inc. et al., 52 F.T.C. Rep. 888 (1956).

where.[479] However, it must be added that there are no statutory provisions nor is there case law dealing with choice-of-laws situations.[480]

[479] Barrera Graf, Unfair Competition in Mexican Law, in University of Miami School of Law, Mexico: a Symposium on Law and Government 91 (1958).

[480] Wengler, Law Concerning Unfair Competition and the Conflict of Laws, 4 Am. J. Comp. L. 167 (1955); Rappaport, Trade-Mark and Unfair Competition in International Conflicts of Laws: an Analysis of the Choice-of-Law Problem, 20 U. Pitt. L. Rev. 1 (1958); Briglia, Choice of Law for the Tort of Unfair Competition, 57 T.M. Rep. 528 (1967). For general information, Pinner, World Unfair Competition Law (1965).

Both countries have ratified a number of international commodity agreements. Their functions in terms of conflict law, however, will not be discussed here.

19. MARITIME LAW

In Mexico, maritime transportation is considered a commercial transaction under article 75, VIII, of the Commercial Code and, consequently, regulated by this Code. However, the respective provisions of the Code (art. 641 to 944) have been replaced by the Law of Maritime Navigation and Commerce, enacted in 1963,[481] and still remain part of the Code. Moreover, additional provisions must be gleaned from the Law on General Means of Communications, dealing with maritime commerce in book three (art. 169 to 305).

TREATY LAW

There are several conventions in force between Mexico and the United States, both multilateral and bilateral, containing, among others, maritime conflict rules. Out of the eleven Brussels maritime conventions adopted between 1910 and 1937, only one, the Convention for the Unification of Certain Rules with Respect to Assistance and Salvage at Sea (1910), was ratified by both countries, and later supplemented by the bilateral Treaty for Sending of Vessels for Purposes of Assistance and Salvage, signed in 1935. Furthermore, the Convention on Safety of Life at Sea signed in London in 1948, and the additional Regulation for Preventing Collisions at Sea are in force in both countries, as is the International Convention for the Prevention of Pollution of the Sea by Oil, signed in London in 1954.

In regard to assistance and salvage operations, the 1910 Brussels Convention[482] provides that no remuneration may be had for saving human lives, but adds a saving clause in favor of "national laws on this subject" (art. 9). The same Convention establishes a uniform statute

---

[481] D.O. Nov. 21, 1963, amended Aug. 20, 1964 in regard to art. 160, 164, 175 and 194-196. Rivera Farber, Observaciones a la Ley de Navegación y Comercio Marítimos, 15 Revista de la Facultad de Derecho de México 189 (1961).

[482] The Convention does not apply to salvage under contract but only to voluntary acts, 8 Boletín de Información Jurídica 238 (1952). In Long v. The Tampico, 16 Fed. 491 (1883), a salvage claim against the Mexican government was allowed on the ground that, first, it did not appear that title passed to the government, and secondly, even if the title passed, the vessel was at the time of salvage not in public service of the Mexican government or in possession thereof.

of limitations period, with the addition that the "grounds upon which the said period of limitation may be suspended or interrupted are determined by the law of the court where the case is tried," i.e., by the *lex fori* (art. 10, para. 2). Contracting countries also reserve the right to "provide by legislation . . . that the said period shall be extended in cases where it has not been possible to arrest the vessel assisted or salved in the territorial waters of the State in which the plaintiff has his domicile or principal place of business" (art. 10, para. 3). It may be added that, according to Mexican law, maritime claims arising out of assistance and salvage at sea are barred after ten years (art. 1047 of the Commercial Code). Under Mexican law foreign vessels are permitted to engage in salvage operations in Mexican territorial waters only in cases of emergency or whenever local authorities have no necessary means at their disposal (art. 192, V, of the Law on General Means of Communication). This rule, however, seems to have been modified in relation to the United States by the bilateral treaty of 1935 which gave both contracting countries the right to assist their own vessels within defined areas of territorial waters of the other contracting country in the Pacific as well as in the Gulf of Mexico (art. I), with the proviso that when engaged in such operations these vessels "shall be subject to the provisions of the laws in force in the country in whose territorial waters such assistance is rendered" (art. III), on the side of Mexico to articles 72 to 87 of the Law on Maritime Navigation and Commerce of 1963.

The Regulation for Preventing Collisions at Sea of 1948 contains elaborate rules of the road on the high seas.[483] They have been relied upon in an American case.[484] There, the Mexican insurance company, subrogated to the shipowner's claim under article 855 of the Mexican Commercial Code, sued the American vessel for the amount of damages paid to the owner of the Mexican vessel arising from a collision in the international waters of the Gulf of Mexico. The court found that the Mexican vessel was engaged in a trawling operation and, therefore, had the right of way over the American vessel which was found to have been without a proper lookout at the critical time. The court gave judgment for plaintiff for a sum expressed in dollars according to the

[483] Collision between a Mexican and Brazilian vessel, 16 Semanario (6a ép.) 9 (1958). Art. 34 of the Law on Maritime Navigation and Commerce (1963) repeats this provision adding that the privilege may be denied in case of lack of reciprocity or in public interest.

[484] La Interamericana, S.A. v. The Narco, 146 F. Supp. 270 (S.D. Fla. 1956). Cf. S. T. Tringali Co. v. Tug Pemex XV, 274 F. Supp. 227 (1967).

rate of exchange on the day when the collision took place.[485]

In respect to the nationality of vessels evidenced by the flag[486] they fly, the Geneva Convention on the High Seas (1958) recognizes to all countries the right "to sail ships under [their]flags on the high seas" (art. 4). The conditions for the grant of nationality to vessels, for the registration and for the right to fly its flag, remain within the powers of each country granting it. However, the Conventions adds a far-reaching proviso:

> There must exist a genuine link between the State and the ship; in particular, the State must effectively exercise its jurisdiction and control in administrative matters, technical and social matters over ships flying its flag.

Vessels sailing under the flag of a country shall be, save in exceptional cases, subject "to its exclusive jurisdiction" (art. 6) ; such flag may not be changed "during a voyage or while in port of call, save in the case of a real transfer of ownership or change of registry" (art. 6). A vessel which uses flags of two or more countries according to convenience, may not claim any of these nationalities and may "be assimilated to a ship without nationality" (art. 6, para. 2). However, a piratical vessel retains its original nationality; its "retention or loss is determined by the law of the country from which such nationality was derived" (art. 18).

NAVIGATION

Generally, navigation[487] in Mexican territorial waters is free to vessels of all nations "subject to the rules of law and international treaties" (art. 189 of the Law on General Means of Communications), which means in accordance with articles 14 to 23 of the Geneva Convention on the Territorial Sea and the Contiguous Zone (1958). Of course,

---

[485] Relying on Liebeskind v. Mexican Light & Power Co., 116 F. 2d 971 (2d Cir. 1941), and Indemnity Mutual Marine Assurance Co. v. United States, 1935 A.M.C. 809.

[486] Helguera, Condiciones en las Cuales los Estados Conceden a los Buques el Derecho de Enarbolar el Pabellón Nacional, 11 (32) Boletín del Instituto de Derecho Comparado de México 73 (1958). See Regulation Regarding the Flag and Registration of Mexican Merchant Vessels, D.O. Aug. 2, 1946, particularly art. 6; 123 Semanario (5a ép.) 2227 (1955).

[487] Ramírez Banos, El Estado y la Marina Mercante, 11 Revista de la Facultad de Derecho de México 349 (1961). For American law, Sinclair, Conflict of Laws Problems in Admiralty, 15 SW. L.J. 1, 1207 (1961); Goss, U.S.A. Legislation and the Foreign Shipowner, 12 J. Industrial Economy 1 (1963); Raymond, The Application of Our Laws to Foreign Merchant Ships, 67 Dick. L. Rev. 289 (1963).

foreign vessels navigating in Mexican waters are by this very act "subject to compliance with the laws of the Republic and with the respective regulations." Similarly, Mexican ports are open to vessels regardless of their flag, while cabotage[488] along the coast and on rivers is limited by statute (art. 190). Foreign vessels may disembark passengers as well as cargo in Mexican ports or continue to other Mexican ports (art. 192, I and II); however, these privileges may be denied because of lack of international reciprocity or because of public interest involved (art. 192, para. 2). Even though certain maritime operations are reserved to Mexican registered vessels, they may be allowed to foreign vessels under a permit issued by the Secretariat of Communications (art. 193 and 195).

Mexican vessels are registered in the Public National Maritime Register (*Registro Público Marítimo Nacional*) as part of the Commercial Register (*Registro Comercial*), as provided in article 96, I, of the Law of Maritime Commerce and Navigation and article 4 of its transitory provisions, in accordance with article 21, XVI, and XVII, of the Commercial Code. Such inscription will suffice to create effects envisaged by the Commercial Code (art. 22).

Vessels are considered movables (art. 106 of the Law of Maritime Navigation and Commerce). Consequently, interests in them may be established in accordance with rules applicable to chattels. However, acts "extinguishing property," meaning apparently transfers of title as well as security interests and other interests *in rem* (*derechos reales*) must be executed in the form of a public document (art. 111) and properly registered (art. 111 and 116, VII). Vessels may also be attached by virtue of valid judgments; however, vessels cleared for departure may not be attached but only detained during the period needed for apprehension of a criminal, recovery of stolen property, or removal of persons who have boarded the vessel improperly (art. 55).[489]

ACTS ON BOARD SHIP: CIVIL

As has been already indicated, Mexican vessels on the high seas are

[488] Regulation Concerning Cabotage, D.O. Sept. 4, 1941.

[489] Seizure of foreign vessel, 70 Semanario (5a ép.) 3389 (1941). General Regulation of Port Police (D.O. Oct. 9, 1941) contains provisions regarding arrests on board foreign vessels (art. 66), or members of the crew (art. 67), or deserters (art. 68); foreign captain's request for assistance (art. 69-70); consular privileges (art. 71-73); acts against Mexican nationals on board foreign vessel (art. 75).

considered to be Mexican territory (art. 2 of the Law of Maritime Navigation and Commerce) . Consequently, Mexican law applies whenever the *lex loci actus* obtains. Mere happenings on board, such as torts, or transactions, such as contracts, will be governed by Mexican law or, more precisely, by federal law as enacted in the federal Civil Code and in the Commercial Code. In addition, there are special provisions included in the federal Civil Code applicable to acts on board vessel. Births occurring on Mexican vessels, apparently without distinction of the nationality of the parents, must be documented by an act containing data listed in articles 58 to 65 of the federal Civil Code, and certified by the captain or the owner of the vessel and two witnesses (art. 70) . Persons thus born become Mexican nationals (art. 1, III, of the Nationality and Naturalization Law) . On the other hand, where a child is born on board of a foreign vessel to Mexican parents, the federal Civil Code refers to article 15, i.e., the *lex loci actus,* thus making the law of the flag controlling at least insofar as formalities are concerned (art. 73) . Where a death occurs on board a Mexican vessel, a document has to be executed as prescribed by article 119 of the same Code; however, there is no parallel provision for deaths on board foreign vessels. Maritime wills, i.e., privileged testamentary dispositions executed on board Mexican vessels when on the high seas (art. 1583 of the federal Civil Code) , available both to Mexicans and aliens, are executed in the presence and under the signature of the captain and two witnesses (art. 1583 and 1584) and noted in the ship's log (art. 1586) ; upon arrival in port, the captain will deposit a copy of the will with the Mexican diplomatic or consular agent while a second copy will be forwarded to the maritime authority (art. 1588) . It is to be kept in mind that such maritime wills retain their effect only if the testator dies on board ship or within one month after debarcation in a place "where, according to Mexican law or to the foreign law, he would be qualified to ratify this will or make a new one" (art. 1591) .

The Law of Maritime Navigation and Commerce has supplied additional conflict rules for juridical acts occurring on Mexican vessels when in foreign territorial waters, or on foreign vessels in Mexican territorial waters (art. 3) :

> When national vessels are in foreign waters, juridical acts related to them *(actos jurídicos relacionados con ellos)* will be subject to Mexican laws insofar as this is compatible with the legislation of the respective foreign State. Reciprocally, foreign vessels when in national territorial or inland waters, will be considered as subject to the laws of the foreign State insofar as this is compatible with the application of Mexican laws.

At first glance, this provision contains three points in need of clarification. The first difficulty arises from the term *actos jurídicos*. Assuming the term is deliberately used to exclude *hechos*, then only voluntary legal transactions will be covered while, by the same token, other events, such as torts, may be excluded. The second difficulty stems from the limitation to acts "related to them." It is not clear whether these acts must be related to vessels or are intended to cover happenings on board of such vessels generally. In any case, the second interpretations seems to be reasonable. The third difficulty originates from the failure to specify the compatibility of the foreign law with the otherwise applicable Mexican law and vice-versa, since the basis for such determination may be general public policy, or the cogent nature of either rules, or merely reasonableness dictated by the particular circumstances.

The same law also provides in article 6 that maritime customs apply as supplementary source of law, in addition to the Commercial Code, the Law of Insurance Contracts, the General Law of Insurance Institutions, the federal Civil Code and the Law of General Means of Communications.

Criminal acts on board vessels are discussed elsewhere in this study.

20. AVIATION LAW

The inherently international nature of aviation has postulated international regulations of aviation as well as domestic legislation aware of international implications. While the first factor leads, generally, to successful international negotiations and treaties, the second remains, at least in regard to choice-of-laws aspects, rather neglected. In respect to both factors, conflict rules applicable to aviation problems between the jurisdictions of both Mexico and the United States, offer the typical interplay between treaty law and domestic legislation.

TREATY LAW

Mexico and the United States have both ratified a number of treaties, multilateral as well as bilateral, dealing with international civil aviation.[490] Among the conventions adopted in Chicago (1944) the Convention on International Civil Aviation as amended in 1954, and the International Air Services Transit Agreement, are binding on both countries. The former restates a number of conflict rules already recognized by both countries, among them national sovereignty over airspace (art. 1 and 2) ; nationality of aircraft to be determined by country of registration (art. 17) ; prohibition of dual nationality of aircraft (art. 18) ; and transfer of aircraft to be controlled by the national law (art. 19). In regard of the rules of the air (art. 12), the Convention distinguishes between two kinds of traffic rules: one requiring every country to adopt measures to "insure that every aircraft flying over or maneuvering within its territory and that every aircraft carrying its national mark, wherever such aircraft may be, shall comply with the rules and regulations . . . there in force," as well as to "insure the prosecution of all persons violating the regulations applicable;" and the second promising that rules for traffic over the high seas will be "established under this Convention" (art. 12). Furthermore, equal national treatment is due to aircraft of all contracting countries in regard to charges for the use of airports and other facilities, by providing that aircraft engaged in scheduled international flights must pay no higher charges than "those that would be paid by its national aircraft engaged in similar international air services" (art. 15, para. 2, b). This provision of the Chicago Convention was invoked in a suit brought by

[490] Bayitch, El Actual Derecho Convencional de la Aviación, 18 Boletín del Instituto de Derecho Comparado de México 723 (1965).

ten Latin American carriers, among them one Mexican, against the Dade County Port Authority operating the Miami International Airport, seeking injunctive relief against, as well as recovery of charges beyond those paid by a group of domestic carriers on the basis of a contract confirmed by the Authority in its first published schedule (1946).[491] The trial court found for the plaintiffs, only to be reversed on appeal. The later opinion relying on article 82 of the Convention and on an ill-conceived notion of most-favored-national treatment, is discussed elsewhere.[492]

It may be added that the same Convention prohibits the seizure or detention of a lawfully present aircraft of another nationality for claims arising out of infringement of patents or similar rights, and against the requirement to deposit security in such cases (art. 27, a), provided that the country whose aircraft is involved offers sufficient protection either by belonging to the International Convention for the Protection of Industrial Property, or offers sufficient protection in its own domestic law (art. 27, c).

Further uniform conflict rules are in force in Mexico and in the United States in consequence of their having ratified the Convention on Unification of Certain Rules Relating to International Transportation by Air, the Warsaw Convention of 1929. The uniform substantive rules applicable to international flights as defined by article 1, are implemented by a number of related conflict rules referring, in most situations, to the *lex fori*. Contributory negligence on the part of the injured passenger will be available as defense, provided such defense is available under the *lex fori* (art. 21), as is the case in Mexico according to article 346, III, of the Law on General Means of Communications. The *lex fori* will also decide whether or not damages may be awarded in the form of periodical payments (art. 22, para. 1), a remedy available under Mexican law (art. 1915, I, of the federal Civil Code). Furthermore, the *lex fori* governs procedure (art. 28, para. 1), as well as the method of calculating the two-year period of limitation

---

[491] Aerovías Interamericanas de Panamá v. Board of County Comm'rs, 197 F. Supp. 230 (S.D. Fla. 1961); rev'd sub nom. Board of County Comm'rs v. Peruansa, S.A., 307 F. 2d 802 (5th Cir. 1962), cert. denied, 372 U.S. 932 (1963).

[492] Bayitch, International Law, 16 U. Miami L. Rev. 240, 259 (1961); also Florida and International Legal Developments: 1962-1963, 18 U. Miami L. Rev. 321, 339 (1963); Grove, International Law: Chicago Convention Interpreted, Discriminatory Airport Charges to Foreign Airlines, 18 U. Miami L. Rev. 482 (1963); Rijks, Airport Charges under Judicial Review, 9 Ned. Tijdsch. Int'l Recht 50 (1962).

established by the Convention (art. 29, para. 2) , a period longer than that found in Mexican law (art. 347, para. 2, or art. 350, para. 3, of the Law on General Means of Communication) . Similarly, the equivalent in the *lex fori* of the notion of "wilful misconduct," or *"dol"* in the French authentic text, will be defined by the *lex fori* (art. 25, para. 1) .[493] The Convention contains also far reaching jurisdictional provisions for the litigation of claims arising under it. According to article 28, such actions

> must be brought, at the option of the plaintiff, in the territory of one of the High Contracting Parties, either before the court of the domicile of the carrier, or of his principal place of business, or where he has a place through which the contract has been made, or before the court at the place of destination.

The difficulties arising from the interpretation of article 28 in federally organized countries, like Mexico and the United States, are discussed elsewhere.[494] Here, it may be added that jurisdictional rules established by the Convention cannot be changed, at least before the occurrence of the damage, by parties' agreement (art. 32) . The same rule applies agreements to arbitrate, except that claims arising from transportation of goods may be subjected to arbitration before as well as after the damage occurs, provided arbitration "is to take place within one of the jurisdictions referred to in the first paragraph of article 28," quoted above. In any case, such arbitration remains "subject to this convention" (art. 32) . Finally, it is to be pointed out that the provisions controlling under the Convention cannot be changed by "deciding the law to be applied" (art. 32) , meaning by choice of law through parties' agreement.

Limitations on liability of air carriers under the Warsaw Convention (art. 22, para. 4) underwent recently dramatic changes initiated by the United States. Relying on article 22, paragraph (1) of the Convention, the United States has, through the Civil Aeronautics Board, published an Agreement to be adopted by domestic and foreign carriers operating in and out of the United States.[495] It raises limits for damages in cases of injury or death of passengers and eliminates one

[493] Acosta, Wilful Misconduct under the Warsaw Convention: Recent Trends and Developments, 19 U. Miami L. Rev. 575 (1965).

[494] McKenry, Judicial Jurisdiction under the Warsaw Convention, 29 J. Air L. & Comm. 205 (1963).

[495] 31 (97) Fed. Reg. 7302 (1966). See Appendix III. Among Mexican carriers Aeronaves de México, S.A., and Compañía Mexicana de Aviación, S.A., have adopted the Agreement.

of the defenses available to carriers under the Convention. In view of the fact that the United States has withdrawn its initial denunciation of the Warsaw Convention, the Agreement is designed to operate within the general scope of the Convention. The definition of an international flight still stands as determining the coverage under the Convention; however, the Agreement added a further qualification, namely that, in order to be affected by the Agreement, a flight, in itself international under article 1, paragraph (2) of the Convention, must also be a flight "which includes a point in the United States as a point of origin, point of destination, or agreed upon stopping place." In regard to flights meeting both requirements, the Agreement provides a new limit of liability for "death, wounding or other bodily injury" of each passenger, within the scope of article 17, of course. Replacing the conventional limitation of $8,300 with a new one, the Agreement raises this limit to the sum of $75,000 exclusive of legal fees, and in jurisdictions "where provision is made for separate award of legal fees and costs," to a limit of $58,000, respectively. While passengers retain under the Agreement the claim to full damages in cases of wilful misconduct (art. 25) and lack of ticket (art. 3) and carriers the defense of contributory negligence (art. 21) in accordance with the *lex fori*, the carriers are deprived of their defense under article 20, paragraph (1) of the Convention, providing that

> The carrier shall not be liable if he proves that he and his agents have taken all necessary measures to avoid the damages or that it was impossible for him or them to take such measures.

As the only exception in this regard the Agreement allows to stipulate that the rights and liabilities of a carrier will remain unaffected "with regard to any claim brought by, on behalf of, or in respect to any person who has wilfully caused damage which results in death, wounding, or other bodily injury of a passenger," a provision intended to discourage sabotage.[496]

[496] For a general discussion, see Lowenfeld & Mendelson, The United States and the Warsaw Convention, 80 Harv. L. Rev. 497 (1967); Caplan, The Warsaw Convention Revitalized, 1966 J. Bus. L. 335; Fitzgerald, Liability Rules in the International Carriage of Passengers by Air and the Notice of Denunciation of the Warsaw Convention by the United States, 4 Can. Yb. Int'l L. 194 (1966); Keiner, The 1966 Carrier Agreements: the United States Retains the Warsaw Convention, 7 Va. J. Int'l L. 140 (1967); Levine, Warsaw Convention: Treaty under Pressure, 16 Clev. Mar. L. Rev. 327 (1967); Mendelsohn, Another View on the Adequate Award in International Aviation Accident, Ins. L. J. 197 (1967); Osinoff, The Warsaw Convention, 2 Texas Int'l L. Forum 207 (1966); Riggs, Termination of Treaties by the

While there are no reported Mexican cases dealing with the Warsaw Convention, a few American cases related to Mexico may be mentioned. The preliminary question whether or not a flight was an international flight within article 1 of the Convention was at issue in Grey v. American Airlines, Inc.[497] It was held that a flight from New York to Mexico City with a scheduled stop in Dallas where the crash occurred, was an international flight in respect to passengers with tickets to Mexico, but not those with tickets for Dallas. Similarly, a flight from Washington, D.C., to Mexico City was held to be international, and wilful misconduct on the part of the carrier found.[498] On the contrary, a flight between San Diego and a Mexican island was not considered within the scope of the Convention because not only was the aircraft not one "for hire" (art. 1, para. 1), but it was also used in "extraordinary circumstances outside of the normal scope of an air carrier's business" in the sense of article 34 of the Convention.[499] The validity of the ticket provision that claims must be presented in writing within 30 days was involved in Sheldon v. Pan American Airways, Inc.[500] In this suit for damages arising from an air accident near Mexico on a flight from Los Angeles, defendant air carrier invoked such limitation. The court held this clause on the ticket not inconsistent with the Convention, stating that the Convention "refers to the time within which an action must be commenced, while the clause of the ticket refers only to the time within which a written claim must be made upon the carrier."[501]

Executive Without Congressional Approval: the Case of the Warsaw Convention, 32 J. Air L. & Comm. 526 (1966) ; Sincoff, Absolute Liability and Increased Damages in International Aviation Accidents, 52 A. B.A.J. 1122 (1966) ; Stephen, The Adequate Award in International Aviation Accidents, Ins. L. J. 711 (1966) ; Bayitch & LeRiverend, La Convencion de Varsovia en la Actualidad, 17 Revista de la Facultad de Derecho de México 845 (1967) ; also in Folchi (ed.), Cuestiones Actuales de Derecho Aeronáutico 96 (Buenos Aires, 1968) ; Mankiewicz, Le Statut de l'Arrangement de Montreal (Mai 1966) . . . , 21 Revue Française de Droit Aérien 384 (1967).

It would go beyond the scope of this study to discuss the compatibility of changes imposed by the Agreement in regard to carriers' defenses, with art. 23 and 32 of the Convention.

[497] 95 F. Supp. 756 (S.D.N.Y. 1950), aff'd, 227 F. 2d 282 (2d Cir. 1955), cert. denied, 350 U.S. 989 (1956).

[498] 186 F. 2d 529 (D.C. App. 1949).

[499] 1953 U.S. & Can. Av. Rep. 423 (Cal. 1953).

[500] 190 Misc. 537, 74 N.Y.S. 2d 578, aff'd, 272 A.D. 1000, 74 N.Y.S. 2d 267 (1947).

[501] Jurisdictional rules of art. 28 of the Warsaw Convention have been litigated in an action against a Mexican air carrier in Woolf v. Aerovías Guest, 1954 U.S. & Can. Av. Rep. 399 (N.Y. 1954). Finding defendant's prin-

In concluding the discussion regarding multilateral aviation conventions binding on both countries, it may be added that Mexico has ratified both the Hague Protocol (1955) as well as the Guadalajara Convention (1961), but not the United States. Consequently, the Warsaw Convention remains in force between the two countries in its original text, except as modified in relation to the United States by recent developments. It may also be repeated here that the Convention on the International Recognition of Rights in Aircraft, signed at Geneva in 1948, even though ratified by both countries, is regarded by the United States as not in force in relation to Mexico, due to unacceptable reservations made by the latter.

Immediate aviation problems between both countries are regulated by the bilateral Air Transport Agreement, signed in 1960 and later repeatedly extended as well as amended.[502] It contains, among others, a few conflict rules. The *lex loci actus* applies to admission or departure of aircraft engaged in international flights (art. 5), and national treatment is assured in article 7 (a):

> Each of the parties may impose or permit to be imposed just and reasonable charges for the use of the public airports and other facilities under its control. Each of the parties agrees, however, that these charges shall not be higher than would be paid for the use of such airports and facilities by its national aircraft engaged in similar international services.

AIRSPACE

The Mexican airspace is defined in article 42 of the federal Constitution as the space "situated over the national territory, with extensions and modifications as established by international law" (art. 42, VI). The same provision includes in the national territory: integral parts of the Federation (I); islands, including rocks and keys within the adja-

---

cipal place of business in Mexico City and the ticket bought in Florida for a round trip from there to Mexico, the court dismissed without prejudice. Of course, the Convention does not apply in actions brought by non-passengers against a Mexican air carrier. In Nickleski v. Aeronaves de México, S.A., 228 N.Y. S. 2d 963 (1962), plaintiff's car was hit in New York by a low flying defendant's aircraft; the court held the carrier responsible under the *lex loci delicti* (N.Y. Gen. Business Law, sec. 251) and gave judgment for plaintiff in the ground that defendant's aircraft "invaded a public highway."

502 Healy, Revision of the Mexican-United States Air Transport Agreement, 1965-1970, 32 J. Air L. & Comm. 167 (1966). For citations, see U.S. Department of State, Treaties in Force: a List of Treaties and Other International Agreements of the United States in force on January 1, 1967, at 134 (1967).

cent sea (II) ; the islands of Guadalupe and Revillagigedo in the Pacific Ocean (III) ; the continental shelf and the submarine shelf of the islands, keys and rocks (IV) ; and waters of the territorial sea to the extent and under conditions established by international law, as well as the inland sea (V). The Law of General Means of Communication also defines the national airspace as the "space over Mexican territory" (art. 306, para. 1), adding that for the purposes of this law Mexican territory includes the territory of the United Mexican States, territorial waters and adjacent islands on both oceans as well as the two islands just mentioned (art. 306, para. 2). Civil aviation within this area is governed by treaties, by the Law of General Means of Communication as well as other laws and regulations in point (art. 307), among them the federal Civil Code (art. 309, para. 2).[503]

AIR TRANSPORTATION

Claims arising from civil aviation activities in Mexico are determined by the Law of General Means of Communication:[504] damage to passengers (art. 342 to 348) ; to cargo and baggage (art. 349 to 450), and to third person on the ground (art. 351 to 355). Should these provisions not suffice, the provisions contained in the Commercial Code will be resorted to (art. 4, II and III), or to the federal Civil Code and Code of Civil Procedure for the Federal District and Territories (art. 4, IV). Finally, consideration shall be given "to the needs of public service whose satisfaction is involved" (art. 4, V). In a recent case, the provision referring to the federal Code of Civil Procedure has been interpreted as exclusive jurisdictional grant to the federal courts in matters of claims arising from aviation accidents.

Considerable difficulties arise on the domestic level in regard to the interplay between the provisions contained in the Law of General Means of Communication and its general (art. 4, IV) as well as special (art. 347, 350, and 355) references to the federal Civil Code, particularly with regard to articles 1913 and 1915 of the latter, and are discussed elsewhere.[505]

[503] Francoz Rigolt, Directivas Mexicanas del Derecho de la Aviación (Mexico, 1958) ; Villafuerte, Ambitos de Validez de la Legislación Mexicana de la Aviación, 21 La Justicia 30 (1961).

[504] Translation in United States Senate Committee on Commerce, Air Law and Treaties of the World 1721 (1965). On aviation litigation, Jurisprudencia (civ.) 4 (1964).

[505] Vaselli, Responsibilidad Contractual e Extracontractual por Muerte del Pasajero en el Transporte Aéreo, 3 (11) Revista de la Facultad de Derecho de México 9 (1955) ; Aguilar Gutierrez, Relaciones entre Respon-

It may be added that compulsory insurance established for air transportation under article 127 of the Law of General Means of Communication covers flights which begin and end in Mexico, probably including a portion of the flight over and a landing in a foreign country (art. 32 of the Regulation of Article 134 [now 127] of the Law of General Means of Communication).

ACTS ON BOARD AIRCRAFT: CIVIL

There is a number of statutory provisions governing acts non-criminal in nature occurring on board Mexican aircraft in flight. In regard to births and deaths, articles 70 to 72 of the federal Civil Code, dealing with such events on board Mexican vessels, apply (art. 309, para. 2, of the Law of General Means of Communication), with the captain functioning as the civil registrar who will "note in the flight log[506] events that occurred on board aircraft in flight and may have legal consequences." Upon landing in a foreign country, the captain reports such events to the local authorities and to the Mexican consul (art. 322).

In a general way, Mexican laws apply to (art. 308, I):

Events and juridical acts occurring on board Mexican aircraft in flight over the national territory or over non-territorial seas as well as over foreign territory, provided that they do not infringe upon the security or the public order of the subjacent state,

a proviso common to Latin American aviation codes but never clearly interpreted. In view of article 12 of the federal Civil Code, events and acts on board foreign aircraft within the national airspace will also be governed by Mexican law, in this case apparently without the proviso just quoted.

Conflict rules applicable to criminal acts on board aircraft are discussed elsewhere in this study.

---

sabilidad y Seguro en el Derecho Aereo Mexicano e Internacional, in Comunicaciones Mexicanas al VI Congreso Internacional de Derecho Comparado, Hamburgo, 1962, at 157 (1962). Absolute liability in air accidents, Jurisprudencia (civ.) 3 (1965).

[506] Regulation Regarding Operation of Civil Aircraft, art. 98, D.O. Nov. 22, 1950.

21. MISCELLANEOUS PROBLEMS

There are problems in the conflict of laws which generate more theoretical interest than practical considerations might warrant, among them renvoi[507] and characterization.[508] In Mexico they have received only scant theoretical treatment.

Equally unproductive remains in Mexico the question of the substantive or procedural nature of the statute of limitations.[509] Article 258 of the General Law of Credit Titles and Operations, discussed elsewhere in this study, may indicate that the *lex fori* will prevail over the *lex causae* as it does in the United States. However, it is to be kept in mind that in the United States the procedural nature of the statute has been, to a considerable extent, eroded by the borrowing statutes.

Constitutional aspects involved in the statute of limitations of the forum or, more precisely, the forum's prohibition against its shortening, was before the United States Supreme Court in Home Insurance v. Dick.[510] There the Supreme Court held that a Texas court could not apply its rule against shortening of the forum's statute of limitations and thus invalidate a non-suit clause included in an insurance contract with contacts pointing overwhelmingly toward Mexican law as controlling: the plaintiff-assignee of the insured, even though a domiciliary of Texas, was a resident of Mexico; the insurance contract was made in Mexico between a Mexican insurer with no contacts with Texas, and an American residing in Mexico; these parties agreed that Mexican law shall control; the premiums were paid in Mexico in Mexican currency; and finally, the vessel was insured only when in Mexican waters where the loss also occurred. In view of this the Court found that "Texas was . . . without power to affect the terms of the contract so made." Moreover, in the opinion of the Court the prohibition of the *lex fori* against shortening the statute of limitations below two years was not a simple statute of limitations affecting remedies of the forum, but rather a pro-

---

[507] Alfonsín, Ensayo sobre la Teoría del Reenvío en Derecho Internacional Privado, 4 (16) Revista de la Facultad de Derecho de México 117 (1954).

[508] Characterization by the *lex fori* of Mexican's domicile in France, 51 (2) Semanario (5a ép.) 1609 (1938).

[509] Philonenko, Prescripción Extinctiva en Derecho International Privado, 2 (5) Revista de la Facultad de Derecho de México 53 (1952).

[510] 281 U.S. 397 (1930).

vision affecting substantive rights and obligations arising out of a contract, valid under Mexican law. Consequently, the ruling of the Texas court resulting in an extension of the time limitation for action agreed upon in the contract, amounted to an "attempt to impose greater obligation than that agreed upon." The mere possibility that defendant's property might be seized "in payment of the imposed obligation," was held to amount to a violation of the constitutional guarantee against deprivation of property without due process of law. After declining the argument that the "constitution does not require the states to recognize and protect rights derived from the laws of foreign countries," the Court held that the rights asserted in this case are not based on the full faith and credit clause but on the fourteenth amendment, available also to aliens, adding:

> Moreover, the parties in interest are American companies. The defense asserted is based on the provision of the policy and on their contracts of reinsurance. The courts of the state, i.e., Texas, confused this defense with that based on the Mexican Code. They held that, even if the effect of the foreign, i.e., Mexican statute was to extinguish the right, plaintiff's removal to Texas prior to the bar of the foreign statute removed the cause of action from Mexico, and subjected it to the Texas statute of limitation. And they applied the same rule to the provisions of the policy. Whether or not that is a sufficient answer to the defense based on foreign law we may not consider; for no issue under the full faith and credit clause was raised. But in Texas, as elsewhere, the contract was subject to its own limitations.

PART FOUR

Criminal Law

22. CRIMINAL CONFLICT LAW

Like substantive rules of private law, substantive criminal statutes need to be defined in regard to their conflict application, particularly since the traditional maxim of the *lex loci delicti* has lost considerable ground. As a consequence, modern criminal codes, among them the Mexican federal as well as most of the state criminal codes, have adopted a number of conflict rules expanding the applicability of criminal statutes beyond the scope of the traditional territorial principle. In the same vein, common law countries have developed substantially identical rules through judge-made law, particularly by interpreting statutory criminal enactments in the light of new trends. Such rules will achieve, of course, international recognition only if they conform not only to treaties in force, if any, but also to generally recognized principles of international law, some of them authoritatively stated in the Case of the S.S. Lotus.[511]

TREATY LAW

As between Mexico and the United States, the Consular Convention of 1942 reserves to local authorities the jurisdiction over criminal acts committed on board private vessels flying the flag of the other contracting country, when located "within the territory or territorial waters" of the other, provided such acts constitute a "crime according to the laws of the receiving State," and subjects the "person guilty thereof, to punishment as a criminal" to the same authorities. A consular officer may intervene in these cases only if he is "permitted to exercise [such powers] by the local law" (art. X, para. 2).

[511] (1927), P.C.I.J. Ser. A, No. 10.

Conflict rules also are found in the extradition treaties in force between Mexico and the United States.[512] The basic Convention, signed in 1899, denies extradition whenever the person to be extradited is charged with a crime which, under the "laws of the place where the fugitive or person so charged shall be found," would not justify his apprehension or commitment for trial "if the crime or offense had been there committed" (art. III, para. 1). In regard to the controlling statute of limitations, the Convention provides that extradition may be denied if "legal proceedings or the enforcement of the penalty for the act committed by the person demanded is barred by limitation according to the laws of the country to which the requisition is addressed" (art. III, para. 3).[513]

The Convention on the High Seas, signed at Geneva in 1958 and binding on both countries, contains significant provisions regarding maritime and air piracy committed on or over high seas or in areas "outside the jurisdiction of any State" (art. 15). The Convention supplies its own definition of such acts (art. 15):

(1) Any illegal acts of violence, detention or any act of depredation,

[512] Franco, El Tratado de Extradición entre México y Estados Unidos, (38) El Foro (4a ép.) 93 (1962); Hernández Romo, El Amparo Contra la Extradición, ibid. 103. Parallel provisions are contained in the interamerican Convention on Extradition (Montevideo, 1933): the requesting country must have judicial jurisdiction over the crime punishable in both countries (art. 1); statute of limitations must not have run in either country (art. 3); the request will be decided in accordance with the domestic legislation of the requested country (art. 8); no extradition for political crimes nor military or religious offenses (art. 4). On political qualification, Huerta Pérez, El Delito Político en el Derecho Penal Mexicano (Mexico, 1963); García-Mora, The Present Status of Political Offenses in the Law of Extradition and Asylum, 14 U. Pitt. L. Rev. 371 (1953); The Nature of Political Offenses: a Knotty Problem of Extradition Law, 48 Va. L. Rev. 1226 (1962); Treason, Sedition and Espionage as Political Offenses under the Law of Extradition, 26 U. Pitt. L. Rev. 65 (1964); Vries & Rodríguez Novas, Territorial Asylum in the Americas: Latin American Law and Practice of Extradition, 5 Inter-Am. L. Rev. 61 (1963). On extradition to the United States, Jurisprudencia (pl.) 72 (1964).

[513] Villareal v. Hammond, 74 F. 2d 503 (5th Cir. 1934) (kidnapping punishable both under Texas and Mexican law). In Fernández v. Phillips, 268 U.S. 311 (1925), the question of dual criminality was not raised. Merino v. United States Marshall, 326 F. 2d 5 (9th Cir. 1964), cert. denied 377 U.S. 997 (1964), reh. denied 379 U.S. 872 (1964). Provision of art. 3 para. (1) of the extradition treaty is not affected by art. 19 of the Mexican Constitution, 36 Semanario (5a ép.) 358 (1932). Fraud committed in Oklahoma shows constitutive elements proving dual criminality, Informe Rendido a la Corte Suprema de la Nación, 1931, at 127.

committed for private ends by the crew or the passengers of a private ship or private aircraft, and directed:

(a) On the high seas, against another ship or aircraft, or against persons or property on board such ship or aircraft;

(b) Against a ship, aircraft, persons or property in a place outside the jurisdiction of any State.

The Convention also provides for the right to seize "a pirate ship or aircraft or a ship taken by piracy and under control of pirates, and arrest the persons and seize property on board," provided this is done "on the high seas or any other place outside the jurisdiction of any State" (art. 19) and executed by "warships or military aircraft, or other ships or aircraft on government service authorized to that effect" (art. 21). As to jurisdiction over such acts, the Convention authorizes (art. 19) :

> The courts of the State which carried out the seizure may decide upon the penalties to be imposed, and may also determine the action to be taken with regard to the ships, aircraft or property, subject to the rights of third parties acting in good faith.

Furthermore, the same Convention regulates hot pursuit[514] of a foreign vessel from its internal or territorial waters into the high seas "when the competent authorities of the coastal State have good reason to believe that the ship has violated the laws and regulations of that State" (art. 23). If the foreign vessel is found in the contiguous zone, the pursuit may "only be undertaken if there has been a violation of the rights for the protection of which the zone was established" (art. 23).

Criminal conflict provisions, both jurisdictional and choice-of-law rules, are included in article 11 of the Convention for the Solution of the Problem of the Chamizal (1963) and are discussed elsewhere in this study.

MEXICAN LAW

Both in Mexico[515] and in the United States legislation in matters of

[514] Sobarzo Loaiza, El Derecho de Persecución de Naves en Alta Mar, 12 Revista de la Facultad de Derecho de México 671 (1962).

[515] 1 Carranca y Trujillo, Derecho Penal Mexicano: Parte General 145 (Mexico, 1955) ; Porte Petit, Legislación Penal Mexicana Comparada (Jalapa, 1946), and Evolución Legislativa Penal de México (Mexico, 1965) ; Pavon Vasconcellos, Manual de Derecho Penal Mexicano: Parte General 102 (Mexico, 1967) ; García Ramírez, Los Límites de la Jurisdicción Penal, 19 Boletín del Instituto de Derecho Comparado de México 301 (1966). Cf. Murray, Crim-

criminal law and procedure is primarily within the powers reserved to the several states. In Mexico, the application of federal criminal legislation is limited to the Federal District and Territories while elsewhere throughout the Republic it applies to "matters of federal concern," such as commerce, labor, transportation, patents, copyrights, and to crimes affecting the Republic as a whole. The coverage of the federal Criminal Code is co-extensive with the jurisdiction of federal courts as defined in article 41, para. I, of the Organic Law of the Judicial Power of the Republic (1935) listing *delitos del orden federal* and, therefore, within the jurisdiction of federal courts:[516]

(a) crimes contained in federal laws and treaties;

(b) crimes listed in articles 2 through 5 of the federal Criminal Code;

(c) those committed abroad by Mexican diplomatic agents as well as by the official personnel of legations and by Mexican in their official capacity or otherwise (*oficiales o comunes*);

(d) those committed in foreign embassies or legations (of course, in Mexico);

(e) those in which the Republic is adversly affected (*sujeto pasivo*);

(f) those committed by a federal official or employee in the performance of his functions or in connection therewith;

(g) those committed against a federal official or employee in the performance of his functions or in connection therewith;

(h) those perpetrated against a federal public service even if such service is decentralized or functioning under a license;

(i) those perpetrated against the functioning of a public federal service or affecting instrumentalities used in such service, even if it should be decentralized or operated under a license;

(j) all those which attack, impair or prevent the exercise of any of the powers reserved to the Federation.

In pursuance of paragraph (b) above, federal courts have jurisdiction and apply federal criminal law to "criminal acts, initiated, prepared

---

inal Procedure in the Federal District and Federal Territories of Mexico, 19 U. Miami L. Rev. 251 (1964).

Federal courts have jurisdiction over crimes committed on board ship within Mexican territorial waters, 129 Semanario (5a ép.) 337 (1956), as well as crimes committed close to islands, 127 Semanario (5a ép.) 233 (1956).

[516] Art. 1 of the Federal Criminal Code provides "This Code shall apply in the Federal District and Territories to criminal acts (*delitos*) within the jurisdiction of courts of general jurisdiction (*tribunales comunes*); and throughout the Republic to criminal acts within the jurisdiction of federal courts."

Press Law (D.O. April 12, 1917) provides in art. 36, "This law shall be binding in the Federal District and Territories in regard to criminal acts of general nature (*del orden común*) as provided therein, and throughout the Republic for what concerns criminal acts within the jurisdiction of federal courts."

or committed abroad whenever they produce or are intended to produce results in the territory of the Republic" (art 2, I) [517] as well as
over continuing crimes (art. 3), i.e., those where the act or omission
committed abroad continues in the Republic, regardless of the nationality of the culprit, provided—in both cases—that the criminal act is
one punishable under the federal Criminal Code. Furthermore, federal
criminal law applies and federal courts have jurisdiction over crimes
committed abroad[518] by a Mexican against other Mexicans or against
an alien, or by an aliens against a Mexican, provided (art. 4):

(I)   The accused is found in the Republic;
(II)   The guilty has not been tried definitely (*definitivamente*) in the
        country where he committed the criminal act;
(III)   The violation of which he is accused is a criminal act both in the
        the country where it was committed and in the Republic.

Finally, according to article 5, the following acts "are considered to
have been committed in the Republic," and fall within the scope of the
federal Criminal Code:

(I)   Criminal acts committed by Mexicans or aliens on the high seas
        on board Mexican vessels;
(II)   Acts committed on board a national military vessel anchored in
        a port or in territorial waters of another nation; this rule in-
        cludes also cases of merchant vessels, provided the culprit was
        not tried in the nation to which the port belongs;
(III)   Acts committed on board a foreign vessel anchored in a national
        port or in the territorial waters of the Republic, provided public
        order is disturbed, or the culprit or the affected person (*ofend-
        ido*) were not members of the crew; if this should not be the
        case, reciprocity applies;
(IV)   Acts committed on board of national or foreign aircraft when
        within national territories or airspace, or national or foreign

[517] Forgery committed abroad but taking effect in the Republic is punishable in Mexico, Jurisprudencia (pl.) 167 (1964).

[518] In case a crime is committed abroad and tried in Mexico, the Federal
Criminal Code applies, having in such situations a "general federal function"
and federal courts have jurisdiction, 13 Semanario (5a ép.) 578, 1322 (1923);
35 Semanario (5a ép.) 1500 (1932); 38 Semanario (5a ép.) 2377 (1933).
Murder committed by a Mexican abroad against an alien is punishable under
art. 4 of the Federal Criminal Code, Jurisprudencia (crim.) 462 (1964); 90
Semanario (5a ép.) 1738 (1947); exclusive jurisdiction of federal courts, 41
(4) Semanario (5a ép.) 31 (1936).

In a criminal case for counterfeiting United States currency the fact that
the pertinent United States statute required to be cited by art. 238, III, of
the Federal Criminal Code only referred to by page in the U.S.C. was considered not sufficient to support *amparo*, 109 (3) Semanario (5a ép.) 1790
(1952).

territorial waters, in cases analogous to those involving vessels in the preceding sections; and

(V)   Acts committed in Mexican embassies and legations.

From the provisions just quoted it appears that Mexico, even though adhering in principle to the territoriality of its criminal statutes, has adopted also the protective principle, not only in regard to the Republic and its various agencies and activities, like the diplomatic and consular services abroad, but also by applying its substantive criminal law to crimes committed abroad against individual Mexican nationals (art. 4) by Mexicans or aliens. In some instances the coverage appears to adopt the principle of nationality by including crimes committed abroad by Mexicans against aliens (art. 4).[519]

The protective principle adopted already in the previous federal Criminal Code (1871) clashed with the American territorialistic position in the famous Cutting case (1887).[520] Cutting, an American national, was indicted and found guilty in a Mexican court for having libelled in his newspaper, published in El Paso, Texas, a Mexican national, the court relying on article 186 of the federal Criminal Code that offenses "comitted in a foreign country . . . by a foreigner against Mexicans, may be punished in the Republic." The United States government protested and demanded "instant release of A. K. Cutting . . . now unlawfully imprisoned at Paso del Norte," taking the position that

---

[519] The alleged fraud in connection with documents of an automobile to be transported from the United States to Mexico was held to have been committed in Puebla, regardless of the fact that the defendant, a United States national, had formed the intention to commit fraud when in New York, consequently within the jurisdiction of state court, Jurisprudencia (pl.) 162 (1964). Similarly, the illegal appropriation of a chattel in the United States, subsequently brought to Mexico and sold there, remains in the jurisdiction of state courts and their criminal codes. A collision in Mexico with a car stolen in the United States is within the coverage of state criminal code since the theft and collision are not interrelated, Jurisprudencia (pl.) 109 (1964). However, federal jurisdiction and law controls the abduction of a woman to the United States and rape there, Jurisprudencia (pl.) 316 (1964), as well as a crime committed on board a Mexican warship in a Mexican port, Jurisprudencia (pl.) 54 (1964), and a crime committed on a Mexican vessel on high seas, Jurisprudencia (pl.) 151 (1964).

Note art. 1 of the draft prepared by the Mexican Academy of Criminal Sciences in 1965, Código Penal Tipo para Latinoamérica 491 (Mexico, 1967).

[520] Ebb, International Business: Regulation and Protection 76 (1964); also Katz & Brewster, The Law of International Transactions and Relations: Cases and Materials 544 (1960), with the translation of the Chihuahua judgment (1886); Moore, Report on Extraterritorial Crime and the Cutting Case, [1887] U.S. For. Rel. 757.

penal laws of a country have no extraterritorial force. Each state may, it is true, provide for the punishment of its own citizens for acts committed by them outside of its territory; but this makes the penal law a personal statute, and while it may give rise to inconvenience and injustice in many cases, it is a matter in which no other government has the right to interfere. To say, however, that the penal laws of a country can bind foreigners and regulate their conduct, either in their own or any other country, is to assert a jurisdiction over such countries and to impair their independence.

The Government not only claimed that an indemnity be paid to Cutting but also urged "in the interest of good neighborhood and future amity, that the statute proposing to confer such extraterritorial jurisdiction, should, as containing a claim invasive of the independent sovereignty of a neighboring and friendly state, be repealed." Mexico in a note of February 16, 1888, stood its ground and stated that the "right which every nation has to impose national conditions upon the entry of foreigners upon its own territory conveys with it the rights within the limits of legislation to hold such foreigners responsible for acts they have committed abroad against that nation, or against any of its citizens or subjects." With respect to the demand to change its legislation in this matter, Mexico countered that the United States "can not request Mexico to modify her legislation in this respect, even supposing that legislation to contain the alleged defect, for the United States themselves in one or more of their territorial entities hold and follow substantially the same legislation." The affair ended when both countries dropped the matter.[521]

By way of illustration, two interesting Mexican cases may be presented. In one[522] the accused, a Mexican national, married his first wife in Sonora in 1949, obtained in 1950 a Chihuahua divorce and married his second wife on September 10, 1951, in a ceremony in New Mexico. On motion of his first wife made in a Mexican court late in September 1951, his Chihuahua divorce was declared to be null; nevertheless, defendant succeeded in obtaining a new divorce decree against his first wife in November of the same year. Found guilty of bigamy and sentenced to three years and three months in prison and a fine of

---

[521] [1888] 2 Foreign Rel. 1114 (1889).

[522] 124 Semanario (5a ép.) 329 (1954). Accused married in the United States four days after obtaining divorce in Mexico, in violation of judicial order not to remarry within one year; after returning to Mexico with her new husband accused was found guilty under 168 of the Federal Criminal Code (resistance to authority), even though the marriage took place abroad, Jurisprudencia (pl.) 164 (1964).

one hundred pesos, he attacked this judgment by *amparo* on two grounds. The first urged that his marriage in New Mexico had no legal effects in Mexico since it was never registered in accordance with article 161 of the federal Civil Code; the court, however, decided that such registration relates only to civil effects of a foreign marriage while for the purposes of criminal responsibility the mere fact of a subsequent illegal marriage suffices. The second attack was directed against the application of Mexican criminal law to an act comitted abroad, i.e., the marriage in the United States, but was equally unsuccessful. The court took the position that article 4 of the federal Criminal Code has adopted in this regard the personal principle and imposed criminal responsibility on Mexican nationals for acts committed abroad against Mexicans and even aliens, provided the accused is found in the Republic and has not been tried abroad for the crime punishable under Mexican as well as under the *lex loci delicti*.

In another case[523] the indictment charged a Mexican national with rape committed in the United States. On *amparo* the Mexican Supreme Court found the lower court's reliance on the *lex loci delicti* to be insufficient to support conviction, since the burden of proving foreign law was upon the public prosecutor, but was not met.

On the interstate level, the effect of criminal judgments in sister states is guaranteed only by the general terms of paragraph (1) of article 121 of the federal Constitution. It may be added that interstate extradition is regulated in article 119 of the federal Constitution, imposing on the states the duty to extradite "criminals of the other State or of foreign countries." This constitutional precept is implemented by the Law Regulating Article 119 of the Constitution, enacted in 1953. It provides, *inter alia,* that extradition may be denied if under the laws of the requested state the act involved is not punishable (art. I), or if the requested state itself has the power to prosecute the crime (art. III).

Acts on Board Ship

Criminal conflict rules controlling acts committed on board Mexican vessels are contained, first, in the Criminal Code for the Federal District and Territories which applies, according to article 1, within the Federal District and Territories to "criminal acts within the powers of courts of general jurisdiction; and throughout the Republic to

---

[523] 124 Semanario (5a ép.) 601 (1954).

criminal acts within the jurisdiction of federal courts." In article 5 the Code provides that acts listed under I, II, and III, already quoted, "shall be considered as committed within the territory of the Republic." Thus, the Code imposes federal criminal law on three classes of acts: (i) those committed on board Mexican vessels when on the high seas, regardless of the nationality of the delinquent; when in a foreign port of foreign territorial waters, then provided the delinquent has not been tried there; (ii) on board Mexican warships when in foreign port or foreign territorial waters regardless of a trial of the delinquent there, a reservation omitted here under the probable assumption that such trial would not be permitted by Mexican naval authorities; (iii) on board foreign vessels, without distinction between merchant and military, when in a Mexican port or in Mexican territorial waters and public order was disturbed or non-members of the crew were involved as victims or delinquents; in case the latter qualifications are not met, the matter will depend on reciprocity granted or exercised by the country of the flag, in addition to treaty law, if any.[523a]

Additional provisions have been supplied by the Law of Maritime Navigation and Commerce of 1963. According to article 4

> Mexican laws apply to crimes and misdemeanors committed on board national vessels, except when committed in foreign waters, the delinquents have been subjected to the jurisdiction of the other country.

In cases of criminal acts and misdemeanors committed aboard foreign vessels when in Mexican waters, the same law provides in article 5 that

> Mexican authority will intervene and apply Mexican laws in cases of criminal acts and misdemeanors committed on board foreign vessels in national waters:
>
> I. If public order is disturbed;
> II. If this is requested by the captain of the vessel or by the consul of the country to which the vessel belongs.

The law also contains in article 6, paragraph (2), a saving clause in favor of treaties. Consequently, consular functions in maritime matters

---

[523a] In Nixon v. United States, 352 F. 2d 601 (5th Cir. 1965) the court affirmed conviction for murder on the high seas under federal statute (18 U.S.C.A. § 1111), the case considered "within the special maritime and territorial jurisdiction of the United States (18 U.S.C.A. § 1, para. 1)." The court added that jurisdiction would have "attached even had the trawler been in Mexican waters since the offenses occurred on a vessel of the United States ownership and registry," relying on United States v. Rodgers, 150 U.S. 249 (1893).

as defined in article X of the Consular Convention of 1942, remain unchanged.

Neither Mexican courts nor Mexican writers have undertaken the arduous task of reconciling conflict rules emanating from the two statutory sources just quoted.

As to jurisdiction, article 8 of the Federal Code of Criminal Procedure provides that in cases of sections (I) and (II) of article 5 of the Criminal Code quoted above, jurisdiction is vested in the federal court where the vessel makes its first landing within the national territory: in cases of section (III), it is vested in the court of the port concerned or of the port where the vessel lands.

Maritime Piracy

Piracy is punishable under the federal Criminal Code as a crime against international law (art. 146), apparently regardless of the nationality of the vessel, of the pirates and without even mentioning a limitation to the high seas. Pirates are defined as (i) members of the crew of a vessel, Mexican, foreign or stateless, who take over another vessel by force of arms, or commit robberies there, or do violence to persons there (art. 146, I), thus excluding persons who are not members of the crew of the pirate vessel; or (ii) those who, being on board a vessel and not necessarily members of its crew, seize the same vessel and hand it over voluntarily to a pirate (art. 146, II).[524]

Additional rules originate from the articles 15 through 22 of the Geneva Convention on the High Seas (1958), already discussed.

Acts On Board Aircraft

Mexican statutory law gives no full answer to the question what law applies to criminal acts committed on board aircraft. First of all, it is to be noted that the matter is regulated in two enactments: in the federal Criminal Code (art. 5, IV), and in the subsequent Law of General Means of Communication (art. 309, II). The second difficulty arises from the fact that the Criminal Code extends to aircraft conflict provisions designed primarily to cover criminal acts on board vessels.

Article 5 (IV) of the federal Criminal Code considers as having been committed "within the territory of the Republic" acts

---

[524] Sobarzo Loaiza, La Pirateria en Derecho Internacional y en Derecho Interno, 14 Revista de la Facultad de Derecho de México 476 (1964); Góngora Pimentel, Estudio sobre el Delito de Piratería, 32 Criminalia 136 (1966).

IV. Committed on board national or foreign aircraft within the territory or airspace or national or foreign territorial waters in cases analogous to those contained in the previous sections in regard to vessels.

The use of technical analogy (any other is prohibited by article 14, paragraph 3 of the federal Constitution) creates considerable difficulties by transposing conflict rules designed for maritime navigation to matters connected with aviation. Attempting to follow this rule, section (I) of article 5, namely that "criminal acts committed by Mexicans or by aliens on board national vessels when on high seas," applies to aircraft, would cover in aviation cases criminal acts by Mexicans or aliens on board Mexican-registered aircraft in flight over the high seas. This rule, however, is not included in section (IV) since the latter applies in terms only to aircraft in flight over the national territory or over national or foreign territorial waters, without including the high seas. Proceeding to section (II), it extends the coverage of the federal Criminal Code to "acts on board national military vessels in a foreign port or in territorial waters of a foreign nation," also including Mexican merchant vessels. Transposed to aircraft this may mean that criminal acts committed on board Mexican aircraft at a foreign airport or on (or over) foreign territorial waters will be punishable under the same Criminal Code. Finally, section (III) of the same article 5 refers to acts "committed on board foreign vessel anchored in a national port or within territorial waters of the Republic," with the provisos already mentioned. Again transferred to aviation, this provision may be understood as including acts on board foreign aircraft at a national airport or in flight over territorial waters of the Republic.

This attempt at reasonable statutory interpretation, however, leaves unanswered two simple questions: what law applies to criminal acts committed on board Mexican aircraft in flight over foreign territory, and what law governs acts committed on board foreign aircraft in flight within the Mexican airspace. The first question is answered in article 309 (II) of the Law of General Means of Communication to the effect that "Mexican laws" apply to

II. Criminal acts that have occurred on board of any aircraft in flight over foreign territory whenever these acts produce effects or are intended to produce them within the Mexican territory.

Here again, a general reference to "Mexican laws" as controlling is used. And again, the assumption may be made that this reference is to be understood not as pointing to one of the several state criminal codes, but simply to the federal Criminal Code. The second question as to the substantive criminal law controlling acts on board foreign aircraft in flight within the Mexican airspace finds no express answer in Mexican statutory law since the federal Criminal Code, as already stated, applies only within the Federal District and Territories (art. 1), including their airspace, and beyond this only to cases specifically stated in articles 2 to 5 of the same Code. The difficulty may be overcome by reliance on the Law of National Property (1944) which lists the airspace over the Republic as belonging to the nation and justifies the application of federal law.

As to jurisdiction, the Organic Law of the Federal Judicial Power may again be cited. It allocates, *inter alia,* to the federal judiciary criminal acts violating federal statutes and treaties as well as those included in articles 2 to 5 of the federal Criminal Code. Furthermore, the Federal Code of Criminal Procedure (art. 9) determines venue, again using the unfortunate technique adopted in article 5 (IV) of the federal Criminal Code, by providing in article 8:

> in cases within sections I and II of article 5 of the criminal code the court within whose territory the national port where the vessel arrives, is situated, shall have jurisdiction; and in cases of section III of the same article, the court having jurisdiction over the port where the vessel is found or where it arrives.

It may be noted that the Convention on Offenses and Certain Other Acts Committed on Board Aircraft, signed at Tokyo in 1963 by the United States, is not yet in force.

Air Piracy

Among the crimes against international law, the Mexican federal Criminal Code deals with piracy (art. 146) which may involve either vessels or aircraft. In regard to the latter, the Code simply provides that rules regarding maritime piracy "shall apply equally to aircraft" (art. 146, III). Following this directive, two types of air piracy emerge. One type may be deduced from section (I) of article 146 which includes as potential offenders "members of the crew of a commercial vessel, Mexican, foreign or stateless, who take over by force of arms any vessel (*embarcación*), or commit robberies there, or do violence to person on board thereof." However, transposed to aircraft, this would be an unlikely form of piracy. The second type of piracy defined in section (II) of article 146 brands as pirates those who "being on board a vessel, seize it and hand it over voluntarily to a pirate," as defined in section (I), a rather improbable event. In any case, following the precepts of strict interpretation of criminal statutes, imposed by the federal Constitution (art. 14, para. 3), it follows that mere seizure of an aircraft is not punishable unless the aircraft so seized is handed over to a person who qualifies under the same Code as a pirate.

AMERICAN LAW

American courts started from a strict territorial principle as expressed, for example, in the American Banana case[525] in the sense that "the character of an act as lawful or unlawful must be determined wholly by the law of the country where the act is done." Continuing this trend, the premises of the United States consulate in Mexico City were considered—improperly—to be United States territory in United States v. Archer;[526] consequently, a perjury committed by a Mexican national there was held as committed within the territorial limits of the United States and punishable by the pertinent federal criminal statute. This position was further supported by the fact that, as a consequence of such act, the perjurer entered the United States. An identical situation was again before a federal court in United States v. Rodríguez.[527] However, the court, quoting from the S.S. Lotus case, overcame the territorial principle. Instead, it relied on the protective principle and applied to an act committed in the same consulate the federal criminal statute on the ground that the "entry by an alien into the United States secured by means of false statements or documents is an attack directly on the sovereignty of the United States," and that Congress possessing the power to protect the United States may "rightfully incorporate [protection] into its legislation, without waiting for action to be taken by foreign governments which would grant the United States the right to exercise jurisdiction." Thus the untenable position that United States consulates abroad are United States territory (the comparable provision of the Mexican Criminal Code relies only on an assumption: *se consideran como ejecutados en territorio de la República* . . ., art. 5, V) was abandoned in favor of the protective principle, even though the appellate court felt that the

---

[525] 213 U.S. 347 (1909). For a general discussion, Jurisdiction with Respect to Crime, 29 Am. J. Int'l L. (supp.) 435 (1935).
[526] 51 F. Supp. 708 (1943).
[527] United States v. Rodríguez, 182 F. Supp. 479 (1960).

latter principle is "less known than the territorial principle," adding that, nevertheless, "a sovereign state must be able to protect itself from those who attack its sovereignty."[528]

A different position seems to have been taken by a California court in People v. Buffum,[529] involving a conspiracy to induce resident women to undergo abortions in Mexico. The court held that "our statutes do not provide a criminal penalty" for an agreement to transport women to Mexico and perform abortions there; moreover, the mere admission of proof of Mexican criminal law in this matter was considered prejudicial error on the ground the jury could have assumed that they have to decide under Mexican law. A different position seems to have prevailed in People v. Burt,[530] the court holding that solicitation in order to extort is punishable under the California Criminal Code (art. 518, 182), even though acts have been committed in Mexico. A similar position prevailed in Ramey v. United States;[531] there the fact that the money to be transported into the United States was obtained from the victim in Nuevo Laredo, Mexico, in conse-

---

[528] Rocha v. United States, 288 F. 2d 545 (9th Cir. 1961), cert. denied, 366 U.S. 948 (1961), noted in 15 U. Miami L. Rev. 428 (1961); followed in Marín v. United States, 352 F. 2d 174 (5th Cir. 1967), where the court upheld conviction for smuggling heroin into the United States from Mexico, a crime "committed against the United States at a time when the offender was corporeally out of the jurisdiction of the United States," but was, even though an alien, "found physically within the Court's jurisdiction" (at 177). George, Extraterritorial Application of Penal Legislation, 64 Mich. L. Rev. 609 (1966). Relying on the Rocha case, the court in Rivard v. United States, 375 F. 2d 882 (5th Cir. 1967) restated fundamental rules as follows:

Under international law a state does not have jurisdiction to enforce a rule of law prescribed by it, unless it had jurisdiction to prescribe the rule . . . It is for this reason that the mere physical presence of the . . . alien appellants before the court did not give the District Court jurisdiction. The question remains whether their conduct without the United States had such a deleterious effect within the United States to justify this country in prohibiting the conduct. The law of nations permits the exercise of criminal jurisdiction by a nation under five general principles. They are the territorial, national, protective, universality, and passive personality principles . . . All nations utilize the territorial principle . . . There are, however, two views as to the scope of the territorial principle. Under the subjective view, jurisdiction extends over all persons in the state and there violating its laws. Under the objective view, jurisdiction extends over all acts which take effect within the sovereign even though the author is elsewhere.

See also Ford v. United States, 273 U.S. 593 (1927); Marín v. United States, 352 F. Supp. 174 (5th Cir. 1965).

[529] 40 Cal. 2d 709, 256 P. 2d 317 (1953).   [530] 288 P. 2d 503 (1955).

[531] 228 F. 2d 774 (5th Cir. 1956), reh. denied, 230 F. 2d 171 (1956).

quence of a conspiracy among defendants which took place in California, was not a valid defense. Similarly, a sham marriage in Mexico of a thirteen year old daughter to defendant's common law husband was held[532] not to be a valid defense on the part of the mother against charges of aiding and abetting statutory rape on her daughter.[533]

American criminal law of the air is discussed elsewhere.[534]

[532] People v. Smith, 23 Cal. Rptr. 5 (1962).

[533] Barnes v. United States, 215 F.2d 91 (9th Cir. 1954) (bringing into United States illegal Mexican immigrants); Ivey v. United States, 344 F.2d 770 (5th Cir. 1965) (getting a "fix" in Mexico); De Lina v. United States, 308 F.2d 140 (5th Cir. 1962) (defendant Mexican's constitutional right to remain silent).

The general attitude of American courts is stated in Ex Parte Martínez, 145 S.W. 959 (Tex. 1912) that "Every citizen of the United States is entitled to a speedy public trial before an impartial jury, and a citizen of a foreign country [Mexico], residing within the borders, charged with crime, is entitled to and should receive all rights, privileges and benefits accorded to one of our own citizen—no more and no less."

[534] Bayitch, International Law, 16 U. Miami L. Rev. 240, 260 (1961); and Florida and International Legal Developments, 1962-1963, 18 U. Miami L. Rev. 321, 342 (1963); Boyle & Pulsiter, The Tokyo Convention on Offenses and Certain Other Acts Committed on Board Aircraft, 30 J. Air L. & Comm. 305 (1964); Mendelson, In-flight Crime: the International and Domestic Picture under the Tokyo Convention, 53 Va. L. Rev. 509 (1967).

PART FIVE

Jurisdictional Conflicts

23. JURISDICTION

Understood in its fullest sense, the term jurisdiction means the legally recognized power to exercise public authority or any kind or parts thereof. On the international level, jurisdictional rules emanate from generally recognized principles of international law, from treaties as well as from domestic law.[535]

Jurisdiction as vested in the several sovereign countries is in general terms expressed in the classical passages from The Schooner Exchange v. McFaddon[536] and from the S.S. Lotus.[537] The same principles are reflected in conventions binding both on Mexico and the United States. The interamerican Convention on Rights and Duties of States, signed at Montevideo in 1933, recognizes a country as having the right

> to organize itself as it sees fit, to legislate upon its interests, administer its services, and to define the jurisdiction and competence of its courts,

which powers include everyone within its territorial limits (art. 9, para. 2):

> The jurisdiction of states within the limits of national territory applies to all inhabitants.

[535] Lenhoff, International Law and Rules of International Jurisdiction, 50 Cornell L. Q. 5 (1964); Goldschmidt, Jurisdicción Internacional, 5 Revista Española de Derecho Internacional 163 (1952); Fragistas, La Compétence Internationale en Droit Privé, (104) Recueil de Cours 165 (1961); Deddish, Judicial Jurisdiction: A Study in International and Comparative Law (1968, unpublished thesis in University of Miami Law Library).

[536] 7 Cranch 117 (1812).   [537] P.C.I.J. Ser. A, No. 10 (1927).

Similarly, the Charter of Bogotá, signed in 1948,[538] emphasizes the pervading aspect of personal jurisdiction:

> The jurisdiction of States within the limits of their national territory is exercised equally over all inhabitants, whether nationals or aliens,

while the jurisdiction over things, corporeal or incorporeal within such territories is assumed to be in no need of clarification.

These treaty rules, however, do not contemplate the problem of sovereign jurisdiction on the international level in all its various aspects, namely legislative, judicial, and administrative.[538a] The problems involving legislation and adjudication are of particular interest here. In analyzing conflict problems, the distinction is fundamental, as stated in the Patiño case[539] by the Mexican Supreme Court:

> In principle, judicial jurisdiction, on the one hand, and legislative jurisdiction, on the other, shall be independent from each other; this means that the fact that the law of one country controls the substantive law does not imply its judicial jurisdiction in the matter. In other words, the fact that judicial jurisdiction is vested in one country does not necessarily mean that the laws of the same country control the substance of the case. This distinction is most useful in private international law, because foreign law could never be applied if the two were inseparable.

Generally speaking, it is well recognized that countries may "extend the application of the laws . . . of their courts to persons, property and

---

[538] 2 U.S.T. 2394.

[538a] In an action involving competing natural gas companies interested in supplying natural gas from the United States to Mexico, the court acknowledged that "it is for the authorities in Mexico, and not for the Commission [i.e. Federal Power Commission], to determine what franchise rights are to be granted across the border. But it is for the Commission to determine what it should authorize on this side of the border, and this determination depends to some extent on the situation across the border when the matter involves the exportation of gas . . . The jurisdiction of the authorities of Mexico over franchise rights in Juarez well might be an important factor in the deciding the issues, but is not a reason for excluding one in the situation of petitioner from being heard; for action by the authorities of Mexico does not control the Commission in the exercise of its own authority, or require the Commission to make the orders here involved. Therefore, it cannot, as it were, delegate to those authorities the determination of petitioner's intervention right." Juarez Gas Company, S.A. v. Federal Power Commission, 375 F. 2d 595 (D.C. 1967).

For tax conflict cases, see Missouri-Illinois Railroad Company v. United States, 381 F. 2d 1001 (Ct. Cl. 1967), and Missouri Pacific Railroad Co. v. United States, 392 F. 2d 592 (Ct. Cl. 1968) (Mexican tax on rentals for railroad cars equivalent to United States income tax and, therefore, creditable).

[539] 30 Semanario (6a ép.) 10, 15 (1960).

acts outside their territory," leaving to countries a "wide measure of discretion," provided, of course, that the adjudication process may take place only "in its own territory," as expressed in the S.S. Lotus case. Whether or not a statute is intended to apply extraterritorially depends, first of all, on the existence *vel non* of the international legislative power allocated to the respective country. If this is the case, then the statute may expressly provide that it shall have extraterritorial application; if the statute is silent, courts may find an implied intent. On the contrary, whenever legislation would extend beyond the scope of powers traditionally allocated to independent countries, neither express intent nor interpretation finding implied intent may give such legislative act international validity.

TREATY LAW

Treaty provisions dealing with judicial jurisdiction are rare. As between Mexico and the United States, only a few scattered provisions may be noted. The most articulate jurisdictional rule is found in the Warsaw Convention (art. 28), already quoted. Another provision dealing with jurisdiction involves consular officers and their functions. According to article X of the Consular Convention of 1942, consular officers are vested with two kinds of quasi-judicial functions. One is their exclusive jurisdiction "over controversies arising out of the internal order of private vessel of his country," provided the vessel and the "persons charged with wrongdoing shall have entered territorial waters or a port within his consular district" (art. X, para. 1). The second function consists in mediating disputes "over issues concerning the adjustment of wages and the execution of labor contracts of the crews." In these cases, however, the consular officer is "without authority to settle disputes," or *a fortiori,* decide them. There also is a reservation in favor of local authorities to the effect that such consular mediation "shall not exclude the jurisdiction conferred on the respective local authorities under existing or future laws of the place." Whenever acts on board a vessel of the sending state constitute a "crime according to the laws of the receiving State, subjecting the person guilty thereof to punishment as a criminal;" the consular officer may not exercise jurisdiction "except as he is permitted to do so by the local law" (art. X, para. 2).

The exercise of civil jurisdiction over foreign vessels passing through territorial waters and persons on board, is subject to article 20 of the Convention on the Territorial Sea and the Contiguous Zone signed at Geneva in 1958. In regard to civil proceedings against vessels passing through the territorial waters, the Convention denies the coastal country the right to "levy execution against or arrest the ship for the purpose of any civil action," except for claims "assumed or incurred by the ship itself in the course or for the purpose of its voyage through the waters of the coastal State" (art. 20, para 2). However, these provisions do not affect the "right of the coastal State, in accordance with its laws, to levy execution against or to arrest, for the purpose of any civil proceedings, a foreign ship lying in the territorial sea or passing through the territorial sea after leaving internal waters" (art. 20, para. 3). In regard to persons on board such vessels, the Convention prohibits the coastal country to "stop or divert a foreign ship" for "the purpose of exercising civil jurisdiction in relation to a person on board the ship" (art. 20, para. 1).

In regard to criminal jurisdiction, the same Convention provides that it "should not be exercised on board a foreign ship passing through the territorial sea" by arresting any person on board or conducting an investigation there. An exception is established for arrests or investigation "in connection with any crime committed on board the ship during its passage," provided (a) the consequences of the crime extend to the coastal country; or (b) the crime is of a kind "to disturb the peace of the country or the good order of the terirtorial sea"; or (c) the "assistance of the local authorities has been requested by the captain of the ship or by the consul of the country whose flag the ship flies"; or (d) such measures are "necessary for the suppression of illicit traffic in narcotic drugs" (art. 19, para. 1). However, such action may not be taken by the coastal country in "connection with any crime commited before the ship entered the territorial sea, if the ship, proceeding from a foreign port, is only passing through the territorial sea without entering internal waters" (art. 19, para. 5), as defined in article 5 of the Convention. On the contrary, the Convention imposes no limitations on the exercise of criminal jurisdiction by the coastal country in accordance with its own laws for the "purpose of an arrest or investigation on board a foreign ship passing through the territorial sea after leaving internal waters" (art. 19, para. 2). The Convention also provides for notification of the consular authority of the "flag State" regarding such actions (art. 19, para. 3).

In regard to jurisdiction over vessels on the high seas, the Convention of the High Seas, signed at Geneva in 1958, grants "ships owned or operated by a state and used only on government non-commercial services" (art. 9), on the high seas "complete immunity from the jurisdiction of any state other than the flag state" (art. 9). The same Convention also provides (art. 11) that proceedings to determine the criminal or disciplinary responsibility of the "master or of any other person of the ship" in consequence of a collision or any other "incident of navigation concerning a ship on the high seas" may be "instituted against such persons [only] before the judicial or administrative authorities either of the flag state or of the state of which such person is a national." The right of hot pursuit of a foreign vessel from a country's internal or territorial waters beyond the territorial waters or the contiguous zone is regulated in article 23 of the same Convention.

Finally, the recent Convention for the Solution of the Problem of Chamizal (1963) contains jurisdictional rules regarding conflicts which might arise from the relocation of the international boundary. It was agreed in article 11 that such relocation shall in no way affect

(b) The jurisdiction over legal proceedings of either a civil or criminal character which are pending at the time of, or which were decided prior to, such relocation;

(c) The jurisdiction over acts or omissions occurring within and with respect to the said portions of territory prior to their transfer.

It may be added that equally unaffected by such relocation shall remain the "law or laws applicable to the acts or omissions referred to in paragraph (c)" (art. 11 d).

JUDICIAL JURISDICTION: MEXICAN LAW

Simply stated, every country has the right to establish, within generally accepted rules of international law, its own system of courts and vest in them the administration of justice,[540] including constitutional safeguards to be observed. In regard to aliens they may be discriminatory within the minimum standards as adopted by international law, or wholly undiscriminatory. The Mexican Constitution has taken the latter position by providing in article 14, paragraph (2) that:

No one shall be deprived of life, liberty, property, possessions or rights without a trial by courts previously established, and in accordance with the essential formalities as well as with laws enacted prior to the fact.

[540] De Pina & Castillo Larrañaga, Instituciones de Derecho Procesal Civil 67 (Mexico, 1961). Jurisdiction and competence discussed in 25 Semanario (5a ép.) 1647 (1929).

There are no discriminatory provisions against aliens in regard to judicial jurisdiction in the Mexican procedural codes, except that certain foreign corporations must hold themselves amenable to local courts. This is, for example, the case of foreign banking institutions under the General Law of Credit Institutions and Auxiliary Organizations of 1941 which requires that they must "submit themselves . . . to the courts of the Republic in all matters related to their business within the national territory," for the benefit of "all persons who may hold claims or shares against the institution, through operations or business effectuated in the Republic and which must be performed therein," a jurisdictional grant wholly within the scope of the American long-arm statutes.[541]

On the interstate level, article 121 of the Mexican Constitution indirectly establishes fundamental jurisdictional rules by stating interstate requirements for full faith and credit.[542] Judgments *in personam* presuppose that the person against whom judgment was rendered, submitted expressly or by reason of his domicile to the court after having been personally summoned to appear in court (art. 121, III, para. 2). On the other hand, no jurisdictional requirements have found expression in regard to adjudication of interests in land (art. 121, III, para. 1). General jurisdictional problems have been discussed recently in a separate opinion filed by one of the justices of the Mexican Supreme Court[543] in the following way:

(1) The legislation of each of the several states has effect only within its own territory and, consequently, can have no effect outside of such state (art. 121, I).

(2) Jurisdiction in the sense of legislative jurisdiction only, cannot be extended to include things or persons outside of the territory of the state.

---

[541] The fact that there is a subsidiary of a foreign corporation in Mexico gives the Mexican courts jurisdiction in matters arising out of dealings between the subsidiary and third persons, 28 Semanario (5a ép.) 1573 (1930). For a discussion of Florida long-arm statutes, Bayitch, Florida: Conflict of Laws, 1964-1966, 20 U. Miami L. Rev. 495, 503 (1966).

[542] Jurisdiction on interstate level, Jurisprudencia (civ.) 210 (1965). In commercial litigation jurisdiction is established primarily by express or implied submission by parties (art. 1092 of the Commercial Code), as defined in art. 1093 and 1094, with limitations in art. 1095. In any case, preference will be given to the court of the place "designated by the debtor as the place where he should be required to pay," or of the place "designated in the contract as the place of performance" (art. 1104). Lenhoff, The Parties' Choice of a Forum, 15 Rutgers L. Rev. 414 (1961); Schwind, Derogation Clauses in Latin American Law, 13 Am. J. Comp. L. 167 (1964).

[543] 56 Semanario (6a ép.) 295 (1960).

(3) By reason of brotherhood between the states belonging to the same federation, the constitution permits that judges of one state pass judgments over citizens or residents of another under the following conditions:

    (a) That they are domiciled in the forum state, or

    (b) That they have submitted to the forum by prorogation, and

    (c) If the litigation concerns immovables situated in another state, the judgment will have effect in the latter state only if its own laws so permit (art. 121, III).

(4) Also because of brotherhood and of justice to be administered in accordance with the needs of the times, place and persons, the substantive legislation (not the procedural) passes from one state to another, like matrimonial regimes, the civil status of persons, article 121, section I, notwithstanding, because the state where the citizens arrive from another, agrees to apply the law of the other state, thus making for the limited purposes of private international law the legislation of the former its own. Conclusions derived from these principles are most fruitful: judges of state A cannot apply their procedural laws to inhabitants of state B or vice versa. Judges of state A cannot apply procedural laws of state B to cases before them even if the substantive relations have arisen in the latter.

The Mexican Supreme Court has held repeatedly that a mere notification of defendants residing in another Mexican state does not meet the requirements of article 121, III, of the federal Constitution and that judgments rendered on this basis do not qualify for interstate recognition. It would follow that service of process is effective only on persons within the state of the forum and not on persons outside of the forum state, also on the authority of section I of article 121 of the Constitution which limits the effect of state laws to their own territory. In one of these cases[544] the Supreme Court expressed its position in the following way:

> The formalities of procedure belong to the domain of the law in force at the place where the competent court sits, i.e., the *lex fori,* which law is considered to be in the nature of international public order. However, it is sometimes difficult to determine the area to which the *lex fori* or the foreign law applies. This is particularly true in respect to summonses in cases where the person cited to appear in the court of one State is a resident of another State. Generally, this problem has been decided by applying the rule *locus regit actum;* consequently, the requirements of the summons are governed by the law of the place where

---

[544] 46 Semanario (5a ép.) 3581 (1935); 47 Semanario (5a ép.) 1821 (1937) (involving interstate situation).

the person to be summoned is found. It follows that the summons to appear in court in a divorce suit, must be served in accordance with the law in force at the place of his residence, if the domicile of the party is known; if not performed in this manner, it is impossible to hold that the party has been properly summoned.

It is a pity, of course, that the Court sidestepped the difference between the power of the forum to have summons served in another jurisdiction, and the manner in which such service is to be performed.

Difficulties in perfecting jurisdiction on the interstate level are due, as already indicated, largely to the fact that Mexican procedural codes are patterned after models designed for unitarian states without a dual system of courts and without sovereign judiciaries vested in the several federal entities, i.e., states.

Not only are rules as to interestate service to perfect jurisdiction unsatisfactory but also those governing jurisdiction of Mexican courts, federal as well as state, on the international level. From article 327, paragraph (2) of the Federal Code of Civil Procedure it would seem that only a proper summons is required in order to perfect jurisdiction over a person outside of Mexico:

> In case the defendant resides abroad, the period to enter proceedings (*emplazamiento*) shall be suitably extended, taking into consideration the greater or lesser facility of communications,

particularly if this provision is read in the light of the position taken by the Supreme Court in the Patiño case that

> There is no provision in our procedural law that a person, national or alien not domiciled in Mexico, would enjoy any exemption from jurisdiction or from procedural laws. Only foreign states or their representatives enjoy such privileges.

These difficulties arising from a short-sighted disregard for international implications of judicial jurisdiction cannot be clarified or removed by falling back on the fundamental principles of jurisdiction as contained, for example, in the Code of Civil Procedure for the Federal District and Territories. According to article 144, jurisdiction (*competencia*) will be determined by four factors: the subject matter; the amount involved; the level of the court in the judicial hierarchy; and the territorial contact (venue, *competencia territorial*), of which only the last may be changed by prorogation (art. 149). Territorial competency follows in most cases the maxim *actor sequitur forum rei*. However, there are numerous exceptions to these rules in cases where jurisdiction is completely independent from the location of either party as, for example, in litigations involving inheritance. There, the court of the last domicile of the deceased is "territorially competent" (art. 156, V and VI).[545]

Particular jurisdictional questions may arise in *amparo* proceedings. There, four parties will usually be involved: the amparo-plaintiff; the authority, judicial, legislative or administrative, which issued the act attacked, termed the "responsible authority": the other private party in cases of bilateral judicial proceedings; and, finally, the federal district attorney (art. 5 of the Organic Law of Articles 103 and 107 of the Federal Constitution). As already stated, *amparo* proceedings are within the exclusive jurisdiction of the federal courts. Their jurisdiction is determined in two ways: where the attacked governmental act is enforceable, the court in whose jurisdiction such enforcement takes or is about to take place, takes cognizance; however, if there is no need for enforcement, the court in whose jurisdiction is located the governmental authority which issued the act under attack (art. 36). All parties must be properly notified (art. 27 to 34). In case the defendant private party resides outside of the seat of the court, notice will be given "by the proper authority" (art. 147, para. 3). This means that in an *amparo* proceeding attacking a Mexican divorce involving nonresident American nationals, for example, jurisdiction will be vested in the federal court at the seat of the Mexican divorce court while both litigants in the divorce suit will only be notified at their residence in the United States.

JUDICIAL JURISDICTION: AMERICAN LAW

In the United States jurisdiction[546] of federal courts is determined by

---

[545] 30 Semanario (5a ép.) 12, 18 (1959). Change of territorial competency (venue) is available also in divorce actions, except where expressly prohibited by statute, e.g., art. 75 of the Code of Civil Procedure of Morelos (1945), providing that "In regard to proceedings involving civil status of persons, competency by reason of territory is not changeable by prorogation (*no es prorrogable*)." Consequently, marital domicile remains the only jurisdictional contact.

[546] Developments in the Law: State Court Jurisdiction, 73 Harv. L. Rev. 909 (1960); Briggs, Contemporary Problems in Conflict of Laws: Jurisdiction by Statute, 24 Mon. L. Rev. 85 (1963); Bayitch, Conflict of Laws in Florida, 1957-1963, 18 U. Miami L. Rev. 269, 275 (1963), and Florida: Conflict of Laws, 1964-1966, 20 U. Miami L. Rev. 495, 503 (1966). In regard to Mexican corporations doing business in the United States, e.g., Compañía Mexicana Refinedora Island v. Compañía Metropolitana de Oleoproductos, 250 N.Y. 203, 164 N.E. 907 (1928); Wells Fargo & Co. of Mexico, S.A. v. McArthur Bros. Mercantile Co., 26 P. 2d 1021 (1933); Latimer v. S.A. Industries

the Judiciary Act, and by state law, constitutional, statutory and case, for state courts, both subject to constitutional standards of due process. A few cases involving Mexico may serve as illustrations. The requirement of doing business on the part of Mexican corporations as defendants was at issue in a number of cases.[547] In another, the enforcement of a subpoena[548] was involved. In an action by the wife against her husband's employer, a foreign railway company, to satisfy her alimony by attaching his wages earned in Mexico, the court[549] held that it has jurisdiction under the rule in Harris v. Balk[550] and that plaintiff is entitled to judgment unless "such judgment when paid would not be an acquitance in the courts of Mexico." From an expert opinion the court concluded that an Arizona judgment would not be a bar or defense to a suit for the same amount in Mexico as it would be here, and held that even though "there is no international rule, or law, or treaty . . . requiring that they [i.e., Mexican courts] give full faith and credit to judgments of this country's courts," the company "ought not to be compelled to pay such debt to an Arizona creditor when it is not possible but probable it would have to pay it again."

Reunidas F. Matarazzo, 175 F. 2d 184 (2d Cir. 1949), cert. denied, 338 U.S. 867 (1949); Compañía de Astral, S.A. v. Boston Metals Company, 205 Md. 237 (1953), 107 A. 2d 357 (1954); Richter v. Impulsora de Revolcadero, S.A., 278 F. Supp. 169 (N.Y. 1967).

Cf. Uniform Interstate and International Procedure Act, text in 11 Am. J. Comp. L. 415 (1962).

[547] E.M. Fleischmann Corp. v. Resources Corp. International, 211 F. 2d 204 (3d Cir. 1954), affirming 114 F. Supp. 843 (1953); cf. 105 F. Supp. 681 (1953); but see Pesquero del Pacífico, S.R.L. v. Superior Court, 201 P. 2d 553 (Cal. 1949). Operation of aircraft in New York by a nonresident (Mexican) corporation makes it amenable to service of process, Hayes v. Aeronaves de Mexico, 222 N.Y.S. 2d 523 (1961), aff'd, 230 N.Y.S. 2d 291 (1962).

[548] S.E.C. v. Minas de Artemisa, S.A., 150 F. 2d 215 (9th Cir. 1945). Note, Subpoena of Documents Located in a Foreign Jurisdiction Where Law of Situs Prohibits Removal, 37 N.Y.U. L. Rev. 295 (1962).

[549] Weitzel v. Weitzel, 27 Ariz. 117, 230 P. 1106 (1924).

[550] 198 U.S. 215 (1905).

24. CIVIL PROCEDURE

It is generally accepted that jurisdictional as well as procedural rules, including those governing evidence, are governed by the *lex fori*. This rule is restated in the Warsaw Convention (art. 28, para. 2) :

> Questions of procedure shall be governed by the law of the court to which the case is submitted.

The same rule obtains also in Mexican law as expressed in the Patiño[551] case:

> The forms regarding procedure are controlled by the law in force in the place where the court sits, i.e., by the *lex fori*, which rule is considered to be one of public international order.

The impact of litispendency in international situations has been litigated in Mexico and in the United States. Mexican courts seem to deny any effect to the fact that the same issue is being litigated between the same parties in a foreign country. In the Patiño case, for example, the Supreme Court stated that there is "no provision in our legislation which would accept litispendency and connexity in relation to courts of various nations, which attitude of Mexican legislation reflects the solution suggested by legal doctrine that litispendency and connexity may intervene only between the courts of the same country." This position was further supported by the argument that the facts of litispendency and connexity have "only internal effect, since litispendency and connexity are designed to avoid contradictory judgments which would share the same authority of *res judicata* as well as the same executory force, without leaving a criterion when to prefer one to the other, assumed, of course, that both originate in Mexican courts.

American courts, however, have adopted a less rigid attitude. An action for damages was dismissed because plaintiff's subsidiary in Mexico has brought in Mexico an action for the same damages; it is significant that the court took this position regardless of the possibility that the statute of limitation of the *lex fori* in the United States might bar the claim after the action in Mexico would have been decided.[552]

[551] 30 Semanario (6a ép.) 12, 63, 100 (1960).   [552] See supra note 547.

EVIDENCE

Various facets of the law of evidence[553] are, as a rule, determined by the *lex fori*. There are, first of all, two treaties to be taken into account in regard to evidentiary documents. One is the Protocol on Uniformity of Powers of Attorney (1940), already discussed. The other is the Consular Convention of 1942.[554] Its article VII, paragraph (2), provides that

> Instruments and documents thus executed and copies and translations thereof, when duly authenticated by the consular officer, under his official seal, shall be received as evidence in the territories of either State, as original documents or authenticated copies, as the case may be, and shall have the same force and effect as if drawn up or executed before a notary or other public officer duly authorized in the State by which the consular officer was appointed; provided, always, that such documents shall have been drawn and executed in conformity to the laws and regulations of the State where they are designed to take effect.

Generally speaking, public documents originating abroad will be recognized in Mexico provided they are authenticated by the diplomatic or consular authorities (art. 131 of the Federal Code of Civil Procedure), public documents being defined as those executed by public officials vested with public trust, within their authority and within the scope of their functions (art. 129).[555] The intrinsic evi-

[553] Alcalá-Zamora, Unificación de la Prueba en el Proceso Civil de los Países Hispanoamericanos, 16 (46) Boletín del Instituto de Derecho Comparado de México 97 (1963).
The immigration status of the witness does not affect admissibility of his testimony, 60 Semanario (5a ép.) 1054 (1939); 95 Semanario (5a ép.) 336 (1948); Cortes Figueroa, Sobre el Testimonio de Extranjeros, 10 (37) Revista de la Escuela Nacional de Jurisprudencia 173 (1948). *Informatio ad perpetuam* involving alien, 127 Semanario (5a ép.) 110 (1956).
The admissibility in evidence of a sum of money taken in Mexico from the person of defendant accused of illegal transportation of currency and bank-robbery (Hardin v. United States, 324 F. 2d 553, 5th Cir. 1963) was attacked on the ground that the seizure was illegal in view of the fourth amendment, but without success on the ground that defendant did not prove that his arrest in Mexico was illegal nor did he offer any proof as to the controlling Mexican law.

[554] Testimony by consular officers in civil, contentious-administrative, labor and criminal cases is regulated in art. II of the Consular Convention of 1962, see Appendix II.

[555] Evidentiary value of a self-serving affidavit executed in the United States, 99 Semanario (5a ép.) 648 (1949); of documents executed abroad, 42 Semanario (5a ép.) 1924 (1960).

dentiary value of foreign documents was discussed by the Mexican Supreme Court in the Patiño case:[556]

> Whoever wants to base his right on a foreign document whose evidentiary value depends of the laws of the place, must also submit foreign laws to be explored by the courts of [this] country; and in case the party does not produce such laws, the conclusion by the court that it is unable to evaluate the documents and that the party involved did not substantiate its allegations, is correct; and it is of no avail that the same party alleges it does not rely on foreign but on Mexican law, as long as the party attempting to prove its claim under foreign law, submits foreign documents.

PROOF OF FOREIGN LAW

One of the particular questions involving evidence concerns the way foreign law is to be proven whenever it shall apply.[557] Since the adage *iura novit curia* applies only to the forum's own law, special rules have developed in regard to proof needed to show the law in force in a foreign country.

Mexican Law

The Code of Civil Procedure for the Federal District and Territories and the Federal Code of Civil Procedure contain in regard to proof of foreign law[558] identical provisions (art. 284 and 86, respectively), repeated in a number of state procedural codes:

> Only facts need to be proved; law only when it is based on foreign laws or on usages, customs or case law (*jurisprudencia*).

The requirements of proof of "usages, customs and case law" includes not only those belonging to foreign legal systems but also those developed in Mexico. Substantially the same rule regarding foreign laws is repeated in the Commercial Code with the addition that "whoever relies on them must prove their existence as well as their applicability to the case" (art. 1197). The reason for the general rule is found in

[556] 30 Semanario (6a ép.) 13, 63, 100 (1960).

[557] Eder, Tentative Notes on Proof of Foreign Law in Latin America, A.B.A. Section on Int'l & Comp. Law, Proceedings, 1961, at 160; Loreto, El Conflicto de Leyes en Materia de Prueba en el Derecho Internacional Privado, (22) Revista de la Facultad de Derecho 9, 19 (Caracas, 1961).

[558] Art. 14 of the new Tamaulipas Civil Code (1961) expressly provides that "interested parties must prove the existence of foreign laws upon which they base their claims." Sister state laws are not foreign laws and not subject to special evidentiary rules, 74 Semanario (5a ép.) 6735 (1943).

the Patiño case.[559] There the court pointed out that "Mexican courts are not organs of foreign laws," and that foreign laws "are not imposed [upon Mexican courts] by their own force but only by virtue of the decision of the legal system which refers to them." Therefore, the burden of proof is upon the party invoking it.[560]

The rule was, again, stated in another opinion[561] in the following way:

> Whoever relies on foreign law must prove its existence as well as applicability in the case. The proof of foreign law need not necessarily be by way of presenting the code or other document, since it is sufficient to prove in a reliable way the text of the law upon which the litigated claim rests; this may be done by information supplied by the Secretariat of Foreign Relations.

In regard to the requirements of showing the applicability of a rule of foreign law to the case before the court, the Supreme Court decided that the information supplied by French diplomatic and consular officers in regard to a contested French matrimonial regime might only be considered as an opinion. After quoting extensively from Lessont's *Teoria General de la Prueba en Derecho Civil* (1906), the Court decided that the proof presented was insufficient. The same position was taken by the Supreme Court in a subsequent case.[562]

Recently, Mexican courts have admitted proof of foreign law by experts. Indeed, there is no reason to exclude expert opinion from the statutory definition supplied in article 143 of the Federal Code of Civil Procedure, admitting expert opinion "in questions involving science or art."

American Law

Common law courts consider law in force in a foreign country as a simple fact. It has to be properly alleged by the party relying on it as well as proven, to be determined by the judge and not by the jury.[563]

---

[559] 30 Semanario (6a ép.) 65 (1960).

[560] 7 Semanario (5a ép.) 1332 (1920); 14 Semanario (5a ép.) 432 (1924).

[561] 124 Semanario (5a ép.) 357, 367 (1955); see also 5 Revista de la Facultad de Derecho de México 280 (1955).

[562] 36 Semanario (6a ép.) 65 (1960).

[563] Sommerich & Busch, Foreign Law: a Guide to Pleading and Proof (1959); Jeffries, Recognition of Foreign Law by American Courts, 35 U. Cinc. L. Rev. 578 (1966); also Schlesinger, Die Behandlung des Fremdrechts im amerikanischen Zivilprozess, 27 Rabel's Ztschr. 54 (1962).

This rule is supplemented by a number of presumptions, the most important among them that foreign law will be considered to be identical with the *lex fori* unless the contrary is proven.[564] This presumption is sound whenever the law of another common law country is to be ascertained. However, its usefulness is doubtful when the foreign law is of the civil law type. In such situations, courts have repeatedly shown reluctance to apply the presumption of identity. Instead, they requested a proof of foreign law to avoid dismissal of the action without or, in some jurisdictions, with prejudice.[565]

In federal[566] as well as in most state courts these rules have been amended or completely changed by statutory enactments, particularly in states which have adopted the Uniform Judicial Notice of Foreign Law Act. As an example, the text of the act as adopted in Florida may be cited:[567]

> The existence and the tenor or effect of all foreign laws may be proven as fact by parol evidence; but if it shall appear that the law in question is contained in a written statute or code, the court may, in its discretion, reject any evidence of such law which is not accompanied by a copy of such code or statute.

In other states different rules prevail. California, for example, has enacted a statute,[568] imposing upon courts the duty to take judicial notice of:

> (4) The law and statutes of foreign countries and of political subdivisions of foreign countries; provided, however, that to enable a party to ask that judicial notice thereof be taken, reasonable notice shall be given to the other parties to the action in the pleadings or otherwise . . . In all these cases the court may resort for its aid to appropriate books or documents of reference. In cases arising under subdivision 4

[564] Mexican law presumed to be identical with the *lex fori*, Blochman Commercial and Savings Bank v. Ketcham, 171 P. 1084 (1918); People v. Spitzer, 208 P. 181 (1922); Nesbit v. MacDonald, 263 P. 1007 (1928); Bobala v. Bobala, 33 N.E. 2d 845 (Ohio, 1940); deYoung v. deYoung, 165 P. 2d 457 (1946); Silveyra v. Harper, 187 P. 2d 83 (Cal. 1947); Glasband v. Hussong, 304 P. 2d 225 (1956); Medina v. Hartman, 260 F.2d 569 (9th Cir. 1958); Bostrom v. Tepeyac, S.A., 225 F.Supp. 222 (Tex. 1963).

[565] Luckett v. Cohen, 145 F.Supp. 155 (1956).

[566] A new rule regarding determination of foreign law is contained in the amended R. 44 of Federal Rules of Civil Procedure, authorizing courts to "consider any relevant material or source, including testimony," the determination of foreign law to be "treated as a ruling on a question of law." Miller, Federal Rule 44.1 and the Fact Approach to Determining Foreign Law, 65 Mich. L. Rev. 613 (1967).

[567] §92.04 Fla. Stat. (1965).

[568] Code of Civil Procedure, art. 1875 (1957).

of this section, the court may also resort to the advice of persons learned in the subject matter, which advice, if not received in open court, shall be in writing and made a part of the record in the action or proceeding.

If a court is unable to determine what the law of a foreign country or a political subdivision of a foreign country is, the court may, as the ends of justice require, either apply the law of this State, if it can do so consistently with the Constitutions of this State and of the United States, or dismiss the action without prejudice.

In Texas the proof of foreign law is regulated by section 3718 of the Texas Statutes which provides that

The printed statute books of . . . any foreign government, purporting to have been printed under the authority thereof, shall be received as evidence of acts and resolutions therein contained.

In Hunter v. West[569] an action was brought on a bill of exchange executed in Mexico in Spanish, later endorsed in Laredo, Texas. Drawee refused to pay and judgment was recovered against the endorser. Appellant contended that Mexican law should have been applied, alleging that Mexican law is in the form of a code; but it was not produced according to Section 3718. The court held Mexican law in the matter to be identical with the *lex fori*. The same rule was followed in the already discussed Bostrom v. Seguros Tepeyac case,[570] the court relying on the argument that "the civil law originally prevailed in both Texas and Mexico."

In relation to Mexican law two particular situations may arise. One, when Mexican or Spanish law, or both, are applicable as the law in force at the time when such law was the law of the land. In these cases Spanish or Mexican law need not to be proven by parties because courts will take judicial notice of the laws of a preceding sovereign.[571] The other situation involves the Texas doctrine already discussed.

FOREIGN JUDGMENTS

Being federally organized, both Mexico and the United States regulate the recognition of judgments on the interstate (including federal-state) as well as on the international level.

---

[569] 293 S.W. 2d 686 (Tex. 1956).   [570] 225 F. Supp. 222, 229 (Tex. 1963).
[571] United States v. Perot, 98 U.S. 428 (1878); Freemont v. United States, 17 How. 542 (1854); United States v. Chaves, 159 U.S. 452 (1895); Crespin v. United States, 168 U.S. 208 (1897); Wells v. Stout, 9 Cal. 480 (1858); State v. Sais, 47 Tex. 307 (1877); Ohm v. San Francisco, 28 P. 580 (1891); Martínez v. Gutiérrez, 66 S.W. 2d 678 (1933).

Mexican Law

Starting with the enforcement of judgments on the interstate level, it must be pointed out that the constitutional precept adopted in Mexico is quite similar even though not identical with its counterpart in the United States, both in regard to language and effect.[572]

It is well known that the American full faith and credit clause does not make sister-state judgments directly enforceable in other states of the Union. Such judgments are only recognized to be judgments for the purposes of the common law action in debt on a foreign judgment, and no more. There is, of course, no counterpart to this background in Mexican law, particularly since the very notion of *entera fé y credito* is utterly foreign to civil law. Just because of this, it seems, it is generally recognized in Mexico that a judgment rendered in one federal unit (state) will be recognized as a judgment in another, and enforced there in non-contentious proceedings[573] without the necessity of a new action upon such judgment. The requirements established, for example, in article 602 of the Code of Civil Procedure for the Federal District and Territories, are:

(I) that the demand is for a sum certain or a specified thing;

(II) that judgments affecting immovables or interests in immovables in the District and Territories, are in accordance with their laws;

(III) that judgments dealing with personal claims or with civil status have been recovered in proceedings based on express submission of the charged party (*persona condenata*) or by reason of domicile;

(IV) that the charged party was personally summoned to appear in court.

Interstate rules regarding enforcement of judgments appear also in the codes of civil procedure in force in the several states. These

---

[572] Briseño Sierra, El Título Ejecutante, 8 (31-32) Revista de la Facultad de Derecho de México 63 (1958). Cf. Nadelmann, Cooperación Interamericana en Materia de Reconocimiento de Sentencias: Algunos Datos Recientes de Interés, 19 Boletín del Instituto de Derecho Comparado de México 517 (1966).

[573] Interstate enforcement, 33 (1) Semanario (5a ép.) 978 (1933); Jurisprudencia (pl.) 146 (1964). Fix Zamudio, Breves Reflexiones sobre la Reglamentación de la Jurisdicción Voluntaria en el Código de Procedimientos Civiles para el Distrito y Territorios Federales . . . 1932, (40) El Foro (4a ép.) 25 (1963). The Civil Code of Oaxaca (1944), for example, has in § 13 (2) an express provision that "Acts involving civil status meeting requirements of the other States, of the Federal District and Territories, shall be valid in the territory of the State of Oaxaca."

rules are, of course, limited by the constitutional maxims contained in article 121. However, without waiting for the promised nation-wide enactment, several states have adopted their own rules. The Code of Civil Procedure of Sonora, for example, stays in article 356 the following provision:

> Judgments rendered by national courts shall take effect in this State [i.e., Sonora] with no more limitations than those established in section III, article 121 of the General Constitution of the Republic, whenever they should be enforced or take effect in another State, in the Federal District or Territories.

It may be added that under the same Code a collateral attack is available to a third party only if a right connected with the judgment is proven, provided the judgment was "the product of fraudulent practices or collusion to the detriment" of the third party (art. 357, I).

Where a judgment has been rendered in a foreign country,[574] the first question is what law will control its recognition and local enforceability, federal or state. There is a view which looks upon foreign judgments as affecting international relations and, therefore, are a matter of federal concern to be controlled by federal procedural law and administered by federal courts. As supporting arguments are adduced article 73, XVI, of the Mexican Constitution as well as the language used in article 605 of the Code of Civil Procedure for the Federal District and Territories, setting up conditions for the enforcement of foreign judgments in general terms "in the Mexican Republic," as distinguished from those provisions of the same Code limited in their applicability to the Code's primary territorial coverage. However, the argument that the matter of foreign judgments was "federalized" as dealing with the status of aliens, was rejected by the Mexican Supreme Court.[575] The Court took the position that the legislation of Sonora regarding foreign judgments has nothing to do with the status of aliens. Not only does this legislation not affect the civil rights (*derechos civiles*) of aliens, but is applicable to nationals

---

[574] 2 Sodi, La Nueva Ley Procesal 35 (Mexico, 1946); Alfonsín, La Ejecución Extranacional de las Sentencias en Materia Civil y Comercial, 18 (70) Anales de Jurisprudencia (2a ép.) 339 (Mexico, 1951); MacLean, Introducción al Estudio de la Extraterritorialidad de las Sentencias, 16 (47) Boletín del Instituto de Derecho Comparado de México 325 (1963); MacLean, La Eficacia de las Sentencias Extranjeras, 18 Boletín del Instituto de Derecho Comparado de México 3 (1965). Form for application in Pallares, Formulario de Juicios Civiles 162 (Mexico, 1956).

[575] 5 Semanario (6a ép.) 121, 127 (1957); Coahuila, 51 (5) Semanario (5a ép.) 2882 (1938); Vera Cruz, 114 Semanario (5a ép.) 153 (1953).

as well as aliens when they demand the recognition of a foreign judgment. Equally, the second argument, based on article 606 of the Code
of Civil Procedure, mentioned above, was rejected as not decisive. Instead, the Court considered the matter of recognition of foreign judgments as one within the powers reserved to the states when it stated:

> There can be no doubt that the Congress of Sonora has the power to
> enact legislation as to requirements to be met in order that foreign
> judgments may take effect in the State, since the people exercises under
> article 41 of the federal Constitution its sovereignty through the federal
> authorities whenever these powers are vested in the federal authorities,
> and through the States in matters regarding their internal affairs; and
> in accordance with article 124 of the Constitution, powers not expressly
> delegated to the Federation, are considered to be reserved to the States,
> and it is apparent that the matter here discussed is not reserved to the
> Federation.

It would follow that the recognition and enforcement of foreign
judgments may be sought not only in federal but also in state courts,
according to the applicable rules of their codes of civil procedure. As
an example of a state code, that of Sonora may be quoted. In general
terms, it provides that foreign judgments "establish no presumption
of res judicata . . . unless their validity is judicially declared" by the
courts of Sonora (art. 356). The party invoking a foreign judgment
must "first apply to have its validity declared by the competent judge.
Such a declaration may also be requested through diplomatic channels,
provided treaties or the principle of reciprocity so permit" (art. 475).
Among requirements for recognition listed in article 480, (section VI
and VII) have no counterpart in the federal procedural codes, namely:
that the foreign judgment must not be "contrary to a decision rendered
by a Mexican court," and there must not be "pending before a
Mexican judge an action involving the same matter, between the same
parties and commenced before [the foreign judgment to be recognized]
became *res judicata*."

For federal courts, article 604 of the Code of Civil Procedure for
the Federal District and Territories provides that foreign judicial
decisions shall have in Mexico the effect determined by treaties; if
there is no treaty, reciprocity shall prevail. Once the requirement of
reciprocity is met, a foreign judgment will be granted enforceability
(*exequatur*) under the following conditions:

(I)   the Court must first make a preliminary finding as to whether or
       not the foreign judgment is contrary to the laws of the Republic,
       to treaties, or to principles of international law; if this should

be the case, the court will deny the application stating reasons
which prevent enforcement (art. 428 of the Federal Code of Civil
Procedure) ; the court also will check the compliance of the application with formal requirements (art. 605, I, of the Code of
Civil Procedure for the Federal District and Territories) ;

(II)   that the judgment was rendered in an action in personam (acción personal) ;[576]

(III)   that the performance of the obligation arising out of such judgment is permissible (licita) in the Republic;

(IV)   that defendant was personally served with the summons to appear
in the foreign court;

(V)   that the foreign judgment qualifies for enforcement under the
laws of the country where rendered;[577]

(VI)   that the judgment meets requirements necessary for its authenticity.

In addition to these requirements,[578] it seems reasonable to assume

[576] A judgment rendered by California court dealing with succession to
land situated in the state of Nayarit was not recognized, not only because
of lack of proof of reciprocity but also because only judgments in personam
will be recognized (art. 785 of the previous and art. 605, sec 2 of the present
Federal Code of Civil Procedure) ; moreover, art. 13 of the then valid federal
Civil Code (now art. 14) subjected interests in land to Mexican laws while
it is unusual for a foreign court to decide questions involving land in a
foreign country, even under the color of a judicial decision, since all Mexican laws affecting public policy, among them interests in land, including those
involving succession, are territorial and exclusive (absolutas), 31 Semanario
(4a ép.) 722 (1907).

[577] Burden of proving finality of a foreign judgment, 131 Semanario
(5a ép.) 604 (1965).

[578] In the Patiño opinion, 30 Semanario (6a ép.) 10, 60 (1960), the
Mexican Supreme Court interpreted art. 605 as containing two elements, one
establishing requirements for recognition, and the other a rule by which
the "Mexican judge declares the recognition in the sense that he accepts the
act of a foreign judicial power as an act of the domestic judicial power.
In the words of the writers, the Court continues, the judge domesticates it
(lo nacionaliza). It follows that no foreign judgment may take effect within
the Mexican territory and bind its functionaries, except not to reach an incompatible decision (res judicata), unless the foreign judgment is trans-
formed into decision by a Mexican court. Thus, the Mexican law confers
upon the Mexican judge the power (misión) to recognize the efficacy in
Mexico of a foreign judgment by means of his own decision (acto de voluntad
de él)."

The Code of Civil Procedure for the Federal District and Territories
further provides (art. 607) that the foreign judgment properly translated
(art. 330) will be submitted to the competent court which will allow enforcement after a hearing (artículo) on the authenticity and conformity with
the requirements of the "national laws" on the basis of briefs (escrito) submitted by parties and on the opinion of the Ministerio Público (50 Semanario, 5a ép., 1415, 1938). However, the court will not consider questions

that foreign judgments must not be open to the objections, listed in article 602 of the same Code, already discussed, since the latter requirements are, even though imposed in regard to judgments on the interstate level, couched in general terms so as to cover also foreign judgments.

A foreign judgment may be produced in a Mexican court for two kinds of consideration: for the granting of *exequatur* as preliminary to its enforcement, for which a formal application (*exhorto*) in accordance with article 599 of the Code of Civil Procedure for the Federal District and Territories is necessary; or only as a foreign public document for purposes of evidence in any judicial proceedings. This latter alternative is available without reciprocity and, of course, without any need to meet the requirements listed in articles 602 and 605 of the same Code. This difference was recognized in regard to a judgment by the Supreme Court of Spain which declared null and void a property agreement between spouses. The Mexican Supreme Court expressly observed that, in this case, the foreign judgment was introduced only for purposes of information (*por ser declarativo*), without a request for *exequatur*.[579]

In relation to the United States, Mexico has no treaty dealing with recognition of judgments. Consequently, Mexico requires proof of reciprocity which is constantly held to exist.[580] The same requirement obtains in the United States in jurisdictions following Hilton v. Guyot[581] where it was found that reciprocity is granted in Mexico to judgments rendered by the courts in the United States.

American Law

In most states of the Union judgments rendered in foreign countries[582]

---

of fact nor the law on which the foreign judgment relies (art. 608), 25 Semanario (5a ép.) 585 (1929).

No recognition to foreign criminal judgments, 39 (2) Semanario (5a ép.) 1862 (1936).

[579] 30 Semanario (6a ép.) 116 (1960).

[580] Cruz v. O'Boyle, 197 F. 824 (1912). On enforcement of American judgments abroad generally, Lorenzen, The Enforcement of American Judgments Abroad, 29 Yale L. J. 188 (1919); Nadelmann, Non-Recognition of American Judgments Abroad and What to Do About It, 42 Iowa L. Rev. 236, notes 114, 115 (1957).

[581] 159 U.S. 113 (1895).

[582] Yntema, Enforcement of Foreign Judgments in Anglo-American Law, 33 Mich. L. Rev. 1129 (1935); Reese, The Status in This Country of Judgments rendered Abroad, 50 Colum. L. Rev. 783 (1950); Lloyd, The Enforceability of Foreign Judgments in American Courts, 37 Notre Dame

are recognized under the doctrine of comity.[583] However, particular circumstances may restrict the scope of this doctrine. This was the case in Banco Minero v. Ross & Masterson,[584] involving a Mexican judgment. After acknowledging that "comity which obtains between foreign governments, upon which the principles of international private law are founded, does not require a state to go further than to give a judgment rendered in a foreign country more respect than would be given a like judgment rendered at home," the court continued:

> It would be pushing comity a way beyond its limits for a state to sanction a wrong done its citizens abroad by recognizing the medium through which the wrong was accomplished, when the means by which it was wrought would be regarded as illegal and inequitable if done within her own territorial limits. An individual may carry his politeness to such an extent as to ignore a wrong done to himself, but a state cannot. The duty she owes to her own citizens forbids that she sanctions or gives color to a wrong done him in a foreign country through the medium of its laws and courts; but she must, if possible, redress his wrongs and protect his rights. Comity reaps no harvest of iniquity in the field of justice.

Specific requirements for the recognition of a foreign judgment have been restated in Banco Minero v. Ross,[585] involving a Mexican judgment against an American national, in the following language:

> There is no difficulty . . . in determining the general principles of law which govern the standing of a judgment of a foreign country in our courts. Where there is a competent court, jurisdiction of the parties and the cause, as opportunity for full and fair trial, regular proceedings according to the course of a system of civilized jurisprudence, likely to secure an impartial administration of justice between the citizens of its own country and those of other countries, with nothing to show either prejudice in the court or in the system of laws, or fraud in the procurement of the judgment, and there is no special reason why the comity

---

Law. 88 (1961); Leigh, Enforcement of Judgments and Awards, in Southwest Legal Foundation, Rights and Duties of Private Investors Abroad 439 (1965); Shaaf, The Recognition of Judgments from Foreign Countries . . . , 3 Harv. J. Leg. 379 (1966); Nadelmann, Los Estados Unidos de América y los Acuerdos sobre Ejecución Recíproca de Sentencias Extranjeras, 4 (14) Revista de la Facultad de Derecho de México 47 (1954); also Sentencias Extranjeras por Una Suma de Dinero en los Estados Unidos y en Canadá, 10 (37-40) Revista de la Facultad de Derecho de México 571 (1960). Cf. Lenhoff, Die Anerkennung and Vollstreckung ausländischer Urteile in den USA, 19 Rabel's Ztschr. 201 (1953).

[583] Yntema, The Comity Doctrine, in 2 Vom deutschen zum europäischen Recht: Festschrift für Hans Dölle 65 (Tübingen, 1963); also 65 Mich. L. Rev. 9 (1966).

[584] 138 S.W. 224, 228 (Tex. 1911).   [585] 172 S.W. 711 (Tex. 1911).

of the United States should not allow it effect, the merits of the case in an action in this country, are not subject to retrial on account of errors of law or face in the rendition of the judgment. Hilton v. Guyot, 159 U.S. 113. But jurisdiction being granted, the chief requisite for the recognition of a foreign judgment necessarily is that an opportunity for a full and fair trial was afforded. This means, not a summary proceeding, though sanctioned by the law of the forum, but an opportunity to be heard upon the proof where it is apparent that the cause involves questions of fact, and to have it considered by an unprejudiced court. These proceedings shown in relation to this judgment make it manifest that the trial in the Mexican court was wanting in these esssential elements. They reveal that the action was one unquestionably resting in questions of fact, and that [the American national] pleaded what would have constituted a good defense, yet that he was denied the right to present it, it not appearing that his offer to supply it was unseasonably made. If it be urged that this was warranted by the Mexican procedure, we are unwilling to give conclusiveness to a judgment which such a process sanctions. The judgment and the recitals which accompany it are a maze of words; but, as we interpret their vague and confused statements, it appears to have been rendered upon no proof whatsoever. It furthermore appears that [the American national] was denied an appeal from the judgment upon what seems to us to have been a frivolous ground; namely, the omission to affix a stamp to the document of appeal. The entire proceeding appears to have been arbitrary in its nature and summary in its execution; and the court [below], in our opinion, properly declined to give the judgment effect.

When it was shown that the Chihuahua court violated some of the fundamental rules of its own special proceedings involving titles to *bancos*,[586] and deviated from the principle that "each and every step necessary to perfect that title must be both pleaded and proved," as "would be the case in special proceedings in a Texas court under the Texas statutes," the Texas court found that the appellant plaintiff also omitted pleading an appraisement as well as that certain notices have not been properly published. Moreover, the court considered the description of the property deficient to such an extent that the land could not have been identified from the judgment without extrinsic aid. Finding also proceedings in Chihuahua to correct this deficiency to have been *ex parte* without notice to persons in possession of the litigated land, the court denied recognition.[587]

[586] San Lorenzo Title & Improvement Co. v. Caples, 48 S.W. 2d 329 (Tex. 1932), aff'd, 73 S.W. 2d 516 (1934).
[587] In Willis v. First Real Estate & Investment Co., 68 F.2d 671 (5th Cir. 1934) the court found that the *banco* in question was in 1905 part of Texas and, therefore, any judicial action on the part of Mexico without effect. Even if Mexican courts would have jurisdiction, the proceedings in Chihua-

If a judicial decision is not final under the foreign *lex fori*, it will not be given effect here. A Chihuahua divorce decree lacking the declaration of finality was not considered final, thus lacking qualifications under section 1915 of the California Code of Civil Procedure.[588] However, a Mexican judgment imposing court assessed costs against the losing American plaintiff in Mexico, was considered not unenforceable in Texas as obnoxious to public policy.[589] The court met

---

hua were conducted "in complete disregard of these requirements" (i.e., art. 727-730 of the Chihuahua Civil Code); the court was aware of the fact that the property was, at least inchoately, a part of Texas and first dismissed proceedings on the ground that "it is not proper to sequestrate property referred to, and the sequestration thereof is refused because the same is outside of the jurisdiction of this court." In the renewed proceedings it conclusively appeared not only that the land was outside of the actual jurisdiction of the court, but that there were persons in possession under American titles. When, notwithstanding these facts which made sequestration impossible and established that the land was not vacant or abandoned, the court undertook to proceed further, all these acts were void for which is essential to a proceeding in rem . . . Further, the proceedings were fatally void because on their face they

> show a complete disregard of the fundamental maxim, *audita* [sic] *alteram partem*. They show that notwithstanding the requirement of the code that those in possession be served with notice of the proceedings and the fact known to the court, that there were persons in possession, no notice was given. A domestic judgment taken under such circumstances would be without force and effect . . . Under these circumstances, the foreign judgment relied on is utterly void and invalid.

Action against a Mexican corporation in receivership in Mexico on a note payable in Texas was successful. The court also denied judgment in favor of an intervening Mexican bank invoking a Mexican judgment against defendant on the ground that "there were no pleadings or evidence to support such judgment. Appellee, i.e., plaintiff, was not shown to be a party to the suit in Mexico . . . nor was the amount presently due on the note shown," Gas Butano, S.A. v. Rodriguez, 375 S.W. 2d 542 (1964).

In Henderson v. Drake, 258 P. 2d 879 (1953), the court, considering sufficiency of service of process on defendants' attorney under Mexican law, held that evidence on the issue of the Mexican judgment was unsatisfactory, in spite of expert's statement that the power should have been filed with a Mexican court.

[588] Estate of George Stanley Cleland, 258 P. 2d 1097 (Cal. 1953).

[589] Compañía Mexicana Radiodifusora Fronteriza v. Spann, 41 F. Supp. 907 (Tex. 1941), aff'd, 131 F.2d 609 (5th Cir. 1942).

Even though adopted only in three states (Illinois, Maryland and Oklahoma), the Uniform Foreign Money-Judgment Recognition Act may be considered as declaratory of general principles prevailing in state courts. A foreign money-judgment, final, conclusive and enforceable where rendered (§ 2) will be enforceable "in the same extent as the judgment of a sister state," i.e., by an action upon a foreign judgment (art. 3), except the judgment is not conclusive (§ 4,a) because it was rendered under a "system

defendant's attempt to evade payment of costs by pointing out that appellant-defendant

> having invoked the jurisdiction of the Mexican courts under the statutes and rules which, if he had recovered the amount he sued for, would have entitled him, in addition thereto, to 12% thereof as cost, and, if he had lost, would subject him to a like judgment for costs, and, now contesting the judgment against him as loser, finds himself a quite unenviable position of trying to take the good without the bad, the sweet without the bitter. If, instead of invoking, he had been dragged into the jurisdiction of Mexican courts . . . he could with better grace have sought relief from it. But it is a poor rule that does not work both ways.

DIVORCE DECREES

Between Mexico and the United States the recognition of divorce decrees granted in the former present an area of conflict law of more than academic interest. The fact that annually hundreds of thousands of divorces are applied for and routinely granted in Mexico to couples who are both nationals and domiciliaries of the United States has created in the United States a host of problems dealt with by the several states in a most varied fashion.

Mexican Divorces: American Law

The recognition of divorce decrees may be considered on three different levels. The first includes the recognition of divorce judgments within the same jurisdiction; the second, the recognition on the interstate level; and the third, on the international level. In the present study

---

which does not provide impartial tribunals or procedures compatible with the requirements of due process of law"; because of lack of jurisdiction over the defendant or over the subject matter. A foreign judgment will not be recognized (§ 4,b) if defendant was not timely notified; if the cause of action is repugnant to the public policy of the state; the judgment conflicts with another judgment; if the proceedings abroad were "contrary to an agreement between the parties under which the dispute in question was to be settled otherwise than in the proceedings in that court"; or in case the foreign court was a "seriously inconvenient forum" and defendant did not appear. However, a foreign judgment shall not be denied recognition in cases enumerated in § 5, among them, when the defendant was served personally within the foreign jurisdiction; when he personally appeared; when the defendant has submitted to the jurisdiction in advance of the suit; if the defendant was domiciled in the foreign state or has a business office there; or he operated "a motor vehicle or airplane in the foreign state and the proceedings involved a cause of action arising out of such operation."

this last group falls in two classes of cases: recognition of Mexican divorce decrees in the United States, and the recognition in Mexico of divorce decrees issued by American courts,[590] to be discussed in the following section.

At the outset, it must be pointed out that there is no treaty in this matter between the two countries nor is there a constitutional provision which would impose upon the courts of either country the duty to recognize foreign divorce decrees. In the United States the full faith and credit clause applies only on the interstate level, thus leaving the matter of recognition of foreign divorce decrees to state law. Some states have enacted statutes in the matter while others follow the frequently changing case law.

In absence of statutory law dealing with recognition of foreign judicial decisions generally, and of divorce decrees in particular, states rely on the broad doctrine of comity,[591] already explained. The recognition requires no special procedure. To have a foreign decree recognized, there is no need for a local *exequatur;* instead, whenever the domestic effectiveness of such a decree is questioned, it may be decided

---

[590] Bates, The Divorce of Americans in Mexico, 15 A.B.A.J. 709 (1929); Berke, Mexican Divorces, 7 (3) Pract. Law. 84 (1961); Efectos de las Sentencias de Divorcio Pronunciadas por Tribunales Mexicanos en el Estado de Nueva York, 14 (41) Boletín del Instituto de Derecho Comparado de México 281 (1961); also in (7) Lecturas Jurídicas 17 (1961); and The Present Status of Mexican Divorces, 36 N.Y.S.B.J. 111 (1964); Cartwright, Yucatan Divorces, 18 A.B.A.J. 307 (1932); Howe, The Recognition of Foreign Divorce Decree in New York State, 40 Colum. L. Rev. 373 (1940); Lenhoff, The Rationale of the Recognition of Foreign Divorces in New York, 16 Fordham L. Rev. 231 (1947); Lindey, Foreign Divorce; Where Do We Go From Here, 17 U. Pitt. L. Rev. 125 (1956); Ploscowe, Mexican Divorces: Where Are They Valid? 36 N.Y.S.B.J. 201 (1964); also in 17 (50) Boletín del Instituto de Derecho Comparado de México 367 (1964); Silverman, Effect of Mexican Divorces in United States, 9 Miami L. Q. 186 (1955); Simak, Legal and Ethical Considerations of Mexican Divorces: a Bibliography, 57 L. Lib. J. 241 (1964); Stern, Mexican Marriages and Divorces, 2 The California Family Lawyer 1571 (1963); Stilley, Recognition in New York of Foreign Nation Divorce Decrees, 17 N.Y.U. Intra. L. Rev. 239 (1962); Sumner, Effect in California of Mexican Divorces, 33 Cal. S.B.J. 15 (1958). Mexican Divorces: Validity in New York State, 21 Alb. L. Rev. 64 (1947); Recognition of Mexican Divorces . . . , 49 Colum. L. Rev. 417 (1949); Mexican Divorce: A Survey, 33 Fordham L. Rev. 449 (1965). For instruction by the Department of State in regard to Mexican divorces, see 2 Hackworth, Digest of International Law 384 (1941). For a survey, Domestic Recognition of Divorce Obtained in Foreign Country and Attacked for Lack of Jurisdiction of Parties, 13 A.L.R. (3d) 1419 (1967).

[591] Hilton v. Guyot, 159 U.S. 113 (1895).

by a declaratory judgment[592] or as a preliminary or collateral issue in another suit, for example, in actions involving alimony, subsequent marriage or divorce, annulment, adultery or succession.[593] Of course, where alimony arrears or other monetary claims are litigated, an action in debt on a foreign judgment or its equivalent lies.

To a limited extent the recognition of a foreign divorce decree

---

[592] E.g., Baumann v. Baumann, 228 N.Y.S. 539 (1928); Herrhammer v. Herrhammer, 129 N.Y.S. 767 (1954); Robinson v. Robinson, 94 N.Y.S. 2d 806 (1949); Grutman v. Grutman, 106 N.Y. 2d 315 (1957); but see Pantelides v. Pantelides, 54 N.Y.S. 2d 841 (1945); Rosenbaum v. Rosenbaum, 309 N.Y. 371, 130 N.E. 2d 902 (1955) noted in 26 Fordham L.Rev. 319 (1957); but not in Florida, Kittel v. Kittel, 164 So.2d 833 (1964). A Mexican divorce decree obtained by wife and declared valid by a California court, effective in New York, Cannon v. Phillips, 255 N.Y.S. 2d 753 (1965).

A marriage celebrated in Grenada, B.W.I., by a court official allegedly without statutory authority, was subsequently divorced in Mexico, thus establishing—impliedly—the validity of the previous marriage. An action was brought by the husband for declaratory judgment against his wife to establish the invalidity of the Grenada marriage and thereby the nullity of the Mexican divorce, including its alimony provision, after the Mexican court denied his petition for relief from the divorce decree on the ground that the court has "no power under Mexican law to reopen the original decree for any purpose whatsoever." However, the unsupported statement by the Mexican lawyer that, under Mexican law, neither party would be barred by the Mexican doctrine of *res judicata* "from litigating in a separate proceeding the validity and effect of a separation agreement incorporated by reference in a divorce decree," was understood by the New York court as granting plaintiff the right to collaterally attack the Mexican divorce decree in Mexico "if the defendant could be brought within the jurisdiction of the Mexican courts." The New York court concluded that "since the rendering nation would permit such an attack, it follows that the plaintiff 'may collaterally attack [the decree] in our courts' and litigate the validity of the marriage which the divorce purportedly terminated," adding that there is "no reason to give more conclusive effect to a foreign judgment that it would be accorded by the courts of the jurisdiction which rendered it." Schoenbrod v. Siegler, 20 N.Y. 2d 403, 283 N.Y. S. 2d 881 (1967), reinstating 50 Misc. 2d 202, 270 N.Y. S. 2d 19 (1966), and reversing 27 A.D. 2d 531, 275 N.Y.S. 2d 575 (1967).

[593] E.g., Harrison v. Harrison, 214 F.2d 571 (4th Sir. 1954), cert. denied, 348 U.S. 896 (1954); Champion v. Champion, 156 N.E.2d 16 (1959); Douglas v. Douglas, 330 P. 2d 659 (1958), cert. denied, 359 U. S. 990 (1960); Astor v. Astor, 120 So.2d 176 (Fla. 1960), cert. denied, 364 U. S. 862 (1960). A New York court found itself without jurisdiction in an action by first wife whose marriage to defendant was divorced in Mexico, for annulment of his second marriage on the ground that New Jersey was the present domicile, i.e., the *res* of the second marriage, regardless of service on defendant in New York, Sachs v. Sachs, 47 Misc. 2d 1050, 263 N.Y. S. 2d 891 (1965).

may be achieved by the equitable doctrine of estoppel[594] which denies a party the right to invoke invalidity of an act to its own advantage against the other party that changed its position in reliance on such act, in this case a divorce decree, even though the foreign decree is intrinsically invalid. This doctrine finds application in situations where, for example, a husband already married obtains a quickie Mexican divorce, marries again and when later his second wife brings an action for divorce and alimony, the husband turns around and urges that the Mexican divorce from his first wife was invalid, that he is still married to her and, consequently, that his second wife is not married to him and cannot bring a divorce action or claim alimony. If wife's reliance on such otherwise invalid Mexican divorce is shown, then courts may hold such divorce valid at least as to her monetary claims and, possibly, even in regard to her status. It so happened that a man was held, at least in matters of alimony, to be married to two living wives.[595] However, under the general principles of equity estoppel is not available to a party who comes into court with unclean hands,[596] has cooperated in the Mexican divorce proceedings,[597] or was actively involved in the procurement of such a divorce, or simply took advantage of such divorce to remarry. However, some jurisdictions, for example New York, deny estoppel in cases of mail-order divorces holding them utterly void as being contrary to public policy.[598]

A foreign divorce decree may not only be contested between the spouses immediately involved but may also be collaterally attacked by third parties,[599] for example, by a subsequent wife or by children

[594] Application of Estoppel to Invalid Divorces, 47 Mich. L.Rev. 574 (1949); Weiss, A Flight in the Fantasy of Estoppel in Foreign Divorce Decrees, 50 Colum. L.Rev. 409 (1950). E.g., Krause v. Krause, 282 N.Y. 355, 26 N.E. 2d 290 (1940); Harlan v. Harlan, 161 P.2d 490 (1945); Harges v. Harges, 261 N.Y.S. 2d 713 (1965); Farber v. Farber, 269 N.Y.S. 2d 608 (1966) (laches).
[595] Bayitch, Conflict of Laws in Florida, 1957-1963, 18 U.Miami L.Rev. 269, 306, note 286 (1963).
[596] E.g., Tonti v. Chadwick, 64 A.2d 436 (N.J. 1949); Landsman v. Landsman, 96 N.E. 2d 81 (1950); Untermann v. Untermann, 117 A.2d 599 (1955).
[597] E.g., Weber v. Weber, 238 N.Y.S. 333 (1933); Alfaro v. Alfaro, 169 N.Y.S. 2d 943 (1958), aff'd, 198 N.Y.S. 2d 318 (1960).
[598] E.g., Harlan v. Harlan, 161 P. 490 (1945); Weibel v. Weibel, 234 N.Y.S. 2d 298 (1962); contra Warrender v. Warrender, 190 A. 2d 684 (N.J. 1963), and Cross v. Cross, 381 P. 2d 573 (1963).
[599] In re Rathscheck's Estate, 90 N.E. 2d 887 (1950), rev'd, 89 N.Y.S. 2d 490 (1949); aff'd, 80 N.Y.S. 2d 622 (1949).

from the divorced or a subsequent marriage in litigations involving inheritance. The availability of such attack is determined by the *lex fori divorcii* which may have adopted in regard to such attacks a strict or a liberal attitude.[600]

Some effect may be granted to an otherwise invalid Mexican divorce under the rule of *res judicata* whenever such divorce was recognized by an American court. The effect is limited to both parties involved in such litigation provided the question of the Mexican divorce decree was directly involved and clearly determined by the decision. Such a finding will be binding upon the same parties in any subsequent litigation in a sister-state by virtue of the full faith and credit command.[601]

It may be added that the filing of a divorce suit in a foreign country or its prosecution may be enjoined by a domestic court, provided there are grounds for equity to intervene.[602] Finally, the recognition in the United States of an irregular Mexican divorce decree may be affected by an attack on such decree at its source, namely in Mexico, by *amparo* in a federal court by showing, for example, lack of jurisdiction under Mexican constitutional standards.

Starting from the commonly accepted doctrine of comity courts, nevertheless, reach different results. These differences arise from the effect given in different jurisdictions to additional factors involved in recognition of judgments rendered abroad, in general, and of divorce decrees in particular. These factors may be arranged in three groups: one, that of adherence, to a greater or lesser degree, to the requirement of domicile as the basis for divorce jurisdiction on the international level; the other, the degree of reliance on the ill defined notion of public policy which, in most cases, turns around the *fraus legis,* consisting of an improper avoidance of the otherwise controlling law of the spouses' domiciliary legislation in matters of marriage and divorce; and the third, the degree of acceptance of jurisdictional provisions as

[600] Foreign Divorce Decree: Collateral Attack by Third Parties, 19 Fordham, L.Rev. 327 (1950) ; Rights of Third Parties to Contest Validity of Foreign Divorce: Annulment, 14 Albany L. Rev. 226 (1950). E.g., Rudnick v. Rudnick, 280 P. 2d 96 (1955) ; Cocco v. Cocco, 181 A. 2d 266 (Conn. 1962).

[601] Slatter v. Slatter, 2 N.Y. 2d 668, 143 N.E. 2d 10 (1957).

[602] E.g., Greenberg v. Greenberg, 218 N.Y.S. 87 (1926) ; contra Newman v. Newman, 44 N.Y.S. 525 (1943), and Armetta v. Armetta, 68 N.Y.S. 2d. 880 (1947), also Rosenbaum v. Rosenbaum, 130 N.E. 2d 902 (N.Y. 1955), relying on Bauman v. Bauman, 165 N.E. 819 (1929), and Lowe v. Lowe, 192 N.E. 291 (1934).

well as jurisdictional findings of the foreign divorce forum.

The first consideration, namely that of domicile, arises from the greater or lesser infusion into an international conflict situation of requirements established by the United States Supreme Court for the interstate recognition of sister-state divorce decrees under the full faith and credit clause. Even though the domiciliary contact is not binding in international situations, it may, nevertheless, be applied on the ground that domestic jurisdictional standards must not be lowered in international situations where, on the contrary, they seem even more desirable. Courts have resorted to them whenever they felt the respect for the principle of domicile or for fairness or justice so requires. As a result, these considerations have prompted American courts in many instances to check the jurisdictional bases of Mexican divorce decrees not only against the Mexican jurisdictional *lex fori* but also against minimum jurisdictional standards applicable to domestic interstate situations. Limited to jurisdictional aspects, these tests do not open the question of the Mexican substantive law, particularly the availability of Mexican divorce grounds which may have occurred in the United States, to American domiciled spouses. Nor do American courts explore their compatibility with the divorce grounds available under the American *lex domicilii*. Only in rare cases would American courts do so under a local statute.

It is indeed surprising to find how little authority is available in regard to the jurisdictional bases and the resulting *res judicata* effect at home, of adjudications in Mexican courts on collateral issues settled in divorce decrees, namely property settlements, alimony to the former spouse and support to children, as well as questions of custody.[603]

---

[603] E.g., Schwartz v. Schwartz, 143 So.2d 901 (Fla. 1962); Lappert v. Lappert, 20 N.Y. 2d 364, 283 N.Y.S. 2d 26 (1967). A number of cases in New York deal with agreements to separate, including property settlement or support or both, subsequently incorporated in a Mexican divorce decree. If such decree is safe from attack, so is the agreement, McLinden v. McLinden, 146 N.Y.S. 2d 679 (1955); Baylek v. Baylek, 206 N.Y.S. 2d 359 (1960); Newman v. Newman, 253 N.Y.S. 2d 405 (1964). However, if it may be shown that the agreement was used as inducement to obtain a foreign divorce, without being incorporated in the Mexican divorce decree, the agreement will be void, Viles v. Viles, 251 N.Y.S. 2d 672 (1964). Estoppel has been considered in Harges v. Harges, 261 N.Y.S. 2d 713 (1965), and Werber v. Werber, 262 N.Y.S. 2d 679 (1965). Later, courts introduced the distinction between incorporation and merger, Laye v. Shepard, 265 N.Y.S. 2d 142, aff'd, 267 N.Y.S. 2d 477 (1966), instilling in Fitzgerald v. Morgenstern, 265 N.Y.S. 2d 467 (1965), the Rosenstiel rationale as to estoppel. Finally, these uncertainties were remedied by an amendment of § 5-311 of the N.Y.

In jurisdictions without statutory law in point, Mexican divorce decrees may be arranged in the following groups: (1) mail-order divorces; (2) divorces with only plaintiff appearing in the Mexican court (*ex parte*) ; (3) divorces with plaintiff appearing personally as well as defendant's attorney; (4) divorces with both parties appearing, accompanied by their local attorneys; (5) divorces obtained by Americans *bona fide* residents of Mexico.

Mail-order divorces include decrees obtained from Mexican courts through the activities of local Mexican attorneys without either party coming to Mexico or appearing personally in court. These divorces are generally considered invalid.[604]

General Obligations Law that a separation agreement will "not be considered a contract to alter or dissolve a marriage unless it contains an express provision requiring the dissolution of the marriage or provides for the procurement of grounds for divorce."

Action for damages resulting from procurement of a fraudulent Mexican divorce, Spindel v. Spindel, 283 F. Supp. 797 (E.D. N.Y. 1968).

Mutual mistake as to validity of Mexican divorce not ground for cancellation of a domestic property settlement, Simpson v. Simpson, 387 S.W. 2d 717 (Tex. 1965).

Support granted to child agreed by parents and incorporated in a Mexican divorce obtained both parents participating, was denied effect in New York because it "in an improvident and inadequate manner offends our public policy and is not entitled to recognition in that respect," since it provides for a child who is domiciled in and is a citizen of New York State and the child was "a party to neither the separation agreement nor the divorce that ensued and is consequently not bound or estopped by the provisions thereof," Rudnick v. Rudnick, 285 N.Y.S.2d 996 (1967). But was enforced in Hambleton v. Palmer, 283 N.Y. S. 2d 404 (1967), on the ground that a "bilateral decree of divorce obtained in Chihuahua, Mexico, as a matter of comity offends no public policy of this state and must be recognized . . . The child support provisions of a foreign divorce decree, incorporating a separation agreement, where it is claimed that the father's right of visitation has been violated, must be complied with until modified, unless the support payments are expressly conditioned and dependent upon visitation."

[604] E.g., Alzman v. Maher, 87 N.Y.S. 60 (1930) ; Vose v. Vose, 21 N.E. 2d 616 (1939) ; Querze v. Querze, 47 N.E. 2d 423 (1943) ; Caldwell v. Caldwell, 81 N.E. 2d 60 (1948) ; recently Busk v. Busk, 229 N.Y.S. 2d 904 (1962). Greenspan v. Greenspan, 18 A. 2d 283 (1941) ; Newins v. Newins, 12 N.Y.S. 2d 377 (1939) ; Steward v. Steward, 89 P.2d 404 (1939) ; Ohlson v. Ohlson, 54 N.Y.S. 2d 900 (1945) ; Considine v. Rawl, 242 N.Y.S. 2d 456 (1963) ; Schotte v. Schotte, 21 Cal. Rptr. 220 (1962). Mail-order divorce no defense against charge of bigamy, Tonti v. Chadwick, 84 A. 2d 436 (1949) ; child from subsequent marriage illegitimate, In re Estate of Weeast, 178 A. 2d 113 (1962). Note, Validation of Mail-order Divorce Through Change of Domicile, 15 U.Chi. L.Rev. 220 (1947). In particular instances Mexican divorces may have a limited effect, e.g., In re Rathscheck's Estate, 90 N.E. 2d 887 (1950) ; Dorn v. Dorn, 112 N.Y.S. 2d 90 (1952), aff'd, 126 N.Y.S. 2d 713

The other groups of Mexican divorces represents cases where plaintiff appeared with local attorney in a Mexican court and served the defendant in the United States by publication or other notice, including registered letter.[605] This kind of divorce is considered in most jurisdictions to be invalid on the ground that the Mexican *lex fori* does not recognize *ex parte* divorces in the fashion of Williams I and II.[606]

(1953) ; Unruh v. Industrial Comm'n, 301 P. 2d 1029 (1956).

For a Mexican view of Mexican divorces, see Barra Mexicana, Tramitación de Divorcios por Parte de Extranjeros no Residentes en México, (4) El Foro (5a ép.) 29 (1966), particularly the opinion of Professor Molina Pasquel (at 39).

[605] E.g., Bonner v. Reandrew, 214 N.W. 536 (Iowa, 1927) ; Golden v. Golden, 68 P. 2d 928 (N.M. 1937) ; Frelingstad v. Frelingstad, 134 N.Y.S. 2d 63 (1954) ; Molnar v. Molnar, 131 N.Y. 2d 120 (1954), aff'd, 135 N.Y.S. 2d 623 (1954) ; Magner v. Hobby, 215 F. 2d 190 (1954), cert. denied, 348 U.S. 919 (1955). In Commonwealth ex rel. Thompson v. Yarnell et ux., 169 A. 370, Pa., (1933), the court held that a Mexican divorce must be recognized until it is established that the divorced party was not in Mexico, was never properly served, was not represented by counsel and "that cause of action arose elsewhere." Mexican divorce obtained without notice to defendant wife void, Risch v. Risch, 395 S.W. 2d 709 (Tex. 1965). In most jurisdictions recognition is declined because of lack of bona fide domicile on the part of the plaintiff, e.g., Newton v. Newton, 179 A. 621 (1935) ; Ruderman v. Ruderman, 82 N.Y.S. 2d 479 (1948) ; Harrison v. Harrison, 214 F. 2d 571 (1954), cert. denied, 348 U.S. 896; Bergeron v. Bergeron, 192 N.E. 86 (1934) ; Bethune v. Bethune, 94 S.W. 2d 1043 (Ark. 1936). Recognition of Mexican Divorce Where Complainant is Present and Respondent by Attorney, 49 Colum. L.Rev. 417 (1949). But recognized in Skolnick v. Skolnick, 204 N.Y.S. 2d 63 (1960); Sonnenberg v. Sonnenberg, 203 N.Y.S. 2d 118 (1960) ; Heine v. Heine, 231 N.Y.S. 2d 239 (1962) , aff'd, 242 N.Y.S. 2d 705 (1963); Guillermo v. Guillermo, 252 N.Y.S. 2d 171 (1964). Subsequent appearance by defendant wife in the Mexican court validates prior divorce decree, including support agreement, Hytell v. Hytell, 254 N.Y.S. 2d 851 (1964).

In Butler v. Butler, 239 A. 2d 616 (D.C. 1968) the court denied validity to a Mexican *ex parte* divorce decree "because under our system of jurisprudence a court must have jurisdiction of the subject matter over which it purports to act, the marriage res in a divorce action, and jurisdiction over the marriage res depends upon a finding of domicile or residence of at least one of the parties to the action within the territorial limits of the court's jurisdiction." Considering it "absurd to say that under the facts of this case [defendant husband] established either a domicile or a bona fide residence in Mexico, and that it is disingenuous to argue that our courts would countenance the suggestion that there was jurisdiction of the marriage in the Mexican court," the court granted wife, who was served with the Mexican suit by a federal marshal, separate maintenance.

[606] 317 U.S. 287 (1942) ; 325 U.S. 226 (1945). In Commonwealth ex rel. Thompson v. Yarnell et ux. 169 A. 370 (Pa. 1933) the court held that a Mexican divorce decree must be recognized until it is established that the

The third group embraces cases where the plaintiff appears in a Mexican court with a local attorney and, at least *quoad forma,* complies with the jurisdictional requirements of the *lex fori,* while the defendant appears only through a local attorney. This type of divorce will be frowned upon by most American courts particularly if it appears that defendant took a trip to Mexico only to obtain divorce. Nevertheless, it stands a better chance to be recognized even though some courts may be willing to entertain objections based on lack of jurisdictional requirements, particularly domicile. Equally suspicious are most American courts in regard to the express submission to Mexican courts and laws and hold that such submission cannot be established by a mere declaration, without genuine ties with the Mexican forum.[607]

The fourth group includes cases where both parties appear personally accompanied by their Mexican attorneys and after formal compliance with the jurisdictional requirements of the *lex fori,* including the production of required documents (e.g., the certificate of local residence) and formal declaration of submission to Mexican courts and laws, obtain the decree. Such divorce decrees have a reasonable chance to survive an attack, unless the court is persuaded that gross improprieties are involved or that a genuine domicile is the only basis for jurisdiction in matters of divorce.

Finally, divorces between Americans, *bona fide* domiciliaries of Mexico, must be mentioned. Their divorces have never been questioned.

Liberal American jurisdictions seem willing to forego penetrating inquiries into the factual basis of jurisdiction and accept the decisions of the Mexican court, particularly where the Mexican decree contains

---

divorced party was not in Mexico, was never properly served, was not represented by counsel and "that the cause of action arose elsewhere," i.e., not in Pennsylvania.

[607] E.g., Molnar v. Molnar, 131 N.Y.S. 2d 120, aff'd, 135 N.Y.S. 2d 623 (1954); MacPherson v. Macpherson, 149 N.Y.S. 2d 525 (1956); Kantorowitz v. Kantorowitz, 249 N.Y.S. 2d 723 (1964) (Mexican divorce not recognized since power of attorney and appearance was fraudulently induced). Ploscowe, Mexican Divorces: When Are They Valid? 36 N.Y.S.B. J. 201 (1964). After a Chihuahua divorce obtained both parties participating, wife cannot claim alimony in New York, Travis v. Travis, 54 Misc. 575, 282 N.Y.S. 2d 1001 (1967). But a prior New York separation decree granting support is not affected by a subsequent Mexican divorce, Lappert v. Lappert, 20 N.Y. 2d 364, 229 N.E. 2d 599 (1967). A separation agreement included in a Mexican divorce decree effective, Fabrikant v. Fabrikant, 19 N.Y. 2d 154, 278 N.Y. 2d 607, 225 N.E. 2d 202 (1967).

express findings and rulings on jurisdiction. Among the liberal jurisdictions appears New York which does not seriously question divorces
of third type, and even less those falling under the fourth. The issues
involved as well as judicial attitudes are exemplified in the recently
decided case Wood v. Wood,[608] falling into the third group of the
above classification. Starting from the general principles of comity, the
court declared it will recognize Mexican decrees, provided

> after an examination of the decree, particularly in matters involving
> the marital status of New Yorkers, we at least accept the basis of juris-
> diction as a proper basis, if we understand jurisdiction, if not on the
> grounds of divorce and the matter of proof; and if on ground of policy
> we should recognize them.

The case involved a Chihuahua divorce, where the plaintiff appeared
personally with her attorney and defendant through his attorney.
Plaintiff had no certificate of residence as required by article 24
of the Chihuahua law, nor did she allege domicile or residence
there. Instead, she submitted expressly to the jurisdiction and laws
of the forum and renounced "all other law that may be applicable
in this case for any reason," in accordance with Chihuahua law,
as did defendant's lawyer. The New York court held the divorce
to be valid in Mexico since the court had jurisdiction. However,
the recognition in New York is, in the opinion of the court, not
determined by the *lex fori*, but by "reference to our commonly understood definition of that term in matrimonial matters." Applying
this principle to domicile or residence, the court held that "we insist
upon the link of some length and of some degree of permanence, actual
or prospective, between the spouses and the sovereignty which assumes
to exercise power over them in relation to the marital status. Unless
there is that link, the sovereignty has no power to act." Therefore,
questions of "jurisdiction of the foreign country, of domicile, or residence of the parties according to our notions, are always open to examination, and we must find that there was a link," since even sister-
states cannot be "given jurisdiction; and domiciliaries of our State
cannot 'renounce' our laws and our control over them." To permit to

---

[608] E.g., Wood v. Wood, 41 Misc. 2d 95, 245 N.Y.S. 2d 800 (1963); 22
A.D. 2d 660, 253 N.Y.S. 2d 204 (1964); cert. denied, 383 U.S. 943 (1966).
Noted in 64 Colum. L.Rev. 968 (1964); 32 Fordh. L.Rev. 581 (1964), and
77 Harv. L.Rev. 1531 (1964). A Florida court recently warned to "beware
of the Ides of March before venturing upon a midsummer night's dream at
a spot south of the border, down Mexico way," Dawson v. Dawson, 164
So.2d 536 (1964).

do so would be "contrary to our public policy in the protection of marriage and morality" of citizens of New York. It must be added that on rehearing the court upheld the ruling resulting in the annulment of the marriage with plaintiff's husband whom she married subsequently to her Mexican divorce, but on narrower grounds, namely that the question of jurisdiction of the Chihuahua court was open to attack in New York since the Chihuahua divorce contained no recital of domicile, residence, or any other substantial contact of the litigants with the foreign court.

Shortly before the amendment of New York Domestic Relations Act in 1966, the seal of approval on migratory divorces of type three was given in Rosenstiel v. Rosenstiel.[609] There, the question whether recognition is to be granted to such a divorce not only on grounds not accepted in New York but where personal jurisdiction over the plaintiff spouse was acquired by his personal appearance in the Mexican court while jurisdiction over the other spouse was established by the appearance and pleadings through an authorized attorney, but without domicile of either party in Mexico, substituted by residence of one of the parties through "a statutory formality based on a brief contact," was squarely before the court. Acknowledging the well established rule that where "a divorce has been obtained without any personal contact with the jurisdiction by either party or by physical submission to the jurisdiction by one, and no appearance or submission by the other, decision has been against the validity of the foreign decree, the court, nevertheless dismissed as immaterial not only the fact that grounds for the foreign divorce are inadmissible in New York, but also the fact that the physical contact "with the Mexican jurisdiction was ephemeral." The court found "some incidents in the Mexican proceedings which are common characteristics of the exercise of judicial power," namely physical presence of plaintiff in the foreign country, his personal appearance in the foreign court, coupled "with the usual incidents and the implicit consequence of voluntary submission to foreign sovereignty." Even though, the court continues, plaintiff did not establish in Mexico what would amount to a domicile in New York, nevertheless he did what was required by the foreign court, namely to establish "residence." This the court considered to be sufficient on the ground that it is all what the "local law of Mexico prescribes." In a rather fancy vein

[609] 43 Misc. 2d 462, 245 N.Y.S. 2d 800, 251 N.Y.S. 2d 565 (1964); 21 A.D. 635, 253 N.Y.S. 2d 206 (1964); 16 N.Y. 2d 64, 262 N.Y.S. 2d 86, 209 N.E. 2d 709 (1965); cert. denied, 384 U.S. 971 (1965). Aftermath in Rosenstiel v. Rosenstiel, 278 F. Supp. 794 (N.Y. 1967).

the court considered plaintiff to be "one party of the two-party contract of marriage [who] carried with him legal incidents of the marriage itself, considered as an entity which came before the court when he personally appeared and presented his petition," apparently under the erroneous assumption that Mexico approves of *ex parte* divorce proceedings. Nevertheless, the court based its reasoning on the "highly mobile era such as ours," where the need arises "on pragmatic grounds to regard the marriage itself as moving from place to place with either spouse." Furthermore, the court considered the appearance of the other spouse by attorney a "further support to an acquired jurisdiction there over the marriage as a legal entity." Jurisdiction being an "imposition of sovereign power over the person," usually exerted "by symbolic and rarely by actual force," the court held that the Mexican court in Juarez has acquired jurisdiction by "physical and personal submission to [its] judicial authority." Bothered by the haunting specter of domicile, the court took refuge behind the proposition that "domicile is not intrinsically an indispensable prerequisite to jurisdiction," citing no other authority than learned writings. And still not satisfied with such general defiance of the traditional domicile, the court found that domicile is "in actual practice complied with by a mere formal gesture having no more relation to the actual situs of the marriage or to the true domicile than the signing the Juarez city register." In concluding, the court conceded that the state of the "true domicile has the closest public interest in a marriage." And pointing to itself as acting in just such a capacity, the New York court held that in a case where one of its domiciliaries establishes a "synthetic domicile" abroad, in this case in Mexico, it makes, in the opinion of the court, in respect to New York's "public interest" no difference whether there is a "formality of one day [or] a formality of six weeks" and decided in favor of the Mexican divorce.

It appears that New York courts stand alone in their acceptance of one-day court affairs in Mexico. In view of the half-hearted enactment there of the Uniform Divorce Recognition Act in 1966, the future trend is difficult to predict. By contrast, the majority position remains well entrenched. A recent Louisiana[610] case, for example, held:

> Under the generally acknowledged principles that the judicial power to grant a divorce is founded on domicile, and because the plaintiff and defendant admittedly went to Mexico for the sole purpose of obtain-

[610] Clark v. Clark, 192 So. 2d 594 (La. 1966).

ing their respective divorces, we hold that the divorces thus obtained were patently invalid and of no effect whatsoever.

It is significant that the court omitted any test of jurisdiction vested in the Mexico court under its own *lex fori*. The court went even so far as to deny to the parties' subsequent marriage the benefit of a putative marriage, pointing out that Louisiana law requires "not only an honest belief, but a reasonable belief" in this respect which the court found lacking in view of the "entire transaction: the three day trip to secure the divorces, the lack of any attempt of notification of the parties' former spouses, and the fact that the parties themselves secured later Louisiana divorces." A similar position was taken, for example, by a Florida court as recently as 1967.[610a] It held that granting recognition to a Mexican divorce decree is a matter of comity, not "a matter of obligation but [one] of deference and respect," thus allowing the court to ponder whether or not "there is some good and valid reason to the contrary." Such reason was found in the possibility that granting recognition would

> permit any party desiring to shed himself of a wife to simply go to a state or a country several thousand of miles away, remain there a few days, and secure a divorce on grounds not even recognized in this State. Should this be permitted, it would violate all principles of morality and justice. Certainly it is not an abuse of discretion, under the facts in this case to refuse to recognize the validity of the Mexican decree.

Turning now to states with statutory law in matters of recognition of foreign divorce decrees, the following types may be identified:

(i) States requiring that the jurisdiction of the foreign divorce court be determined in accordance with the foreign *lex fori;* this requirement is included in the California statute. There are also states denying recognition to foreign *ex parte* divorce decrees by requiring the foreign divorce court to acquire not only the jurisdiction over the subject matter but also over both parties (Maine,[611] Massachusetts[612]).

[610a] Kittel v. Kittel, 194 So. 2d 640 (Fla. 1967).

[611] Maine Rev. Stat. ch. 166, § 67 (1954):
When residents of the State go out of it for the purpose of obtaining a divorce for causes which occurred here while the parties lived here, or which do not authorize a divorce here, and a divorce is thus obtained, it shall be void in this state; but in all other cases, a divorce decreed out of the state according to the law of the place, by a court having jurisdiction of the cause and of both parties, shall be valid here.

[612] Massachusetts Anno. Laws, ch. 208 § 39 (1958):

(ii) States denying recognition to foreign divorce decrees obtained in
fraudem legis ("by going into another jurisdiction in order to obtain
divorce") ; this rule adopted in the Uniform Divorce Recognition Act
is in force in California, Louisiana, Montana, Nebraska, New Hampshire, North Dakota, Rhode Island, South Carolina, Washington, Wisconsin, and now partly in New York.[613] The same rule obtains also in
Maine, Massachusetts, and New Jersey.[614] (iii) States inquiring into
the divorce grounds, both those of the foreign as well as their own *lex
fori*. In these jurisdictions recognition will be denied if the foreign divorce was granted on a ground which occurred when parties lived in
the domestic jurisdiction, or for grounds not recognized there,[615] e.g.,

---

A divorce decreed in another jurisdiction according to the laws thereof
by a court having jurisdiction of the cause and of both parties shall be
valid and effectual in this Commonwealth; but if an inhabitant of this
commonwealth goes into another jurisdiction to obtain a divorce for
a cause occurring here while the parties resided here, or for a cause
which would not authorize a divorce by the laws of this Commonwealth,
a divorce so obtained shall be of no force or effect in this Commonwealth.

Von Mehren, Validity of Foreign Divorces, 45 Mass. L.Q. 23 (1960).

[613] Domestic Relation Law, § 250 as amended in 1966:
Divorces obtained outside of the state of New York. Proof that a person
obtaining a divorce in another jurisdiction was (a) domiciled in this
state within twelve months prior to the commencement of the proceedings therefore, and resumed residence in this state within eighteen
months after the date of his departure therefrom; or (b) at all times
after his departure from this state and until his return maintained a
place of residence within this state, shall be prima facie evidence that
the person was domiciled in this state when the divorce proceeding was
commenced.

Cf. 1 Foster & Freed, Law and Family: New York 370 (1966).

[614] New Jersey Rev. Stat. § 2:50-35 (1937) :
Full faith and credit shall be given in all courts of this state to a decree
of annulment of marriage or divorce by a court of competent jurisdiction
in another state of the United States when the jurisdiction of such court
was obtained in the manner and in substantial conformity with the
conditions prescribed in sections 2:50-9, 2:50-10 and 2:50-11 of this title.
Nothing herein contained shall be construed to limit the power of any
court to give such effect to a decree of annulment or divorce by a court
of a foreign country as may be justified by the rules of international
comity; provided, that if any inhabitant of this state shall go into another state or country, in order to obtain a decree of divorce for a
cause which occurred while the parties resided in this state, or for a
cause which is not ground for divorce under the laws of this state, a
decree so obtained shall be of no force or effect in this state.

Warrender v. Warrender, 190 A. 2d 684 (1963), aff'd, 200 A. 2d 123 (1964).

[615] See supra n. 612. Cf. Commonwealth ex rel. Thompson v. Yarnell
et ux., 169 A. 370 (Pa. 1933) (Mexican divorce will be recognized until,
inter alia, it is established "that the cause of action arose elsewhere") .

Massachusetts. (iv) Finally, there are states with statutes referring generally to international comity (New Jersey, Wisconsin).[616]

In most states statutory schemes consist of combinations of types just enumerated. For example, California adopted elements (i) and (ii); Maine (i), (ii), and (iii), as did Massachusetts, with New Jersey and Wisconsin combining (ii), (iii), and (iv).

Among the states with pertinent statutory law the most significant case law has developed in California. The California Code of Civil Procedure provides in article 1915 that

> A final judgment of any other tribunal or a foreign country having jurisdiction, according to the laws of such country, to pronounce judgment, shall have the same effect as is the country where rendered, and also the same effect as final judgments rendered in this state.

This statute only seems but does not grant foreign judgments what is guaranteed under the full-faith-and-credit clause to judgments rendered by sister states.[617] Neither do California courts rely simply on statutory jurisdictional requirements of the Mexican divorce court. Instead, since Scott v. Scott,[618] California courts emphasize public policy involved a foreign adjudication of domestic marital relations in cases where the foreign court "has no legitimate interest in the marital status of the parties, when the sole purpose of seeking the divorce in a foreign court is to evade the laws of the state." It must be added that

---

[616] Wisconsin Stat. § 247.21 (1941):
Full faith and credit shall be given in all the courts of this state to a decree of annulment of marriage or divorce by a court of competent jurisdiction in another state, territory or possession of the United States, when the jurisdiction of such court was obtained in the manner and in substantial conformity with the conditions prescribed in sections 247.05 and 247.06.
Nothing herein contained shall be construed to limit the power of any court to give such effect to a decree of annulment or divorce, by a court of a foreign country as may be justified by the rules of international comity; provided, that if any inhabitant of this state shall go into another state, territory or country for the purpose of obtaining a decree of divorce for a cause which occurred while the parties resided in this state, or for a cause which is not ground for divorce under the laws of this state, a decree so obtained shall be of no force or effect in this state.

[617] Ryder v. Ryder, 2 Cal. App. 2d 426, 37 P. 2d 1069 (1934).

[618] 51 Cal. 2d 249, 331 P. 2d 641 (Cal. 1958). Harlan v .Harlan, 70 Cal. App. 2d 657, 161 P. 2d 490 (1945); Estate of Edgett, 188 Cal. App. 2d 700, 10 Cal. Rptr. 552 (1961); Schotte v. Schotte, 203 Cal. App. 2d 28, 21 Cal. Rprt. 220 (1962).

California has enacted also the Uniform Divorce Recognition Act[619] declaring of no force or effect in California a divorce obtained in another jurisdiction "if both parties to the marriage were domiciled in this State at the time the proceeding for the divorce was commenced." An able discussion of the California law is available elsewhere.[620]

A few states have statutory provisions dealing with foreign divorces only on the interstate level (e.g., Delaware, Kansas, Indiana), leaving the matter of divorces rendered in foreign countries to be decided by case law in the light of the "rules of international comity," as expressed in the Delaware statute.[621]

Cases involving recognition of Mexican annulment decrees are rare. An interesting situation was litigated in Hearst v. Hearst.[622] In this action for separation and support brought by his fourth wife, the defendant husband urged that his marriage to plaintiff in Juarez within four hours after obtaining a Chihuahua divorce from his third wife was invalid because the divorce decree was interlocutory in nature. The court denied this point, but considered the effect to be given a Chihuahua nullity judgment obtained by the Chihuahua State Attorney in his action brought the same year against the judge of the civil register in Juarez as well as against both parties involved in the present action demanding that the marriage in Juarez be declared a nullity and expunged from the register, on the ground of fraud perpetrated upon the judge in charge of the civil register. This action was successful with all parties appearing in court except the present plaintiff who was served in California forty-eight hours before the hearing. The New York court found the Mexican nullity judgment to be without effect against the present plaintiff, relying on Mexican law which allows defendants one day for every 40 kilometers journey to the court. Since distance from the place in California where service on the present plaintiff was performed, and the court was approximately 980 miles,

[619] Cal. Civil Code, art. 150—50.4 (1960). Sohnlein v. Winchell, 41 Cal. Rptr. 145 (1964).

[620] Stern, Mexican Marriages and Divorces, in 2 The California Family Lawyer 1571 (1963).

[621] 45 Laws of Delaware, ch. 225, p. 225, p. 906 (1945).

Conflict rules determining the law controlling family status for purposes of social security benefits are contained in §416 (h), 42 U.S.C., as amended in 1964. Cf. Trivanovitch v. Hobby, 219 F.2d 762 (Cir. 1955), and Dwyer v. Folsom, 139 F. Supp. 571 (1956); also DeSylva v. Ballentine, 351 U.S. 570 (1956). Effect of Mexican divorce decree in tax matters, Borax's Estate v. C.I.R., 349 F. 2d 666 (5th Cir. 1965).

[622] 150 N.Y. S. 2d 746 (1955).

the court found that plaintiff should have been given forty-two days to appear and answer, instead of forty-eight hours available to her. This the New York court considered to be a violation of due process under article 14 and 16 of the Mexican constitution and, therefore, denied recognition to the nullity judgment.[623]

American Divorces: Mexican Law

Compared with the torrential flow of Mexican divorce decrees into the United States, the movement in the opposite direction is, for obvious reasons, insignificant. In dealing with American divorce decrees, Mexican courts will apply article 605 of the Code of Civil Procedure for the Federal District and Territories, or the procedural codes in force in the several states, as the case may be. It is interesting to note that in spite of the prevailing position that recognition of foreign divorce de-

---

[623] Reluctance to recognize Mexican divorce decrees is noticeable in other countries, e.g., Argentina (90 Journal de Droit International 185, 1963); Brazil (Valladao, Ineficacia, no Brazil, dos Divorcios Novos Casamentos de Mexico, 79 Arquivos de Ministerio de Justica e Negocios Interiores 11, 1961); Austria (Abel, Non-recognition of a Mexican Divorce Decree in Austria, 10 Int'l & Comp. L.Q. 189, 1961); France (Patiño case, Court de Cassation, Chambre Civile, May 15, 1963, 90 Journal de Droit International 1015, 1963). There, a prior French decree granting separation but declining divorce (40 Revue Critique de Droit International Privé 648, 1951) was upheld against the attack by husband invoking the Mexican divorce obtained in 1958. This latter decree was attacked in the French court not only as contrary to French jurisdictional rules because the Mexican court had no territorial jurisdiction (*territorialement incompétent*), but also that the Mexican court applied the law in force in the Federal District although the Bolivian law controlling as the national (Bolivian) law common to both spouses referred to Spanish law as the lex loci celebrationis which does not recognize divorce, all this in spite of the fact that the Mexican court found the husband to be domiciled in Mexico. Without deciding these points the French court, *sua sponte*, invoked the res judicata effect of the 1950 French decree denying divorce which bars the recognition in France of any foreign decision inconsistent with it. This ground alone, in the opinion of the court, being of "pur droit" justifies the decision of the court below, regardless of other grounds upon which it is attacked. Cf. 53 Revue Critique de Droit International Privé 506 (1964). Recently a Chihuahua divorce between two New York domiciliaries was also denied recognition, 91 Journal du Droit International [Clunet] 810 (1964) and 66 Revue Critique de Droit International Privé 340 (1967). For Great Britain, Mountbatten v. Mountbatten, (1959) P. 43; for Italy, 3 Revista di Diritto Internazionale Privato e Procesuale 587 (1967).

In general, Sommerich (ed.), Recognition of Mexican Divorces in Europe, 1 Int'l Lawyer 39, 202 (1966); and Wiesner, Recognition of American Divorces in France, Spain, and Latin America, 2 Comp. Jur. Rev. 144, 185 (1965).

crees is an international matter and, consequently, within the legislative and judicial powers of the Union, the Mexican Supreme Court recognized, as already indicated, the power of a state, namely Sonora, to decide the recognition of an American divorce decree in accordance with its own Code of Civil Procedure.[624]

The question of interstate recognition of divorce judgments in Mexico is regulated by section III of paragraph 2, article 121 of the Constitution, already set forth. As we have seen, in order to qualify for interstate full faith and credit, a divorce decree rendered in one Mexican state must have been rendered by a court having jurisdiction by reason of an express acceptance of jurisdiction (implied submission seems insufficient), or because the party against whom the decree was rendered (not necessarily the defendant) was domiciled there, and in all cases on the condition that such party was summoned personally and not by publication. The prevailing opinion seems to indicate that the requirement of personal service applies only to non-residents who may, provided local procedural code permits, be summoned by publication. However, in no case would summons by publication, even if authorized under the local procedural code, meet the constitutional requirements.

As already pointed out, Mexican procedural codes are not drafted with the fact of coexisting federal entities (states) in mind. Consequently, any interpretation is unavoidably conjectural, particularly since even courts seem not to be aware of complex questions of interstate jurisdictional adjustments. With this understood, we may procede with the assumption that the notion of "judgments involving personal rights" (*sentencias sobre derechos personales*) according to the language of the Constitution, include divorce decrees and, furthermore, that the "acts of civil status" (*actos del estado civil*) do not include the status established through judicial proceedings. This distinction between judicial pronouncements and simple status acts is supported by article 24 of the Code of Civil Procedure for the Federal Dis-

---

[624] Art. 97 of the Civil Code of Veracruz requiring local registration of sister state divorce judgments was held unconstitutional on two grounds: first, because states cannot legislate in matters within the scope of art. 121 of the federal Constitution, and second, because the same constitutional rule imposes upon states the duty to recognize status acts without any additional local qualifications, Jurisprudencia (civ.) 633; cf., ibid., 50 (1964).

A separation agreement entered into in Los Angeles (Cal.) and involved in an interstate jurisdictional dispute regarding divorce was resolved under art. 33 and 24 (IV) of the Federal Code of Civil Procedure, 100 Semanario (6a ép.) 12 (1967).

trict and Territories which defines civil status as dealing with questions regarding, among others, marriage, annulment and divorce. Thus, acts of civil status accomplished in non-contentious proceedings, for example, registration of marriage, adoption, recognition of paternity, remain outside of the scope of section III and fall within section IV of the same constitutional article.

25. JUDICIAL ASSISTANCE

At the present time, there is no treaty law in this matter in force between Mexico and the United States.

MEXICAN LAW

Proceedings involving letters rogatory[625] received from abroad or sent abroad by Mexican courts are considered a matter of federal concern and consequently regulated by federal law, namely the Federal Code of Civil Procedure (art. 108 of the Code of Civil Procedure for the Federal District and Territories). In article 302 it provides that letters rogatory (*exhortos*) shall be governed primarily by international conventions, but where such conventions are lacking, domestic law obtains.

In brief some of the significant provisions may be stated. Mexican courts will accept letters rogatory directly from the foreign requesting court (art. 302, IV); of course, transmittal through diplomatic channels is also available. In any case, letters rogatory must be authenticated by the Mexican diplomatic or consular officer in the requesting country. Letters rogatory in a foreign language must be accompanied by a Spanish translation (art. 271) which the other party must have the opportunity to check for accuracy (art. 132).

Testimony in a Mexican court under letters rogatory will be taken in accordance with the *lex fori* (art. 165–187). The procedure is oral, answers being given to questions put by counsel (art. 173). In case the witness is a public official or resides outside of the seat of the court, written interrogatories are permitted (art. 174, 175). Cross-examination is possible (art. 175). Testimony is recorded by the court in its own words, but verbatim questions and answers may be recorded at the request of the parties (art. 181). Witnesses are not sworn: they only promise to tell the truth (art. 176).

---

[625] Briseño Sierra, Cooperación Internacional en Materia de Derecho Procesal Civil en México, Communicaciones Mexicanas al VI Congreso Internacional de Derecho Comparado, Hamburgo, 1962, at 97 (1962); Jones, International Cooperation in Judicial Procedures: Background Relating to the Laws, Doctrine and Jurisprudence of the American Republics, 12 Am.J. Comp. L. 231 (1963).

In matters of commercial jurisdiction art. 1073 and 1074 of the Commercial Code apply.

It may be added that testimony is available also through consular officers who may, under article VII (1) (a) of the Consular Convention of 1942, "in pursuance of the laws of their respective countries . . . within their respective districts, (a) take and attest the depositions of any person whose identity they have duly established."

Documentary evidence may also be secured by letters rogatory (art. 135). Of course, the documents requested must be clearly identified (art. 137).

In cases where service of process on persons in Mexico is requested by foreign courts or parties engaged in a foreign litigation, letters rogatory also may be used (art. 298 and 314).

Letters rogatory issued by Mexican courts are transmitted through diplomatic channels. The signature of the requesting Mexican judicial authorities shall be authenticated by the Secretariat of Government and the latter's authentication, in turn, by the Secretariat of Foreign Relations (art. 302, I). Authentication may be dispensed with if the laws or practice of the requested country do not require it (art. 302, II). The diplomatic channel will be bypassed and the letters rogatory forwarded from the Mexican court directly to the requested foreign court whenever the laws of the requested country so permit. Similarly, authentication will be needed only to the extent required by the laws of the requested country (art. 302, III).

Mexican courts also may entrust letters rogatory to secretaries of Mexican legations as well as to consular officers in case the moving party so desires (art. 302, V). Finally, letters rogatory may be handed over to parties concerned for execution and return to the court (art. 109 of the Code of Civil Procedure for the Federal District and Territories).

AMERICAN LAW

Rules of judicial assistance in force in the United States,[626] federal as well as state, will only be briefly outlined. At the outset it should be noted that both federal and state courts may be requested to act on judicial assistance. In pursuance of such motions, courts may issue letters rogatory addressed to judicial authorities of foreign countries.

[626] Smit & Miller, International Cooperation in Civil Litigation: a Report on Practices and Procedures Prevailing in the United States (Milano, 1961); Jones, International Cooperation in Judicial Procedures, 12 Am.J. Comp.L. 231 (1963); McCusker, Some United States Practices in International Judicial Assistance, 37 Dep't State Bull. 808 (1957); Smit, International Aspects of Federal Civil Procedure, 61 Colum.L.Rev. 1031 (1961).

In regard to state courts, their own statutory rules apply while federal rules obtain throughout the system of the federal judiciary.

Generally, the Department of State has the "power, directly, or through suitable channels, (1) to receive a letter rogatory issued, or request made, by a foreign or international tribunal, to transmit it to the tribunal, officer or agency in the United States to whom it is addressed, and to receive and return it after execution."[627] The Department is equally authorized to "receive a letter rogatory issued or request made, by a tribunal in the United States, to transmit it to the foreign or international tribunal, officer, or agency, to whom it is addressed, and to receive and return after execution." However, these provisions do not preclude a direct transmittal between the domestic and foreign courts.

Starting with federal courts faced with a letter rogatory or similar request from a foreign court, such court will, provided the person involved resides within its jurisdiction, order to appear and give testimony or produce a document or other thing "for the use in a proceeding in a foreign or international tribunal" before a person appointed by the federal court. This appointment will confer the authority to "administer oath and take the testimony or statement." The procedure is, in principle, governed by the requested forum's own law; nevertheless, the order of appointment may prescribe that it "be in whole or in part the practice and procedure of the foreign country."

Whenever "service of a document issued in connection with a proceeding in a foreign country or an international tribunal" is requested of a foreign court,[628] the federal district court where the person to be served resides or is found, may order such service as well as "direct the manner of service." Of course, this does not "of itself, require the recognition or enforcement in the United States of a judgment, decree, or order rendered by a foreign or international tribunal."

In case a federal court permits a deposition to be taken abroad, it will follow Rule 28 (b) of the Federal Rules of Civil Procedure as amended in 1963. This deposition may be (i) on notice before a person authorized to administer oaths, either under the lex loci or under

---

[627] 28 U.S.C.A. § 1781, amended in 1964 by an Act to improve judicial procedure for serving documents, obtaining evidence, and proving documents in litigation with international aspects (78 Stat. 995). Revitalization of International Judicial Assistance Procedure of the United States; Service of Documents and Taking of Testimony, 62 Mich.L.Rev. 1375 (1964). Consult also 22 C.F.R., partic. § 92, as amended, 32 F.R. 11775 (1967).

[628] 28 U.S.C.A. § 1696 as amended in 1964.

the laws of the United States; (ii) before a person commissioned by the American court; (iii) or by a letter rogatory. If the parties have so agreed in writing, the deposition also may be taken "before any person, at any time or place, upon any notive, and in any manner and when so taken may be used like other depositions."[629]

Finally, a court of the United States may issue a subpoena requiring the appearance in the United States as a witness of a "national or resident of the United States who is in a foreign country," provided the court finds this to be "in the interest of justice, and, in other than criminal action or proceeding . . . that it is not possible to obtain his testimony in admissible form without his personal appearance or to obtain the production of the document or other thing in any other manner."[630]

State law in this matter is of three types. One applies the Uniform Foreign Deposition Act (1920),[631] providing that whenever testimony is to be taken on a demand originating from a foreign country

> Witness may be compelled to appear and testify in the same manner and by the same process and proceedings may be employed for the purpose of taking testimony in proceedings pending in this state.

The second type follows closely the federal model while the third type has developed distinct rules of its own as, for example, New York.[632]

It may be added that recently a Uniform Interstate and International Procedure Act has been approved (1962). It covers a broad area of international procedural matters, including requirements to establish jurisdiction over persons outside of the adopting state, even in a foreign country (sec. 1); service of process in such situations (sec. 2); the taking of depositions abroad (sec. 3); the determination of foreign law (art. 4), and the proof of official records (sec. 5). Presently the Act has been adopted only in Arkansas, Oklahoma and the Virgin Islands.[633]

[629] 28 U.S.C.A. § 1781 (a) (2). Smit, New Federal Rules of Civil Procedure Regulating Service and the Taking of Depositions in a Foreign Country, 11 Am.J. Comp.L. 436 (1962).

[630] 28 U.S.C.A. § 1783; contempt proceedings are regulated in 28 U.S.C.A. § 1784.

[631] Uniform Foreign Deposition Act (1920).

[632] Art. 310 of the Civil Practice Act.

[633] Arkansas Stat. 27-2501/7 (1963); Oklahoma Stat. § 1701.01 (1965); Virgin Islands 5, § 4901–4943 (1965); Smit, The Uniform Interstate and International Procedure Act Approved by the National Conference of Commissioners on Uniform State Laws: a New Era Commences, 11 Am.J. Comp.L. 415 (1962).

26. COMMERCIAL ARBITRATION

Neither Mexico nor the United States has ratified the Convention Regarding the Enforcement of Foreign Arbitral Awards (Geneva, 1927), or the United Nations sponsored Convention on Recognition and Enforcement of Foreign Arbitral Awards (1958), and there are no bilateral agreements on this subject in force between them.[634] The only exception is a specific provision found in the Warsaw Convention (1929), allowing arbitration agreements for claims arising from transportation of goods (art. 32), provided the arbitration "is to take place within one of the jurisdictions referred to in the first paragraph of article 28," i.e., of the domicile of the carrier, or its principal place of business, or of the place where the transportation contract was made, or of the place of destination.

MEXICAN LAW

In Mexico private arbitration is regulated by federal as well as by state law[635] in the various codes of civil procedure and in the federal Commercial Code (art. 1051). Limiting this discussion to the law in force in the Federal District and Territories, adopted in a considerable number of states, it may be pointed out that the agreement to arbitrate must be in writing (art. 611 of the Code of Civil Procedure for the Federal District and Territories) and cannot refer to matters expressly exempted in article 615, namely support, divorce, except questions of proprietary interests, annulment of marriage, and questions involving personal status, except pecuniary questions involved in filiation (art. 339 of the federal Civil Code). Arbitration follows the rules established for courts, unless the parties have agreed otherwise (art. 619). Arbitrators must decide the issue "according to rules of law, unless other-

[634] Bayitch, Treaty Law of Private Arbitration, 10 Arb.J. 188 (1955); Hynning, International Commercial Arbitration, 48 A.B.A.J. 236 (1962); Mihm, International Commercial Arbitration in Latin America, 15 Arb. J. 17 (1959).

[635] Crawford, Arbitration Procedure in Mexico, 4 Arb. J. 152 (1940); Fernández del Castillo, El Arbitraje Comercial en la Legislación de México, 9 (26) Boletín del Instituto de Derecho Comparado de México 55 (1956); Briseño Sierra, El Arbitraje en el Derecho Privado (Mexico, 1963); Siqueiros, El Arbitraje Comercial en México, 15 Revista de la Facultad de Derecho de México 703 (1965), and Commercial Arbitration in Mexico, in University of Texas School of Law, Mexican-American Colloquium, Proceedings (1966).

wise directed in the arbitration agreement, for example, to reach an amicable settlement or to decide according to conscience (art. 628). Once rendered, the award is forwarded to the courts for enforcement (art. 632).

There is no statutory rule on the enforcement of foreign arbitral awards.[636] Using the rule of analogy, foreign arbitral awards will be treated like foreign judgments and locally enforced under the same conditions, one of which is reciprocity.

AMERICAN LAW

Insofar as not regulated by treaties or by the federal statute, the enforcement of foreign arbitral awards is a matter of state law.[637] Some of the states have modern statutes granting foreign arbitral awards enforceability; among them the pertinent statute in force in Florida[638] may be quoted:

(1) The term "court" means any court of competent jurisdiction of this state. The making of an agreement or provision for arbitration subject to this law and providing for arbitration in this state shall, whether made within or outside this state, confer jurisdiction on the court to enforce the agreement or provision under this law, to enter judgment on an award duly rendered in an arbitration thereunder and to vacate, modify or correct an award rendered thereunder for such cause and in the matter provided in this law.

(2) Any judgment entered upon an award by a court of competent jurisdiction of any state, territory, the Commonwealth of Puerto Rico, or foreign country, shall be enforceable by application as provided in section 57.26 and regardless of the time when said award may have been made.

The Uniform Arbitration Act (1955)[639] does not provide for the enforcement of awards rendered abroad. States will follow case law

---

[636] Alacala-Zamora, La Ejecución de las Sentencias Arbitrales en México, 11 (32) Boletín del Instituto de Derecho Comparado de México 45 (1958), also in 1 Rapports Généraux du 5e Congres International de Droit Comparé, Bruxelles, 1958, at 345 (1958).

[637] Sturges, A Treatise on Commercial Arbitration and Awards 910 (1930); Conflict of Laws in Commercial Arbitration, 16 Arb. J. 183 (1961). La Nacional Platanera v. North American Fruit & S.S. Corp., 84 F.2d 881, 1936 (action by Mexican corporation to direct parties to arbitrate); Almacenes Fernández, S.A. v. Golodetz, 148 F.2d 625, 1945 (stay of action by a Mexican corporation for contractual damages until arbitration); Tubos de Acero de México, S.A. v. Dynamic Shipping, Inc. 249 F. Supp. 583 (1966) (arbitration agreement through agents).

[638] § 682.18 Fla. Stat. (1967).   [639] Uniform Arbitration Act (1955).

which considers recognition of foreign arbitral awards a matter of comity. Within this general policy, courts may deny foreign arbitral awards the authority needed in actions upon such foreign award if they find, for example, that there was no jurisdiction over the American defendant, no proper service, or no opportunity to be heard.

PART SIX

Appendices

APPENDIX 1

CIVIL CODE FOR THE FEDERAL DISTRICT AND TERRITORIES (1928)

Preliminary Title

Art. 1. Provisions of this Code apply in the Federal District and Territories in matters of general nature, and in the entire Republic in matters of federal concern.

Art. 2. Legal capacity is equal for men and women; consequently, women are not subject by reason of their sex to any restriction in regard to acquisition and exercise of private rights (*derechos civiles*).

Art. 3. Laws, regulations, circulars and any other disposition of general applicability become binding and take effect within three days from their publication in the official gazette.

In order that laws, regulations, etc., may be considered published and binding in places outside of where the official gazette is published, one day more must elapse for every 40 kilometers of distance, or fraction thereof exceeding one half kilometer, in addition to the period established in the preceding paragraph.

Art. 4. In case the law, regulation, circular, or a disposition of general application determines the day it begins to take effect, it becomes binding from that day, provided it was published before.

Art. 5. No law or governmental disposition shall have retroactive effect to the detriment of anybody.

Art. 6. The will (*voluntad*) expressed by individuals cannot exempt from the duty to obey the law, nor can the will change or modify it. Only those private rights may be waived which do not directly affect public interest, provided the waiver is not prejudicial to rights of third persons.

Art. 7. The waiver permitted in the previous article has no effect unless given in clear and precise terms so that there can be no doubt as to the right to be waived.

Art. 8. Acts executed against the contents of prohibitive laws or against public interest shall be null, except in cases of a law to the contrary.

Art. 9. The law may only be abrogated or repealed by another subsequent law declaring this expressly or containing provisions incompatible, totally or partially, with the previous law.

Art. 10. Disuse, customs or contrary practice cannot be invoked against the duty to comply with the law.

Art. 11. Laws establishing an exception from general rules apply only to cases expressly covered by the former.

Art. 12. Mexican laws, including those regarding the status and capacity of persons, apply to all inhabitants of the Republic, be they nationals or aliens, domiciliaries or transients.

Art. 13. Juridical effects of acts or contracts made abroad and to be performed within the territory of the Republic shall be governed by the provisions of the present Code.

Art. 14. Immovables situated in the Federal District and Territories as well as movables found there shall be governed by the provisions of this Code even if the owners should be aliens.

Art. 15. Juridical acts shall be, in regard to everything related to form, governed by the law of the place where they have been made. However, Mexicans and aliens residing outside of the Federal District and Territories are free to subject themselves to forms prescribed by this Code whenever the act shall be performed within the mentioned territorial limits.

Art. 16. Inhabitants of the Federal District and Territories are under a duty to exercise their activities as well as use and dispose of their assets (*bienes*) in a way not prejudicial to the community, subject to the sanctions established by this Code and other respective laws.

Art. 17. Whenever somebody by taking advantage of extreme ignorance, apparent inexperience or of extreme poverty of another, obtained an excessive benefit apparently disproportionate when compared with what he on his part has undertaken, the injured party has the right to demand the rescision of the contract, and in case this is impossible, an equitable reduction of its obligation.

The rights granted in this article last one year.

Art. 18. Silence, obscurity, or insufficiency of the law does not authorize the judge or courts to decline resolving a controversy.

Art. 19. Judicial controversies of a civil nature shall be decided in accordance with the language of the law or its legal interpretation. In case of lack of law, controversies shall be decided according to general legal principles.

Art. 20. Whenever there is a conflict between rights and there is no express provision of the law applicable, the controversy shall be decided in favor of the party who tries to avoid damages rather than in favor of the one who seeks to gain an advantage. In case the conflict arises between equal rights or rights of the same kind, the controversy shall be decided by taking into consideration the best obtainable equality between the contestants.

Art. 21. Not knowing the law is no excuse for noncompliance with it; nevertheless, judges may, taking into consideration the apparent intellectual backwardness of some individuals, their remoteness from means of communication or their deplorable economic situation, and with the consent of the Public Ministry, exempt them from sanctions which they may have incurred by not complying with the law which they did not know, or, if possible, grant them a period to comply, provided always that the laws involved do not directly affect public interest.

APPENDIX 2

CONSULAR CONVENTION BETWEEN THE UNITED STATES OF AMERICA AND THE UNITED MEXICAN STATES, SIGNED AT MEXICO, ON 12 AUGUST 1942

The President of the United States of America and the President of the United Mexican States, being desirous of defining the duties, rights, privileges, exemptions and immunities of consular officers of each country in the territory of the other country, have decided to conclude a convention for that purpose and have appointed as their plenipotentiaries:

The President of the United States of America:

George S. Messersmith, Ambassador Extraordinary and Plenipotentiary of the United States of America in Mexico, and

The President of the United Mexican States:

Ezequiel Padilla, Secretary of Foreign Relations;

Who, having communicated to each other their respective full powers, which were found to be in good and due form, have agreed upon the following Articles:

Article I

1. Each High Contracting Party agrees to receive from the other High Contracting Party, consular officers in those of its ports, places, and cities, where it may be convenient and which are open to consular representatives of any foreign States.

2. Consular officers of each High Contracting Party shall, after entering upon their duties, enjoy reciprocally in the territories of the other High Contracting Party all the rights, privileges, exemptions and immunities which are enjoyed by consular officers of the same grade of the most favored nation, there being understood by consular officers Consuls General as well as Consuls and Vice Consuls who are not honorary. As official agents, such officers shall be entitled to the high consideration of all officials, national or local, with whom they have official intercourse in the State which receives them.

3. The Government of each High Contracting Party shall furnish free of charge the necessary exequatur of such consular officers of the other High Contracting Party as present a regular commission signed by the chief executive of the appointing State and under its great seal; and shall issue to a subordinate or substitute consular officer duly appointed by an accepted superior consular officer with the approbation of his Government, or by any other competent officer of his Government, such documents as according to the laws of the respective States shall be requisite for the exercise by the appointee of the consular function; provided in either case that the person applying for an exequatur or other document is found acceptable. On the exhibition of an exequatur, or other document in lieu thereof issued to a subordinate or substitute consular officer, such consular officer or such subordinate or substitute consular officer, as the case may be, shall be permitted to perform his duties and to enjoy the rights, privileges, exemptions and immunities granted by this Convention.

4. Upon the death, incapacity, or absence of a consular officer having no subordinate consular officer at his post, secretaries or chancellors, whose official character may previously have been made known to the Government of the State in the territory of which the consular function was exercised, may temporarily exercise the consular functions of the deceased or incapacitated or absent consular officer; and while so acting shall enjoy all the rights, privileges, exemptions and immunities that were granted to the consular officer.

5. A consular officer or a diplomatic officer of either High Contracting Party, a national of the State by which he is appointed and duly commissioned or accredited by such State, may, in the capital of the other State, have the rank also of a diplomatic officer or of a consular officer, as the case may be, provided that and for so long as permission for him to exercise such dual functions has been duly granted by the Government of the State in the

territory of which he exercises his functions as a consular officer and to which he is accredited as a diplomatic officer, and provided further that in any such case the rank as a diplomatic officer shall be understood as being superior to and independent of the rank as a consular officer.

Article II

1. Consular officers, nationals of the State by which they are appointed, and not engaged in any private occupation for gain within the territory of the State in which they exercise their functions, shall be exempt from arrest in such territory except when charged with the commission of an act designated by local legislation as crime other than misdemeanor and subjecting the individual guilty thereof to punishment by imprisonment. Such officers shall be exempt from military billetings, and from service of any military or naval, administrative or police character whatsoever.

2. In criminal cases the attendance at court by a consular officer as a witness may be demanded by the plaintiff, the defendant, or the judge. The demand shall be made with all possible regard for the consular dignity and the duties of the office; and there shall be compliance on the part of the consular officer.

3. In civil, contentious-administrative and labor cases, consular officers shall be subject to the jurisdiction of the courts of the State which receives them. When the testimony of a consular officer who is a national of the State which appoints him and who is not engaged in any private occupation for gain is taken in civil cases, it shall be taken orally or in writing at his residence or office and with due regard for his convenience. The officer should, however, voluntarily give his testimony at the opportune moment of the trial whenever it is possible to do so without serious interference with his official duties.

4. A consular officer shall not be required to testify in criminal, contentious-administrative, labor or civil cases, regarding acts performed by him in his official capacity.

Article III

1. Consular officers and employees in a consulate, nationals of the State by which they are appointed, and not engaged in any private occupation for gain within the territory of the State in which they exercise their functions, shall be exempt from all taxes, National, State, Provincial and Municipal, including taxes on fees, wages or salaries received specifically in compensation for consular services, and they shall be exempt from all kinds of charges incident to the licensing, registration, use or circulation of vehicles. However, they shall not be exempt from taxes levied on account of the possession or ownership of immovable property situated within the territory of the State in which they exercise their functions or taxes levied against income derived from property of any kind situated within such territory or belonging thereto.

2. The exemptions provided in paragraph 1 of this Article shall apply equally to other officials who are duly appointed by one of the High Con-

tracting Parties to exercise official functions in the territory of the other High Contracting Party, provided that such officials shall be nationals of the State appointing them and shall not be engaged in any private occupation for gain within the territory of the State in which they exercise their functions; and provided further that permission for them to exercise such official functions has been duly granted by the Government of the receiving State. The Government of the State appointing such officials shall communicate to the Government of the receiving State satisfactory evidence of the appointment and shall indicate the character of the services which will be performed by the officials to whom the exemptions are intended to apply.

Article IV

1. Each High Contracting Party agrees to permit the entry free of all duty of all furniture, equipment and supplies intended for official use in the consular offices of the other High Contracting Party, and to extend to such consular officers of the other High Contracting Party as are its nationals and to such members of their families and suites as are its nationals, the privilege of entry free of duty of their baggage and all other personal property whether accompanying the officer or his family or suite to his post or imported at any time during his incumbency thereof; provided, nevertheless, that there shall not be brought into the territories of either High Contracting Party any article, the importation of which is prohibited by the law of such High Contracting Party, until requirements in accordance with the appropriate law have been duly met.

2. The exemptions provided in paragraph 1 of this Article shall apply equally to other officials who are duly appointed by one of the High Contracting Parties to exercise official functions in the territory of the other High Contracting Party, provided that such officials shall be nationals of the State appointing them. The Government of the State appointing such officials shall communicate to the Government of the receiving State satisfactory evidence of the appointment and shall indicate the character of the services which are to be performed by the officials to whom the exemptions are intended to apply.

3. It is understood, however, that the exemptions provided in this Article shall not be extended to consular officers or other officials who are engaged in any private occupation for gain within the territory of the State to which they have been appointed or in which they exercise their functions, save with respect to Governmental supplies.

Article V

1. Consular officers may place over the outer door of their respective offices the arms of their State with an appropriate inscription designating the nature of the office, and they may place the coat of arms and fly the flag of their State on automobiles employed by them in the exercise of their consular functions. Such officers may also fly the flag of their State on their offices, including those situated in the capitals of the respective countries. They may likewise fly such flag over any boat or vessel employed in the exercise of the consular functions.

2. The quarters where consular business is conducted, correspondence to which the official seal of the consulates is affixed, and the archives of the consulates shall at all times be inviolable, and under no pretext shall any authorities of any character of the State in which such quarters or archives are located make any examination or seizure of papers or other property in such quarters or archives or to which the official seal is affixed. When consular officers are engaged in business within the territory of the State in which they exercise their functions, the files and documents of the consulate shall be kept in a place entirely separate from the place where private or business papers are kept. Consular offices shall not be used as places of asylum. No consular officers shall be required to produce official archives in court or to testify as to their contents.

Article VI

1. Consular officers of either High Contracting Party may, within their respective consular districts, address the authorities, National, State, Provincial or Municipal, for the purpose of protecting the nationals of the State by which they were appointed in the enjoyment of rights accruing by treaty or otherwise. Complaint may be made for the infraction of those rights. Failure upon the part of the proper authorities to grant redress or to accord protection may justify interposition through the diplomatic channel, and in the absence of a diplomatic representative, a consul general or the consular officer stationed at the capital may apply directly to the Government of the country.

2. Consular officers shall, within their respective consular districts, have the right:

    (a) to interview and communicate with the nationals of the State which appointed them;

    (b) to inquire into any incidents which have occurred affecting the interests of the nationals of the State which appointed them;

    (c) upon notification to the appropriate authority, to visit any of the nationals of the State which appointed them who are imprisoned or detained by authorities of the State; and

    (d) to assist the nationals of the State which appointed them in proceedings before or relations with authorities of the State.

3. Nationals of either High Contracting Party shall have the right at all times to communicate with the consular officers of their country.

Article VII

1. Consular officers, in pursuance of the laws of their respective countries, may, within their respective districts:

(a)   take and attest the depositions of any person whose identity they have duly established;

(b)   authenticate signatures;

(c)   draw up, attest, certify and authenticate unilateral acts, translations, testamentary dispositions, and transcripts of civil registry of the nationals of the State which has appointed the consular officer; and

(d)   draw up, attest, certify and authenticate deeds, contracts, documents and written instruments of any kind, provided that such deeds, contracts, documents and written instruments shall have application, execution, and legal effect primarily in the territory of the State which shall have appointed the consular officer.

2.   Instruments and documents thus executed and copies and translations thereof, when duly authenticated by the consular officer, under his official seal, shall be received as evidence in the territories of either State, as original documents or authenticated copies, as the case may be, and shall have the same force and effect as if drawn up or executed before a notary or other public officer duly authorized in the State by which the consular officer was appointed; provided, always, that such documents shall have been drawn and executed in conformity to the laws and regulations of the State where they are designed to take effect.

Article VIII

1.   In case of the death of a national of either High Contracting Party in the territory or the other High Contracting Party, without having in the locality of his decease any known heirs or testamentary executors by him appointed, the competent local authorities shall at once inform the nearest consular officer of the State of which the deceased was a national of the fact of his death, in order that the necessary information may be forwarded to the persons interested.

2.   In case of the death of a national of either High Contracting Party in the territory of the other High Contracting Party, without will or testament whereby he has appointed testamentary executors, the consular officer of the State of which the deceased was a national and within whose district the deceased made his home at the time of death, shall, so far as the laws of the country permit and pending the appointment of an administrator and until letters of adminstration have been granted, be deemed qualified to take charge of the property left by the decedent for the preservation and protection of such property. Such consular officer shall have the right to be appointed as administrator within the discretion of a court or other agency controlling the administration of estates, provided the laws of the place where the estate is administered so permit.

3.   Whenever a consular officer accepts the office of administrator of the estate of a deceased countryman, he subjects himself in that capacity to the jurisdiction of the court or other agency making the appointment for all

necessary purposes to the same extent as if he were a national of the State by which he has been received.

Article IX

1. A consular officer of either High Contracting Party shall within his district have the right to appear personally or by authorized representative in all matters concerning the administration and distribution of the estate of a deceased person under the jurisdiction of the local authorities, for all such heirs or legatees in the estate, either minors or adults, as may be nonresidents of the country and nationals of the State by which the consular officer was appointed, unless such heirs or legatees have appeared, either in person or by authorized representatives.

2. A consular officer of either High Contracting Party may on behalf of his nonresident countrymen collect and receipt for their distributive shares derived from estates in process of probate or accruing under the provisions of so-called Workmen's Compensation Laws or other like statutes, for transmission through channels prescribed by his Government to the proper distributees, provided that the court or other agency making distribution through him may require him to furnish reasonable evidence of the remission of the funds to the distributees.

Article X

1. A consular officer shall have exclusive jurisdiction over controversies arising out of the internal order of private vessels of his country, and shall alone exercise jurisdiction in situations, wherever arising, between officers and crews, pertaining to the enforcement of discipline on board, provided the vessel and the persons charged with wrongdoing shall have entered territorial waters or a port within his consular district. Consular officers shall also have jurisdiction over issues concerning the adjustment of wages and the execution of labor contracts of the crews; provided that their intervention will have a conciliatory character, without authority to settle disputes which may arise. This jurisdiction shall not exclude the jurisdiction conferred on the respective local authorities under existing or future laws of the place.

2. When an act committed on board a private vessel under the flag of the State by which the consular officer has been appointed and within the territory of the territorial waters of the State by which he has been received constitutes a crime according to the laws of the receiving State, subjecting the person guilty thereof to punishment as a criminal, the consular officer shall not exercise jurisdiction except in so far as he is permitted to do so by the local law.

3. A consular officer may freely invoke the assistance of the local police authorities in any matter pertaining to the maintenance of internal order on board a vessel under the flag of his country within the territory or the territorial waters of the State by which he has been received, and upon such request the requisite assistance shall be given.

4. A consular officer may appear with the officers and crews of vessels under the flag of his country before the judicial authorities of the State by which he has been received for the purpose of observing proceedings or of rendering assistance as an interpreter or agent.

Article XI

1. A consular officer of either High Contracting Party shall have the right to inspect within the ports of the other High Contracting Party within his consular district, the private vessels of any flag destined to and about to clear for ports of his country, for the sole purpose of observing the sanitary conditions and measures taken on board such vessels, in order that he may be enabled thereby to execute intelligently bills of health and other documents required by the laws of his country and to inform his Government concerning the extent to which its sanitary regulations have been observed at ports of departure by vessels destined to one of its ports, with a view to facilitating entry of such vessels, provided that the captain of the vessel shall have requested of the consular officer the issuance or visa of the appropriate bill of health.

2. In exercising the right conferred upon them by this Article, consular officers shall act with all possible despatch and without unnecessary delay.

Article XII

1. All proceedings relative to the salvage of vessels of either High Contracting Party wrecked upon the coasts of the other High Contracting Party shall be directed by the consular officer of the country to which the vessel belongs and within whose district the wreck may have occurred, or by some other person authorized for such purpose by the law of such country and whose identity shall be made known to the local authorities by the consular officer.

2. The local authorities of the receiving State shall immediately inform the consular officer, or the other authorized person to whom reference is made in the foregoing paragraph, of the occurrence, and shall in the meantime take all necessary measures for the protection of persons and the preservation of the wrecked property. Such authorities shall intervene only to maintain order, to protect the interests of the salvors, if the salvors do not belong to the crew of the wrecked vessel, and to ensure the excution of the arrangements which shall be made for the entry and exportation of the salvaged merchandise, such merchandise not to be subjected to any customs charges unless intended for subsequent consumption in the country where the wreck has occurred.

3. When the wreck occurs within a port, there shall be observed also those arrangements which may be ordered by the local authorities with a view to avoiding any damage that might otherwise be caused thereby to the port and to other ships.

4. The intervention of the local authorities shall occasion no expense of any kind to the owners or operators of the vessels, except such expenses as may be caused by the operations of salvage and the preservation of the goods saved, together with expenses that would be incurred under similar circumstances by vessels of the country.

Article XIII

Honorary Consuls or Vice Consuls, as the case may be, shall enjoy, in addition to all the rights, privileges, exemptions, immunities and obligations enjoyed by honorary consular officers of the same rank of the most favored nation, those rights, privileges, exemptions, immunities and obligations provided for in paragraph 3 of Article I and in Articles V, VI, VII, VIII, IX, X, XI and XII of the present Convention, for which they have received authority in conformity to the laws of the State by which they are appointed.

Article XIV

1. This Convention shall be ratified and the ratifications thereof shall be exchanged in the City of Mexico.

APPENDIX 3

LIABILITY LIMITATIONS OF WARSAW CONVENTION AND HAGUE PROTOCOL

Order Approving Agreement

Adopted by the Civil Aeronautics Board at its office in Washington, D.C., on the 13th day of May, 1966.

The Convention for the Unification of Certain Rules Relating to International Transportation by Air, generally known as the Warsaw Convention, creates a uniform body of law with respect to the rights and responsibilities of passengers, shippers, and air carriers in international air transportation. The United States became a party to the Convention in 1934, and eventually over 90 countries likewise became parties to the Convention. On November

15, 1965, the U.S. Government gave notice of denunciation of the Convention, emphasizing that such action was solely because of the Convention's low limits of liability for personal injury or death to passengers. Pursuant to Article 39 of the Convention this notice would become effective upon 6 months' notice, in this case, May 15, 1966. Subsequently, the International Air Transport Association (IATA) made efforts to effect an arrangement among air carriers, foreign air carriers, and other carriers (including carriers not members of IATA) providing the major portions of international air carriage to and from the United States to increase the limitations of liability now applicable to claims for personal injury and death under the Convention and the Protocol. The purpose of such action is to provide a basis upon which the United States could withdraw its notice of denunciation.

The arrangement proposed has been embodied in an agreement (Agreement CAB 18900) between various air carriers, foreign air carriers, and other carriers which has been filed with the Board pursuant to section 412 (a) of the Federal Aviation Act of 1958 and Part 261 of the Board's economic regulations and assigned the above-designated CAB number.

By this agreement, the parties thereto bind themselves to include in their tariffs, effective May 16, 1966, a special contract in accordance with Article 22 (1) of the Convention or the Protocol providing for a limit of liability for each passenger for death, wounding, or other bodily injury of $75,000 inclusive of legal fees, and, in case of a claim brought in a State where provision is made for separate award of legal fees and costs, a limit of $58,000 exclusive of legal fees and costs. These limitations shall be applicable to international transportation by the carrier as defined in the Convention or Protocol which includes a point in the United States as a point of origin, point of destination, or agreed stopping place. The parties further agree to provide in their tariffs that the carrier shall not, with respect to any claim arising out of the death, wounding, or other bodily injury of a passenger, avail itself of any defense under Article 20 (1) of the Convention or the Convention as amended by the Protocol. The tariff provisions would stipulate, however, that nothing therein shall be deemed to affect the rights and liabilities of the carrier with regard to any claim brought by, on behalf of, or in respect of any person who has willfully caused damage which results in death, wounding, or other bodily injury of a passenger.

The carriers by the agreement further stipulate that they will, at time of delivery of the tickets, furnish to each passenger governed by the Convention or the Protocol and by the special contract described above, a notice in 10 point type advising international passengers of the limitations of liability established by the Convention or the Protocol, or their higher liability agreed to by the special contracts pursuant to the Convention or Protocol as described above. The agreement is to become effective upon approval by this Board, and any carrier may become a party to it by signing a counterpart thereof and depositing it with the Board. Withdrawal from the agreement may be effected by giving 12 months' written notice to the Board and the other carrier parties thereto.

As indicated, the decision of the U.S. Government to serve notice to denounce the Convention was predicated upon the low liability limits therein for personal injury and death. The Government announced, however, that it would be prepared to withdraw the Notice of Denunciation if, prior to its effective date, there is a reasonable prospect for international agreement on limits of liability for international transportation in the area of $100,000 per passenger or on uniform rules without any limit of liability, and if pending such international agreement there is a provisional arrangement among the principal international air carriers providing for liability up to $75,000 per passenger.

Steps have been taken by the signing carriers to have tariffs become effective May 16, 1966, upon approval of this agreement, which will increase by special contract their liability for personal injury or death as described herein. The signatory carriers provide by far the greater portion of international transportation to, from, and within the United States. The agreement will result in a salutory increase in the protection given to passengers from the increased liability amounts and the waiver of defenses under Article 20 (1) of the Convention or Protocol. The U.S. Government has concluded that such arrangements warrant withdrawal of the Notice of Denunciation of the Warsaw Convention. Implementation of the agreement will permit continued adherence to the Convention with benefits to be derived therefrom, but without the imposition of the low liability limits therein contained upon most international travel involving travel to or from the United States. The stipulation that no tariff provision shall be deemed to affect the rights and liabilities of the carrier with regard to any claim brought by, on behalf of, or in respect of any person who has willfully caused damage which results in death, wounding or other bodily injury of a passenger operates to diminish any incentive for sabotage.

Upon consideration of the agreement, and of matters relating thereto of which the Board takes notice, the Board does not find that the agreement is adverse to the public interest or in violation of the Act and it will be approved.

Accordingly, pursuant to the provisions of the Federal Aviation Act of 1958, and particularly sections 102, 204 (a) , and 412 thereof:

It is ordered, That: 1. Agreement CAB 18900 is approved.

This order will be published in the FEDERAL REGISTER.*

---

* 31 Federal Register 7302 (May 19, 1966) .

Indices

TABLE OF AMERICAN CASES

TABLE OF MEXICAN STATUTES

INDEX BY SUBJECTS